Understanding Marvelous Designer

A Guide f

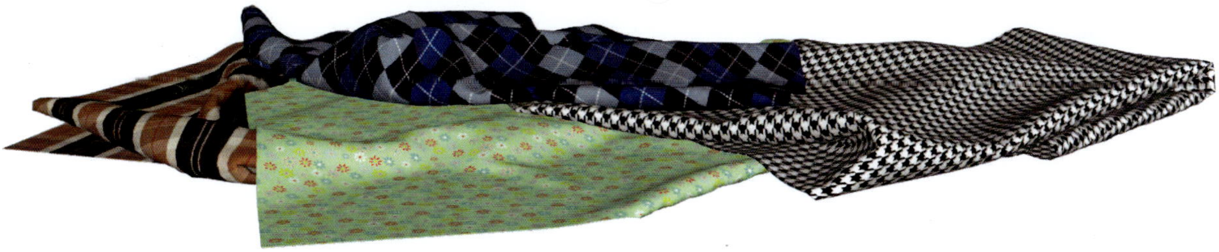

by Lori Griffiths

Lori Griffiths, Vancouver, WA

Lori@FearlessMakers.com

Visit the author's website at - www.FearlessMakers.com

First Edition

ISBN 978-0-9983342-8-8

Contents

Preface

I created this book to teach you how to use the tools in Marvelous Designer to make the best clothing you've ever made in the shortest amount of time. Marvelous Designer is not a complicated program, but it can be extremely confusing for people who don't know how to sew. I'm fortunate because I've been sewing since I was a child and drafting my own patterns for over ten years. I have also had some computer graphics (CG) experience, so MD made sense to me straight away.

You may be wondering what qualifies me to teach MD. I started using MD back in its version 2 days. At the time, I was teaching others how to sew in the real world and MD was a great way to illustrate real sewing techniques in videos. Some CG artists found my work on YouTube and asked me to create MD tutorials for them.

I've been serving the MD community ever since with a website called Fearless Makers (www.FearlessMakers.com), a Marvelous Designer User Forum (www.MarvelousDesignerHelp.com) and a YouTube channel (www.youtube.com/c/LoriGriffiths) with over 10,000 subscribers.

In early 2016 CLO, the company that owns Marvelous Designer, honored me with the distinction of Marvelous Designer Evangelist to acknowledge my contributions.

I recognized that one of the biggest problems for MD users was generating patterns. I came up with a viable solution and created PatternMaker PRO, which drafts patterns that can be used in Marvelous Designer. Most of the garments found in this book are based on PatternMaker PRO patterns (www.PatternMakerPRO.com).

My methods for using MD differ from many other CG artists that create tutorials for the program. Because of my real-world sewing background, I use traditional sewing techniques and patterns in Marvelous Designer. This results in garments that fit the avatars properly and will animate just like the real thing. I'm going to share that knowledge with you, so that you can create clothing in less time, that is more realistic than you ever thought possible.

Acknowledgments

I would like to gratefully acknowledge the individuals who made this book possible.

I would be remiss in not thanking CLO, the company behind Marvelous Designer. They've created a program that is truly worthy of a book. I hope my contribution helps to grow MD usage and popularity.

As with most authors, I have read the contents of this book so many times I no longer see what is written. Louis was a second set of eyes that helped me see where improvements were needed and errors were hiding. Brook worked through the projects and kindly shared his valuable feedback. Neither of you had a surplus of time, yet you both came through for me. I can't thank you enough.

It is easy to write when motivated, but it can become drudgery when not. My little cheerleader, Morgaine, provided encouragement when needed. Gramercy My Lady.

Last, but most appreciated, are my special family. To Maggie and Roxy for reminding me that food and affection are much higher priorities than a silly book, you bring heart to all things.

Wayne is my one, my only and my forever. I never would have attempted such an undertaking without his love and support. Thank you is such an understatement.

Marvelous Designer Quick Reference

3D Window Toolbar

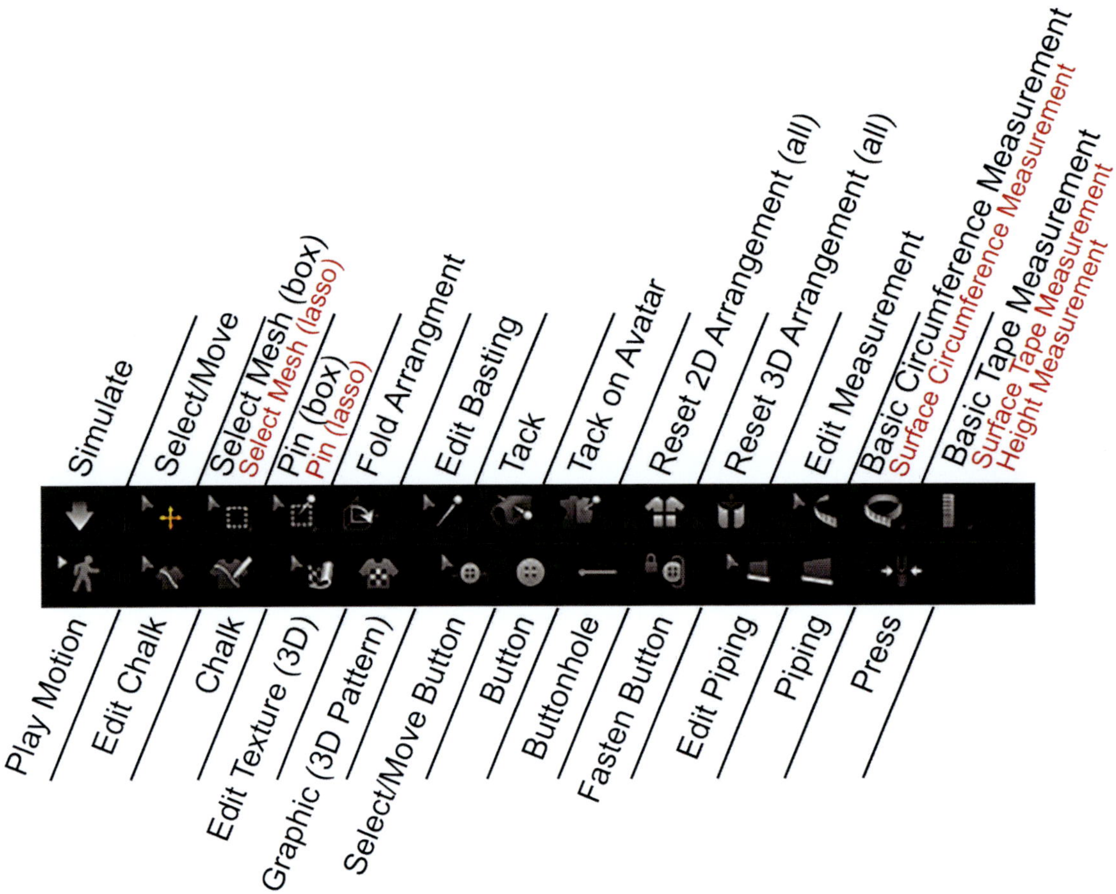

Selections marked in red are buttons hidden behind the exposed button. Click and hold to show hidden items.

2D Window Toolbar

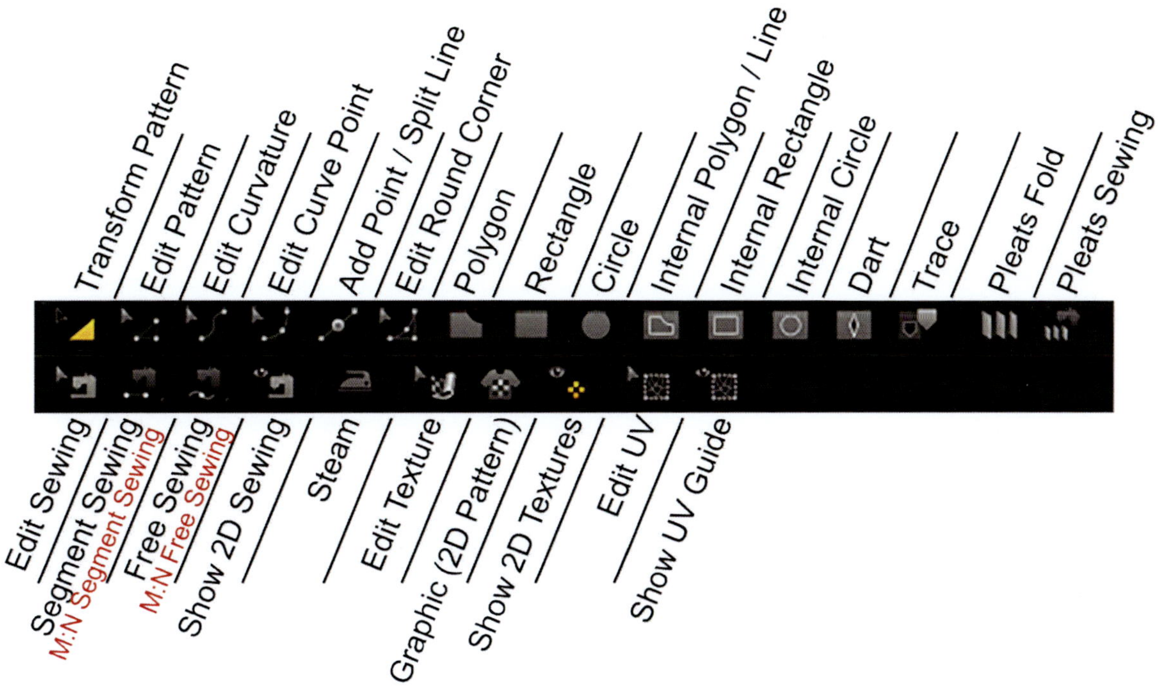

Selections marked in red are buttons hidden behind the exposed button. Click and hold to show hidden items.

3D Window Expanding Buttons

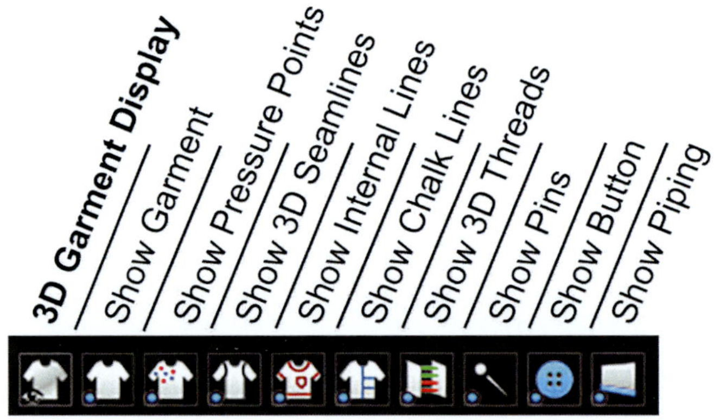

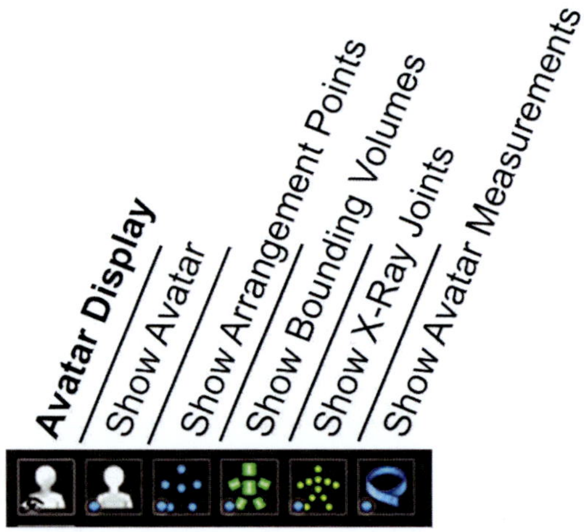

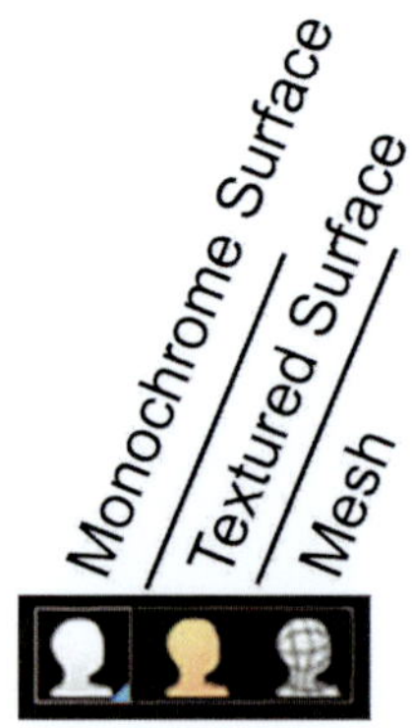

Introduction

This book is focused on teaching you two things. First, you'll learn how to locate and use all the tools and perform all the actions within Marvelous Designer. Second, you will learn what you need to know about garment construction.

Just to make things more interesting, every chapter has a quiz on the material it contains. I've also included projects for you to complete based on the theory taught in the book.

Who This Book is For

This book is for CG artists interested in learning real-world sewing methods and terminology as they apply to the CG industry and Marvelous Designer in particular. This book is intended to be a very comprehensive learning tool providing you with garment industry definitions and images of real garments for reference. After explaining concepts, I will provide instructions or suggestions to achieve these same effects in CG using Marvelous Designer.

Most of you are given sketches or images of garments and asked to re-create them. To do that successfully, you'll need to understand how garments are constructed and how the different "looks" are achieved. This book will teach you those skills.

You need to have very little, if any, knowledge of real-world garment construction to make the most of this book. However, you should have experience with your computer, its operating system and basic computer functionality. If you have some CG knowledge, that's great, but knowledge of CG is not necessary, to succeed with this book.

There are some topics found in sewing books that I will skip completely or only briefly describe. These are topics that simply don't apply to CG garments, in my opinion. For those of you who know how to sew, please understand that these omissions are intentional. If you want to sew real-world garments, there are things, beyond the scope of this book, that you will need to learn to do so successfully.

Companion Website

I've set aside a portion of the Fearless Makers website dedicated to you, the readers of this book at www.FearlessMakers.com.

This book is full of images including screenshots, illustrations and photographs. You'll find large versions of all of these on the website, if you want a better look.

You'll also find supplemental material, including full MD project files, that correspond to *Chapter 26 - Projects*. Visit Fearless Makers to access everything for free.

What You Need

All you need to follow along with the book and create the projects is Marvelous Designer. If you don't currently subscribe to MD, they offer a free trial that you can download. This is a great way to learn the program in order to decide if you want to buy it.

Conventions

In an attempt to be thorough, there are some sewing techniques explained that can't currently be accomplished with MD alone. My 3D graphics software of choice is Blender. I have provided a few images of these techniques created using Blender as inspiration for your work. These are clearly noted, so you don't come away thinking you missed something in MD.

As with any software program, MD has a lot of different ways to do the same thing, which include buttons in the program, pop-up menus available by right clicking and the main menu bar. We all like to do things differently, so all of these methods have been included in this book and are shown as follows:

A button may be shown individually or in a series. The correct one will be lit up or outlined like this:

This is a series of selections off the main menu:

Display > Avatar > Show All Avatars

This is a pop-up menu accessed with a right click (RC):

RC 3D Background > Show All Avatars

Quizzes

Quizzes have several types of questions. There are fill-in-the-blank questions with the number of words required.

1) MD is the abbreviation used throughout the book for ______________ ________________.(two words)

Some questions will be True or False.

2) You must have CG and sewing experience to use this book.

❍ True ❍ False

The last type is multiple choice. If the question states "choose all", then you should select one or more as your response.

3) The Fearless Makers website includes the following for free (choose all):

❍ A. YouTube Videos

❍ B. MD Project Files

❍ C. Marvelous Designer Software

❍ D. Written Tutorials

A "choose one" has only one correct answer.

4) There are six projects included in this book located in (choose one):

❍ A. Chapter 26

❍ B. Chapter 18

❍ C. Chapter 30

The answers to all the quizzes are in the Appendix, at the back of the book.

Projects

Instruction books are a great way to learn, but they don't provide hands-on experience. Until you actually work with MD, it is hard to understand how the tools function and the real purpose of the techniques.

It was important to me that you have the opportunity to try out as many of the tools and techniques in the book as possible. I've created six projects specifically for this purpose.

They start out easy with project #1 and progress to the most advanced project #6. Everything you need to know to re-create these projects is included in the book. In the first couple projects, I even include page numbers so you can look things up quickly.

You can find all the assets for the projects, including my final project files, over on the Fearless Makers website.

Chapter 1 - About Marvelous Designer

What is Marvelous Designer?

Many of you may be wondering exactly what Marvelous Designer is. Is it a 3D graphics program? Sort of. Is it a 2D CAD program? Yes, a bit. Is it a 3D modeling program? Absolutely not.

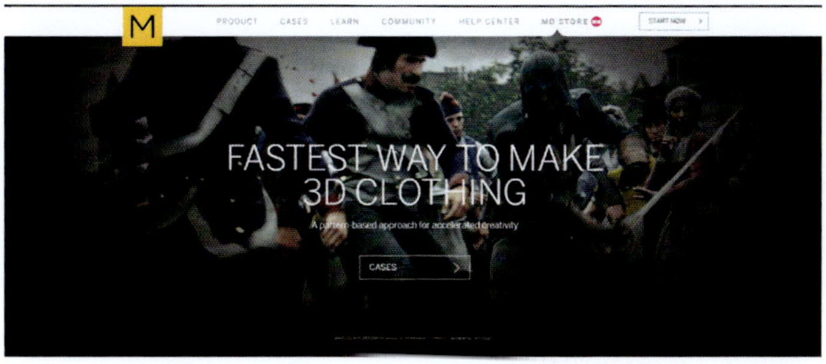

Figure 1-1. MD Website

Perhaps the best way to understand what MD is, would be to learn where it came from. CLO are the owners and creators of Marvelous Designer located in South Korea.

The CLO product is fashion design software made specifically for the apparel industry. It allows for accurate, on-spec, true-to-life garment simulation based on imports of real DXF patterns applied to scalable models. It allows fashion designers to spec out and try different things without spending any money on fabric or mockups.

A while back, CLO realized that they could offer a modified version of their software to CG hobbyists. They called this Marvelous Designer. You can't import DXF patterns or re-size the avatars, but you can draw out garments and perform simulations. This was very popular with folks in the Poser and Daz communities. CLO made some improvements to MD over the years, but it was clearly not their primary product.

Then MD started to get the attention of professional CG artists and studios. Suddenly many long-requested features that had been promised for years started to show up in the software as CLO got serious about MD.

The program doesn't fit into any existing niche of software. It's a hybrid and it is truly one-of-a-kind. There is nothing else like it in the marketplace today.

If you're a CG artist or game designer, you may not have planned on learning to sew. You won't have any problems with the 3D and 2D interfaces, but you are going to have to learn some terminology that you are probably not familiar with.

You can use MD without learning to sew and use pattern techniques. I refer to this as "sculpting" in MD. You start out with basic pattern shapes in the 2D Window and start moving things around until it looks good. You can find examples of this process all over the web and this is what many people choose to do.

As someone who is used to taking the measurements of a real person, hand drafting patterns and then sewing them into garments, I see clearly how the sewing process influenced the origin of MD. In my opinion, the best way to use the program is to invest the time to learn how sewing works in real life.

On their website, MD boasts that professional studios such as Weta Digital, Passion Pictures, and Ubisoft are using their software to speed up their production pipeline and create more accurate clothing. I'll teach you the skills you need to become part of that elite group of CG artists.

Versions and Backward Compatibility

This book was written and illustrated using MD version 6 on a Windows 10 computer. MD is available for Windows, Mac and Linux.

MD is very version specific. Version 6 was a major upgrade and much of the functionality changed. You will need version 6 to open the completed project files created for the Projects chapter.

You can typically open older MD projects with the newer version, but you can't open projects created with a new version with an older one. Even opening older projects with a new version can be problematic. For example, when I open projects created with older versions, version 6 throws a warning about symmetric patterns.

When MD has a new version in beta, they've been making the beta available to everyone to use and test. For me, the best way to test is to put the beta into production. This can be a mistake, because of versioning. Sometimes, MD will close the beta and then wait a bit before releasing the final version. Be aware that during this time, you can't access those projects created with the beta. The older stable version won't be able to open them. Yes, I learned this lesson the hard way.

When a new version is available, you can download it from your account on the MD site. Sometimes there can be issues with new releases that aren't discovered until after it has been distributed. For this reason, I keep a folder of all MD versions as they are downloaded. If there is a problem, it is easy to remove the software from my computer and re-install an older version.

You can locate the current version of your software by selecting:

Help > About

MD Easter Eggs

MD tries very hard to include as many features and functions as possible in the software. They do listen to their users. Finding a way to invoke these features can be challenging. There are only so many buttons and shortcuts available.

As you probably know, an "Easter egg" in software is a hidden message or feature that is not easy to find and undocumented. Unfortunately, some of the functionality of MD is best described this way. It is not the least bit intuitive and many of us stumble upon it.

One action they use is a right-click while dragging. This is an awkward maneuver that does not happen naturally, yet there are features exposed this way that you can't get to by any other means. I've included the ones I'm aware of in this book and it may be the only place they have ever been documented, short of a forum post somewhere.

What Marvelous Designer is Not

That may be a strange heading, but despite how good MD is, some of you may have unrealistic expectations about what Marvelous Designer can do. I've been contacted by many people who want to use MD to create a real-world clothing line. They want to create their patterns in MD and then export them out to produce real clothing. MD can't do this.

As a matter of fact, there is currently no 3D cloth simulation software that can do this. Even Optitex software, which is tens of thousands of US dollars and an apparel industry standard, can't do this.

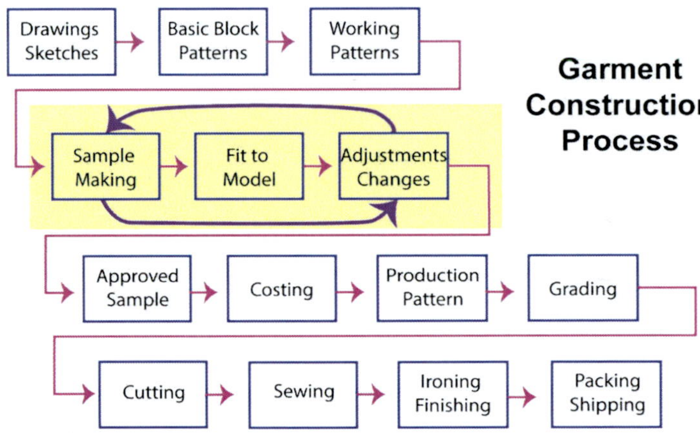

Figure 1-2. Fashion Industry Garment Construction Process

The area highlighted in yellow on the diagram is the part of the garment construction process that used to be done by hand. The samples had to be handmade and fitted to models for review. That has been replaced with 3D cloth simulations.

You'll see in the diagram that the actual, real patterns are generated before the simulations. When the simulation is approved the patterns move on in the process. They are not generated during the cloth simulation process.

3D cloth simulations are far too forgiving to result in a usable pattern that would actually fit someone. Virtual fabric has a lot more give than real fabric does. Although you can achieve some amazing results for CG work, it simply doesn't transition to the real world.

Chapter 1 Quiz

1) CLO are the creators of Marvelous Designer.

❍ True ❍ False

2) Marvelous Designer is a 3D sculpting program like ZBrush.

❍ True ❍ False

3) You can use Marvelous Designer to make real-world patterns for sewing.

❍ True ❍ False

4) Marvelous Designer originates in (choose one):

❍ A. Russia

❍ B. China

❍ C. South Korea

❍ D. France

Chapter 2 - Set Yourself Apart

Fashion Designers & Illustrators

Although this book was created with CG artists in mind, those aren't the only people who will benefit from it. I didn't start using MD because I needed clothing for 3D characters. I used it to illustrate real-world sewing techniques. In the process, I've had the opportunity to try hundreds of new designs and concepts without spending a cent on fabric or models.

Marvelous Designer gives you the ability to sew anything you can imagine. It's the perfect program for budding fashion designers and illustrators. You can create an entire line of clothing just to see it come to life. MD, and this book, use real-world terms and processes so you will learn to sew using only your computer. You can also learn more about how fabric drapes and the different properties and possibilities of materials, all virtually.

Opportunities for You

Figure 2-1. Chinese Lantern Original Design

There are many opportunities available for users of MD outside of the traditional CG world. A while back I was approached by a clothing manufacturer that wanted to use MD garments to visualize his product line.

He was using a photography studio to create images for his website. This was expensive, and finding garments that fit the model perfectly to highlight his quality of work was a real challenge. He thought that creating these garments virtually made more sense.

I took on the challenge and created over 500 garments for him. MD by itself was not capable of creating the level of detail and realism that was necessary, so

I used Blender to finish each one. The final images do not include a model, so there is no distraction from the garment itself. I set up the garments in Blender in such a way that he could easily change the color and material for every garment at any time in the future. If something isn't selling, he can change it to update his catalog. More and more manufacturers and retailers are getting wise to this process. I've heard from several wanting to do the same thing.

I've also been contacted by companies that are creating virtual try-on software. This is the next big step in online retailing. They are primarily focused on the cloth animation and website functionality and they don't specialize in the 3D garments. They are looking for people to do the garments for them.

Just look at the number of clothing manufacturers to get some idea of the quantity of work that will be needed. Every design will need to be made virtually. People skilled in MD will be in high demand.

There are lots of opportunities out there for people who sew virtually and they will only increase over time.

Chapter 2 Quiz

1) You can't make a living using MD to create virtual garments.

❍ True ❍ False

2) MD garments can be used as a selling tool on real-life clothing retail websites.

❍ True ❍ False

3) You can create photorealistic clothing using MD exclusively.

❍ True ❍ False

4) MD can be used by fashion designers to visualize their ideas.

❍ True ❍ False

Chapter 3 - Getting Started in MD

After you purchase your subscription to MD, you'll have a page on your account where you can download the software. Download the appropriate version for your operating system and install it just like you do for any other program.

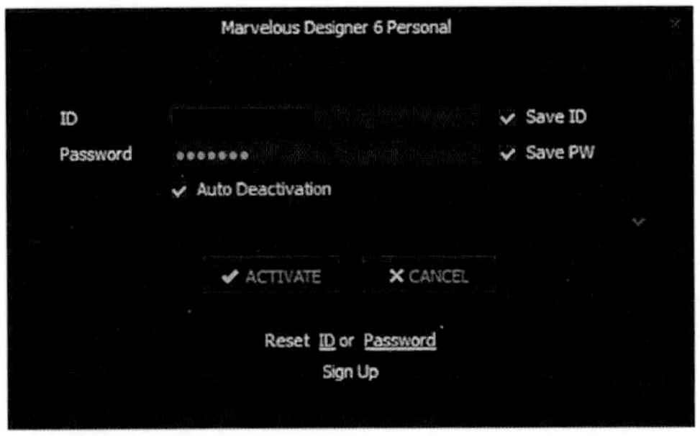

Figure 3-1. License Manager

When you start the program, you'll see a licensing dialog box. Enter in your ID and Password. Check the boxes to save these, if you don't want to enter them every time you start the program. I would strongly suggest you check the Auto Deactivation box, too.

For those of you who are new to subscription software, I'll explain what deactivation means.

The deactivation process ensures that you are only running one instance of the program for your assigned ID and password. This is how the software company makes sure you don't run their program on multiple machines concurrently or share it with friends. If you had two machines, you could deactivate the software on one machine and then you could activate it on the other.

The Auto Deactivation is there to deactivate the software automatically when you close the program. This is a very good idea, because you can lock yourself out very easily. For instance, if you get a prompt to download a new version and you install it without deactivating the old version, you'll be locked out. You'll have to contact the company to fix it and that can take days. I always leave the Auto Deactivation box checked.

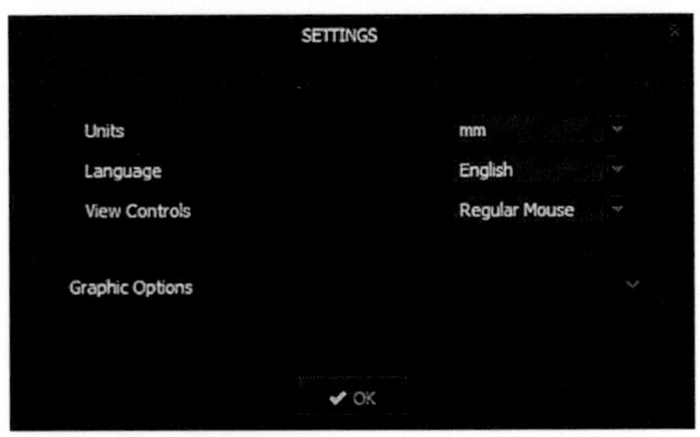

Figure 3-2. Startup Settings

Click Activate to authenticate your credentials and open the program.

If this is the first time you've opened the program, MD may open a dialog box called Settings. The only thing that I would suggest you change is the Language, if you prefer one other than English.

All of the other items shown in this dialog box can be changed at any time within the program. There is no need to do so here.

MD will open the program to a blank project with no avatar or garments. You can change what loads up when you open the program by selecting -

Settings > User Settings > Default Files > Avatar & Garment

You can find all the default avatars to add to your scene by selecting -

Avatar > Avatar Editor > Avatar Style tab

Shortcuts

At the top of the 2D and 3D windows you'll see a series of buttons. These are all shortcuts that apply to the window below them. You can decide which buttons are displayed by showing and hiding the different types.

Display > 3D Toolbars / 2D Toolbars

RC the empty area of the 3D or 2D button bar

At the top, far right of the program area you'll find some other shortcut buttons that are links to the MD site. These are located to the right of your user name. They are labeled Notification, My Page, Issue Reporting and Store.

The Notification and My Page buttons will open your browser to your MD account where you can set your preferences. The Issue Reporting button will open your browser to the MD issue reporting form where you can submit requests and bug reports. The Store button takes you to the MD store, where you can purchase MD garments.

Layouts & Panels

I'm not going to go through every button, menu item and possible selection in the program. It's pointless and would be a waste of your time. I think you'll learn these things much easier when they are used in the proper context.

As you work your way through this book, you'll learn how to use all of the features at the appropriate time. The rest of this chapter is meant to give you an overview so you'll be more familiar with what each of the windows is and how you can move around in the program.

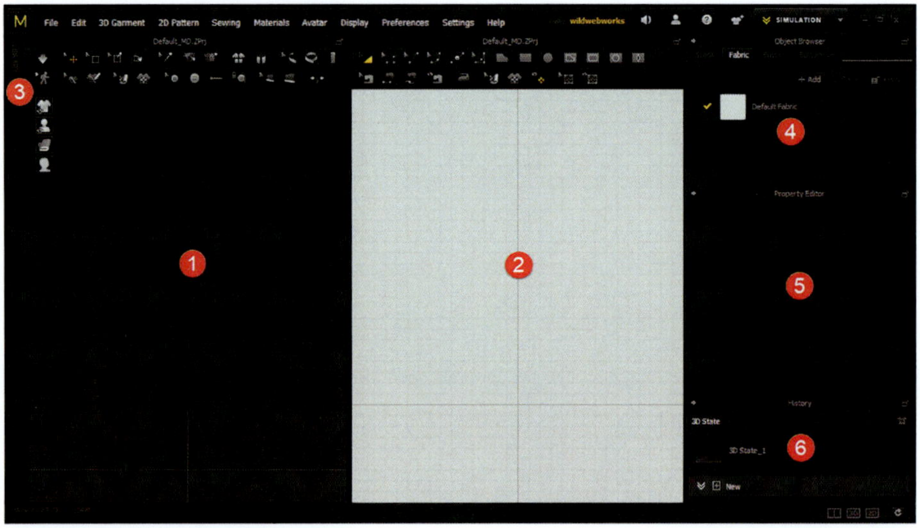

Figure 3-4. Marvelous Designer Program Layout

The two primary windows of the program are the 3D Window on the left (#1 Figure 3-3) and the 2D Window on the right (#2). The 3D and 2D windows can be shown individually or together within the program. Down in the lower right of the program you'll see four window display buttons shown below.

Figure 3-3. Window Display Buttons

The first button is the default layout with both windows open. The 3D button hides the 2D Window and the 2D button hides the 3D Window. The Reset Layout button returns it to the default layout.

In addition to the two main windows you have panels down the left and right sides. On the left is the Library (#3). On the right you'll find the Object Browser (#4), Property Editor (#5) and History (#6) panels.

Panels have three different view states. They can be minimized, opened within the program or opened in their own window. The Library is minimized by default. Click the word Library to open the panel.

At the top of each open panel is an arrow icon and a maximize icon. The 3D Window and 2D Window also have maximize icons at the top.

Click the arrow to minimize the panel. Click the maximize icon to put the panel in its own window. You can now drag that window anywhere you wish. The individual window can be placed outside the program on another monitor, for example. You can also drag the window within the program and drop it in a different location. The program will highlight in gray where the window can be dropped. This allows you to customize the layout any way you want.

You can also use the menu to show/hide and open/close windows by selecting -

Display > Window > Select Window

Please be aware that if you uncheck Open/Close using the menu, you will no longer be able to see a label for it in the program. Closing it is not the same as minimizing it. You'll have to use the main menu to get it back.

You can also change the width of any window or panel. Hover your mouse over the bar separating them and you'll see a double bar with arrows. Click and drag to make them wider or narrower.

MD Help

MD provides a Help button on the main menu that contains a link to the MD manual online as well as other tools to assist you in learning the program.

I've created a special forum just for MD users that you might find useful. You can post questions and get help from other users. The forum is located at MarvelousDesignerHelp.com.

If you are interested in video tutorials, there are many available on my website at FearlessMakers.com. there are also free project files in the store that correspond to the videos.

Moving Around

The 3D Window is three-dimensional, which means you can move along three axes. Not only can you move side-to-side (X axis) and up and down (Y axis), you can also move forward and back (Z axis). This allows you to navigate around the Avatar and see things from every angle. This is similar to the movement in standard 3D graphics programs like Blender or Maya.

The 2D Window is two-dimensional allowing movement in only the X and Y axis. You can only move up, down, left and right. You can equate this to the UV editor in 3D graphics programs or a 2D CAD program.

The actions of pan, zoom and rotate are all customizable.

Settings > User Settings > View Controls

Take note of the controls that MD has chosen by default for each of these actions.

You'll notice there is a drop-down list at the very top right, which is set to Default Preset. Your other choices include Regular Mouse, Maya, 3dsMax, Style CAD and Tablet. If you have experience in any of these other programs, MD will behave in a manner you are more accustomed to.

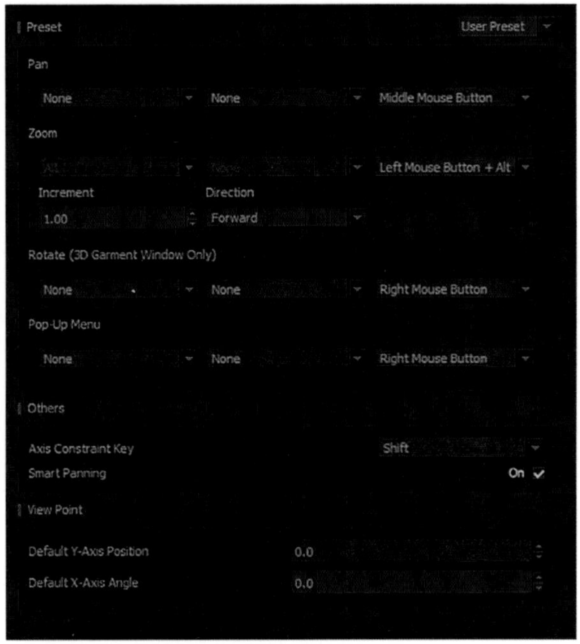

Figure 3-5. User Settings - View Controls

You are free to change any or all of the Pan, Zoom and Rotate individual options. When you do so, the preset will change to User Preset.

Panning

The action of panning locks you in the X and Y axis. You can move up and down, and side to side. You see a little gripping hand icon when panning. The default control for this action is the middle mouse button.

Zooming

The action of zooming locks you in the Z axis. You can move forward and back. Zooming is the Alt key and your left mouse button, or your scroll wheel, by default. Your cursor will change to an up/down icon.

You can set the Increment of the zoom to move slower or quicker, depending on your preference. You can also change the Direction of the zooming. If you are accustomed to another application that zooms in a different direction, you can change MD to match.

Rotating

Rotating spins the Avatar and garments around. The center of the floor plane is the rotation point, regardless of what you have selected. This is very strange compared to most programs and can be a bit disorienting. If you are working on a garment that is not centered to the floor plane, rotating around it can be quite a challenge. You can also tilt up and down while rotating.

Rotating is done by default using the right mouse button. Your cursor will change to a two arrow circle. In the User Settings, the Rotate section states that it is for the "3D Garment Window Only" because the 2D Window does not have the Z axis.

It is very easy to lose your Avatar, if you aren't familiar with moving around in 3D space. To bring everything into view select -

Display > Viewpoint > Zoom Extents All

RC the 3D background > Zoom Extents All

This also works for the 2D Window.

You can also set your view to a specific angle.

Display > Viewpoint

RC the 3D background > Select View

The options include Front, Back, Left, Right, Top, Bottom and 3/4 view.

2D Pattern Window

The 2D Pattern Window is where you will create and edit your patterns. The window consists of a flat plane, with the ability to move in the X and Y axis only.

The 2D Window most resembles a 2D CAD or UV editor interface. There is a grid on the plane to assist you in drawing your patterns. You can choose to show or hide the grid by selecting -

Display > Show 2D Grid

If you want to snap to the grid -

RC the 2D background > Snap to Grid

In the center of the window you'll see a gray silhouette of your Avatar. This silhouette will change as you change avatars and always reflect the "real" outline of the Avatar in your 3D Window.

There is a direct correlation between where the patterns are on the Avatar silhouette and where they will be in the 3D Window. If a pattern is on top of the Avatar in the 2D Window silhouette, it will be in front of the Avatar in the 3D Window. Keep your patterns as close to the silhouette as possible, so you don't have to chase them down in the 3D Window when arranging them.

The features of the 2D Window, including buttons and methods, are covered in later chapters in this book.

3D Garment Window

You should understand that MD is not a 3D modeling program. It applies gravity, mass and wind to planes that are draped or pinned to the Avatar in the 3D Window. The Avatar is simply a collision object. You can't sculpt, extrude or manipulate the geometry in the 3D Window. See *Chapter 4 - 3D Garment Window*, for more details.

Object Browser

The Object Browser is located at the far, top right of the program by default. It contains four tabs, Scene, Fabric, Button and Buttonhole.

Scene

The Scene tab includes a tree hierarchy of all the objects in the scene located in the 3D Window. Every pattern is listed along with all the Seam Line Pairs (sewing seams). The Avatar is also listed in detail, including joints, if they exist. You can use the Scene tab to select items, rather than selecting them in the 3D Window.

Fabric

The second tab in the Object Browser is the Fabric tab, which has a list of fabrics. There will always be a Default_Fabric in the list. You can add fabric by using the Add (+) button.

You can also copy an existing fabric by selecting the fabric and clicking the Copy button. It can take some time to get a fabric set up exactly as you want it. If you need another fabric with the same settings, but perhaps in a different color, you can just copy it and make the necessary changes.

When you select a fabric to set its properties, the fabric will have an orange check-mark next to it. Always make sure you have the intended fabric selected, when you start making changes.

To assign a fabric to patterns, use the Transform tool and select one or more patterns in the 2D Window. The Assign button will light up and you'll see a small assign button next to each fabric. Click that button and all the selected patterns will now be assigned to that fabric. Whenever you have a pattern selected, its assigned fabric name will show in orange, so you know which one is assigned to that pattern.

If you want to delete a fabric, you must make sure that there are no patterns assigned to it. A fabric with no assignments will have a trashcan button next to it. Click the trashcan to delete the fabric. You can't delete the Default_Fabric. Learn more about fabric and its properties in *Chapter 9 - Fabric.*

Buttons & Buttonholes

The last two tabs in the Object Browser are the Button and Buttonhole tabs. These reflect the buttons and buttonholes you have created for your project. You can learn more about these in *Chapter 20 - Other Details.*

Property Editor

The Property Editor is a very dynamic component. Its contents will vary depending on what item you have selected. The editor will show all of the properties of your selection that can be changed. Those properties are covered in detail as each item is described throughout this book.

Library

The Library is located to the far left of the program and is minimized by default. You can open it by clicking the label Library. The Library is a place for you to organize your files and directories and create shortcuts. Rather than browsing through your file system, you can put often used files here and open them with a simple click.

MD provides a default list of files and directories. You can modify this file list using the add (+) button at the top. When you select a directory in the list, the bottom portion of the Library shows you the contents of that directory. You can choose to display these files in icon (thumbnail) or list view by using the List View / Icon View toggle button in the upper-right of the contents section.

History

The History creates an entry for every significant action that you take. These entries are created for you automatically. If you make an error or want to undo an action, simply click one of the previous items to revert.

In addition to the entries that MD makes, you can select specific States to save. These might be major milestones in your progress with the project.

To save a State, simply click the little shirt with a plus sign in the upper right corner of the History panel. A new State will be added under the default 3D State_1 that MD creates on start-up. You can remove a state or give it another name by selecting -

RC the state > Delete / Rename

If you want to revert to a saved state, simply double-click the state name. MD will display a warning about history loss. Click OK to proceed.

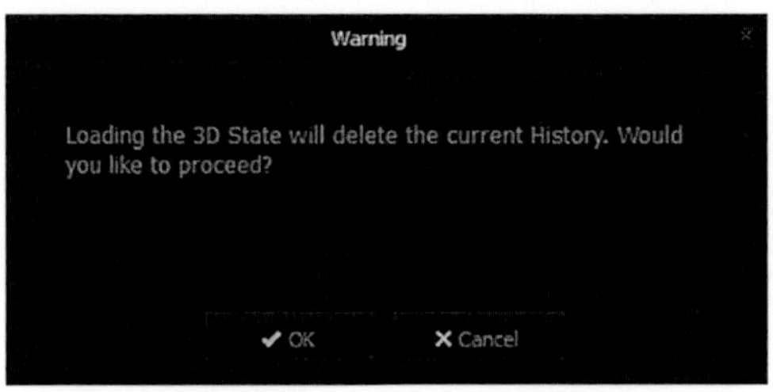

Figure 3-6. State Warning

Chapter 3 Quiz

1) The layout in MD is fixed and you can't rearrange the panels.

❍ True ❍ False

2) Almost all tools can be selected using buttons or through menu choices.

❍ True ❍ False

3) You can undo your last action with (choose all):

❍ A. Control/Command Z

❍ B. Using the History Panel

❍ C. Edit > Undo

4) The 2D window has (choose one):

❍ A. X, Y, Z Axes

❍ B. Z, X Axes

❍ C. Y, X Axes

Chapter 4 - 3D Garment Window

The 3D Garment Window is the part of MD that most closely resembles other 3D graphics programs. It is a 3D space with X, Y and Z axes. The Avatar is placed in the center of the space by default. Patterns that are created in the 2D Window are placed here, where you will arrange and simulate them. Simulation applies gravity and mass to the patterns and uses the Avatar as a collision object.

Environment

MD refers to the 3D space within the 3D Window as the Environment. It consists of a floor, lighting and a background. If you want to know the current size of the 3D Window select -

Display > Show 3D Garment Window Size

Background

By default, MD gives you a background image with a gray gradient. You can change the background by selecting -

Display > Format Background

RC the 3D background > Format Background

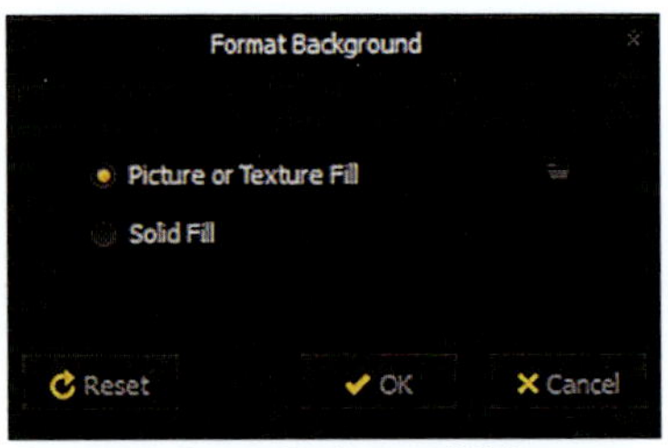

Figure 4-1. Format Background Dialog

You can choose Solid Fill and then select a color using the Color Picker. If you select Picture or Texture Fill, you can choose an image file off your computer.

To return the background to the default, select the Reset button in the Format Background dialog box.

Figure 4-2. Customized Background

Floor Grid

There is a grid on the floor in the 3D space. You can change the visibility of the Axes and Grid Lines with -

Preferences > 3D Grid Brightness

If you want to hide or show the grid select -

Display > Show 3D Grid

Lighting

MD includes two light objects in the scene that you can adjust.

Display > Show Light Controller

Use the Object Browser to select either light object to see its properties in the Property Editor. Both lights are Directional lights.

Figure 4-3. Light Direction and Color Change

The light located between the Avatar's feet has the Attached On Camera property set to On.

You can change the Ambient Color, Diffuse Color and Specular Color of each light.

You can change the name of the light by typing in the Name field and you can move the light around in the 3D Window using the Gizmo.

Shadow

There is a shadow of your Avatar shown on the grid. To hide or show the shadow select -

Display > Show 3D Shadow

RC the 3D background > Show 3D Shadow

Changes in the Light object will change how the Avatar shadow is thrown in the scene. If you are taking snapshots of your 3D Window with PNG transparency, you may want to hide the 3D shadow.

Wind

You can turn on Wind in MD to make your garments flutter during simulation.

Display > Show Wind Controller

You can use the Gizmo to position the cone so it blows in any direction you like.

Figure 4-4. Wind Object Activated

Select the gray cone that appears in the 3D Window and the Property Editor will show all the options available for controlling the wind. You can name the wind controller and control it with the Activate On/Off. There are two types of wind to choose from.

The Spherical type will blow in every direction starting from the controller object in the 3D Window and blowing outwards in a spherical shape.

The Planar type will only blow in the direction that the cone is pointing. Planar type is infinite and does not originate at the controller object, so placement is irrelevant.

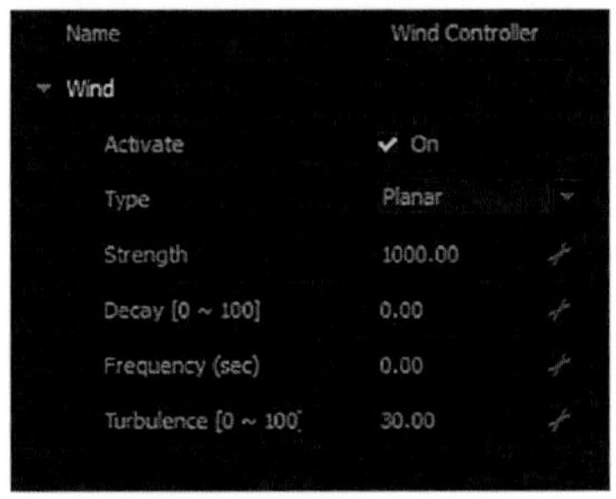

Figure 4-5. Wind Properties

The Strength sets the intensity with higher values being a stronger intensity. Decay is the fall off and sets how far the wind will go before growing weaker and diminishing. Use the Frequency setting to create in intermittent wind that blows on and off over time. Turbulence sets how erratic the wind is, with a higher value increasing the turbulence. Set this low for a soft, gentle breeze.

Toolbar

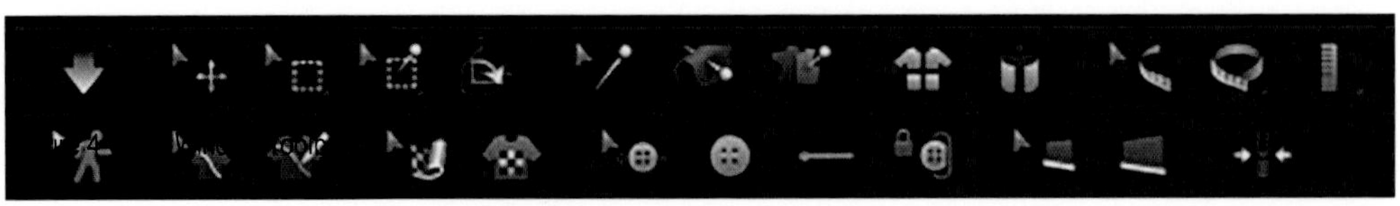

There is a bar at the top of the 3D Window with a series of buttons. These are all shortcuts for performing actions in the 3D Window. All of these actions are available in the main menu. You can control what is displayed on the bar by selecting -

Display > 3D Toolbar

RC the 3D toolbar background > Select/Deselect Toolbars

These shortcuts will be discussed in context throughout this book. Watch for buttons that have a gray bottom right corner. These buttons have other buttons hidden within them. Click and hold on the button and other options will display.

Window Buttons

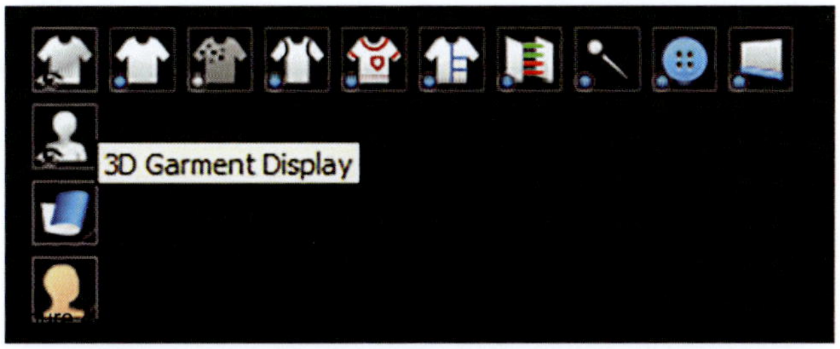

There are four icon buttons in the 3D Window itself. These are special buttons that have more options hidden within them. If you hover over an icon, it will expand out to the right and show all the different options. These options are all active/inactive toggle buttons. They are grayed out when inactive. They are displayed in color when they are active and the dot on the button will turn blue. All of these are shortcuts that control what displays in the window. These options are all available off the main menu, too.

Gizmo

Gizmo is the name that MD gives the manipulator in the 3D Window. It gives you the ability to move objects in the scene in any direction.

The Gizmo is color coordinated according to the axis. Red indicates the X axis, which is side-to-side in 3D space. Blue is the Z axis, for moving forward and backward. Green is the Y axis, for moving up and down.

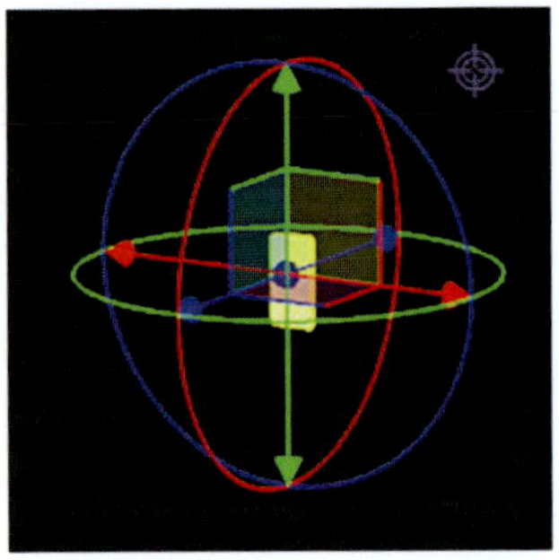

Figure 4-8. Gizmo

The Gizmo includes lines with arrows and circles for every axis. If you click and drag on any of them, the object will move and be constrained in the direction indicated by the color. The lines with arrows are for translating your object in a straight path. The circles are for rotating your objects.

In the center of the Gizmo is a box, and this allows free placement, not constrained to any axis. Select an object, click in the box and drag to move the object anywhere you like. Be careful with this, particularly if you are new to 3D space. You can move objects much further than you intended very quickly.

If you want to select more than one object, select the first one, hold down Shift and then select the others. You'll see that the Gizmo disappears after your second selection. After you have selected all your objects, release the Shift key and click once. The Gizmo will reappear and control all of the objects you have selected.

Unified vs Divided

The default Gizmo is set to Unified, which means that you can select, move and rotate using only this one tool. If you prefer, you can set the Gizmo to Divided.

Settings > User Settings > Other > Gizmo > Divided

This will turn the Gizmo into three separate tools based on shortcut keys. Select the "Q" key to go to Select mode, the "W" key for Move mode and the "E" key for Rotation mode.

Please note that selecting the Divided Gizmo will override any existing shortcuts associated with the Q, W and E keys.

Orientation

You can control the orientation of the Gizmo itself in 3D space.

Preferences > Gizmo > Screen Coordinates/Local Coordinates/World Coordinates

RC the 3D background > Gizmo > Screen Coordinates/Local Coordinates/World Coordinates

In Screen Coordinate mode, the Gizmo never changes. The X axis line will always run left to right, the Z front to back and the Y up and down. The Gizmo is fixed to your screen view, which is basically a flat plane. The easiest way to illustrate what happens is for you to select an object in the scene, so you can see the Gizmo, and then rotate the scene (not the object). In my opinion, this is the most confusing of all the choices and difficult to use.

If you switch it to Local Coordinates, the Gizmo takes on the orientation of the object you have selected. The origin for rotation is now the center of the object itself. It does not take into consideration the location of the object in the scene. Use the Local Coordinates when using the X-Ray Joints to pose your Avatar.

If the Gizmo is set to World Coordinates, the Gizmo will orient objects in respect to the world, which is the entire 3D space. I know this is really confusing and hard to explain. My recommendation is that you work with the local and world settings and find which of those is the easiest for you to use. I prefer the World Coordinates setting, but it is a matter of personal preference.

Freezing Patterns

You can freeze patterns in the 3D Window by selecting -

Edit > Context Menu > 3D Garment > Freeze

RC the pattern in 3D or 2D window > Freeze

When you freeze a pattern it will turn blue and simulating will no longer effect it. However, all the seams are still intact and the rest of the garment will simulate normally.

Freezing is very helpful, as it reduces computer resource usage on large patterns. It is also very beneficial when working with layers, you can freeze lower patterns as you stack more on top. Frozen patterns are still collision objects and unfrozen patterns will simulate around them and collide with them.

Showing & Hiding Patterns

You can choose to show or hide patterns in the 3D Window. You can hide or show the entire garment (all patterns) using the toggle.

Display > 3D Garment > Show Garment

You can hide individual patterns by selecting the pattern and -

Display > 3D Garment > Hide/Show 3D Pattern

RC the pattern in the 3D or 2D window > Hide/Show 3D Pattern

To see hidden patterns select -

Display > 3D Garment > Show All 3D Patterns

RC the background or a pattern in the 3D window > Show All 3D Patterns

All of these processes change the visibility of the patterns only. The sewing remains intact and simulations will continue to work as usual, the pattern is just invisible.

If you want to zoom in on one particular pattern -

Display > Viewpoint > Focus Zoom

RC the pattern > Focus Zoom

Activate & Deactivate Patterns

Freezing, showing and hiding patterns has no effect on the sewing. All attached pieces will still be sewn to the affected pattern and it will collide with other patterns and the Avatar. You can deactivate a pattern by selecting -

Edit > Context Menu > 3D Garment > Deactivate (Pattern Only)

RC the pattern in the 3D or 2D window > Deactivate (Pattern Only)

The pattern will turn transparent and freeze in place. The pattern is no longer a collision object and becomes invisible to all the patterns around it. The sewing is still intact and the seams are still active during simulation.

If you want to deactivate the sewing on a pattern, but not the pattern itself, select the pattern and -

Figure 4-9. Sewing and Pattern Deactivated

Edit > Context Menu > Sewing > Deactivate Sewing (Selected)

RC the pattern in the 2D window > Deactivate Sewing (Selected)

This is a quick way to release the seams on a pattern for testing, without actually deleting them. To reactivate the sewing on all patterns select -

Sewing > Activate Sewing (All)

To reactivate sewing on one pattern select -

Edit > Context Menu > Sewing > Activate Sewing (Selected)

RC the pattern in the 2D window > Activate Sewing (Selected)

If you want to completely deactivate the pattern and all its sewing, select -

Edit > Context Menu > 3D Garment > Deactivate (Pattern & Sewing)

RC the pattern in the 3D or 2D window > Deactivate (Pattern & Sewing)

Although you can still see the pattern in the window, it is completely invisible to everything else in the scene. The sewing is deactivated and none of the attached patterns will recognize it. Simulations behave as though it isn't there at all.

Taking a Snapshot

One very nice feature of the 3D Window is the ability to take a snapshot of your current scene. You can position your Avatar and other objects any way you wish and then create an image. To take a snapshot select -

File > Snapshot > 3D Window

First, MD will ask for the name of the image and where you wish to save it. When you click Save, a dialog box will open.

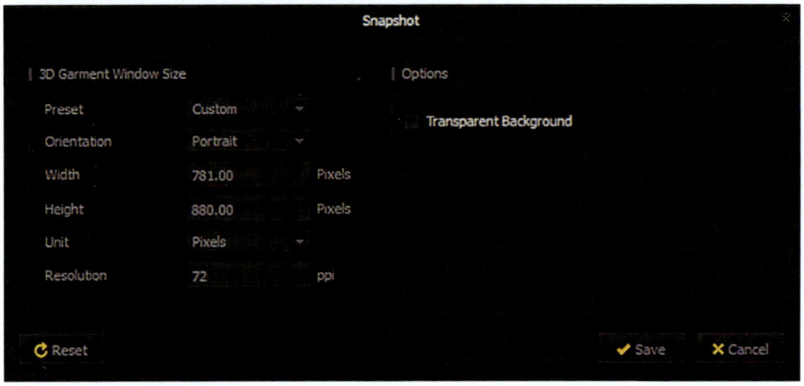

Figure 4-10. Snapshot Dialog

The 3D Garment Window Size section allows you to select from a list of Preset sizes or enter your own custom size. When you size the window yourself by entering the Width and Height, you need to tell MD what Unit of measure you're entering. You can choose pixels, inches, centimeters or millimeters. The Resolution refers to the ppi of the image, which is pixels per inch. If you're creating an image for the web, you can keep this lower, around 72. If you're creating an image to print, set this higher, to 300 or more.

The second section is Options and only contains the Transparent Background checkbox. If you want MD to ignore the background in the scene, check the box. The snapshot is saved as a PNG file, so if you set the background as transparent, it will actually be transparent, not white.

Even if you set the background to transparent, any shadows in the scene will still be in the image. To turn off shadows deselect -

Display > Show 3D Shadow

RC the 3D background > Show 3D Shadow

Chapter 4 Quiz

1) When using the Planar type of Wind (choose one):

❍ A. Place the cone where you want the wind to originate.

❍ B. Point the cone in the direction you want the wind to blow.

❍ C. The wind will blow in a spherical shape from the cone.

2) 3D Window snapshots are JPG files with an opaque background.

❍ True ❍ False

3) The Gizmo can be oriented to (choose all):

❍ A. World Coordinates

❍ B. Avatar Coordinates

❍ C. Local Coordinates

❍ D. Screen Coordinates

4) When it comes to lighting (choose one):

❍ A. You can change the color and direction of both lights.

❍ B. You can change the color of both lights, but not the direction.

❍ C. You can change the color of both lights, but the direction of only one.

Chapter 5 - Avatar Measurements & Fit

Garment Design

A fashion designer will illustrate their design for a garment by using parts of prior work as a basis or drawing something from scratch. When you are designing your garments, don't be concerned with stealing someone else's design. Some of the most expensive fashion houses design their entire lines by taking images of prior work, theirs as well as other's, and picking elements that they want to re-use or modify.

Although this hasn't been challenged legally in regard to CG, in the real world, you can't copyright or patent a garment. That's why designers don't hesitate to copy one another. You are free to recreate whatever fashions you find. However, you should be careful of logos and brands.

Since you can't patent a purse any more than a dress, the designers set themselves apart by using logos in their fabrics. A Gucci purse is quickly identified not by its design, but by the logo splashed all over it. You can't put the Gucci logo on your 3D purses. That's copyright infringement and you'll get in a lot of trouble for that.

It becomes the patternmaker's responsibility to create a pattern that results in the final garment matching the designer's vision and requirements. The patternmaker typically uses one of two techniques to create a pattern that matches the design. Those techniques are draping and drafting.

Draping is done by very experienced tailors and seamstresses. It uses fabric, pins and a dress form as a basis. The fabric is draped on the dress form and then manipulated and pinned in place. It is a very tactile process requiring a high degree of skill. The high fashion houses, like Chanel, use the draping technique to create their garments for fashion shows and clientele. Technically, you could drape your garments in MD using pins, but it would be extremely cumbersome.

Drafting is done using slopers, also referred to as basic blocks. These base patterns are manipulated by adding or removing fullness using the Slash and Spread technique. This is the process that I used when I created the program PatternMaker PRO that drafts patterns automatically for MD.

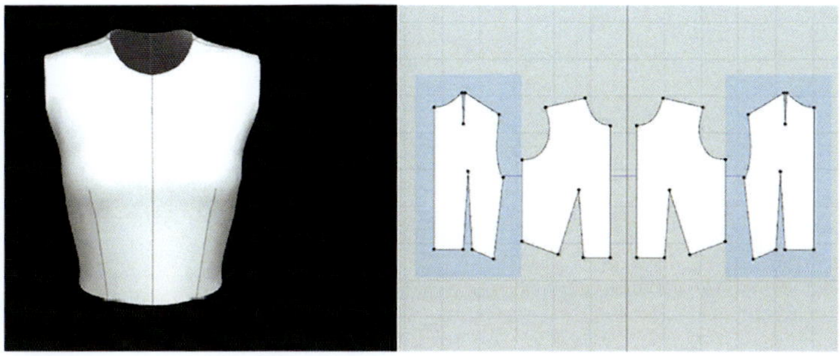

Figure 5-2. Female Bodice Sloper

Ease

There are two kinds of ease that are used in the generation of patterns. The first is wearing ease and the second is design ease. The patternmaker will determine the amount of design ease that is required in order for the garment to drape on the body as the designer intended.

All real-world garments must contain wearing ease to allow for movement and comfort. If patterns are drafted using only the body's measurements, the wearer couldn't move around or sit down. Wearing ease is the number of inches or centimeters added to the actual body measurements to allow the wearer to live in the clothes. Wearing ease is generally less than one inch added to specific measurements.

In MD, we don't need to worry too much about wearing ease. Our avatars aren't gallivanting around in the software and they don't complain when their clothes are too snug. For the most part, you do not need to concern yourself with wearing ease.

Design ease is added fullness beyond wearing ease incorporated into a pattern to create a specific silhouette, as dictated by the fashion designer. These variations are almost limitless, but manufacturers often designate several specific categories.

Real-world sewing patterns include a reference to design ease right on the package. Here's a chart from Butterick, a real-world sewing pattern company, that shows you the large variance in fit.

Misses' Ease Allowances (Inches)

Silhouette	**Bust Area** Dresses, Blouses, Skirts, Tops, Vests	Jackets	Coats	**Hip Area** Skirts, Pants, Shorts, Culottes
Close Fitting	0" – 2 7/8"	N/A	N/A	0" – 1 7/8"
Fitted	3" – 4"	3 3/4" – 4 1/4"	5 1/4" – 6 3/4"	2" – 3"
Semi-Fitted	4 1/8" – 5"	4 3/8" – 5 3/4"	6 7/8" – 8"	3 1/8" – 4"
Loose Fitting	5 1/8" – 8"	5 7/8" – 10"	8 1/8" – 12"	4 1/8" – 6"
Very Loose Fitting	Over 8"	Over 10"	Over 12"	Over 6"

Misses' Ease Allowances (Centimeters)

Silhouette	**Bust Area** Dresses, Blouses, Skirts, Tops, Vests	Jackets	Coats	**Hip Area** Skirts, Pants, Shorts, Culottes
Close Fitting	0 – 7.3 cm	N/A	N/A	0 – 4.8 cm
Fitted	7.5 cm – 10 cm	9.5 cm – 10.7 cm	13.3 cm – 17 cm	5 cm – 7.5 cm
Semi-Fitted	10.4 cm – 12.5 cm	11.1 cm – 14.5 cm	17.4 cm – 20.5 cm	7.9 cm – 10 cm
Loose Fitting	13 cm – 20 cm	14.8 cm – 25.5 cm	20.7 cm – 30.5 cm	10.4 cm – 15 cm
Very Loose Fitting	Over 20.5 cm	Over 25.5 cm	Over 30.5 cm	Over 15 cm

http://butterick.mccall.com/ease-chart-pages-456.php

Figure 5-3. Butterick / McCall Ease Chart

There are five different categories of fit, from close fitting, which would be like a sloper with wearing ease, all the way up to very loose fitting. Just changing the design ease of a garment makes a huge difference in how it looks.

Regardless of the ease of the design, the ultimate goal is that the garment fits the person wearing it. Fashion designers have specific intentions on how the garment drapes, as well as comfort and style. Even though a design may include a dropped shoulder line or an over-sized bodice, the basis of the pattern always fits the intended model size.

Fit in MD

You may think this information is interesting, but has no application to your work in MD. However, understanding fit is very important to your CG garments. You too must come up with a design to start with. It could be a sketch or image. Then you need to create the basic patterns in the 2D Window.

You'll need to recognize the difference between a garment that does not fit well and one that does. A garment may be very loose fitting, with a lot of ease, but at its core it still fits the Avatar.

Here are two images of the female default B Avatar. The dress on the left was drafted using her measurements. I purposely added a lot of ease at the bust, waist and hips. You can see that the dress is very loose fitting, but it is still based on her own measurements. It still "fits" even though it is roomy.

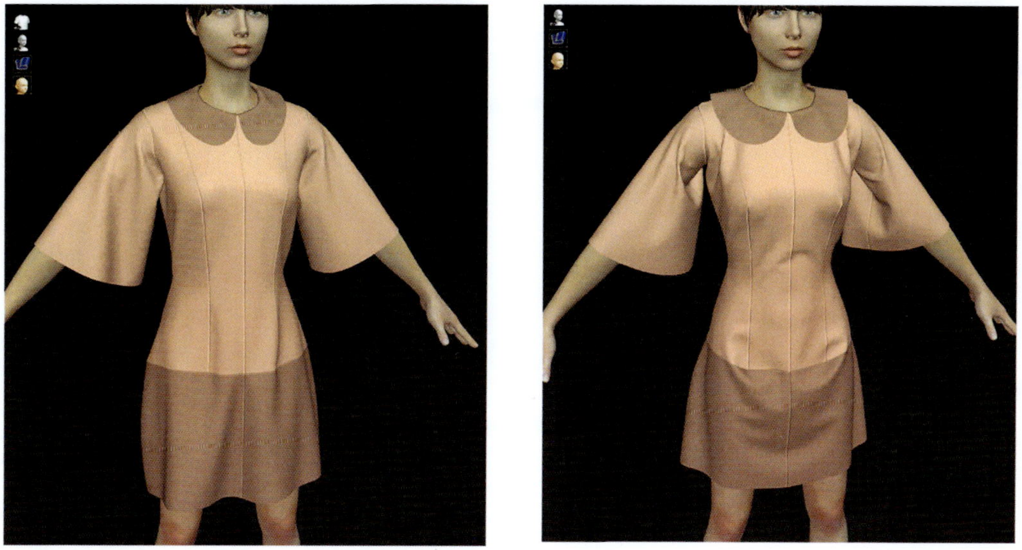

Figure 5-1. Female B Avatar - B Avatar Dress on Left, C Avatar Dress on Right

On the right is the same dress on Avatar B. This time I drafted the patterns using the default MD female Avatar C measurements. The dress is too big in some places and too small in others. It fits very badly. You can tell that it was not made to fit her.

This distinction is very important. You can vary the ease on a pattern to make it form fitting or loose, but it should be based on the avatar's measurements. You can't make one shirt and use it on all of your characters just scaling it up and down. It won't look realistic.

Measuring Avatars in MD

The ability to measure your avatars is a fairly recent addition to MD. If you are generating patterns outside of the program using real-world drafting techniques, you'll need a full set of measurements. For example, PatternMaker PRO requires measurements to create patterns.

If you are just going to draft your patterns directly in the 2D Window, you can often save a lot of time by having some of your Avatar's measurements available for reference. For example, if you were drafting out a skirt, it would be nice to know the distance from the Avatar's waist to the skirt hem edge.

MD includes a group of five measurement tools for you to use. If the measurement tools are hidden select -

Avatar > Measurement

RC the 3D toolbar > Measurement Toolbar

Figure 5-4. Measurement Tool Button Dropped Down

The buttons on the toolbar show the basic tools. Click and hold the buttons with a gray corner to expand for more options.

Most of the default MD avatars come with their own complete sets of measurements. To see the complete measurement set in MD select -

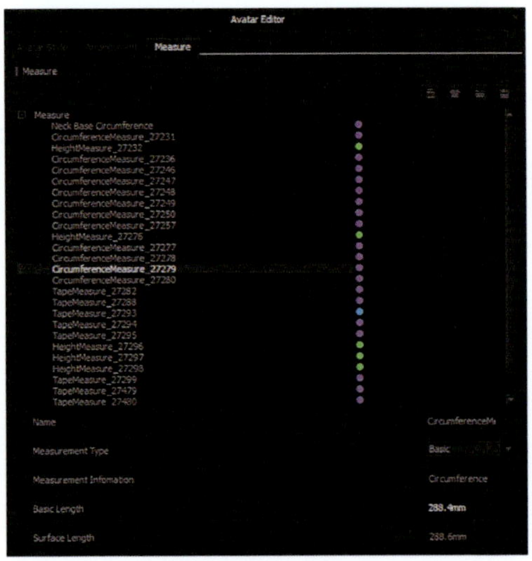

Figure 5-5. Avatar Editor Measure Tab

Avatar > Avatar Editor > Measure tab

Each time you create a measurement, MD adds it to the list of Measure objects. Each type of measurement has a different color indicator. Basic is purple, Surface is blue and Height is green.

You can show and hide measurements by selecting/deselecting the Show box or clicking the colored circle next to each one in the list.

You can change the name of the measurement to whatever you like. You can also see the Measurement Type, Information, and Lengths.

You can open an existing set of measurements, save the current set as a .mea file or delete individual measurements using the buttons in the top right of the Measure tab.

When you select an individual measurement in the list, MD will highlight that particular measurement in the 3D window. If you can't see the measurements drawn on your Avatar, select -

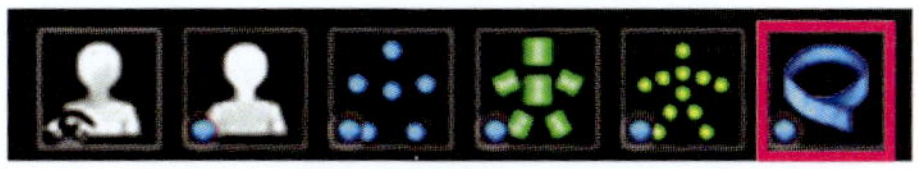

Display > Avatar > Show Avatar Measurements

Surface vs Basic

Before you begin to measure, you need to understand the distinction between a Surface measurement and a Basic measurement. If you wanted to measure the distance between the bust apex on this Avatar, you click on one side and then double click on the other to stop the path. Doing this with the Basic Tape tool, you get a straight measurement from point to point as shown in the image.

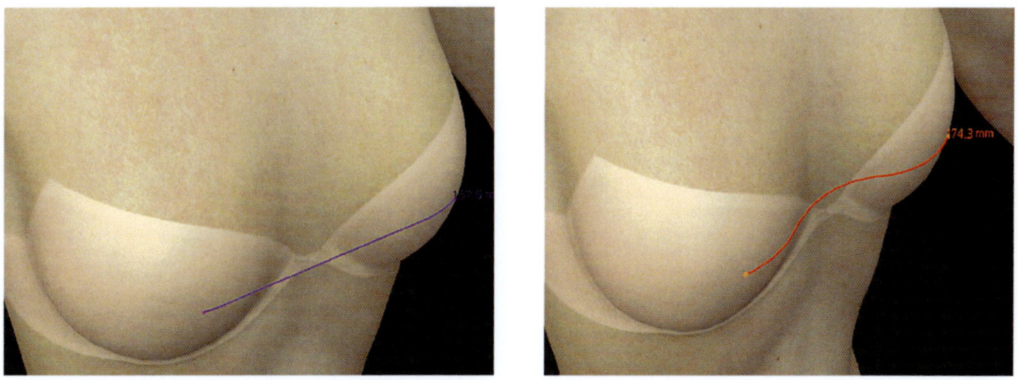

Figure 5-6. Apex to Apex Measurement Using Basic Tape on Left and Surface Tape on Right

If you repeat this process with the Surface Tape tool, you'll see that it conforms to the body. The Surface measurement will be longer, and in some cases, a lot longer than the Basic.

If you think about how cloth lays across the body, you'll understand that the Basic measurement is more realistic for drafting patterns. A shirt is not going to pull in between the breasts. For that reason, you should use the Basic tools, as opposed to the Surface tools, most of the time.

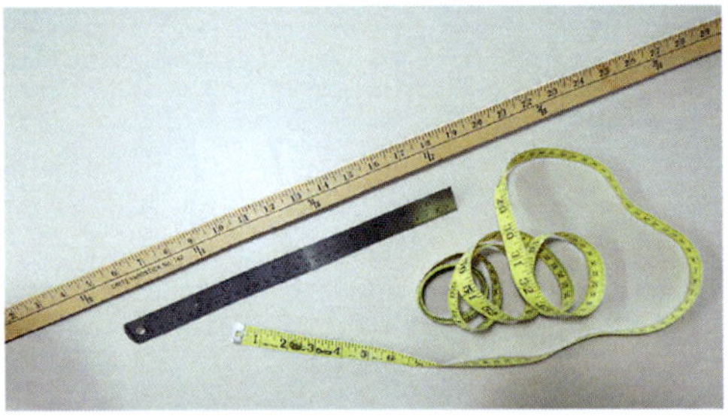

To help you visualize the difference, think of the Basic tools as a stiff ruler or yardstick and the Surface tools as a flexible sewing measuring tape.

Figure 5-7. Yardstick, Metal Ruler, Sewing Tape Measure

You can change a Basic measurement to Surface measurement, or vice versa. With the measurement selected in the Measure tab of the Avatar Editor, use the Measurement Type drop-down to change the type.

Tape Tool

Avatar > Measurement > Basic / Surface Tape Measurement

To use the tape tools, click once at the start point and double click at the end point to stop. You can have as many points as you need in the path between the start and end points to hold the tape to the body.

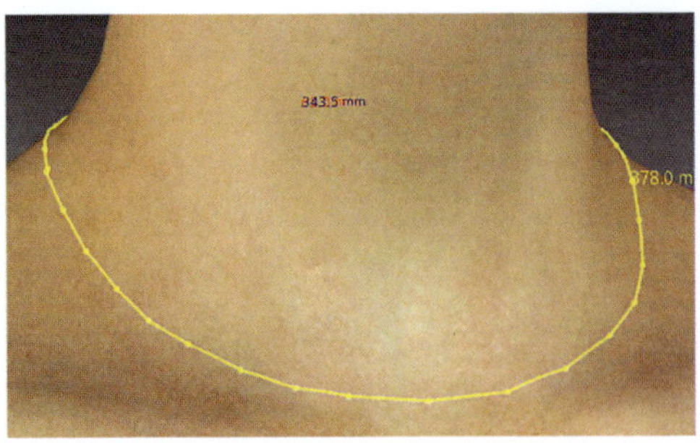

For example, when taking the neck measurement, you'll have to place points all the way around to create a nice curve. Note that the Circumference Measurement Tool rarely works for measuring the neck.

Figure 5-8. Basic Tape Used on Neck

Circumference Tool

Avatar > Measurement > Basic / Surface Circumference Measurement

The next tool is the Circumference Tool and it is available in both Basic and Surface.

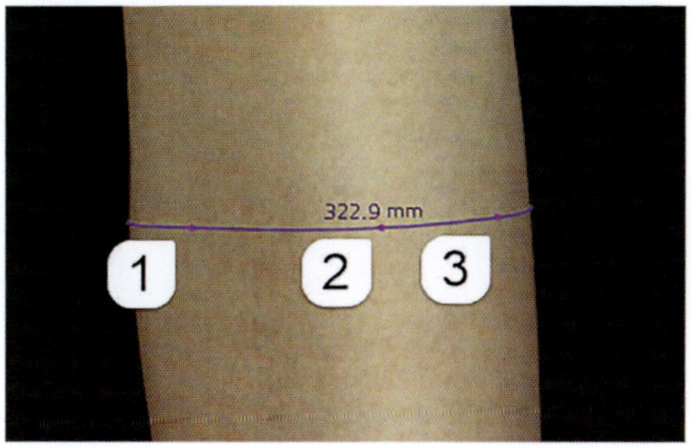

Figure 5-9. Creating Circumference Measurement

To use the Circumference tool, click once to set the starting point (#1 in image).

Then click again a small distance from the first click in the direction you want the circle path to go (#2 in image).

Wait just a moment and you'll see that a third point has been added and it's tied to your mouse. By moving the mouse, you can change the angle of the circle's path. When you get this angle where you want it, click again to set (#3 in image).

Height Tool

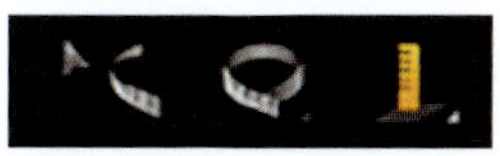

Avatar > Measurement > Height Measurement

The last tool is the height measurement. Click a point on the Avatar to measure from the floor to this point. You'll see that MD draws a yellow plane on the floor showing the origination point.

If you don't want the origination on the floor, select the Edit Measurement tool, click the plane and drag it up where you want it.

The Height tool is unique because it is the only tool that allows you to have a point not touching the avatar. It behaves like a yardstick, with no flexibility.

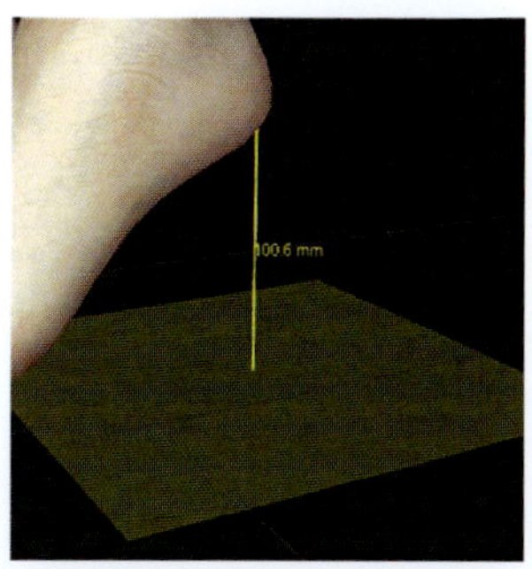

Figure 5-10. Height Measurement Floor Plane

Edit Measurement Tool

Avatar > Measurements > Edit Measurement

Although you can't really edit a measurement, such as moving a point, you'll want to use the Edit Measurement tool to select existing measurements.

Once you've selected a measurement, you can view its properties, make changes or delete it. You'll notice that a measurement's properties are only located on the Measure tab. They do not show in the Property Editor.

Chapter 5 Quiz

1) The Surface Tape measurement tool (choose one):

❍ A. Measures from the floor to the end point.

❍ B. Measures following the curve of the avatar from point to point.

❍ C. Measures straight from point to point.

2) A ski jacket would have more ease than a t-shirt.

❍ True ❍ False

3) Adding design ease doesn't change the silhouette of the garment.

❍ True ❍ False

4) You can change either end point of a tape measurement with the Edit Measurement tool.

❍ True ❍ False

Chapter 6 - Drafting Patterns

In the real world, a sewing pattern is a template that is laid on top of the garment fabric. The template is used to cut out the fabric. Then the fabric pieces are sewn together into a garment.

Sewing patterns are drafted using the measurements of a person or body model using rulers and curves. Below is an illustration showing the measurements used to draft a front female bodice.

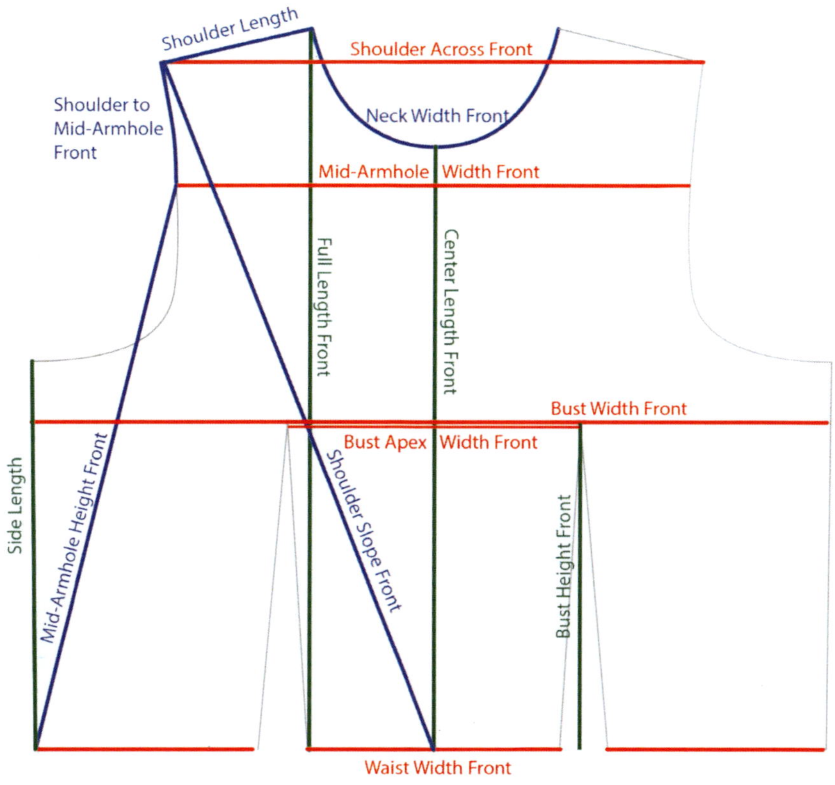

Figure 6-1. Front Bodice Measurement Key

A set of very basic patterns are drafted and test fit on the model. These patterns are called slopers or basic blocks. They have no design ease or decorative elements. They are intended to fit the model very closely.

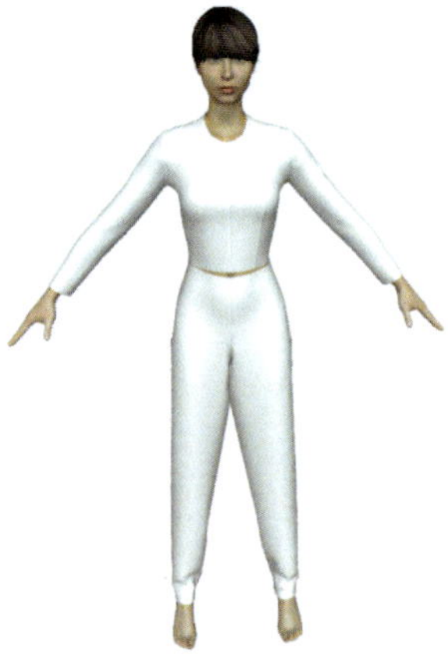

Figure 6-2. Slopers on MD Default Avatar

These sloper patterns are then manipulated to create new designs. A common method that is used to adjust the patterns is called the Slash and Spread technique.

The process for manipulating a sloper into a cowl neckline is shown below.

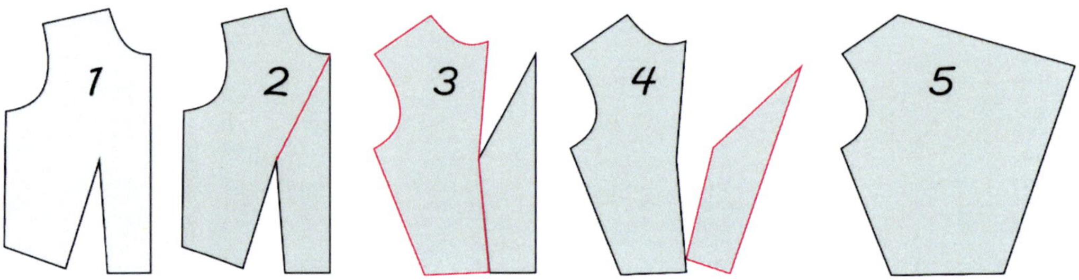

Figure 6-3. Cowl Bodice Drafting Process

Here are the steps taken:

1. The standard front bodice sloper.

2. The pattern is slashed from the bust point to the center front neck point.

3. The left side of the pattern is rotated to close the bust waist dart. This transfers the dart up to the neck.

4. The right side of the pattern is rotated out the distance the designer designates as the cowl spread.

5. The final pattern.

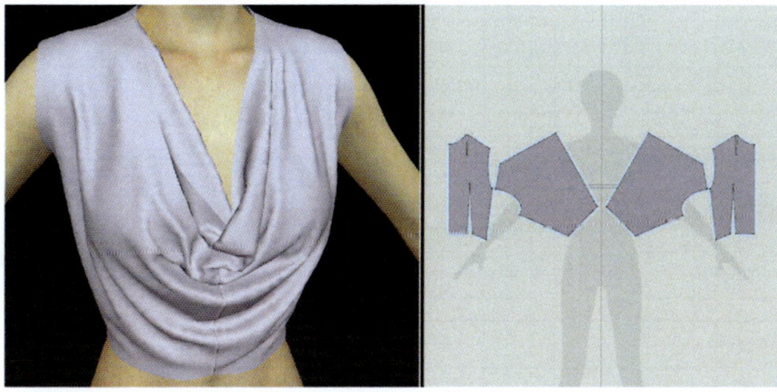

Figure 6-4. Final Cowl Pattern Completed

Here is the final pattern in MD. You'll notice the front bodice is rotated in the 2D Window so the pattern is laid on the bias to get a nice drape. You'll learn more about that in the *Grainlines & Pattern Layout* section in *Chapter 9 - Fabric.*

Drafting may be a bit confusing, but if you hope to make something other than shorts and t-shirts, you'll need to understand these concepts. The program that I created, PatternMaker PRO, creates patterns from slopers using this very same technique. The cowl pattern above was created with that program automatically. The image to the right shows the draft before hiding all the working geometry.

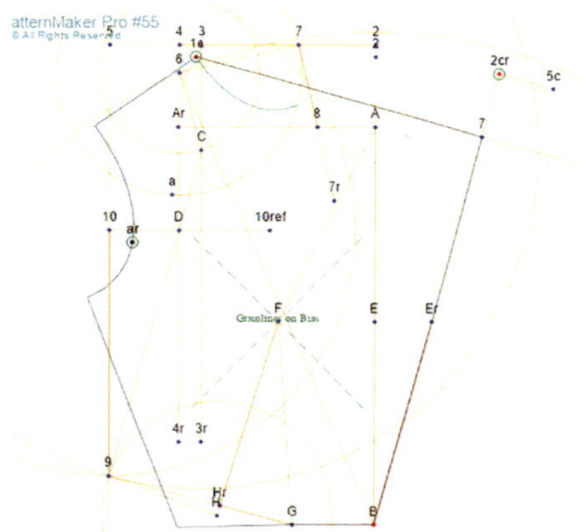

Figure 6-5. PatternMaker PRO in Action

You can clearly see that the process illustrated previously was used here. It doesn't matter if you Slash and Spread with JavaScript, with a 2D CAD program, right in the MD program or with pencil and paper; it's all the same process.

You can purchase pattern drafting books or find patterns on the web to use. Your primary goal is to create basic slopers for your character. Then you can start manipulating those patterns to create more designs.

MD has added a lot of tools recently that facilitate slashing and manipulating patterns in the 2D Window. I don't think this is by coincidence. They know that people need to have these tools to create more advanced and realistic garments.

If you want to learn more about pattern drafting, here are some of the books that I own. My very favorite book, and the easiest one to understand, is *Modern Pattern Design* written in 1942.

The most thorough book, providing a huge amount of designs, is the *Patternmaking for Fashion Design*. It is also the most expensive. You may be able to find used copies of all of these, or even borrow them from your library, to save some money.

Barnfield, Jo, and Andrew Richards. *The Pattern Making Primer.* Hauppauge: Barron's Educational Series, 2012. Print.

Joseph-Armstrong, Helen. *Patternmaking for Fashion Design*. 4th ed. Pearson, 2006. Print.

Kawashima, Masaaki. *Fundamentals of Men's Fashion Design: A Guide to Tailored Clothes*. New York: Fairchild Publications, 1980. Print.

Kim, Myoungok, and Injoo Kim. *Patternmaking for Menswear: Classic to Contemporary*. Fairchild, 2014. Print.

McCunn, Donald. *How to Make Sewing Patterns.* San Francisco: Design Enterprises of S.F., 1977. Print.

Pepin, Harriet. *Modern Pattern Design*. Funk & Wagnalls, 1942. Print.

Roberts, Edmund, and Gary Onishenko. *Fundamental of Men's Fashion Design: A Guide to Casual Clothes.* 2nd ed. New York: Fairchild Publications, 1985. Print.

Rosen, Sylvia. *Patternmaking.* Pearson, 2004. Print.

Working with Half Patterns

In most cases, your patterns will be symmetrical, meaning that the right and left sides are the same pattern mirrored. Drafting and modifying only one pattern and using symmetry in MD will cut your workload in half. You'll learn more about this process in *Chapter 7 - Arranging Patterns*.

Pattern Drafting Tools

In the real world, the process of drawing out templates used for cutting fabric to be made into clothing is called drafting patterns. MD provides a number of virtual pattern drafting tools for you to work with.

Polygon Tool

2D Pattern > Create > Polygon

The Polygon tool is used to draw a pattern that is *N*-sided. The *N* is a variable that stands for as many sides as needed. You create the shape by clicking on the 2D Window grid to set the first point, moving to where you want the next point and clicking again.

Repeat this process until the shape is done and then click on the first point you created to stop. Now the shape is closed and complete. The tool will not release until the shape is closed.

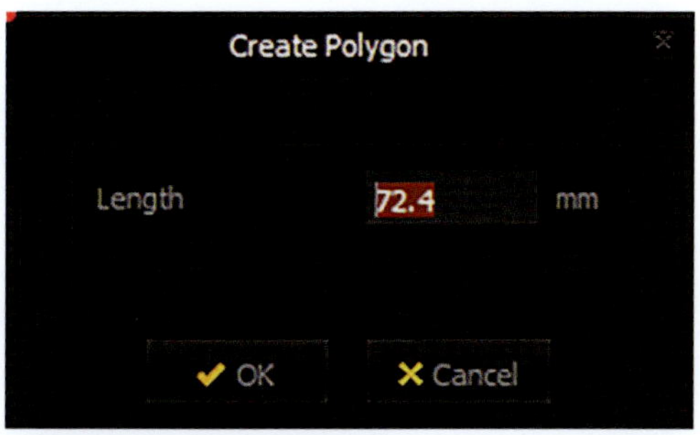

Figure 6-6. Create Polygon Dialog

To make points a specific distance from one another, right-click and a dialog box will open.

Enter the distance you want this point to be from the prior one and click OK.

Rectangle Tool

2D Pattern > Create > Rectangle

The Rectangle tool draws a box shape. There are two ways to use this tool: freestyle and precise. To draw freestyle, click and drag in the 2D window. The first point will be the upper left corner of the rectangle.

If you want the rectangle to be perfectly square, hold down the Shift key as you click and drag.

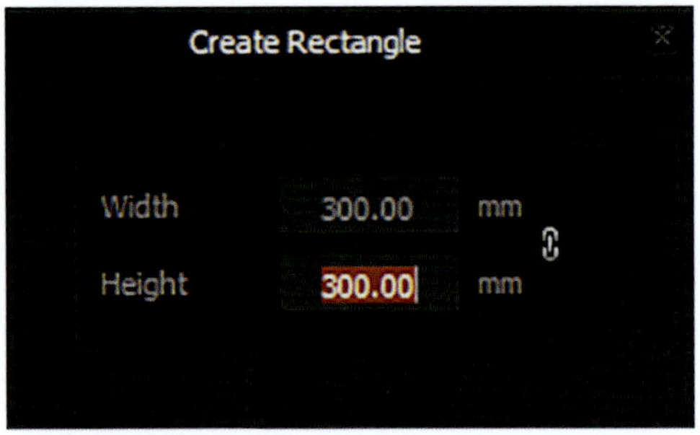

Figure 6-7. Create Rectangle Dialog

To create a precise rectangle, just click in the 2D Window (no drag).

The Create Rectangle dialog box will open allowing you to enter the precise Width and Height of your rectangle.

If you want the rectangle to be perfectly square, click the chain link icon and MD will make sure that Width and Height are the same number.

Circle Tool

2D Pattern > Create > Circle

The Circle tool works with the same two methods as the Rectangle tool.

You can draw freestyle, by clicking and dragging in the 2D window. The first click is the center of the circle and the circle will radiate out from that point.

To create a precise circle, click in the 2D Window and a Create Circle dialog will open. Enter the Diameter of the circle.

Figure 6-8. Create Circle Dialog

When you are drawing circles, you may not know the diameter. You may wish to draw the circle using the radius or the circumference. Refer to the following illustration for the math to convert from one to another.

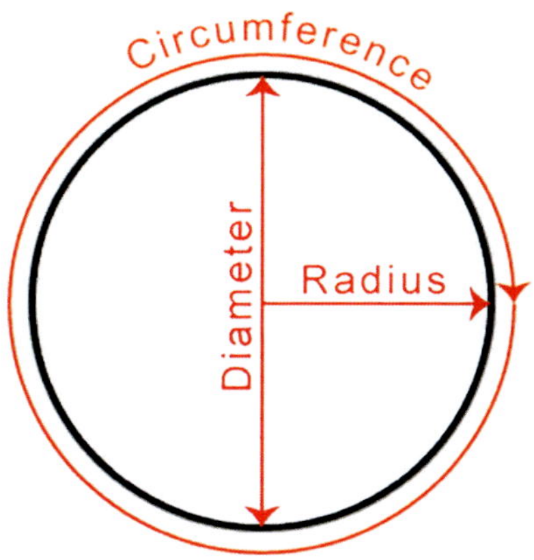

Circumference / 3.14 = Diameter

Radius x 2 = Diameter

Figure 6-9. Circle Formulas

Selecting & Editing Your Patterns

There are several ways to select and edit your patterns. You can edit individual elements, like points and segments with the Edit Pattern Tool, or the entire pattern with the Transform Pattern tool. The right-click menu will be different depending on which tool you are using.

Show Line Length

Editing will be easier, if you can see the lengths of all the lines as you work.

Display > 2D Pattern > Show Line Length

RC the 2D background > Show Line Length

Edit Pattern Tool

To use the Edit Pattern tool, select -

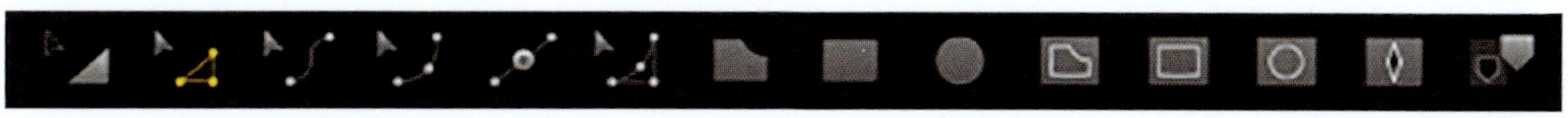

2D Pattern > Edit > Edit Pattern

This tool allows you to select a point or a segment (line between points). You can also select multiple objects by holding down Shift while selecting. Once you've made your selection, drag to move the selection.

If you have any fabric textures on your patterns, they will disappear when you select this tool. To see them again select the Show 2D Textures button in the 2D toolbar.

To keep your movement perfectly vertical, horizontal or at 45°, hold down the Shift key as you drag. This will constrain your movement to the purple dashed lines shown in the image.

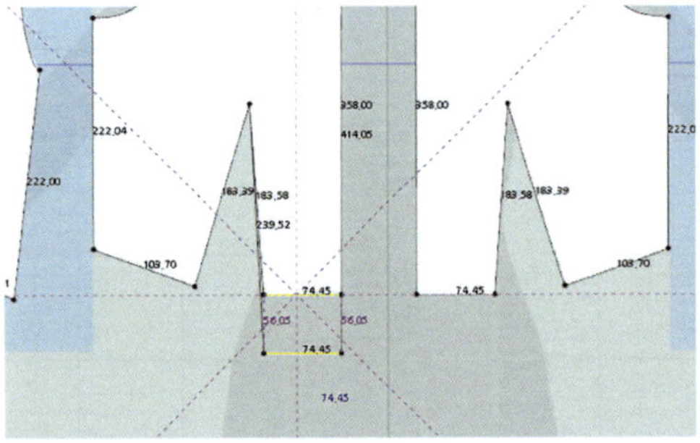

Figure 6-10. Hold Shift While Dragging to Constrain

You may want to adjust the length of a line, but need to keep the angle the same. To do this, hold down your Control key as you drag. It will preserve the original angle of the line as you adjust it.

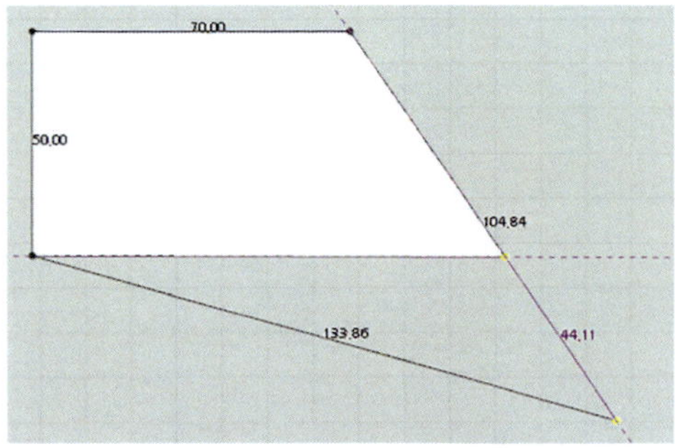

Figure 6-11. Hold Control While Dragging to Keep Angle

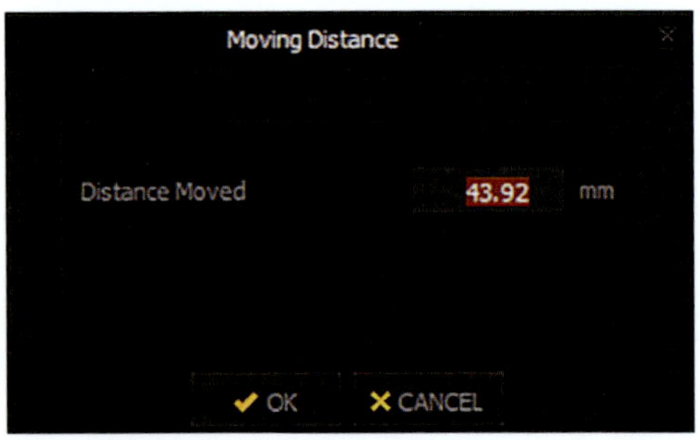

Figure 6-12. Moving Distance Dialog

You can also move a precise distance with the Edit Pattern tool. While you are dragging, right click your mouse. This will open a dialog box where you can enter an exact distance to move.

As you move things, MD will show you the distances in purple. Those amounts are dynamic and will change as you move your mouse. This lets you know how much you have moved, so you can place things more precisely.

Snapping

By default, MD will snap to the pattern when drawing. This is convenient, particularly when you are drawing internal geometry. To change this setting select -

Preferences > Snap to Pattern

RC > Snap to Pattern

You can also snap to the grid as you are drawing by selecting -

Preferences > Snap to Grid

RC the 2D background > Snap to Grid

Aligning Points

When you are modifying your patterns, you'll be moving points around a lot. Sometimes you need your points to be in perfect alignment.

Align to X or Y Axis

You can align your points in a straight line on the X or Y axis automatically. Select all the points that you want to align and then -

RC > Align > To Point (X Axis) / To Point(Y Axis)

The order of your point selection will make a difference. The last point selected is the target point. All others will align to the target point position.

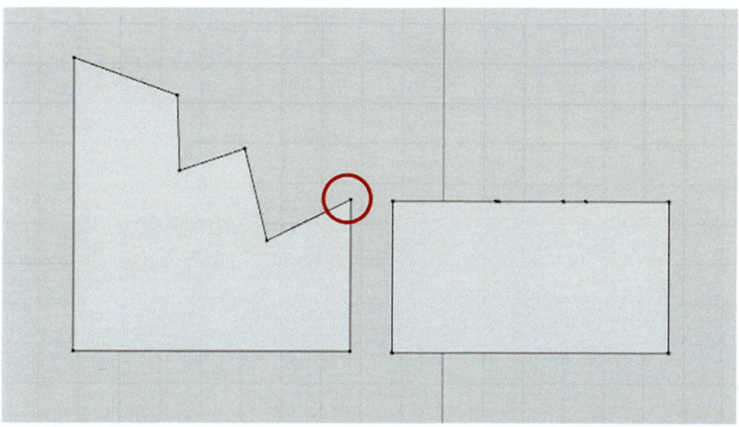

Figure 6-13. Before (left) and After (right) Using Align to X Axis (All top points were selected with the circled point selected last)

Align to Direction

You can align points to a particular direction. The order that you select the points is irrelevant. MD will use the point that is the furthest in the direction selected as the alignment point. The Center and Middle options will find the median between the furthest Left and Right or Top and Bottom respectively. Select all the points you want to align then -

RC > Align >Left / Center / Right / Top / Middle / Bottom

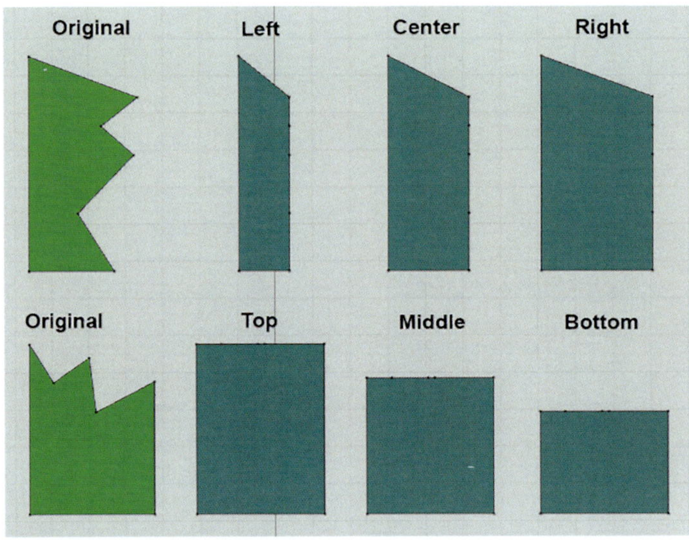

Figure 6-14. Align Points to Direction

These alignment options are also available for you to use on full patterns when arranging them in the 2D Window.

Using Your Keyboard

When you want to move in very precise increments, you can use the arrow keys on your keyboard. By default, MD will move 10 mm for every arrow key press. You can change this value to anything you like by selecting -

Preferences > 2D Pattern Window Properties

The setting is in the Property Editor under Arrow Key Movement. The Arrow Key Movement setting does not always persist. You may need to reset it.

Transform Pattern Tool

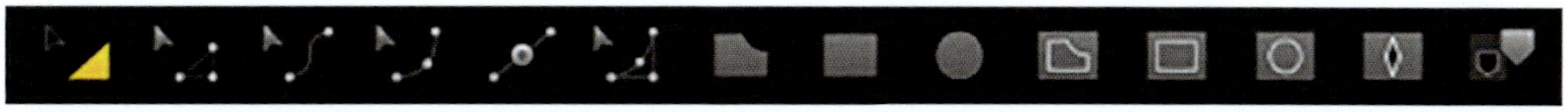

2D Pattern > Edit > Transform Pattern

This tool allows you to select and transform entire patterns. You can select one pattern or multiple patterns by holding down the Shift key as you select them. The Transform Pattern tool works as follows (refer to image):

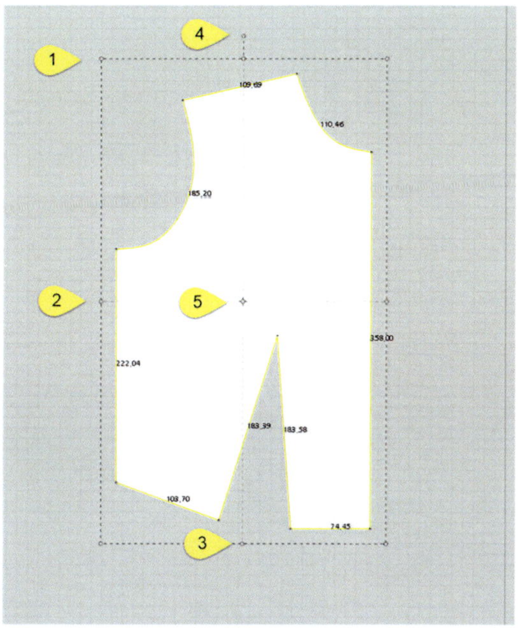

Figure 6-15. Transform Pattern Tool Functions

Point 1 - To re-size the pattern, you can click and drag on any of the four corners of the dashed rectangle. The top left corner is labeled #1 in the illustration. Resizing using the corners will not distort the pattern.

Point 2 - You can make the pattern wider. Click and drag on the left or right middle points on the vertical lines of the rectangle. The left point is labeled #2. This will distort the pattern.

Point 3 - To make the pattern taller or longer, click and drag on the top or bottom middle points on the horizontal lines of the rectangle. The bottom point is labeled #3. This will distort the pattern.

Point 4 - You can rotate the pattern. Click and rotate at the top point labeled #4. Hold down Shift to rotate in 45° increments. The pattern will rotate using the center point #5 as the rotation axis.

Point 5 - The point #5 is the default rotation point. You can change the location of the rotation point. Click the point and move it where you want it within the rectangle. Now when you rotate, the new location will be the rotation axis.

Resizing by Percentage

It is also possible to resize your pattern by a specific percentage. While you are dragging on any of the points around the box, right click your mouse. The dialog box contents will be different depending on which point you were dragging.

If you are dragging one of the center points on the vertical sides, the box will ask for Width. If you are dragging one of the center points on the horizontal sides, it will ask for Height. If you are dragging any of the four corners, the box will have Height and Width options.

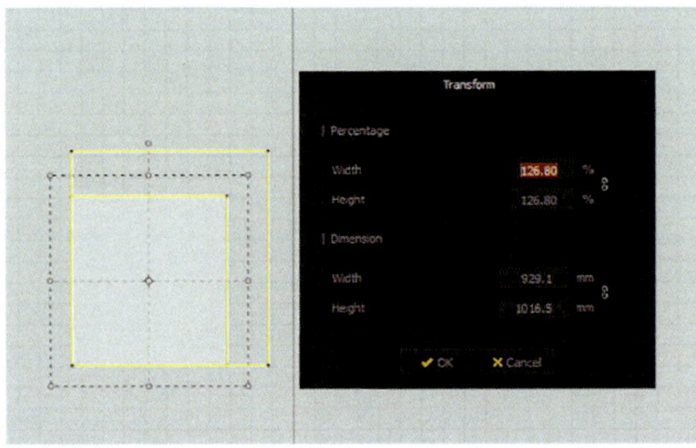

Figure 6-16. Transform Dialog

You can enter a specific percentage to increase or decrease the Height or Width of the pattern. By default, MD locks the percentages to each other to keep the pattern in proportion. If you want to change them by different percentages, click the chain link to unlock them.

You can also change the dimensions of the pattern by entering size values, instead of a percentage. Again, the values are locked by default. Unlock them to change the proportion of the pattern.

Select All with Same Property

There is another feature associated with the Transform Pattern tool called Select All with Same Property. This feature allows you to select multiple objects at the same time based on shared properties. Your options will change depending on where you use the tool.

RC > Select All with Same Property > Select Property

If you right-click on a pattern, your options include Particle Distance, Layer and Fabric. When you choose an option, all patterns that have the same value of the selected property as the pattern you right-clicked will be automatically added to your selection.

If you right-click on an internal line your options include Fold Strength, Fold Angle and Fold Rendering. Select an option and all other lines with that property will be added to your selection.

Curves

Nearly every pattern you draw will need to have curves in it. There are a number of ways to create curves, but they can only be created after your pattern is drawn. You can't draw curves dynamically, while initially drawing the pattern, they are added after your pattern shape is completed.

Edit Curvature Tool

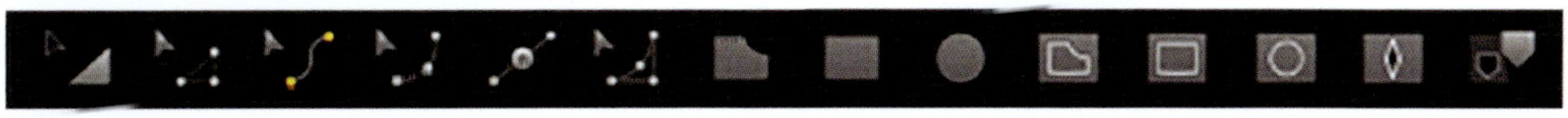

2D Pattern > Edit > Edit Curvature

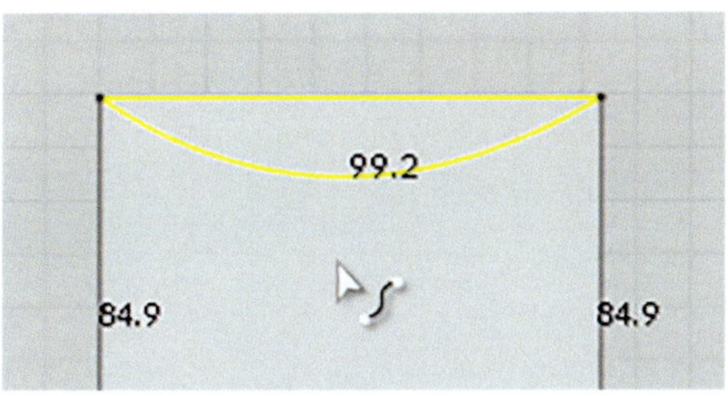

Figure 6-17. Edit Curvature Tool

The Edit Curvature tool changes a straight line or segment into a curve.

Click on a line and drag in the direction you want the curve to go. You can see your original line and the new curve as you are dragging. This tool will create a Bezier curve, which MD calls a three-point curve.

Edit Curve Point Tool

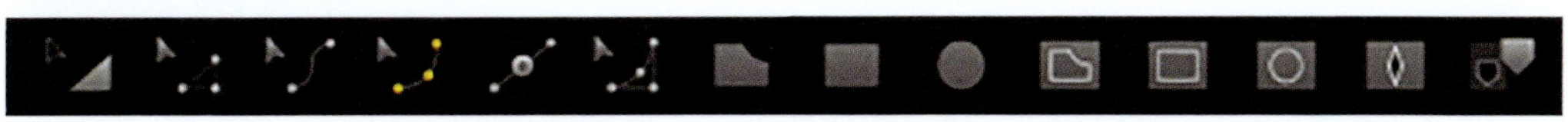

2D Pattern > Edit > Edit Curve Point

The Edit Curve Point tool is very similar to the Edit Curvature tool, but it has some added benefits. The tool can be used to add or edit curve points. Curves added with this tool are fit to the curve, which MD calls free curves. There can be multiple free curve points between segment points.

When editing, the advantage of this tool lies in the visualization of the point. Curve points will be shown on the pattern, so they are easy to select and move.

Curve points created with the Edit Curvature tool and Round Corner tool will be offset, as a Bezier control point.

Curve points created with the Edit Curve Point tool and the Convert to Curve Point method will be fit to the curve. Any type of curve can be edited with the Edit Curve Point tool.

You can delete a curve point by selecting it and using your Delete key or -

RC > Delete Point

You can delete all the curve points between any two segment points. Select the segment with the Edit Pattern tool and -

RC > Delete All Curve Points

Converting Curve Point to Point

If you want to convert a curve point to a standard segment point select the curve point and -

Edit > Context Menu > 2D Pattern > Convert to Segment Point

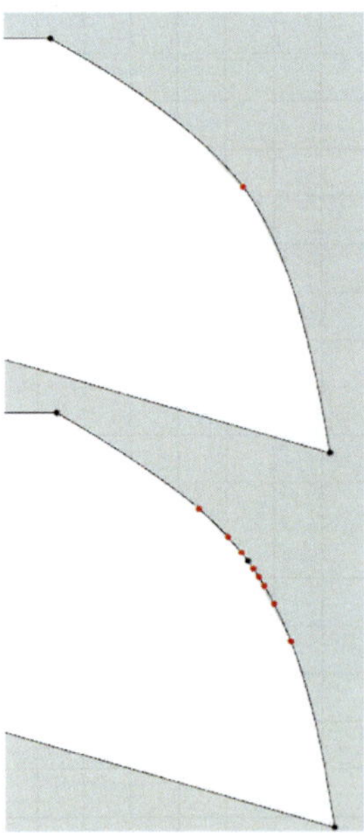

RC > Convert to Segment Point

MD will convert the curve point and it will add as many additional curve points as necessary to keep the curve intact. In the image, the top pattern was the original.

On the bottom pattern you can see the new standard segment point is black in the center but many curve points were added by MD to hold the curve shape.

Figure 6-18. Converting Curve Point (top) to Regular Point (bottom)

Converting Point to Curve Point

In some cases, you will want to turn a standard segment point into a curve point. There are two different methods for doing so, each with very different results.

Convert to Curve Point Method

To convert a regular point to a curve point, select the standard segment point and then select -

Edit > Context Menu > 2D Pattern > Convert to Curve Point

RC > Convert to Curve Point

The pattern in the image was a perfect square, then the top left corner was converted to a curve point.

You can see that the original corner point became the inline fit point for the curve extending the curve out to the corners at the top right and bottom left.

Figure 6-19. Regular Point Converted to Curve Point

Edit Round Corner Tool

2D Pattern > Edit > Edit Round Corner

The second way to convert a standard point to a curve point is to use the Edit Round Corner Tool.

Click on the standard segment point and drag to round off the corner. You can decide how round the corner becomes.

Figure 6-20. Edit Round Corner

You can see this is very different from the Convert to Curve Point method. The corner point is now a Bezier control point with two other points added to hold the square shape beyond the curved corner.

Add Points / Split Line

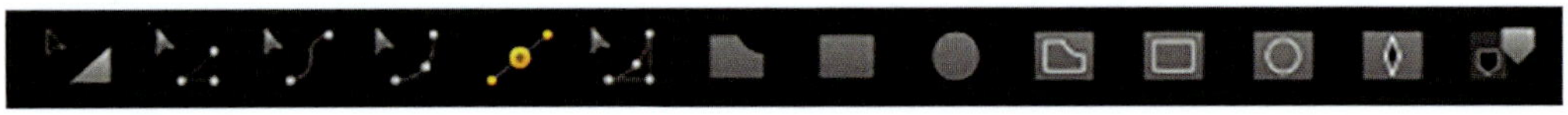

2D Pattern > Edit > Add Point / Split Line

As you are editing your patterns, you will often need to add additional points to the lines. There are two ways to use this tool.

For the first method, hover the cursor over the line segment. MD will show you the line lengths to either side of the proposed point. Click to set the point.

The second method is much more precise and has additional options. With the tool selected, right click the line. You can also select the line with the Edit Pattern tool active and -

RC > Split

This will open a Split Line dialog box with three options for setting the new point.

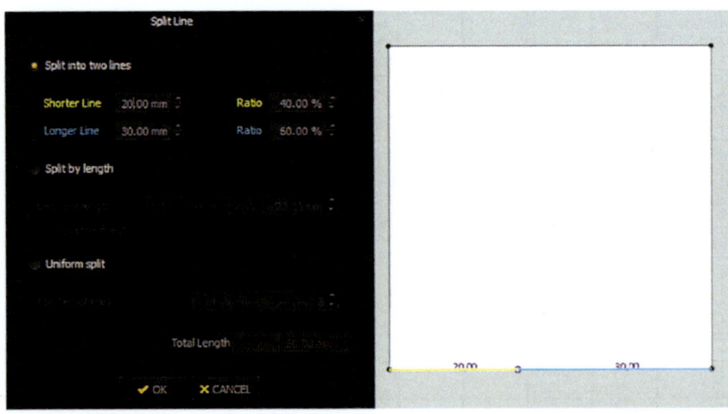

Figure 6-21. Split into Two Lines

The Split into Two Lines section shows you the new length of the lines to either side, as well as the ratio. Enter a number in any box and the others will change automatically.

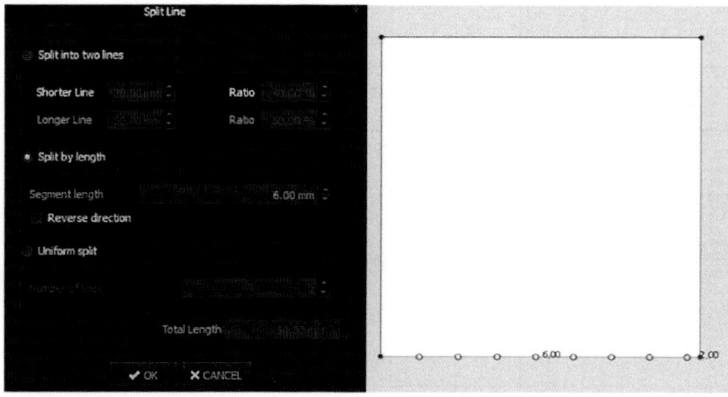

Figure 6-22. Split By Length

The Split by Length section allows you to enter a length to create multiple segments of equal size, if the line is evenly divisible by the length. If not, you will have an odd sized remainder segment.

For example, if you have a line that is 50 mm long and you want it split into segments of 6 mm each, it would create nine total segments; eight of them 6 mm long and the last one 2 mm long.

Be careful with this! This is not a uniform split and if there is a remainder, the last segment will be a different length. If MD starts the division from the wrong starting point, select the Reverse Direction checkbox.

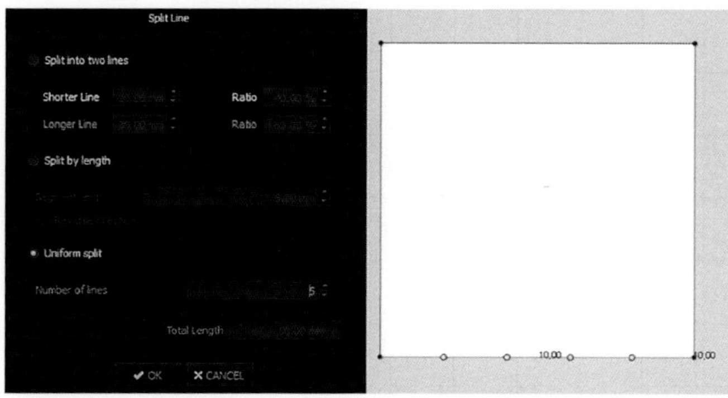

Figure 6-23. Uniform Split

The Uniform Split section allows you to split the line into uniform lengths that MD will calculate. All you have to provide is the quantity of segments, not points, you want created.

Offset Pattern Outline

You can extend the outside edge of a pattern without distorting its shape.

This can be applied to one segment or multiple segments with the Edit Pattern tool or the entire pattern outline with the Transform Pattern tool.

To use this feature, make your selection then -

RC > Offset Pattern Outline

A dialog box will open with various options. Distance tells MD how far out you want the offset to be. You can specify more than one offset and MD will move one Distance for each Number of Offset. The Total Distance will be shown in the box.

By default, you will see a reference line on your pattern showing where the old line was. If you would prefer that this becomes an internal line, check the Create Internal Line box.

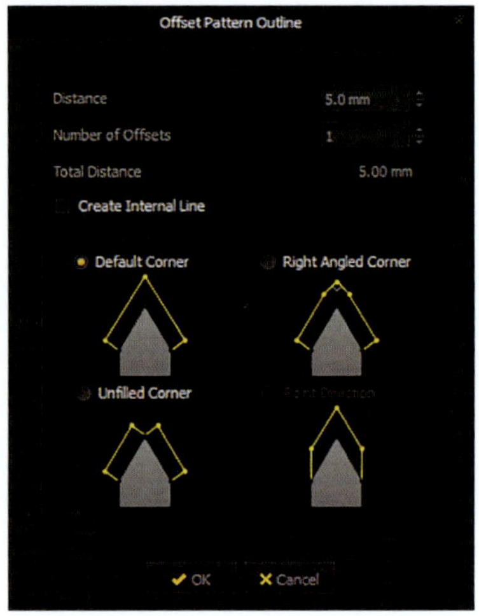

Figure 6-25. Offset Pattern Outline Dialog

MD offers you four different options for turning the corners on your offset.

View the diagrams in the dialog to see what each will do. The results will be quite different, depending on your choice.

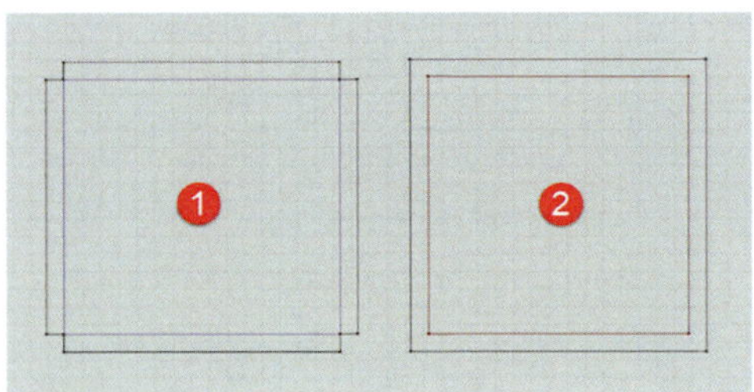

Figure 6-24. Offset Pattern - #1 Unfilled Corner, #2 Default Corner with Create Internal Line

There are a number of uses for this tool outside of making a pattern larger. You can use it when designing unique patterns, since it provides nice reference lines or internal lines at a very precise distance. Also, the Unfilled Corner option creates a pattern that can be sewn into a box very easily.

Internal Geometry

So far we've covered all the different ways to create and edit your basic pattern shapes. There are many other things you'll want to add within those shapes and that's where internal geometry comes into play.

You'll want to create internal shapes to sew pattern pieces, like pockets, to your basic patterns. You also need to create holes within the pattern for shaping or special designs.

To see your internal geometry in the 3D Window select -

Display > 3D Garment > Show Internal Lines

Internal Geometry must be drawn within an existing pattern. It can't be used within the 2D Window alone.

Internal Line

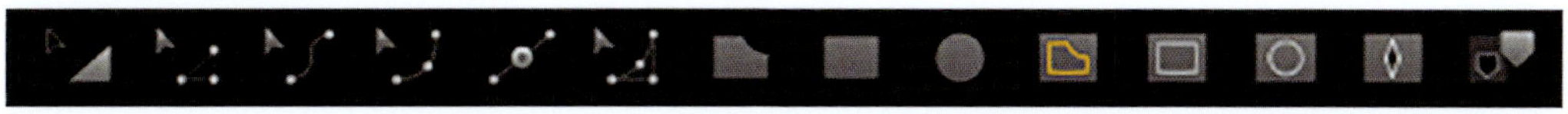

2D Pattern > Create > Internal Polygon / Line

Although all patterns must be closed shapes, Internal Lines may be left open. For instance, creating internal lines on three sides to sew a pocket on a shirt. This tool allows you to draw closed or open shapes on the pattern.

Use this tool just as you did the Polygon tool, but you don't have to close the shape. An internal shape can be a single line, if you wish.

Internal Offset Line

You may need to draw a line an exact distance from a pattern edge or another internal line. This works for fold lines on sleeve edges, hems and casings. Select the line (or multiple lines using Shift) and select -

Edit > Context Menu > 2D Pattern > Offset as Internal Line

RC > Offset as Internal Line

The Offset as Internal Line dialog will open with several options.

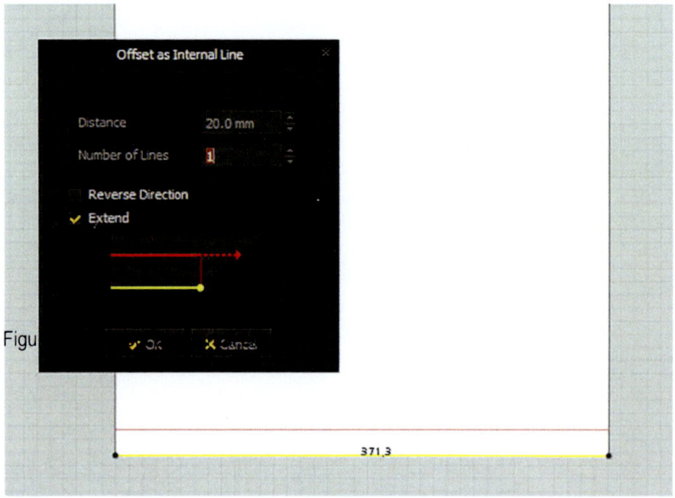

Enter the Distance to offset in the first box. Look in the 2D Window and make sure the line has offset to the desired side of your selected line. If not, check the Reverse Direction box.

The next option is the Number of Lines you need. Each additional line will be the same Distance apart from the previous one. The last option is to Extend the offset line. If your offset line is set at a position on the pattern that will make it longer edge-to-edge than your original line, you can have MD extend it automatically by checking the Extend box.

Internal Rectangle

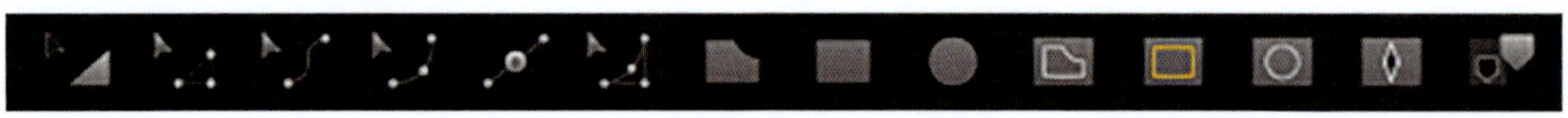

2D Pattern > Create > Internal Rectangle

Internal Rectangles are perfect for pockets and casings. The tool operates just like the standard Rectangle with all of the same features.

Internal Circle

2D Pattern > Create > Internal Circle

Internal Circles can be used to create holes on your patterns. This tool works the same as the standard Circle tool, including all of the same features.

Darts

2D Pattern > Create > Dart

This tool creates a double dart in your pattern. This type of dart is used primarily for shaping a garment so that it fits the Avatar more closely. Click on the pattern where you want the top of the dart and then drag downward to create the correct length. Move your cursor right or left to widen the dart at the center. This is an internal shape that creates a cutout in the pattern.

You can learn more about darts in *Chapter 13 - Shaping Cloth.*

Editing Internal Geometry

Internal shapes can be edited in the same way that standard pattern shapes are, using either the Edit Pattern or Transform Pattern tools. All of the curve tools and techniques will work on internal geometry, too.

You can select only the internal geometry in order to modify it separately from the outer pattern. To be sure that you are editing only the internal geometry, make sure that it is highlighted, but the pattern is not. If you accidentally select the pattern along with the internal geometry, click the background of the

2D window, or another pattern, to release the selection and try again. Since internal geometry is always the child of a pattern, changes to the pattern will affect the internal geometry.

Distribute

MD Gives you the option to space your internal shapes an equal distance apart vertically or horizontally on the pattern. Select the internal shapes and -

Edit > Context Menu > 2D Pattern > Distribute > Horizontally/Vertically

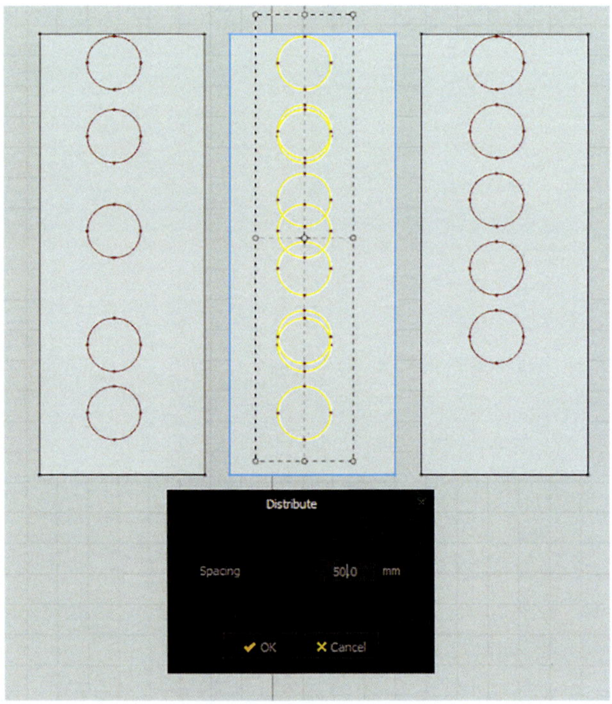

Figure 6-27. Distribute - Before (left), During (center), Result (right)

RC > Distribute > Horizontally/Vertically

MD opens the Distribute dialog box asking for the precise spacing. You'll also see a preview that includes the original position and the new spacing.

Extend / Trim

You can automatically extend or trim Internal Lines. To do this -

RC the line > Extend/Trim to Pattern Outline

This will cut the Internal Line, if it extends beyond the edge of the pattern.

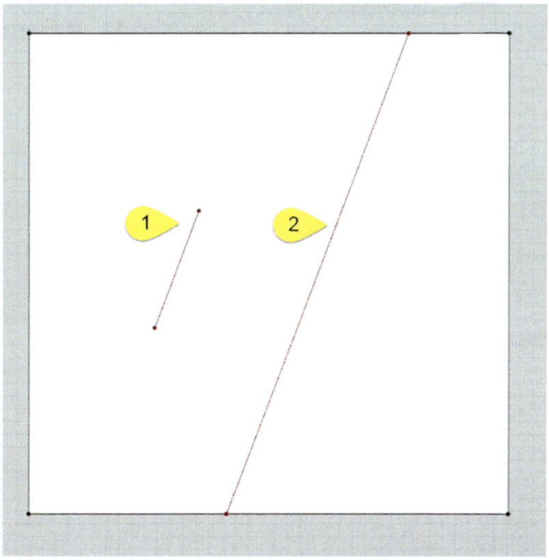

If the line is within the pattern, it will extend the line to the pattern edge. This happens at both ends of the line.

Figure 6-28. Extend Trim - #1 Original, #2 Extended with Points Added

If you want to extend or trim the line and create points where the line intersects the pattern, select -

RC the line > Extend/Trim & Add Point to Pattern Outline

Merging Points

You have the option to merge the points of Internal Lines. To merge two points, hold Shift, select the points and -

RC > Merge to Point

The selection order does matter. The last point selected will be where the points merge. The first point will move over to the second point position.

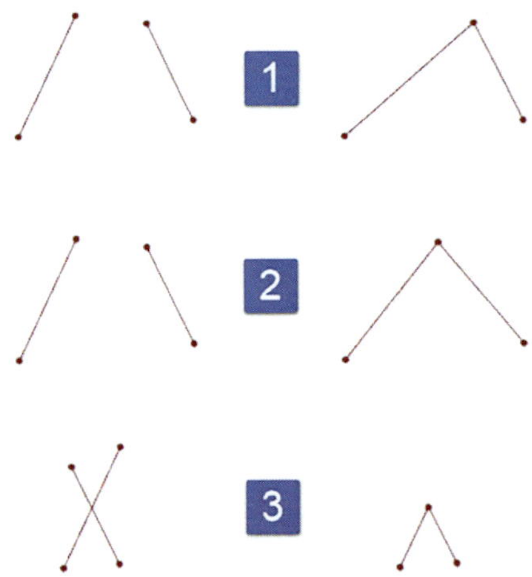

Figure 6-29. Intersect & Merge

If you would prefer that the points merge in the middle of the distance between them, select the points and -

RC > Merge to Average

If you have two Internal Lines that cross over each other, you can merge them on the intersection. Select the ends that you want trimmed off and -

RC > Intersect & Merge

In the image, the original lines are shown at the left. The top points were selected.

#1 Merge to Point

#2 Merge to Average

#3 Intersect & Merge

If you've created two internal lines and they overlap at one point, you can choose to join the points and create one shape. Select the two internal lines and then -

RC > Join Overlapping Points

Creating Holes

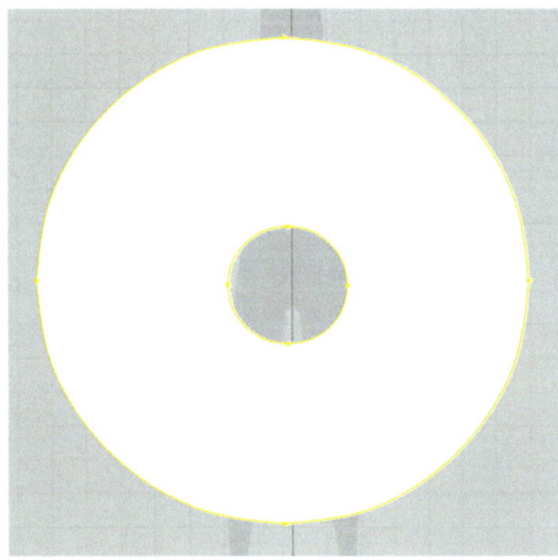

Figure 6-30. Convert to Hole - Creates Cut out for Waist

You may need to cut out shapes in your garment. You can leave the hole empty, or you can sew a different pattern into the hole.

You can create a hole out of any closed shape that you've made in the pattern. It could be an Internal Polygon, Internal Rectangle or Internal Circle. Once you've drawn the internal shape, switch to the Transform Pattern tool -

RC the shape > Convert to hole

Shapes to Patterns / Patterns to Shapes

If you had a shirt that needed a pocket, you could draw the pocket pattern and then draw a matching Internal Line on the shirt to sew it to. This takes two-steps and MD provides two alternate methods that are much quicker and more precise.

Internal Shape to Pattern

If you don't have the pocket or other pattern drawn, create the internal shape where you want the pattern to go. In this example, you would draw out your pocket with an Internal Line or Rectangle on the shirt. Then, using the Transform Pattern tool, select the pattern and -

Edit > Context Menu > 2D Pattern > Clone as Pattern

RC > Clone as Pattern

Place the new pattern in the 2D Window anywhere you like.

Pattern to Internal Shape

If you already have the pocket or other pattern drawn, you can create an internal shape from it. Select the pattern with the Transform Pattern tool and then -

Edit > Context Menu > 2D Pattern > Clone as Internal Shape

RC > Clone as Internal Shape

Place the new internal shape on any pattern you wish.

Marking with Chalk

When you are designing garments, you can use chalk to draw on the patterns. You can mark where you would like to cut the pattern or add embellishments.

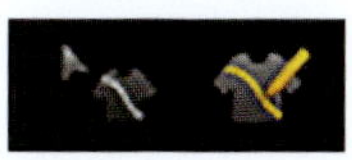

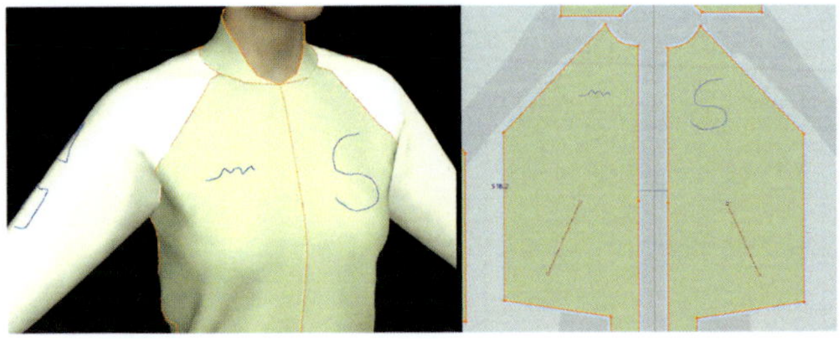

Figure 6-31. Using Chalk

Chalk marks show up on the pattern in the 3D and 2D Windows. You can draw across multiple patterns with one stroke. Click and drag to draw and release to stop.

If you can't see your chalk markings in the 3D Window, select -

Display > 3D Garment > Show Chalk Lines

You can't edit a chalk mark, but you can delete them. Use the Edit Chalk tool by selecting -

Click on the chalk mark and hit Delete. Notice that if your mark crosses over a seam line, only part of the mark will be deleted. MD separates the mark at each seam, even if you drew it in one stroke. You'll have to select the marks individually on each pattern to delete them.

Cutting & Slashing Patterns

You may need to chop up a pattern into multiple pieces and sew them back together. Perhaps you're making a patchwork type effect or want to create a lot of seams throughout the pattern.

You may also choose to do your pattern modifications using the Slash & Spread technique, which will require lots of pattern cutting.

If you're cutting the pattern from edge to edge with one cut, you'll use the Cut method. If you're cutting within the pattern, you'll use the Trace tool.

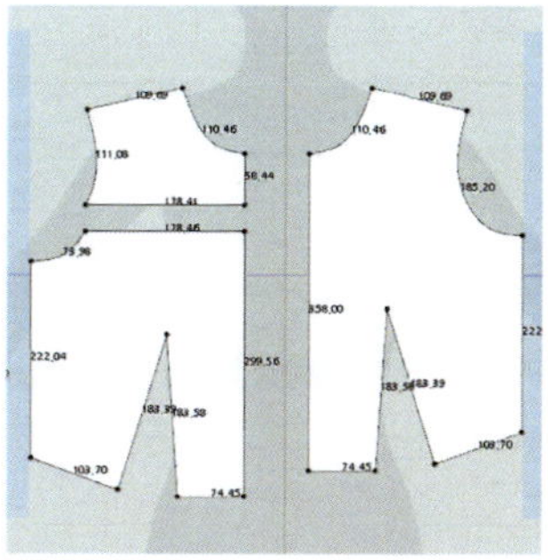

Figure 6-32. Pattern Cut on Left

Cut

Use the Internal Polygon/Line tool to draw across the pattern from edge to edge where you want to cut. With the Edit Pattern tool select the Internal Line and -

Edit > Context Menu > 2D Pattern > Cut

RC > Cut

When you Cut a pattern, MD will cut any Seam Line Pairs on the cut lines and sew them back together. This doesn't always work well and you can be left with very tiny unintended seams. You may want to remove any seam lines on edges that will be cut before cutting.

When you use the cut features, MD can create segment points that lie too close to each other. This makes it difficult to move or edit your patterns. If this happens you can delete the overlapping points automatically by selecting -

RC the 2D background > Delete All Overlapping Points

Cut & Sew

MD also gives you the option to Cut & Sew in one step. MD will automatically create a Seam Line Pair at the cut line and sew it back together for you. With the Edit Pattern tool select the internal line and -

Edit > Context Menu > 2D Pattern > Cut & Sew

RC > Cut & Sew

Trace

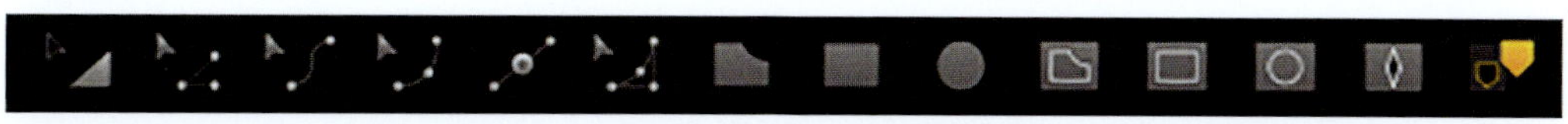

You may want to chop up a pattern into pieces that are completely inside the pattern and not touching any edges. You may also want to use the same technique to create an internal shape. You'll use the Trace tool for both.

First, use the internal tools to draw your shapes within the pattern. Then activate the tool by selecting -

2D Pattern > Trace > Trace

After selecting the tool, hold Shift and select all the lines that surround the shape. The lines must create a closed shape, MD will not trace an open shape.

To create a pattern, with all the lines selected, choose -

Edit > Context Menu > 2D Pattern > Trace as Pattern

RC > Trace as Pattern

MD will place the new pattern in the 2D Window attached to the mouse. Click to place the pattern wherever you want in the window.

To create an internal shape, with all the lines selected, choose -

Edit > Context Menu > 2D Pattern > Trace as Internal Shape

RC > Trace as Internal Shape

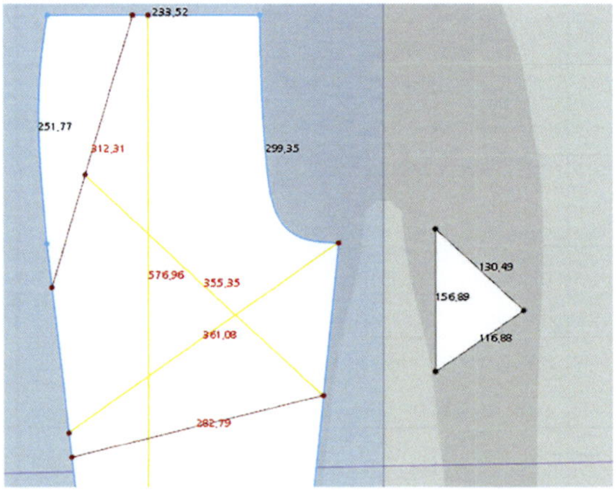

Figure 6-33. Pattern Trace

MD will place the internal shape directly over the lines that you selected. Select the shape with Transform Pattern tool to move it. Be aware that the internal shape belongs to that pattern. You can't drag it over to another pattern to use it.

Be careful when selecting your lines to Trace. If you have more than one closed shape in the lines, MD will choose the largest one. It may be necessary to add points to your Internal Lines to break up the selection more.

The image shows the trace lines selected in yellow. The resulting pattern is shown to the right in the image.

Chapter 6 Quiz

1) Patterns must always be closed shapes.

❍ True ❍ False

2) You can alternate between the Polygon / Line tool and the Curve tool as you are drawing your patterns.

❍ True ❍ False

3) You can make the following conversions with one click (choose all):

❍ A. Convert an internal shape to a pattern.

❍ B. Convert circle to a rectangle.

❍ C. Convert a pattern to an internal shape.

❍ D. Convert a curve point to a standard point.

4) You can create holes in your patterns using (choose all):

❍ A. The internal circle tool.

❍ B. The dart tool.

❍ C. The internal rectangle tool.

❍ D. The circle tool.

Chapter 7 - Arranging Patterns in the 2D Window

Before Duplicating

There is a way to speed up the process of sewing your patterns together. If you are making a bodice, for example, you will create one half of the front and half of the back. Before you duplicate these patterns, sew everything together. Sew all the darts, the shoulders and the side seam for this set. Arrange the patterns in the 3D Window using arrangement points or the Gizmo. You can't simulate them without the opposing side, but you can sew and arrange them. Then make your duplicates using the methods described below.

MD is very smart and will duplicate not only your patterns, but all the sewing and arranging. This is a tremendous time saver and working with half of the patterns makes it much less confusing for beginners and experts alike.

Duplicating Patterns

After you have drawn all of your patterns, it's time to arrange them in the 2D Window. For the most part, only one side of patterns are drafted. You'll want to create the other side of the pattern and MD provides several ways to accomplish this.

Before you duplicate a pattern, it is important that you understand the difference between a pattern that is symmetric and one that is asymmetric. A symmetric pattern doesn't have to be a perfect square or rectangle. If you cut the pattern down the center vertically, the two halves are mirror images. An asymmetric pattern is different on each side. If you cut it in half vertically, the sides would not mirror each other.

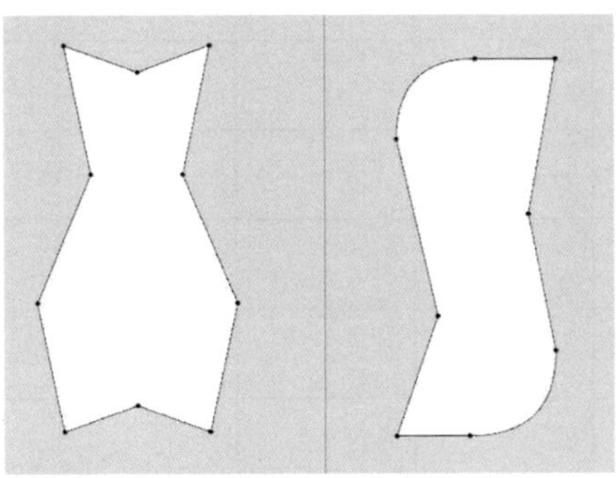

Figure 7-1. Symmetric on Left, Asymmetric on Right

In the image, the pattern on the left is symmetric and the one on the right is asymmetric.

Remember that symmetry in MD is across the Y axis. Even if your pattern is symmetric across the X axis (horizontally), these techniques will not apply.

Copy & Paste

If you need to duplicate a pattern, you can simply copy and paste. This works well for simple patterns like pockets. Each pattern must be edited separately and changes to one will not change the copy.

Copy & Mirror Paste

Most of the time, when you create a duplicate pattern you want it to be a mirror image of the original. If you have half a top for the right of the Avatar, you need to mirror it over for the left. Select the pattern, copy it and -

Edit > Context Menu > 2D Pattern > Mirror Paste

RC > Mirror Paste

This will create a mirror image of the original and each pattern must be edited separately.

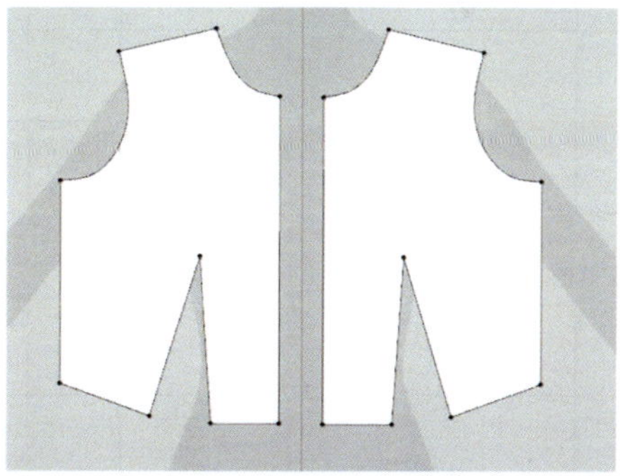

Figure 7-2. Pattern Copied & Mirror Pasted

Unfold

You can create a mirror image of a pattern and merge it with the original in one step. Select the line or lines that you want to mirror across (the mirror axis) and -

Edit > Context Menu > 2D Pattern > Unfold

RC > Unfold

The result is one pattern mirrored across the axis you selected. The pattern can be edited just like any other pattern.

I don't suggest this technique because edits have to be done manually to each side of the unfolded pattern. You can't unfold a pattern, if the resulting pattern would cross over itself in any area.

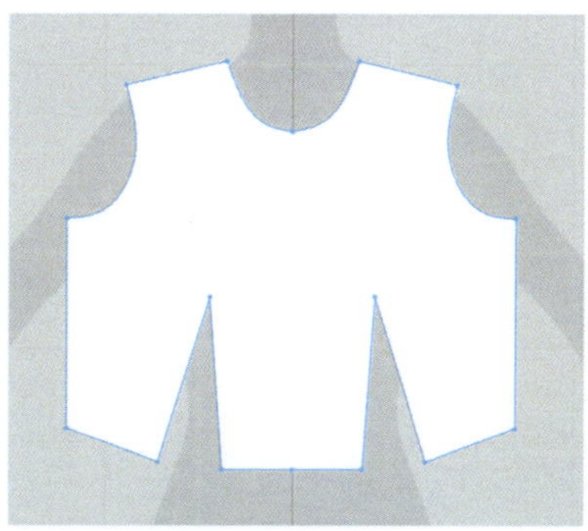

Figure 7-3. Pattern Unfolded

Clone as Symmetric Pattern

MD allows you to create a mirrored duplicate pattern that is linked to the original. This is an enormous time saver and one of my favorite tools. Select the pattern and -

Edit > Context Menu > 2D Pattern > Clone as Symmetric Pattern (with Sewing)

RC > Clone as Symmetric Pattern (with Sewing)

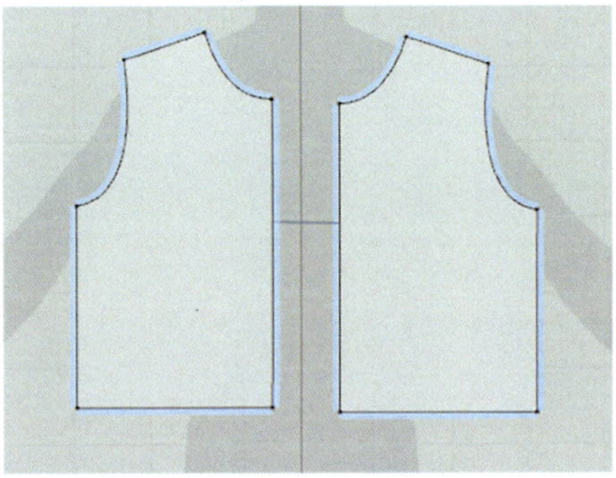

Figure 7-4. Pattern Cloned as Symmetric

You'll see the patterns outlined in blue and connected with a small blue line.

They are linked together and any changes made to one pattern will be automatically reflected in the other. This includes any sewing that you do. All you have to do is sew up one pattern and the other is instantly done.

If you delete a cloned pattern, the symmetry will be removed and the pattern will be deleted, but the other will remain.

If you need to remove symmetry, you can do so by selecting the pattern and -

Edit > Context Menu > 2D Pattern > Remove Symmetry

RC > Remove Symmetry

Now the patterns are completely separate and edits to one will not be made to the other.

I recommend that you use cloning almost exclusively. The only exception would bean asymmetric garment that differs on each side.

Symmetrization

If you have two identical patterns that are not symmetrically linked, you can link them. Select the two patterns and -

RC > Symmetrization

The patterns will now be linked and edits to one will update both.

Symmetric Merge

When you are done with all of your pattern editing, it is very simple to make these two sides into one pattern. Select the line to be shared between the patterns, where the patterns will join, and then-

RC > Merge

The two pieces will be merged together into one. The pattern that you right clicked will stay in its original position and the other one will move to connect to it.

You can't merge a pattern if the resulting pattern would overlap itself.

Stacking Patterns

Even though the 2D Window only has an X and Y axis, you do have layers. Every pattern is its own layer in MD, which allows you to stack them on top of each other.

Don't confuse the pattern layer in the 2D Window for layers in the 3D Window. These are two completely different things and there is no correlation. Layers in the 3D Window allow you to "layer" the clothing. If a coat is worn over a shirt, the coat would be a higher layer. Layering in the 3D Window is used only for simulation and it is a temporary action.

Pattern stacking in the 2D Window is like stacking pieces of paper. You can more easily edit the pattern on top.

2D Window pattern stacking is particularly useful when you are tracing out patterns, like patterns from PatternMaker PRO. You can decide where the pattern is in the stack. You have four different options:

- Bring Forward - This will bring the pattern one layer towards the top.
- Bring to Front - This will bring the pattern to the very top.
- Send Backward - This will send the pattern one layer towards the bottom.
- Send to Back - This will send the pattern to the very bottom.

To change the layering of a pattern, select the pattern then -

RC > Order > Bring/Send

Moving Patterns

Rotate

There are a number of rotation options for you to choose from to get your patterns precisely rotated. To rotate a pattern select -

Edit > Context Menu > 2D Pattern > Rotate > Clockwise / Counterclockwise (45°/90°)

RC > Rotate > Clockwise / Counterclockwise (45°/90°)

To rotate a pattern so that the selected segment is horizontal select -

Edit > Context Menu > 2D Pattern > Rotate > X-Axis

RC > Rotate X-Axis

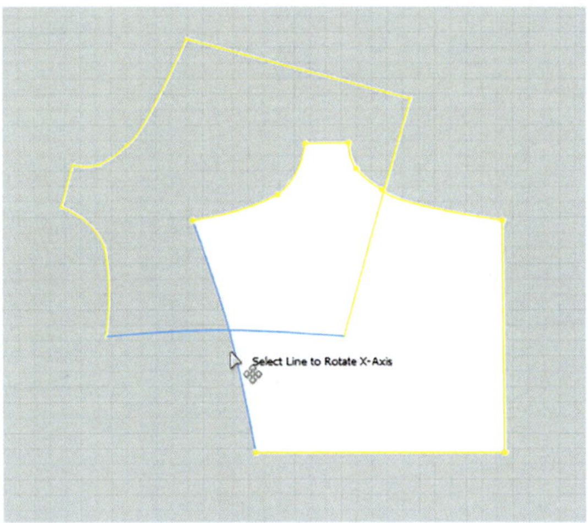

Figure 7-5. X Axis Rotation Preview

MD will ask you to "Select Line to Rotate X-Axis", which is the segment that will establish the rotation amount.

MD will show you an outline preview of how the pattern will be rotated. Click to finalize the rotation and MD will rotate the entire pattern to make the selected line as straight as possible horizontally, along the X-axis.

To rotate a pattern so that the selected segment is vertical select -

Edit > Context Menu > 2D Pattern > Rotate > Y-Axis

RC > Rotate Y-Axis

MD will ask you to select the line as the rotation basis. Then MD will rotate the entire pattern to make that line as straight as possible vertically, along the Y-axis.

To rotate a pattern so that a selected segment is parallel to a selected segment of another pattern select -

Edit > Context Menu > 2D Pattern > Rotate > Parallel To

RC > Rotate Parallel To

This is a two step selection process. MD will first ask you to "Select Line to Match", which is the target segment. Once selected, that segment turns red.

Next, MD will ask you to "Select a Rotation Line". This is the segment that will be rotated so it is parallel to the target segment, taking the rest of the pattern with it. MD will show you an outline of how the pattern will be rotated. Click to finalize the rotation.

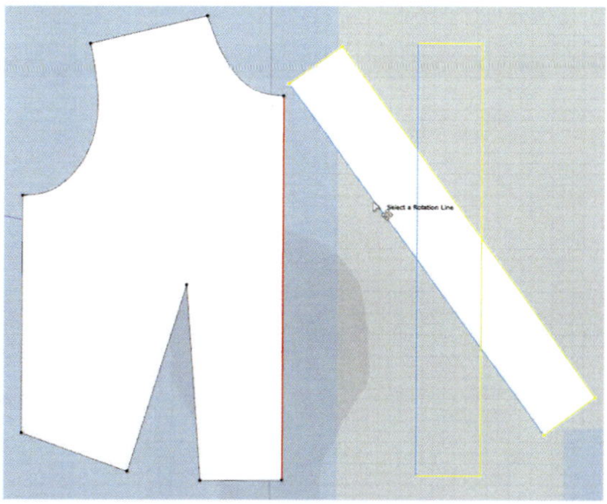

Figure 7-6. Preview of Parallel to Rotation, Target Segment is Show in Red

Distribute

In *Chapter 6 -Editing Internal Geometry - Distribute* you learned all about distributing your internal shapes within a pattern. You can use this same feature to distribute your patterns evenly within the 2D Window. Select the patterns to distribute and -

Edit > Context Menu > 2D Pattern > Distribute > Horizontally/Vertically

RC > Distribute > Horizontally/Vertically

Align

All of the options you have for aligning points are also available to use on full patterns in the 2D Window. Select the patterns you want to align and -

RC > Align > To Point (X Axis) / To Point(Y Axis)

RC > Align >Left / Center / Right / Top / Middle / Bottom

This feature is discussed in detail in *Chapter 6 - Selecting & Editing Your Patterns - Aligning Points.*

Zoom

When you are zoomed far away from a pattern and want to zoom up to it, so it fills the entire window, select -

RC the pattern > Zoom to Selected

If you want all of your patterns to show in the 2D Window select -

Display > Viewpoint > Zoom Extents All

RC the 2D background > Zoom Extents All

Assigning Fabric

There are a number of ways for you to assign a fabric to a pattern. With the pattern selected, you can use the drop-down list in the Property Editor in the Fabric section. You can also use the Assign to Selected Patterns button on the Fabric tab of the Object Browser. Perhaps the simplest way is to just drag and drop the fabric on a pattern in the 2D Window.

If you want to revert the fabric on a pattern to the Default_Fabric, select -

Edit > Context Menu > Materials > Reset to Basic Fabric

The final way to assign a fabric is to create a new fabric and assign it in one step. Select the pattern then -

Edit > Context Menu > Materials > Assign to New Fabric

RC > Assign to New Fabric

This creates a new fabric on the Fabric tab and assigns it to the selected pattern. You can also do this with multiple patterns selected and they will all be assigned the new fabric.

The new fabric is just like the Default_Fabric with no preset assigned or special properties. Learn more about fabric properties in *Chapter 9 - Fabric.*

Locking Patterns

If you want to prevent accidental edits or selections, you can lock all patterns by selecting -

2D Pattern > Lock > Lock All Patterns

RC 2D background > Lock All Patterns

You can also lock all Internal Lines with -

2D Pattern > Lock > Lock All Internal Lines

RC 2D background > Lock All Internal Lines

Picking Point

When you select a pattern in the 3D Window, you'll see a blue dot appear on the pattern. MD refers to this as a picking point. There will be a corresponding blue point shown in the 2D window on the same pattern. This is very useful when you are trying to find an area to edit using the 3D pattern. If you want to hide this point in the 2D Window, select -

Display > 2D Pattern > Show Picking Point

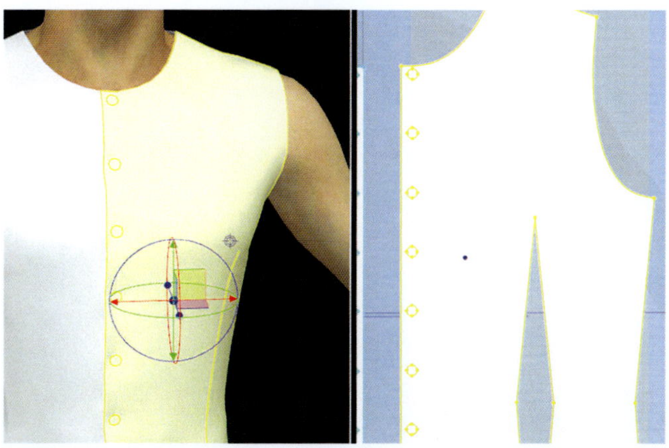

Figure 7-7. Picking Point

Chapter 7 Quiz

1)You can't edit symmetric patterns.

❍ True ❍ False

2) Use the Edit Pattern tool to resize the entire pattern and move it in the 2D Window.

❍ True ❍ False

3) You can assign fabric (choose all):

❍ A. To multiple patterns at once with the Assign button.

❍ B. To one pattern at a time with drag and drop.

❍ C. To multiple patterns using the Fabric button.

❍ D. To one pattern at a time with the Property Editor - Fabric Property.

❍ E. To one pattern with right click, Assign to New Fabric.

4) Which statement is NOT correct (choose one):

❍ A. Bring Forward - This will bring the pattern one layer to the top.

❍ B. Bring to Front - This will bring the pattern to the very top.

❍ C. Send Backward - This will bring the pattern two layers to the bottom.

❍ D. Send to Back - This will send the pattern to the very bottom.

Chapter 8 - Seams & Basting

Seams

The term "seam" is something you will hear a lot. Seams are the lines of stitching that join together individual garment sections.

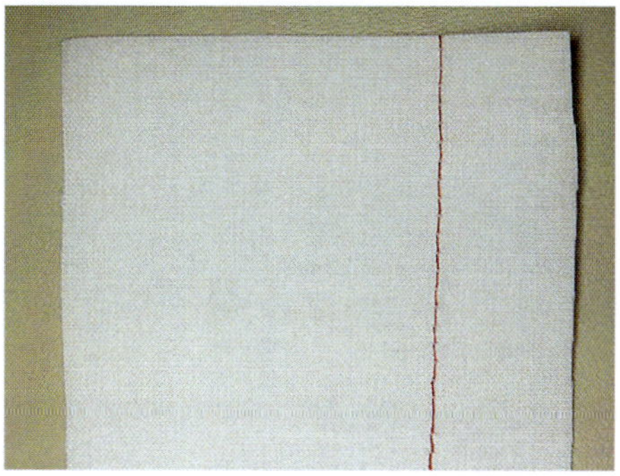

Figure 8-1. Real-World Seam

This image is a real seam. You can see the two pieces of fabric on top of each other with stitching. That stitching is the seam. There must be a seam whenever two pieces of fabric are joined.

MD shows the seams in the 3D Window by applying a color to them. If you want to hide the seams select -

Display > Sewing > Show 3D Seamlines

In the image to the right, the seam has been ironed open with the right side facing the camera. You can't see the stitches anymore, just the two pieces of fabric joined together. This is the way that seams look in MD.

Figure 8-2. Seam Pressed Open, Right Side Up

In real-world sewing, seams are a very big deal. How the seam is made dictates not only how it looks on the garment, but how strong it is. Some seams are appropriate for the thinnest materials and others hold up to the strains of utility clothing made of strong canvas. There are many, many types of seams.

Seam Allowance

You will see the term "seam allowance" when referencing real patterns. Seam allowance is added to the edge of every pattern piece. You need this extra material under the foot of the sewing machine when stitching.

In MD, we can sew edge to edge and we don't need a seam allowance. Therefore, we don't need different types of seams. We just "sew" one piece to another. However, when you get into texturing your finished garments, you will want to consider the finished look of real seams because they can have an enormous effect on how a garment looks.

Seam Finishes

You may also see reference to seam finishes in sewing. Seam finishes are techniques used on the seam allowance to prevent the seam allowance edges from fraying or wearing over time. These finishes are necessary, because if the seam allowance fails, the seam will fail next and the garment will come apart.

Figure 8-3. Frayed Seam Allowance

For MD, you don't need to concern yourself with seam finishes, unless you want a photorealistic garment that is turned inside out.

Seamline Pairs & Segment Sewing

There are two ways to sew a seam in MD. One is Segment Sewing and the other is Free Sewing. In MD, a segment is simply the edge that connects two points. To use Segment Sewing select -

Sewing > Segment Sewing

To use the tool, you just click the edge of a pattern and then the edge of another pattern or the same pattern. Now those two edges are sewn together. It doesn't matter if the edges are the same length or not. If one is longer than the other, the excess on the long edge will be gathered.

If you open the Scene tab in the Object Browser, you'll see you just created an object called a SeamLinePairGroup. Each pair has a unique identifying number. If you look over in the 3D Window, you can see the sewing. If you can't see your seams, select -

Display > Sewing > Show 3D Threads

The seam lines in a pair are the same color. This is very handy when things start to get complicated. You'll notice you have a small perpendicular line on each seam line. This translates to a notch in a real-world pattern. We'll talk more about pattern notches later.

Typically, you will only see your seam line pairs in the 2D Window when you are working with the seam tools. If you want them to display all the time, then select -

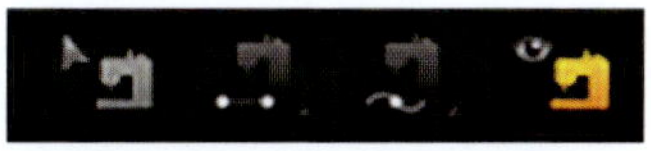

Display > Sewing > Show 2D Sewing

If you would like to hide a seam line pair, select -

Display > Sewing > Hide Sewing (Selected)

To show all seam line pairs, including those that you've hidden, select -

Display > Sewing > Show Sewing (All)

If you want the length of each seam displayed, select -

Display > Sewing > Show 2D Sewing Lengths

Free Sewing

Segment Sewing only allows you to sew one segment to one segment. Free Sewing has a lot more options. To use Free Sewing select -

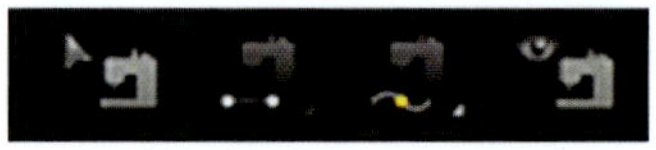

Sewing > Free Sewing

Click to start the seam anywhere on an edge, drag to the place where you want to stop and click to end. The seam line you've created can be a partial segment or it can include many segments, either is acceptable. You define the start and stop points.

To make the other half of the seam, click on another pattern edge, draw the seam line and click to stop. The two lines of the seam line pair can be different lengths, and the excess will be gathered.

Free Sewing has a couple unique features. As you are drawing the seam line, MD shows you some numbers. The first number is the difference between your first seam line and your second seam line. In parentheses, you will see the length of the first seam line, a slash, then the length of the second seam line. If the difference between the two seam lines is less than 1", the numbers will display in blue. If the difference is more than 1", the numbers will be red. This is very dynamic and changes as you move your mouse.

The other thing you'll see is a blue dot. MD is using the length of the first line to show you an end point on the second line. If you end the second line on that dot, the two lines will be the same length. Notice I said "if", you don't have to stop on the dot. You can end the seam before it or after it, too.

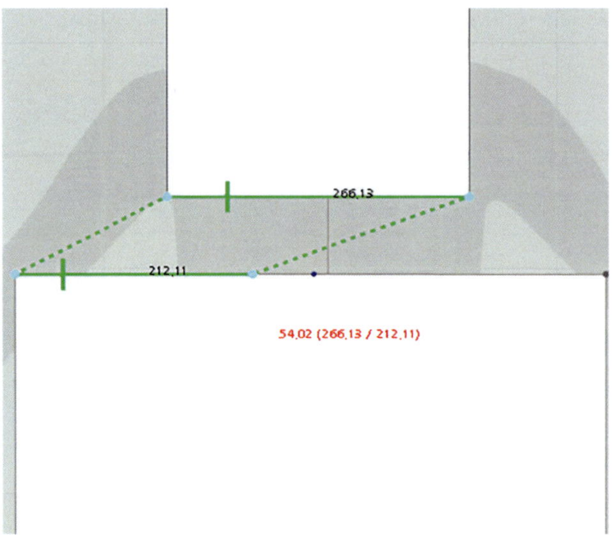

Figure 8-4. Free Sewing Blue End Dot

M:N Sewing

When you sew using the basic Segment and Free Sewing tools, you select one length for the first seam line and another length for the second. These are sewn together to complete the seam line pair. If you are using the Segment Sewing tool, you can only select two segments sewn to each other. Using the Free Sewing tool, you can select a length between points, but you are still confined to choosing only two lengths to sew together.

The M:N sewing tools are very different. The "M" and "N" are variables that represent the value of one or more. The M:N means that you can sew one or more lengths to one or more lengths. The "M" is the first seam line of the pair and the "N" is the second seam line.

M:N Segment Sewing

The M:N Segment Sewing tool restricts you to sewing only full segments, but you can choose more than two. The button is hidden behind the regular Segment Sewing tool in the toolbar. To select the tool choose -

Sewing > M:N Segment Sewing

After selecting the tool, MD asks you to "Select a segment to begin M sewing". Click on a segment for the first half of the seam line pair. The seam will be a bright yellow color.

Now MD directs you to "Press Enter to complete M Sewing". If you want to include more segments in the first half of the seam line pair, select them. You can choose as many segments as you want. If you accidentally select a segment during this process that you don't want included, hit the Delete key to step back. Hit your Enter key when you are done.

The next MD prompt asks you to "Select a segment to begin N Sewing". Select one or more segments for the second half of the seam line pair. As you make these selections, note that the first half of the seam line pair is now a bright green color so you can distinguish between the "M" and "N" selections.

MD will prompt you to "Press Enter to complete N Sewing". Add as many additional lengths to the second half of the seam line pair and hit Enter to finish.

The seam line pair will be one single color, just like any other pair, even though there are multiple segments involved.

M:N Free Sewing

The M:N Free Sewing method is similar to the M:N Segment Sewing method but now you can start and stop the seams anywhere you want. You are not restricted to full segments. The button is hidden behind the regular Free Sewing tool in the toolbar. To select the tool choose -

Sewing > M:N Free Sewing

After selecting the tool, MD will ask you to "Click on a point or segment to begin M Free Sewing". After setting your end point, MD prompts you to "Press Enter to complete M Sewing". You can continue to add to the first half of the seam line pair or hit the Enter key to end your selections. If you accidentally click somewhere you didn't intend, hit the Delete key to step back.

MD will ask you to "Click on a point or segment to begin N Free Sewing". As you are sewing, you'll see that you have that same blue dot reference point that you have when you are Free Sewing. This shows you the distance you have left, if you want to create the second half of the seam line pair the same length as the first.

Create one or more lengths of Free Sewing for your second seam line. MD will ask you to "Press Enter to complete N Sewing". Hit the Enter key when you are done with your selection. The seam lines will all be the same color and linked.

You may see older tutorials referring to the One-to-Many technique. You

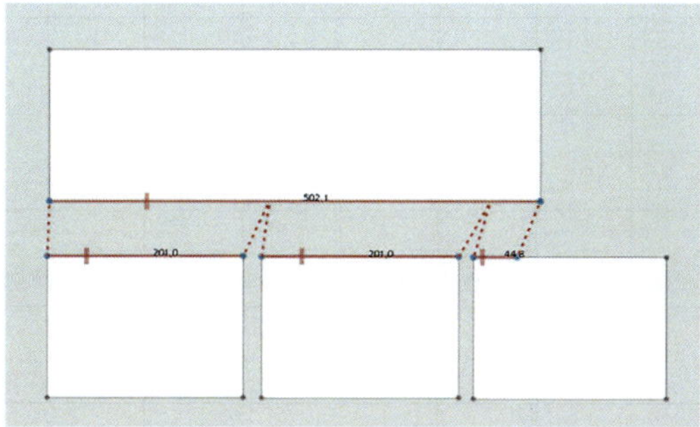

Figure 8-5. M:N Free Sewing Complete with Linked Seams (all one color)

can still do this using the regular Free Sewing and Segment Sewing tools and holding down Shift after you select the first segment. Don't let up on the Shift key until you've selected all the connecting segments. This was the old method before the new M:N buttons were added. You can't sew many-to-many using this mcthod.

Delete & Unlink M:N

To delete the entire seam line pair of M:N sewing, select any seam line length with the Edit Sewing tool and Delete. This will remove the entire sewing set.

If you want to delete only portions of the seam line, you need to separate the sets first. Using the Edit Sewing tool select any seam in the set and -

RC > Unlink M:N Sewing

MD breaks the set into separate pairs as shown. Now you can delete or edit the each pair individually.

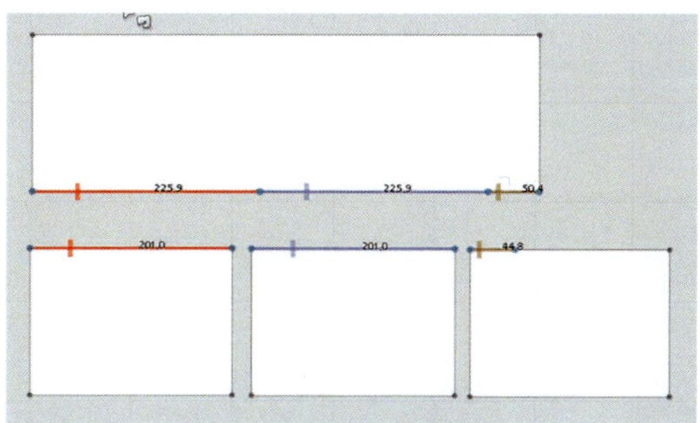

Figure 8-6. M:N Free Sewing Unlinked Seams

Seam Line Distribution

In the image on the previous page, the top pattern edge is 502.1 mm sewn to the lower patterns with edges of 201 mm, 201 mm and 44.8 mm. The ratio of the seam lines, 502.1:446.8, is 88%. MD spread the excess between all three pieces automatically. You may think that MD would sew straight across with no excess until the last seam, but that's not how it works. All gathering will be evenly spread across the seam lines for you, if one side of the seam line pair is longer than the other.

Editing Seams

You can edit your seams after you have completed them by selecting -

Sewing > Edit Sewing

Select a seam by clicking on any seam line of it. That seam will be brightly colored and the others will dim somewhat. As you mouse over the seam, you will be shown the measurements.

To make edit the seam, select the start or end point of any seam line in the pair. Then drag it where you want it. You'll notice that the little blue dot will appear once again to guide you in making matching line lengths. To delete a seam, just select it,

RC > Delete Sewing

or hit your Delete key on the keyboard.

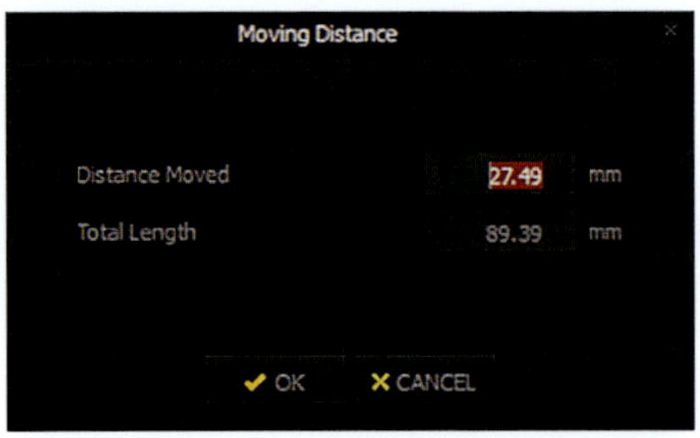

Figure 8-7. Moving Distance Dialog

If you want to move the seam point a specific distance, right-click as you are dragging. The Moving Distance dialog will open where you can type an exact length to move. It also shows you the Total Length.

You can also use the Edit Sewing tool to make multiple selections quickly. The selection is based on the value of a seam line property. With the tool selected -

RC a seamline pair > Select All with Same Property > Select Property

Your property options include Fold Strength and Fold Angle. All other seam line pairs that have the same value of Strength or Angle will be added to your selection automatically.

This is a great feature to use when you need to tweak settings for similar seams all at once.

Add Points at Seam Ends

Using the Free Sewing tools, it is possible to start or stop a seam at any place along the edge of a pattern without starting or stopping on a pattern point. If you re-size a pattern after creating a seam line that does not rest on a pattern point, that seam line length will change.

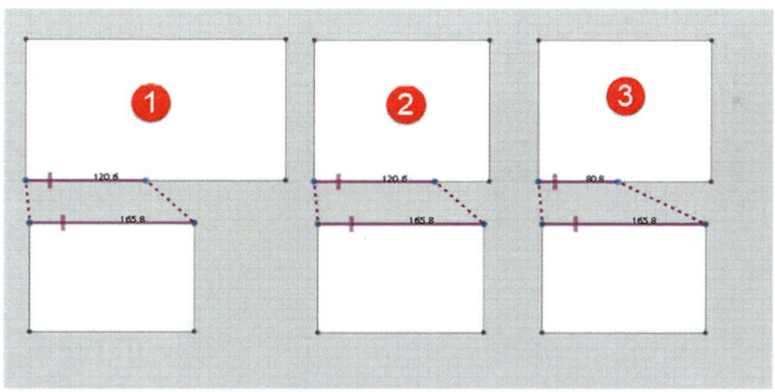

Figure 8-8. #1 Original, #2 Point Added and Re-sized, #3 Re-Sized

In the image above #1 shows the original pattern pieces. The top seam line is 120.6 mm and the bottom is 165.8 mm. In #2 a point was added to the top seam line on end and then the pattern was re-sized. The seam continues to be 120.6 / 165.8. On #3, the pattern was just re-sized without adding a point. The seam line is now 80.8 / 165.8.

If you want to make sure that your seam line stays the same length regardless of edits to the pattern, you will want to create a new pattern point at the "floating" seam point. To add a point at the seam line start select -

RC > Add Point to Pattern on Start

To add a point at the seam line end select -

RC > Add Point to Pattern on End

You may want to create a pattern point just so you can see where the seam ends when you are in pattern editing mode.

Pattern Notches

Here's a real front bodice pattern where you can see the triangular notches. The back pattern piece has corresponding notches.

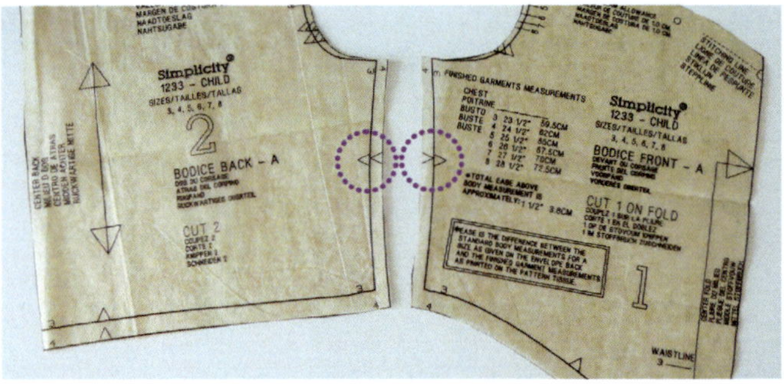

Figure 8-9. Real Pattern Notches

When the fabric is cut out, these notches are cut in the fabric. After the pattern is removed, the front and back fabric pieces are laid with right sides together and these notches are used to line up the two pieces.

When you use a sewing tool in MD and start at the top of a vertical segment, the notch is at the top. When you start at the bottom, the notch is at the bottom. If you sew a seam with notches at opposite ends, MD will flip the pattern over when it sews the seam. MD works just like real-world sewing.

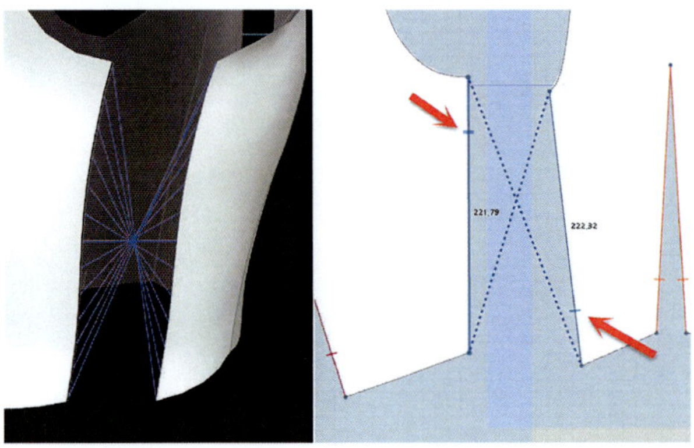

Figure 8-10. Crossed Seam

There are times when you will intentionally reverse a seam, but these are an exception. To fix a crossed seam, select one of the seam lines with the Edit Sewing tool, then -

Edit > Context Menu > Sewing > Reverse Sewing

RC > Reverse Sewing

Always check over in the 3D Window to make sure that your seam looks correct, with nice parallel threads, before simulating.

Seam Properties

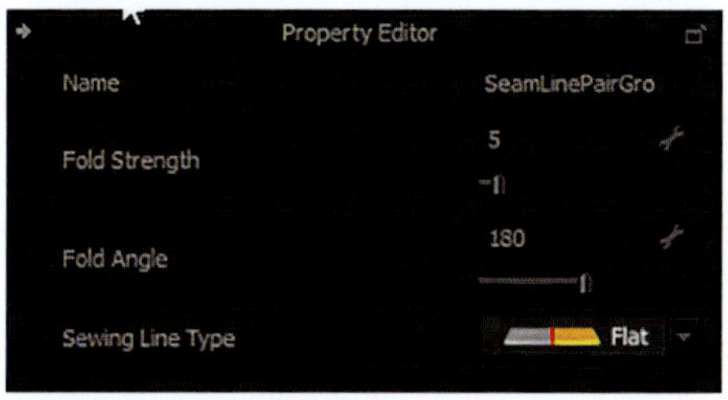

Figure 8-11. Seam Properties

There are a number of properties that you can set for seams in the Property Editor. Select a seam with the Edit Sewing tool to see them.

The Name field gives you the unique number for that side of the seam line pair. You can change the name and it will show up on the Scene tab of the Object Browser.

Many of your seams will be sewn flat, with one edge sewn to the other with the patterns side-by-side. The default Fold Strength of 5, Fold Angle of 180° and Sewing Line Type Flat will accomplish this. If you have one pattern that you are sewing on top of another, you may want to switch to a Sewing Line Type Turned. This is useful for collars and folded cuffs.

A Fold Angle of 180° will keep the seam flat. If the Fold Angle is closer to 0°, the seam will bend pulling the right sides of the fabric together. If the Fold Angle is closer to 360°, the seam will bend pulling the wrong sides of the fabric together. See *Chapter 13 - Shaping Cloth - Pleats* to learn more about fold angle.

Pattern Layout for Quick Sewing

I lay out my patterns as shown in the next image. When sewing, I can work across the screen and all my seam lines are positioned right next to each other. It's very fast and reduces confusion.

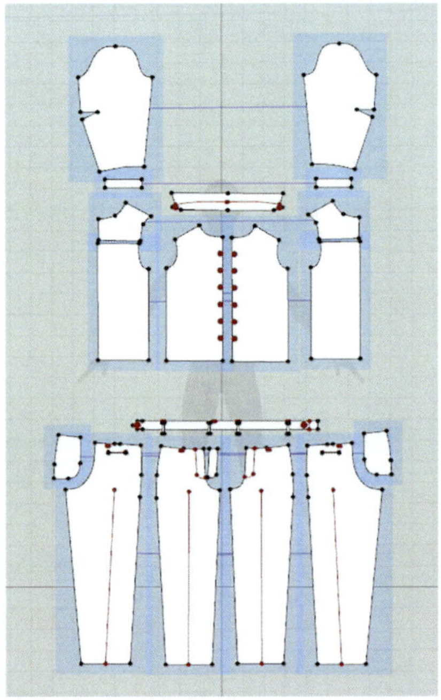

Figure 8-12. My Layout

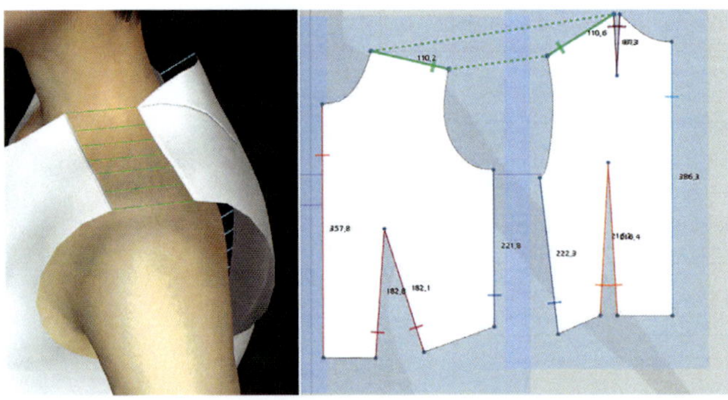

Figure 8-13. Shoulder Seam Layout

Seam lines for the shoulders will appear to be crossed in the 2D Window. You need to remember that you will flip the back patterns in the 3D Window so the wrong side is facing the body.

It can get very confusing trying to remember what is flipped and what isn't. The easiest way to stay clear on this is to look at the notches in relation to features of the pattern. For example, the shoulder seam on the left front has the notch closest to the armhole. The shoulder seam on the left back has the notch closest to the armhole. The notch placement is the same and the seam is correct. When in doubt, just check the 3D Window to make sure.

Basting

Real-world basting is similar to a seam, but it is usually temporary. The stitches are long and loose, sewn either by hand or machine, so they can be easily removed. They are used when holding garment sections together until they can be sewn, or to create gathers. In MD, you can use tacking and pinning to create temporary holds from one pattern to another, to the pattern itself or to the Avatar.

Tacking

You may find that a seam is not an option when you are attaching patterns to each other. You may want to Tack a scarf in place or have the Avatar hold up a skirt in her hand. Using tacks is a great way to achieve unique placement of patterns where sewing isn't appropriate. To use this tool, select -

Sewing > Tack

Click on the first point of the Tack and then the second point. When you simulate, these two points will come together.

If you want to Tack a pattern to the Avatar, select -

Sewing > Tack on Avatar

Click on the pattern to tack and then click on the Avatar. The Avatar will stay stationary on simulation, but the pattern will pull to the second Tack point you placed on the Avatar.

You can edit an existing Tack by using the Edit Basting tool.

Sewing > Edit Basting

Select the tool and click one of the Tack points. The selected point will turn yellow and the line connecting the points will be dashed. You can drag the point to a new position, or hit delete to remove both tack points.

Pinning

A Pin is a collection of multiple points on a pattern that you want pinned to the Avatar. You can select an area of the pattern to Pin using the Box or Lasso selection. The Lasso option is hidden behind the box. To use the tools, select -

3D Garment > Pin (Box / Lasso)

The patterns in the 3D Window will now appear as mesh showing the triangles or quads. Click and drag to select the area to Pin.

To Pin the selected mesh to the Avatar select -

Edit > Context Menu > 3D Garment > Attach Pin to Avatar

RC the mesh or pin > Attach Pin to Avatar

When you simulate, that portion of the pattern will attach itself to the closest part of the Avatar.

If you want to detach a single Pin, select it and -

Edit > Context Menu > 3D Garment > Detach Pin from Avatar

You have the option to work with all Pins. To detach all the Pins from the Avatar, select -

3D Garment > Detach All Pins from Avatar

RC the pattern > Pin > Detach All Pins from Avatar

RC the mesh or pin > Detach All Pins from Avatar

If you want to reattach all the Pins select -

3D Garment > Attach All Pins to Avatar

RC the pattern > Pin > Attach All Pins to Avatar

RC the mesh or pin > Attach All Pins to Avatar

To delete a single Pin, select it then -

Edit > Context Menu > 3D Garment > Delete Selected Pin

RC the mesh or pin > Delete Selected Pin

To delete all Pins on one or more specific patterns, select them -

RC > Pin > Delete All Pins on Selected Patterns

To delete all Pins, select -

Edit > Context Menu > 3D Garment > Delete All Pins

RC the mesh or pin > Delete All Pins

RC the pattern > Pin > Delete All Pins

Mesh Selection

Mesh selection allows you to isolate a portion of the garment to roll up vertically or horizontally. This isn't something that is used often, but you might find it helpful on occasion. You can select an area of the pattern using the Box or Lasso selection. The Lasso selection is hidden behind the box. To use the tools, select -

3D Garment > Select Mesh (Box / Lasso)

The patterns in the 3D Window will now appear as mesh showing the triangles or quads. Click and drag to select the area.

The areas of the pattern that have been selected with the Lasso or Box can be rolled. With the Mesh tool still active select -

Edit > Context Menu > 3D Garment > Roll Up Vertically / Horizontally

RC > Roll Up Vertically / Horizontally

You can also convert your mesh selection to a pin by selecting -

RC > Create Pin

You can show or hide your Pins in the 3D Window by selecting -

Display > 3D Garment > Show Pins

Order of Make

When sewing in the real world, there is generally an order to the assembly of the garment. This is referred to as the "order of make". Each garment is constructed in a precise order because some things have to be sewn before others. There are some steps that are easier to do before other steps have taken place.

In MD, the order is not nearly as important. It is a good idea to work logically, so you don't get confused. Many times it is better to sew the base patterns first and then add the details, such as outside pockets and trims.

If you are creating a layered ensemble, you should always sew and simulate the garments closest to the body first. You may choose to freeze those base layers as you add more to prevent penetration or intermingling between the layers. When everything is completed, you can unfreeze and do a final simulation.

Chapter 8 Quiz

1) When sewing a seam, MD provides these visual feedback clues (choose all):

❍ A. Individual length of each seam line.

❍ B. A blue point showing where the second seam line must stop.

❍ C. The difference between the lengths of the seam lines.

❍ D. The position of the notch for each seam line.

2) Mark which statements are correct regarding seam line pairs (choose all):

❍ A. Sew one pattern to another pattern.

❍ B. Sew one pattern to multiple patterns.

❍ C. Sew multiple patterns to one pattern.

❍ D. Sew multiple patterns to multiple patterns.

3) If you wanted to sew only part of one pattern segment to another pattern, which tool would you use (choose one)?

❍ A. Segment Sewing Tool

❍ B. Free Sewing Tool

❍ C. M:N Segment Sewing Tool

4) Pattern notches on a real-world pattern are completely different from the pattern notches in MD.

❍ True ❍ False

Chapter 9 - Fabric

MD refers to the pattern or design of the fabric as its Texture. That is the term we will use throughout this chapter.

Figure 9-1. Colored Yarns Woven

Fabric texture that is created during manufacturing uses the yarns to create distinct tactile texture (weave) and color.

Color can also be applied to a fabric after it has been manufactured. One method is to print the design on top of the fabric along its entire width and length.

You can apply either type of texture to your fabric in MD using an image file.

Figure 9-2. Printed Fabric

Right Side & Wrong Side

All fabric in the real world has a front side and a back side. It doesn't matter if the fabric is knit or woven, those two sides can be very different. It is up to the designer to decide which side will be facing out on a garment.

Real-world sewing terminology is Right Side and Wrong Side. The right side is the side you want facing out and the wrong side faces the body. Since we are working in 3D, front and back are far too confusing. We will use the terms Right Side and Wrong Side.

We want the normals to be on the Right Side of the fabric, facing away from the avatar. See *Chapter 11 - Arranging Patterns* for more information on normals.

Fabric Property Editor

When you select a fabric from the Object Browser Fabric tab, the properties of the fabric will be displayed in the Property Editor. You can save the current Fabric as a .zfab file using the Save button. Use the Open button to include a saved fabric in the current project. Give your fabric a unique name by typing it in the Name field or select -

RC > Rename

The Object Browser list will update with your new fabric name. This makes it easier to keep track of your fabrics and easily apply them to patterns.

Choosing Colors

You will need to choose colors for many fabric properties. MD includes an advanced Color Picker to make these choices. Click any of the colored boxes in the Material section to open the picker.

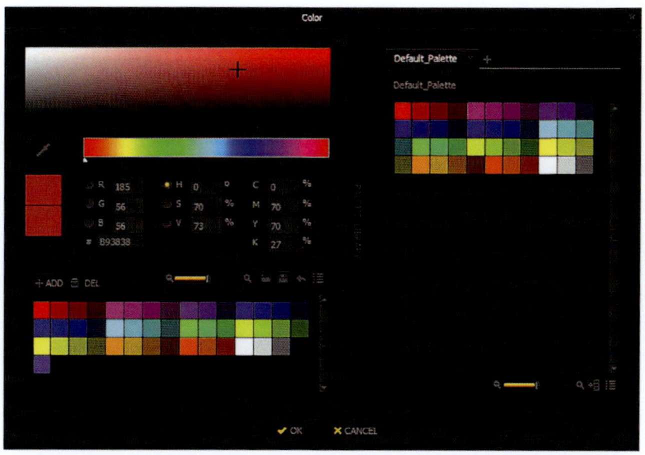

Figure 9-3. Color Picker

There are two distinct sections to the Color window. You'll see a picker on the left and a Palette Library on the right. There are many ways to create a custom color. The uppermost box on the left contains one hue with all the possible value and saturation levels. To change the hue, click and drag the arrow in the second box (to the right of the eyedropper) and the top box will change. Click anywhere in the top box to select a color.

You can also enter a color using RGB, Hex, HSV or CMYK values. If there is a color in your scene somewhere that you want to use, click the eyedropper tool to activate it and then click the color in the scene. When you select a color, the swatch under the eyedropper will update with that color.

If you want to save a color for use later, click the Add button and the swatch will be added to the lower swatches box. To delete a swatch, select it in the swatch box and click Delete. To make the swatches bigger, drag the slider or click on the plus and minus icons. You can also view the swatches in three modes; swatch only, swatch with name single column or swatch with name four columns. To change the view, click the list icon (far right button) in the swatch box.

If you've created a lot of swatches, and you want to save them for use in other projects, click the Save as Palette button. Enter a name for the palette of swatches and it will be saved as an .aco file. If you want to open an existing palette, click the Open Palette button. MD will ask you if you want to keep the existing swatches or delete them before opening the palette. If you keep the swatches, they will stay in the swatches box and the swatches from the opened palette will be added to the box.

The Palette Library contains one Default Palette. You can open existing palettes from the library by clicking the plus sign at the top. The process works just like the swatches side. You can copy all the swatches from an open palette to the swatches box by selecting the Copy to Custom Palette button. MD will ask if you want to clear the swatches box before they are copied over, or if you want to add them.

You can also control how the swatches in the library are displayed by using the buttons in the lower right corner. You can hide the library by clicking on its name between the two windows.

You can also open libraries you've created in other programs, such as Adobe, that have the file extension .aco or .ase.

Fabric Material Properties

Select the arrow next to Material to show all the options. You'll see three tabs; Front, Back and Side. You can change the material properties of one fabric to

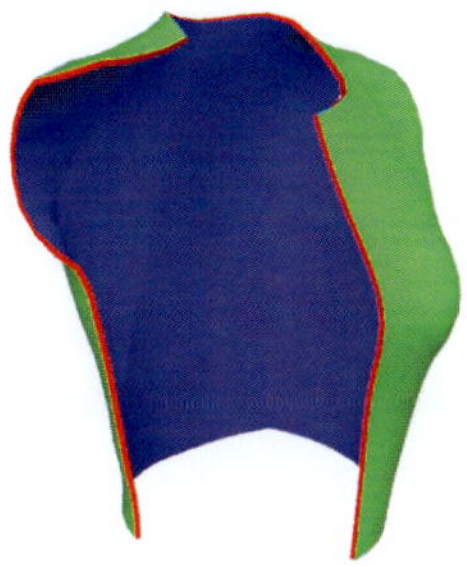

Figure 9-5. Pattern Sides - Green Right Side, Blue Wrong Side, Red Edge Side

differ on all sides. Front refers to the right side of the fabric, Back refers to the wrong side of the fabric and Side is the depth or thickness.

By default, MD will apply the Front material to the back and side. To make different choices, uncheck the Use Same Material as Front box on the Back and Side tabs.

Texture

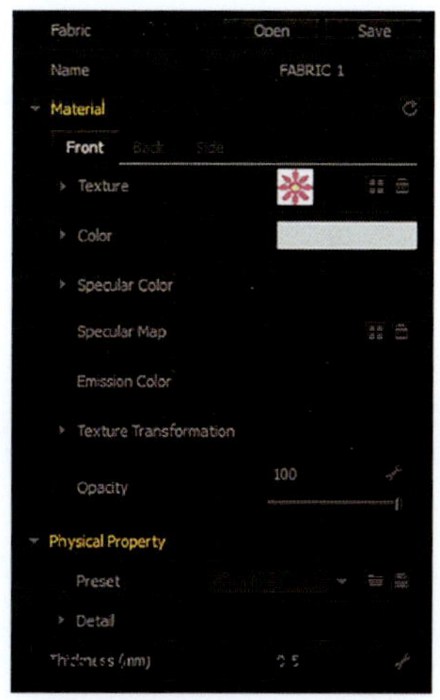

Next to the word Texture, you'll see a four square icon for choosing files. If you click that, you can apply an image file that you've created outside MD as the texture of your fabric. MD will accept jpg and png images.

When people trained in CG hear the word texture, they are expecting a bump map. Texture in MD is only color. Your Texture image can be a gray-scale image and you can apply a solid color over the entire thing, but it still isn't a bump map. I know, this is really confusing, but that's how MD works.

MD will automatically tile your Texture for you, just like any other 3D program. You can adjust the sizing of the tiles and that is covered in the *Printed & Patterned Fabrics* section of this chapter.

If you open the Texture section, you'll see the second item is the Normal Map. Again, you have the Choose File button to select the file from your computer. You can apply a real normal map (blue-pink-green colors, not a gray-scale). Use the Intensity slider to make adjustments. This map does not change the shape of your mesh at all. If you use a normal map that has big shapes on it, the illusion will be ruined quickly by the straight profile at the sides of your garment. To remove the Normal Map, click the circled arrow button.

Next is the Desaturation section. This applies only to a Texture image that you've applied. Turning on Desaturation will remove all the color from your image. Use the Shadow Intensity and Shadow Brightness sliders to make fine tuned adjustments.

To delete a Texture, simply select the trashcan icon on the Texture line. If you want to delete the Texture using the 3D or 2D windows, select a pattern and -

Edit > Context Menu > Materials > Delete Texture

Color

The next material property is Color. This is the overall color of the fabric. Click the box next to the word Color to open the Color Picker. Color is applied over the top of any Texture images you may have defined. Fine tune your Color using the Ambient Intensity and Diffuse Intensity sliders. To remove color from a texture image, set it to pure white. Note that the default color applied to fabric in MD is not pure white. It is a very pale gray.

Specular

Specular Color is the color of the light of a specular reflection. Click the color box to change the light color reflecting off the fabric. The Shininess slider allows you to set how reflective the fabric is. At higher settings, the fabric looks similar to plastic. To remove Specular Color set the color to pure black.

You can apply a Specular Map to your fabric in much the same way as applying a Texture map. With a Specular Map, the image will only be visible at points of reflection on the fabric.

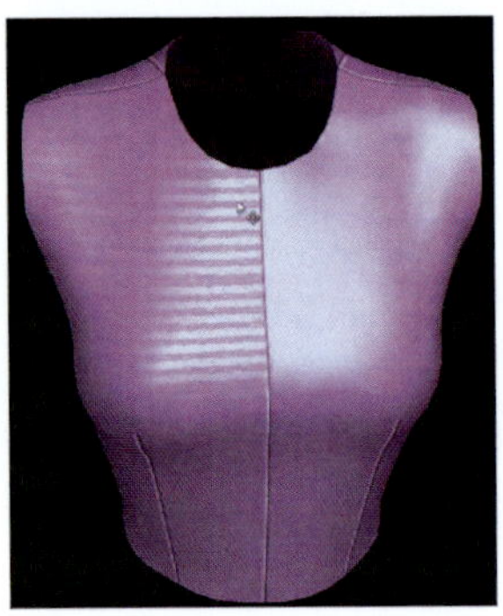

Figure 9-6. Specular Applied

In the image, the bodice color is purple and the Specular Color is aqua. In the image, the Specular Color is applied to the entire bodice. On the left, a striped Specular Map was used.

Emission

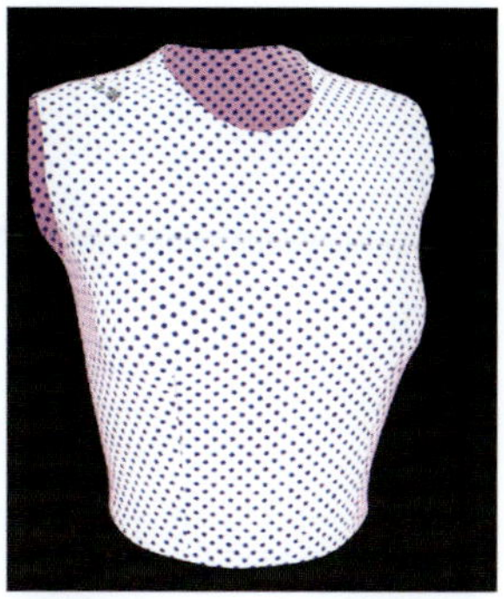

Figure 9-7. Dark Pink Emission

The Emission Color property makes your fabric glow, or emit light. You can choose the color that is emitted. To remove Emission Color, set the color to pure black. Emission Color will blend with any Textures or colors that have already been applied.

In the image, the Texture is a white background with blue polka dots. The Emission Color is a dark pink.

Texture Transformation

Texture Transformation will show you numerically any changes you have made using the Edit Texture Tool which is described in detail later. You can also enter numbers directly to more precisely control the transformation of your textures.

Opacity

The last fabric property is Opacity. Opacity controls the transparency of your fabric. Set at 100% your fabric is completely opaque. At 0% your fabric would be completely transparent. This setting applies to the entire piece of fabric.

If you want to create lace, which should have only sections of transparency, use a png Texture map image that contains its own alpha channel.

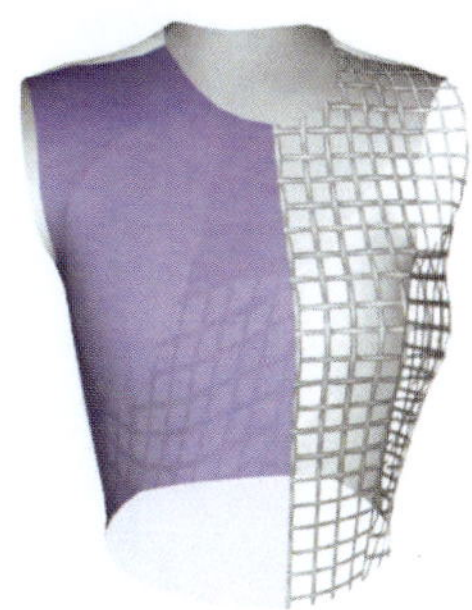

Figure 9-8. Opacity

In the image, the right side has a png image with alpha transparency and the left is a solid color with Opacity set at 50%.

You can also change the entire garment to transparent in the 3D Window by selecting -

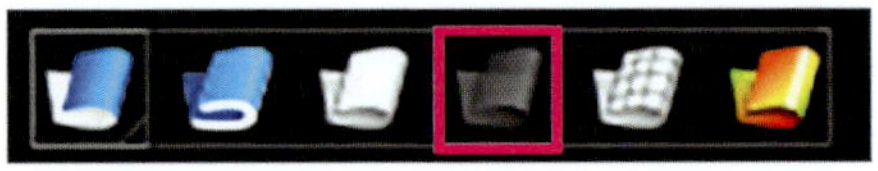

Display > 3D Garment Rendering Style > Transparent Surface

This is a quick way to view your Avatar in relation to the garment. This does not change the fabric opacity setting, only the visibility in the 3D Window.

Fabric Physical Properties

With a fabric selected, open the Property Editor and select the arrow next to Physical Property to show all the options. You must have a good understanding of fabric physical properties, if you hope to create realistic garments.

Fabric Presets

Figure 9-9. Fabric Presets

MD includes 22 fabric presets that you can choose from. You can also create your own presets as a .zfab file with unique properties. Use the Open and Save buttons on the Preset line to save your own presets and open others you've created. This does not save the fabric itself, just the physical properties like any other preset. If you want to save the complete fabric, use the Save button at the very top of the Property Editor above the fabric name.

Each one of these presets has a name that is prefixed with a letter. The first designation is D for Draft. These simulate the quickest and are good for preliminary work.

The R designation is for Reality. These resemble 90% of the real fabric physical properties associated with the fabric name given. This does come with a price, as the simulation speed can be slower. The S designation is for Subsidiary Materials. These are non-fabrics applied in special situations.

Each of these presets has a fabric name, like denim or cotton. These are general names. The problem is that there are many types of denim and cotton. Each type has its own characteristics and these names are pretty worthless, in my opinion.

Thankfully, in addition to the name, MD provides the physical characteristics of each of these. Those are what you need to understand. These characteristics will determine how your garment moves, drapes, stretches and bends. Open the Detail section under Preset to see these properties.

You will find a table in the Appendix listing all of the Preset properties. It's much easier to look at this, rather than names, when deciding what fabric is correct for each pattern piece or garment. Let's learn some of these terms, so you can make good fabric choices.

Fabric Properties

Below is an illustration showing a piece of woven fabric. The threads in the horizontal direction are called the Weft and the threads in the vertical direction are called the Warp.

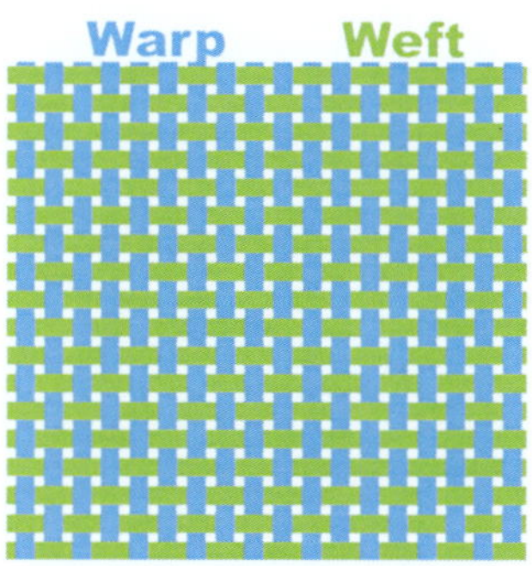

Figure 9-10. Warp & Weft of Woven Fabric

If you look at the MD preset table, you can see that most of the property settings are designated as warp or weft. There is Stretch, Bending, Buckling Ratio and Buckling Stiffness. In most of these, the warp and weft are set to the same numbers. If the numbers are different, a garment will drape and fold differently depending on how it is cut out of the fabric.

The warp and weft Stretch numbers indicate the strength of repulsion against elasticity. In other words, how hard will the fabric fight against stretching. The higher the number, the more it fights. The Rib Knit has more stretch across the warp (20) than it does the weft (32).

Shear is neither warp (vertical) nor weft (horizontal), it is on the diagonal. Increase the shear intensity to the same value as the warp and weft for fabric with little elasticity, like Cotton (23). Decrease the shear intensity in relation to the warp and weft for fabrics that have elasticity, like Rib Knit (9).

The warp and weft Bending numbers indicate the strength of the repulsion against bending. The fabrics with higher strength are more stiff and won't bend easily. Full Grain Leather is very stiff with a setting of 90.

The Buckling Ratio controls how much force is needed to easily bend the fabric. Fabrics that bend easily will have a ratio closer to 100%, like 30s Cotton Jersey (96%). Fabrics with a ratio closer to 0% require a lot of force to bend, like Denim (10%).

The Buckling Stiffness value works in conjunction with the Bending values. The actual intensity of the fold is the Bending value multiplied by the Stiffness value and then divided by 100. If the Bending Weft is 60 and the Buckling Stiffness Weft is 80, the actual intensity of the fold is 48. A higher fold intensity is a stiffer fabric.

Internal Damping has to do with fabric bounce during simulation. If you increase the value, the fabric will bounce slowly like its underwater. If the value is decreased, the fabric will bounce around more quickly. MD assigns the value of 1 to all presets.

The Density of a fabric is its weight or mass. A piece of wool is much more dense than a piece of lightweight nylon. MD sets all Draft fabrics at a density of 35 and the Reality fabrics at 27. I don't have a logical explanation for this.

The Friction Coefficient affects the friction between fabrics or a fabric and the Avatar. MD sets all the preset fabrics at a friction coefficient of 3.

I know all of this is a bit overwhelming. The best way to approach it is to find something you know in the real world that is at the high and low ends of the spectrum. You know what leather is and you know what knits are. So compare the Leather and a Jersey (Jersey is knit). You probably will use some fabric that is in between these extremes. If you want something stiffer, find a fabric that has settings closer to those of Leather. If you want something that drapes better, find something closer to the Jersey.

Fabric Thickness

The last setting in the Property Editor is Thickness. MD includes the ability to add depth to your fabric. To see this select -

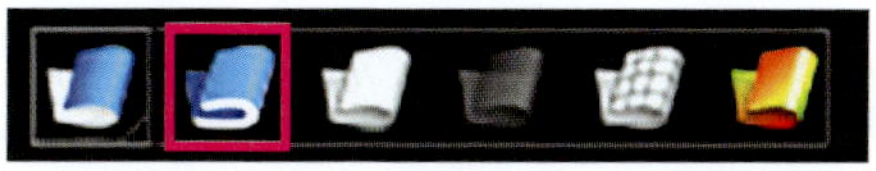

Display > 3D Garment Rendering Style > Thick Textured Surface

Use the Thickness setting to adjust how much depth your fabric has in the 3D Window. You can set different fabrics to different thicknesses to achieve different looks.

Reset Fabric

If you want to clear all the settings you've applied to your fabric select -

RC the fabric on the Fabric tab > Reset

This will revert the fabric back to the default settings and patterns assigned to that fabric will be changed.

Grainlines & Pattern Layout

How your patterns are laid out in the 2D view makes a very big difference in how the garments will simulate and drape. Even though all you see in the 2D Window is color and/or textures on your fabric, you need to remember that it has physical properties. It has a warp and a weft direction. You control the orientation of your pattern to the warp and weft using the grainline of the pattern.

Understanding Warp & Weft

Most patterns are laid out like the image. The grainline on the pattern is lined up with the warp threads. This is referred to as laying the pattern "straight-of-grain" and it gives a garment structure. It will hold its shape because it is square to the threads. You can also line the pattern up on the weft threads, if you want.

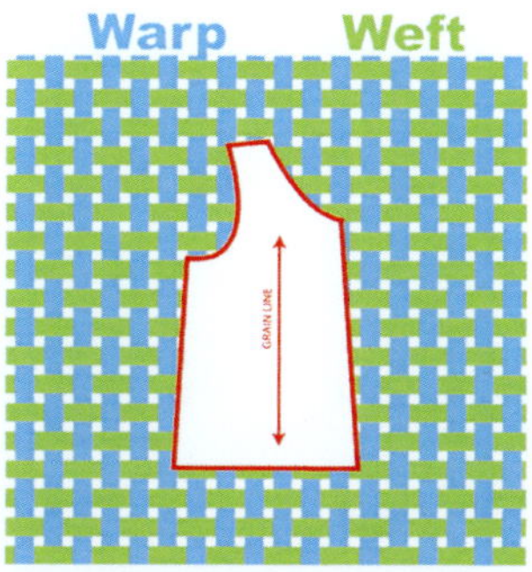

Figure 9-11. Straight-of-Grain Layout

Remember in the Fabric section when we spoke about the fabric properties being different between the warp and weft? If there is a difference between the two values, then laying the grainline on the warp will produce different results than if you laid it on the weft.

There is another direction to fabric called the Bias. If you lay out your pattern on the bias, it will lose its structure. The warp and weft are 45° out of square and the garment will buckle more easily.

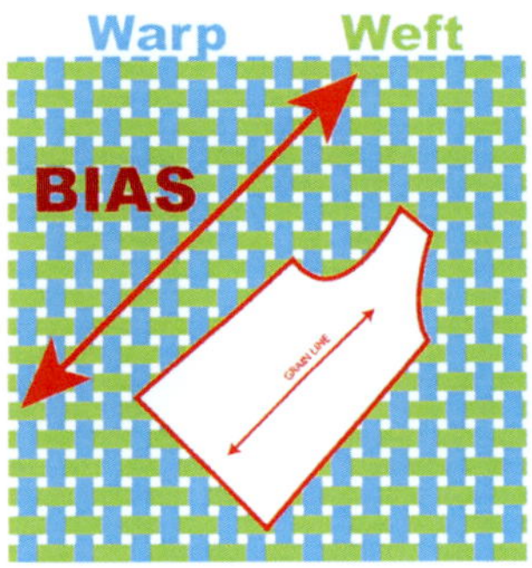

Figure 9-12. Bias Layout

If you create something that is supposed to appear very slinky, like a form fitting dress, and you set the fabric to cotton it won't look right. If you change the setting to satin and then lay the pattern on the Bias, it's going to drape much better and hug the body.

Grainline

Every pattern that you draw has a grainline. MD places a very pale line on the pattern to show you the current grainline orientation. You can see the grainlines on the patterns by selecting -

Display > 2D Pattern > Show Grainline

RC 2D Background > Show Grainline

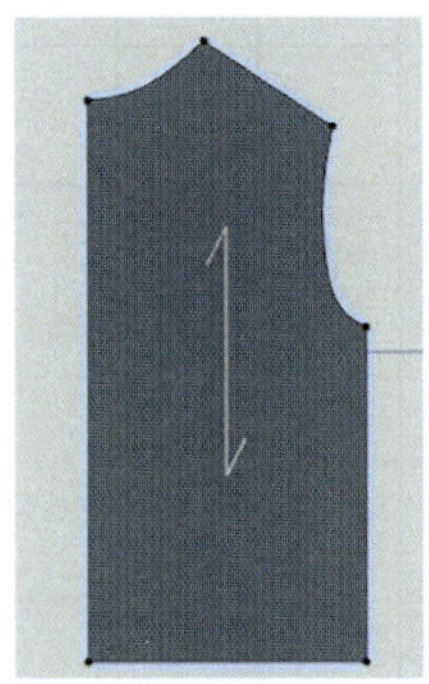
Figure 9-13. Pattern Grainline in Pale Gray

This grainline will determine the orientation of your pattern to the warp and weft regardless of the pattern layout.

MD in all their wisdom has given you the option to change the orientation of the grainline without changing the orientation of the pattern. I think this just serves to confuse everyone more, but there are several ways to do it.

With the grainline selected using the Edit Texture tool select -

Edit > Context Menu > Materials > Align Grain to X-Axis / Y-Axis

You can also change the grainline by changing the Grain Direction property in the Property Editor in the Fabric section. The pattern will not rotate, but the grainline will. Note, if you have a texture on your fabric, the texture will rotate with the grainline.

The other way to rotate the grainline is to use the Edit Texture tool on the grainline itself. When you select a pattern with the tool the grainline will become darker and show three green points, one at the top, middle and bottom of the line.

Hover over the top and bottom points and your cursor turns into the rotation icon. Click and drag to rotate. The center point turns the cursor into a move icon and you can move the grainline. Note that the fabric texture will move and rotate, too.

We'll get into the Edit Texture tool more later in this chapter, but understand that if you use the Edit Texture transform tool (show in the upper right of the 2D Window), the grainline will not move.

I understand that this is very confusing and I wouldn't have thrown this at you if it weren't very important. My suggestion is that you do not rotate the grainline separate from the pattern. Rotate the entire pattern instead. That way when you open your projects two months from now, it will be obvious which patterns are not laid on the straight-of-grain. Refer to the Cowl Pattern image in *Chapter 6 - Drafting Patterns* for a good reference.

Printed & Textured Fabrics

When you sew with a fabric that is printed or woven with a texture, you have to consider how the fabric texture will align at the seams and how balanced the fabric texture is across the body. When using a plaid or striped fabric, darts can look very bad, if the fabric isn't aligned properly.

Editing Textures

To make changes to your fabric orientation select -

Materials > Texture > Edit Texture (2D)

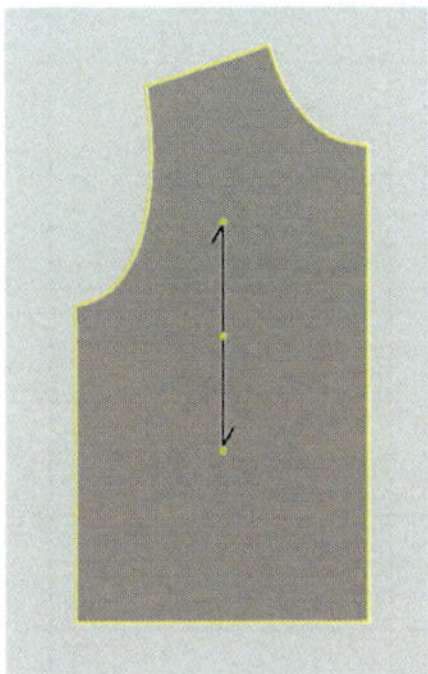

Figure 9-15. Edit Texture Tool

Using the Edit Texture tool, click and drag the fabric side-to-side and up and down until it lines up nicely. You'll want to do this for each pattern keeping a close eye on the seams where the fabric textures meet. This is another reason for keeping your patterns on the straight-of-grain. You can easily line up fabric prints at seams to create an even transition from pattern to pattern on the garment.

It may be impossible to line up the print between pattern pieces. In this case, you should rotate the print drastically. Shirt yokes and waistbands are perfect examples.

You may choose to lay these out at 45° or 90° angles, so the distinction is obvious and purposeful. This was done on the waistband of the plaid skirt in the image.

Figure 9-14. Plaid Skirt with Rotated Waistband

If you want to rotate or scale the fabric, you need to use the orange Edit Texture transform tool in the top right of the 2D Window.

This tool is only visible when you have the Edit Texture tool active and a pattern selected. Remember this allows you to transform your fabric texture without moving the grainline.

MD automatically tiles your texture image and you can use this tool to make adjustments.

Click and drag the boxes shown in the image.

#1 Scale the fabric in the vertical direction. This distorts any textures .

#2 Scale the fabric uniformly in all directions at once. No distortion to textures.

#3 Scale the fabric in the horizontal direction. This distorts any textures.

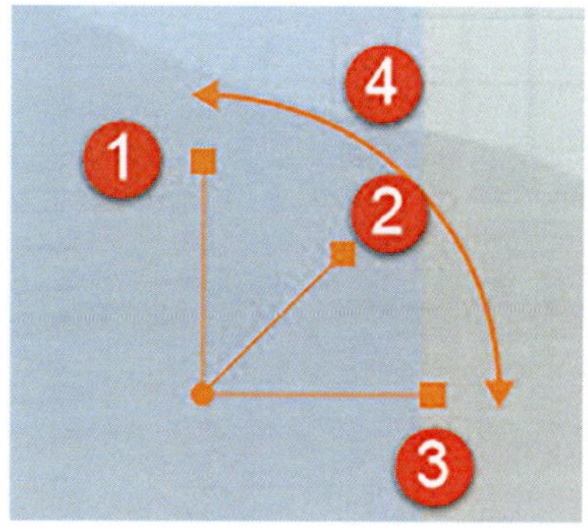

Figure 9-16. Edit Texture Transform Tool

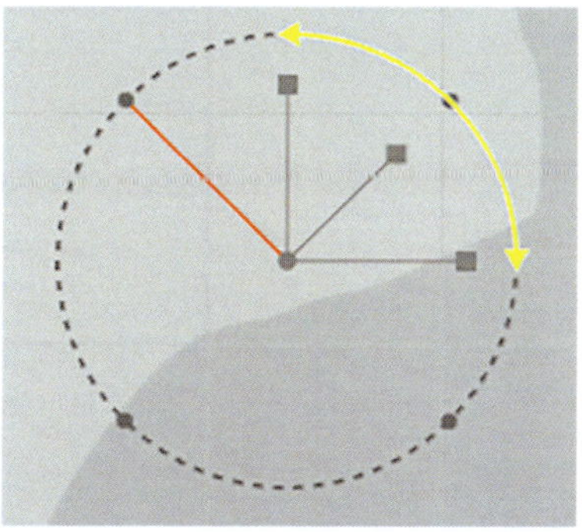

Figure 9-17. Edit Texture Transform Tool Rotation

You can also rotate the fabric to align it a particular way. Click on the arrowed arc at #4 and a circle will appear. This circle will help you to better visualize how much you have rotated the fabric and make more precise movements.

Please note that any transformations done to the fabric applies to the entire fabric, not just that pattern. If that fabric is applied to multiple patterns, the transformation will happen on all of them. If you only want to transform the fabric texture on one pattern, make a copy of the fabric and assign it to only that pattern before transformation.

If you make a mistake and want to reset the fabric to its original angle select -

Edit > Context Menu > Materials > Reset Fabric Angle

If you want more precise movements, select the fabric and open the Texture Transformation in the Property Editor. You can enter a precise Angle, Width and Height. You can also select Lock Aspect Ratio, so that you don't distort the texture of the fabric.

You can flip the texture of a fabric by selecting the pattern it is on and then -

Edit > Context Menu > Materials > Flip Texture Horizontally / Vertically

You may find it easier to move the texture from the 3D Window.

Materials > Texture > Edit Texture (3D)

You can also use the layout of a stripe or plaid to create a new design on the garment. If you put the texture at 45°, you can create a chevron effect. Just make sure the stripes match up where they meet at the seam.

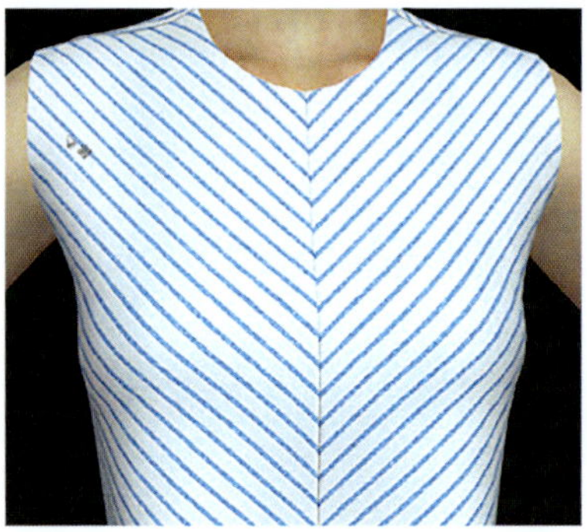

Figure 9-18. Chevron Using Texture Rotation

The last consideration for textured fabrics is the placement on the body when the garment is complete. If you are using a fabric that has large designs, like flowers, make sure the designs end up in a flattering place on the body. You don't want a big design element off-center, as this will make the garment look lopsided.

Fabric Graphics in MD

You may need to place an image on your garment in a particular place to represent a logo or other graphic. You don't want the image repeated (tiled) on the fabric like a texture, you want one particular placement. To do this in the 2D window, select -

Materials > Graphics > Graphic (2D Pattern)

MD will open a file browser dialog for you to select your image. After selecting the image, click on the pattern where you want the graphic.

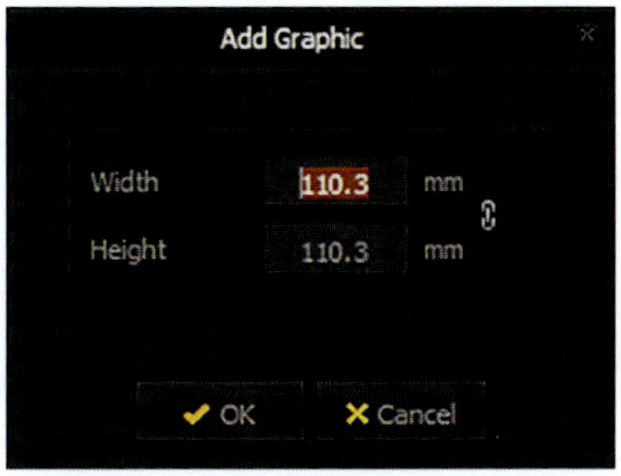

Figure 9-19. Add Graphic Dialog

You will have an Add Graphic dialog box where you can enter exact dimensions.

You can edit the graphic after it is placed by rotating and resizing using the Transform Pattern tool.

If you want to flip the direction of your graphic, you can use the Transform tool or select -

RC > Flip Horizontal / Vertical

If you want precise rotation, select -

RC > Rotate > Select Rotation

It is not possible to move a graphic to another pattern piece after it has been placed. However, you can copy the graphic and paste it on another pattern using the standard copy/paste methods.

If you prefer to place your graphic in the 3D Window, select -

Materials > Graphics > Graphic (3D Pattern)

This allows you to control exactly how the graphic lines up on the draped garment.

You may want a graphic to appear in the same place on a matching symmetric pattern. To do this -

RC > Duplicate to Symmetric Pattern

If you find that the box containing your graphic is larger than your pattern, you won't be able to select the pattern for editing. You can't use the Order feature to put a graphic

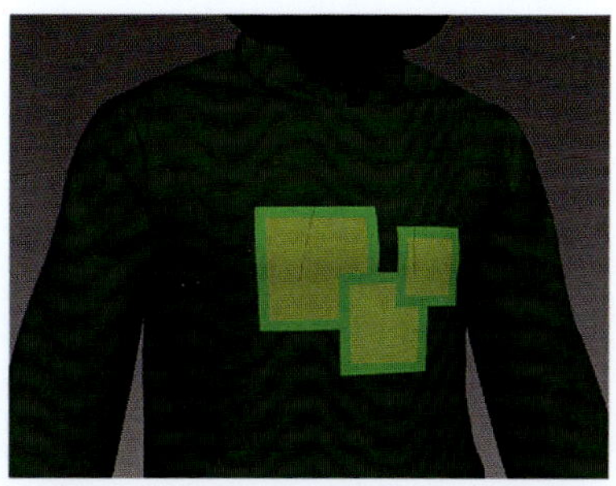

Figure 9-20. Hooded Sweatshirt with Graphic

behind a pattern. Instead, you can lock the graphic, so it can't be selected, and then you can select the pattern behind it.

2D Pattern > Lock > Lock All Graphics

Hide Textures

As you are working with patterns, textures can be distracting. MD will automatically hide textures as long as you have the Edit Pattern tool selected. If you want to hide them at other times select -

Display > Materials > Show 2D Textures

All of your patterns will now be a uniform color in the 2D Window.

You can also hide your textures in the 3D Window by selecting -

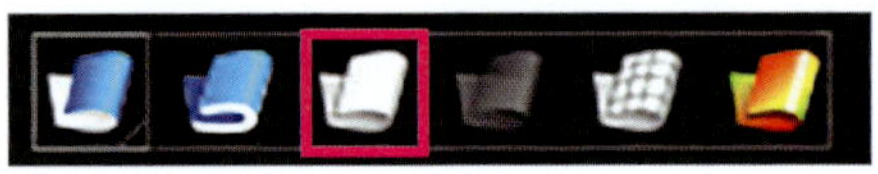

Display > 3D Garment Rendering Style > Monochrome Surface

Refreshing Textures

If you make changes to your fabric and you don't see them in the window, you can force MD to perform a refresh. To do this select -

RC the 3D or 2D background > Refresh Textures

xTex

MD has a partnership with a company called Vizoo. They sell a product called xTex that is a texture creator. Incorporating xTex compatibility started with the CLO product, but it now shows up in MD. To load an xTex texture -

RC the fabric on the Fabric tab in the Object Browser > Import xTex File

RC the fabric on the Fabric tab in the Object Browser > Import (add) xTex File

You'll get a dialog box stating that displacmeent and alpha maps are not supported. Click the OK button and you can select an xTex file. Not only will you get the Texture loaded up, but he Normal Map will be populated as well. You will probably need to adjust the Intensity of the Normal Map to see it in MD.

The files created with their system are very high quality. You can learn more about the xTex product by visiting www.vizoo3d.com.

Tracing Patterns

You can find pattern images online or in catalogs and use them in MD. All you need to do is trace them out.

You'll also need to know how to do this, if you want to do the projects in this book. I will be supplying you pattern drafts out of PatternMaker PRO and those are png files.

To trace a pattern in MD first you need to create a pattern for your image. Use the Rectangle tool to draw out a box.

With the Transform tool selected -

RC > Assign to New Fabric

Select the new fabric in the Object Browser. Click the open file button on the Texture property and select your image. Use the Edit Texture tool to move the image around in the rectangle so you can see all of it. You may need to resize your rectangle, if you made it too large or small.

If you are using PatternMaker PRO drafts, the images are already scaled properly. If the image came from another source, you will most likely need to scale it. Use the Edit Texture tool's transform option in the upper right of the 2D Window.

Now you'll need another fabric for tracing. Create a new fabric and set the Opacity to 0. You'll use this when drawing so you can see the image underneath.

Use the Polygon / Line tool to trace around your image. It is easiest to do a rough trace with the entire image visible and then go back and adjust the points and add curves when you are zoomed in.

As you are editing your shape, the image (texture) may disappear. Just select the Show 2D Textures button to bring the image back into view.

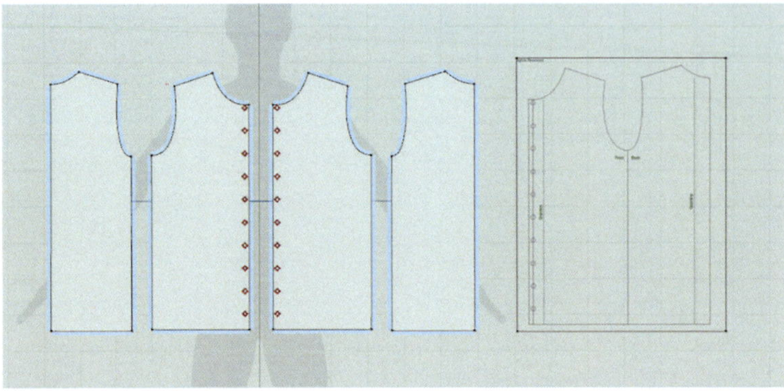

Figure 9-21. Tracing Patterns

In the image above, the rectangle with the image applied is on the far right. The image was traced and then the patterns were Cloned as Symmetric Pattern.

Make note of any markings on the image that you need for reference later. You will want to remove the rectangle with the pattern image before you simulate. At a minimum, hide it in the 3D Window. It is very large and combined with the image itself, it takes a lot of computer resources when simulating.

Strengthen

You may want to make a pattern less flexible and more stiff. You can create a new fabric with a fabric preset that is appropriate, but MD offers a quick way to achieve the same result. Select your pattern and -

Edit > Context Menu > 3D Garment > Strengthen

RC the pattern in the 3D or 2D window > Strengthen

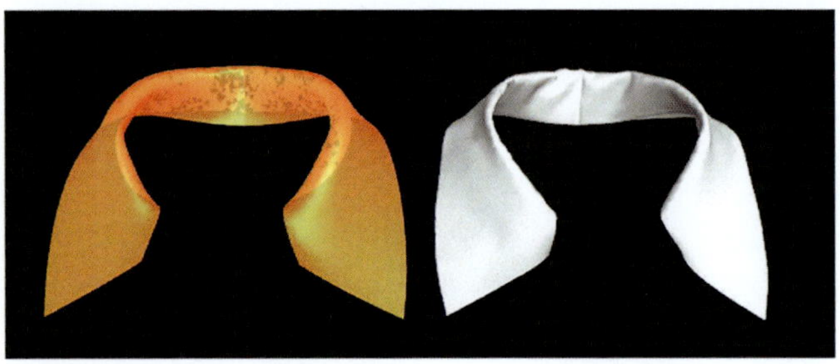

Figure 9-22. Same Collar, Strengthened on Left

Your pattern will turn orange, so you know that Strengthen has been applied. When you simulate it, it will stiffen up and the flexibility will decrease.

Chapter 9 Quiz

1) In most cases, the wrong side of the fabric faces out and the right side faces the avatar.

❍ True ❍ False

2) The Fabric Texture Normal Map can be either gray channels or red/blue/green channels.

❍ True ❍ False

3) How you lay out your patterns in the 2D Window makes a difference in how the patterns will drape in the 3D Window.

❍ True ❍ False

4) You can set the following properties on your fabric (choose all):

❍ A. Transparency

❍ B. Print/Image

❍ C. Shininess

❍ D. Stretch

❍ E. Glow

Chapter 10 - Pattern Properties

Pattern Name

Every pattern in the 2D Window has its own properties. Select the pattern to show all the options in the Property Editor. The first item is Name. You can give unique names to each of your patterns. This name will display in the Object Browser Scene tab.

You can display the pattern names on the patterns in the 2D Window by selecting -

Display > 2D Pattern > Show Pattern Name

You can also show the pattern names in the 3D Window by selecting -

Display > 3D Garment > Show Pattern Names

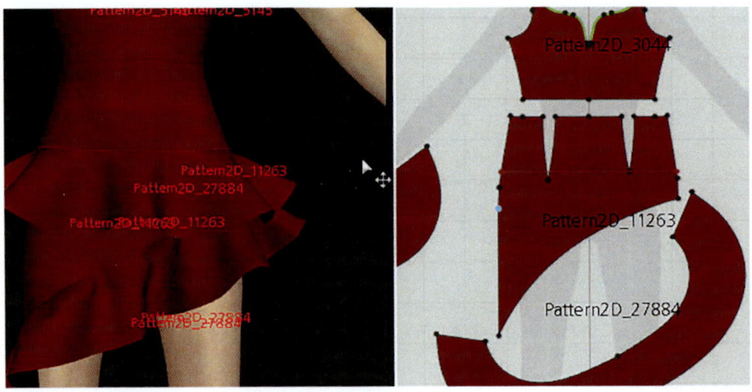

Figure 10-1. Pattern Names in 3D and 2D Windows

Line Length

Next is the section called Selected Line. Click the arrow next to the section name to open all the options. If the entire pattern is selected, Line Length values reflect the outline of the pattern. If you have one or more line segments selected, this will show you the total length of the selection. The 2D Line Length is the length of the line in the 2D Window and the 3D Line Length is the length of the line in the 3D Window.

If the line selection is on a symmetric pattern, you'll see two additional values called + Symmetric Line Length. This is the total of the selection plus the symmetric linked copy. Essentially, it will be two times the value of the selection alone.

This section also shows whether you have turned on Elastic or Curved Side Geometry. Learn more about Elastic in *Chapter 13 - Shaping Cloth.*

Curved Side Geometry

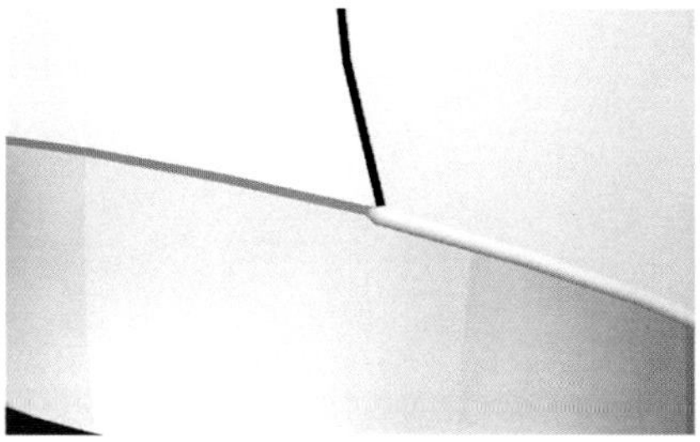

Figure 10-2. Curved Side Geometry

We discuss adding Thickness earlier. Once you have the thickness, you can choose to curve the edges of the pattern. The image shows curved side geometry applied on the right side.

This looks more realistic than leaving it square. When you have curved side geometry active, you can set the Curvature with the percentage slider. You can also set it to Double-Sided. This is a great feature that causes your garment to appear to have lining or facing. See *Chapter 19 - Finishing Edges* for an example.

Simulation Properties

The next section is Simulation Properties. This is where you set the Particle Distance for the pattern, as well as other properties that apply only to simulation. Learn more about Particle Distance in *Chapter 21 - Mesh / Geometry.*

Layer

When you layer one pattern over another, collisions can become a problem. MD is not sure which layer should be on top or underneath. The Layer property is a way to tell MD what your intentions are. All patterns are on layer "0" by default. The "0" layer is the layer closest to the Avatar.

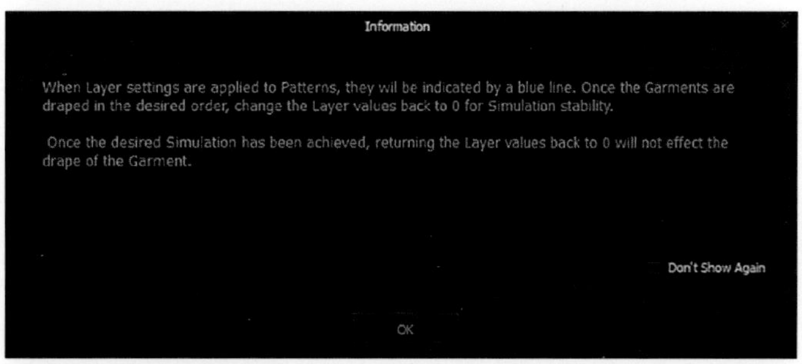

Figure 10-3. Layer Warning

As you stack other patterns on top, you can give them higher values.

Use this with caution and only when necessary. It does cause problems for the program and MD will warn you about this when you set anything to another Layer. The layer will be outlined in a different color to alert you that layering is active. Once you have your garment situated, you should return all patterns to layer "0".

Shrinkage

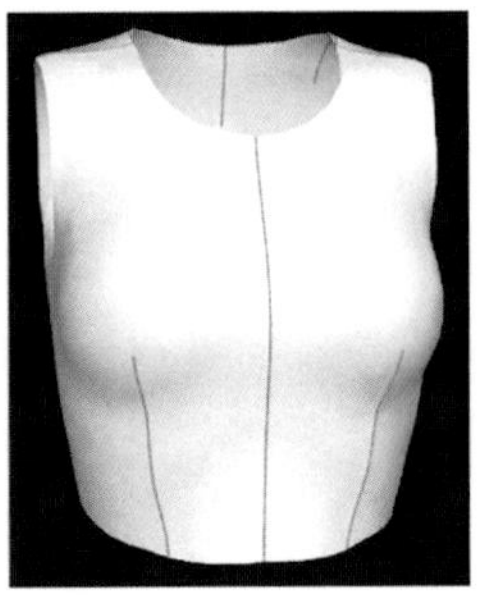

Figure 10-4. Bodice Shrunk to 80%

You are probably familiar with what happens when you wash a garment in hot water and dry it on high. The garment will shrink.

The Shrinkage Warp and Shrinkage Weft settings do this to your patterns. If the Shrinkage is set to greater than 100%, the pattern will grow. If it is set to less than 100%, it will shrink.

The bodice above was a very well fitted bodice and then it was shrunk to 80%. You can see how tight it has become.

Shrinkage is a handy way to make a garment fit differently. You'll end up with more creases and pulling when you shrink it.

The garment will hang loosely, if you grow it. The bodice to the right was a very well fitted bodice and then it was shrunk to 120% (which made it grow).

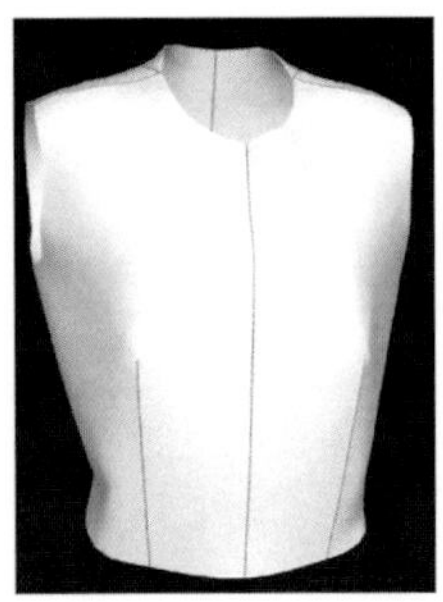

Figure 10-5. Bodice Shrunk to 120% (grows)

Thickness

There are two properties in regard to additional thickness. One is Collision and the other is Rendering. These are very different things.

Collision thickness is the space that surrounds the pattern. This space is not filled, it is invisible. This will push your pattern away from collision objects, be they other patterns or the avatar. In some instances, you will want your pattern spaced a good distance from other objects so they don't collide or even touch.

The Rendering thickness is the actual thickness you see in the 3D Window. You can see your pattern grown in depth as this value is increased. You'll note that both of these are marked as "additional". This thickness will be added to the selected pattern in addition to any thickness set elsewhere. For example, if your fabric applied to the selected pattern has a thickness, any value here will add to that.

Pressure

The Pressure setting is used to apply force to your pattern. You can set this using a number in the field or using the slider. A positive number will send the force in the direction of the normals. It will push the fabric in the direction of the right side of the fabric. A negative number will send the force opposite the normals, pushing to the wrong side of the fabric.

Figure 10-6. Pillows Made in MD (textured and rendered in Blender)

Typically, you will use pressure when two layers of patterns are sewn together, like a pillow. If you are using it on a garment, you will get different results depending on if the pattern with pressure is pushing against the Avatar or another pattern.

Fabric

The next section is dedicated to fabric properties. The Fabric item shows the fabric that has been applied to the pattern. You can use the drop-down menu to select a different one.

The Grain Direction field allows you to enter a number for changing the direction of the grainline on your pattern. We discussed this in *Chapter 9 - Fabric.*

This number is a rotation percentage. If you type in 45, the grainline will rotate 45°. This allows you to rotate the grainline without moving the pattern at all. I suggest you use the pattern tools to rotate the pattern, and the grainline will follow.

Solidify

There are many things you'll want to do to your garments to make them appear more realistic. Perhaps you need a sleeve scrunched up over the elbow or a pair of pants pulled up over the knee.

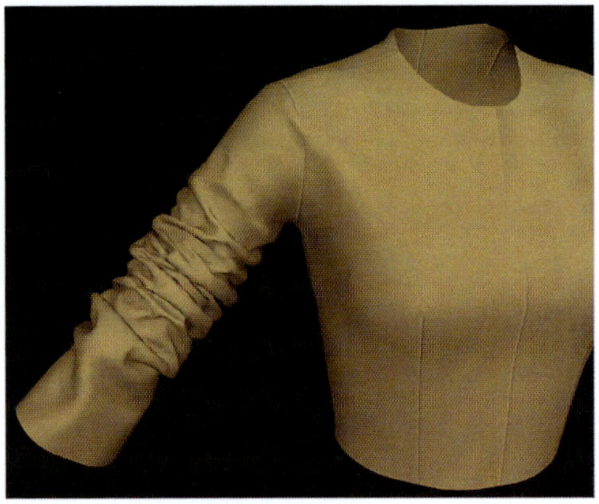

Figure 10-7. Solidify Applied to Sleeve

Pinning and freezing do not work well for these effects. The pins become too obvious and frozen patterns do not simulate. In these cases, the solidify feature works perfectly.

Interact with your patterns while simulating to get the placement desired. Stop the simulation and select -

Edit > Context Menu > 3D Garment > Solidify

RC the pattern in the 3D or 2D window > Solidify

Now when you simulate the pattern it will hold, but still remain flexible for animation and posing.

Arrangement

The Arrangement section gives you all the information regarding how the pattern was arranged in the 3D Window using Arrangement Points. If the pattern wasn't arranged using points, "not assigned" is selected.

The Point Name is the Arrangement Point that was used. The Shape Style shows whether it was arranged Curved or Flat. The Position X, Position Y and Offset are the properties of the Arrangement Point on its Bounding Volume. The Orientation setting can be used to rotate or spiral the pattern, depending on the pattern shape. All of these settings can be changed on a per pattern basis to help you arrange the pattern precisely.

Miscellaneous

The last section is for Miscellaneous information, which is primarily mesh geometry information. The Mesh Type tells you whether the pattern is made of triangles or quads. You are also given the Face Count and Vertex Count on the selected pattern.

Chapter 10 Quiz

1) Use the Layer feature in the Property Editor whenever possible.

❍ True ❍ False

2) The Pressure property is appropriate for the following (choose all):

❍ A. Quilting

❍ B. Inflatables

❍ C. Pillows

❍ D. Aprons

❍ E. Mattresses

3)The Arrangement property shows "not assigned", if you don't use Arrangement Points to place your patterns.

❍ True ❍ False

4)The 2D and 3D Line Length is not accurate if your pattern is one of a symmetric set.

❍ True ❍ False

Chapter 11 - Arranging in the 3D Window

Arrangement Points & Bounding Volumes

Although you can use the Gizmo tool in the 3D Window to arrange your flat patterns, MD provides a quick and easy way to do this automatically.

Arrangement Points (AP) and Bounding Volumes (BV) allow you to place your patterns precisely around the Avatar before simulating. Not only is this convenient, it is sometimes necessary. The default pattern position is flat and getting a circular pattern piece, like a cuff or waistband, to simulate properly from a completely flat start is almost impossible.

Another bonus to using Arrangement Points is that patterns positioned on the back of the Avatar will be flipped for you automatically, so the normals are facing the correct way.

To view existing Arrangement Points and Bounding Volumes, select -

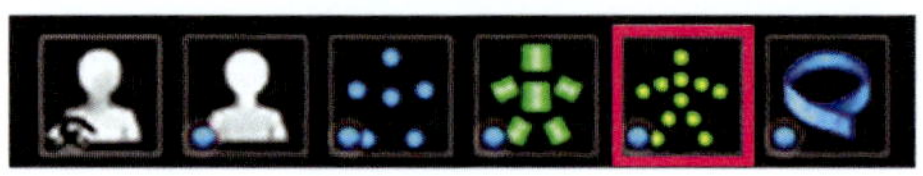

Display > Avatar > Show Arrangement Points

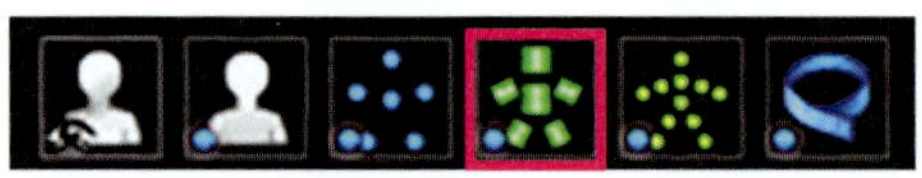

Display > Avatar > Show Bounding Volumes

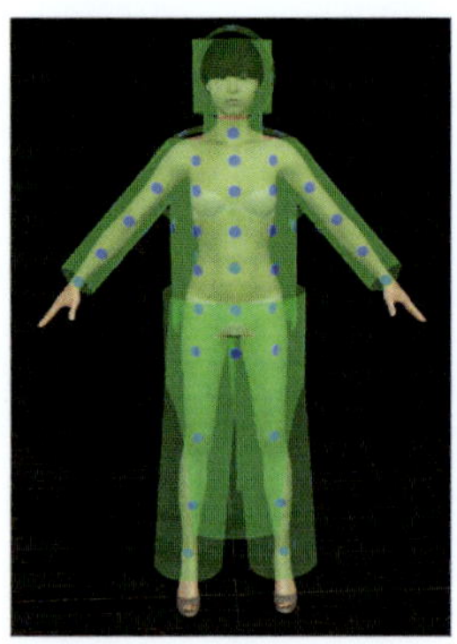

Figure 11-1. Bounding Volumes (green) & Arrangement Points (blue)

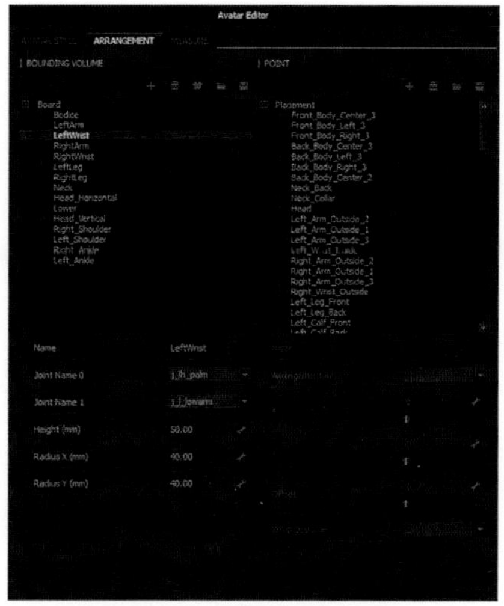

Figure 11-2. Avatar Editor Arrangement Tab

To see the list of points and volumes select -

Avatar > Avatar Editor > Arrangement tab

The Arrangement tab consists of two panes. You have the Bounding Volumes on the left and the Arrangement Points on the right. There are buttons at the top right of each pane to Add or Delete an item, Open a set or Save a set.

The MD default avatars come with a full set of Bounding Volumes (BV) and Arrangement Points (AP). When you begin to work with your own custom avatars, you'll need to create these yourself. You can create new sets by opening and editing an existing set from a different Avatar or starting from scratch.

If you want to bring in an existing set, use the Open button in the Bounding Volume pane and locate a saved BV file (.pan). Do the same for the AP file (.arr). Make sure that the two files were created together originally and work together.

If you are creating AP and BV from scratch, you might find it helpful to take a screenshot of one of the MD avatars, with the arrangement display on, for reference while you're working.

You can't create Arrangement Points without Bounding Volumes. The points are attached to the volumes.

Creating Bounding Volumes

Working in the Bounding Volume pane, select the Add button (plus sign). You'll see you have a cylinder in the 3D window. Use the Gizmo to place the cylinder where you want it. You use the Height and Radius values to shape the cylinder.

Height is how tall the BV is. Radius X is the width, side to side and Radius Y is the depth, front to back. Your goal is to surround the Avatar with the cylinder. For the most part, you don't want to penetrate the Avatar, keep it away from the body. Remember that this defines where the pattern will lay and you want it a bit away from the Avatar. This gives the program more time to sew seams before they collide with the Avatar.

There is one Bounding Volume that I always add down on the floor. When you are working with wide patterns that have a lot of gathering, such as a full skirt, it is nice to have a really big circular Arrangement Point.

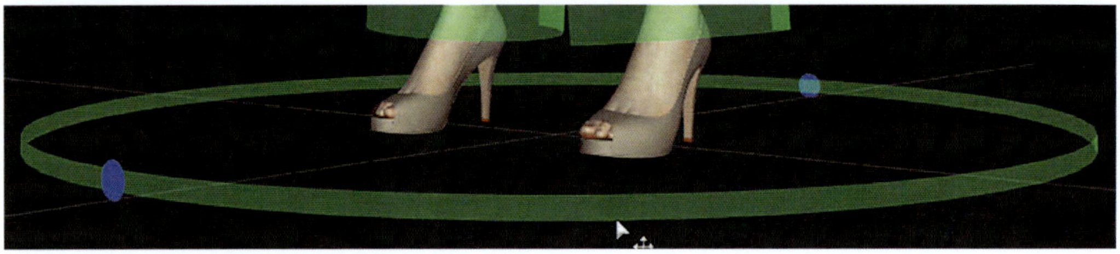

Figure 11-3. Custom Bounding Volume at Floor Level

Make sure to name your Bounding Volume. Use something descriptive and make sure you note whether it is the left or right on symmetrical cylinders. Repeat this process for all the BV you want around your Avatar. Refer to the MD default reference screenshots you took to get an idea of good placement.

Creating Arrangement Points

To create Arrangement Points, select the Add button (plus sign) in the Point pane. Arrangement Points are children of Bounding Volumes. You can't place a point without it referencing a BV. Select a BV from the Arrangement BV drop-down list. Now you know why the names of your BV are important.

Use the X, Y, Offset and Wrap Direction values to place the point where you want it. The X value designates the placement on the X axis, or around the BV cylinder left and right. The Y value is on the Y axis for placement up and down on the BV.

Offset determines how closely the AP will "hug" the Bounding Volume. You can put the point directly on the cylinder at 0, behind it with a negative number and in front of it with a positive number.

The Wrap Direction is not overly obvious. The MD manual says nothing about it and the only distinction I could find was the lapping behavior. If the setting was Down, it lapped the left side of a piece over the right on placement. If the setting was Up, it lapped the right side of the piece over the left. Of course, this only applies if the pattern piece is long enough to encircle the BV and then overlap itself.

If the blue AP dots displayed in the 3D view are too large or small, you can adjust their size by selecting -

Settings > User Settings > Others

There is a section here called Arrangement and you can set the Default Arrangement Point Size to anything you like. You can also set the Default Arrangement Shape Type to Flat or Curved. I'd recommend leaving this Curved.

Think about the Arrangement Point as you place it and which type of patterns will use it. Create as many points as you want. You can always change these settings or add more in the future. As you work with the program more, you'll learn which AP and BV work the best for you.

Testing & Saving Arrangement Sets

I suggest that you create a folder for each of your avatars. You can put all the files associated with it there for easy access. You can create a project containing no clothing that includes the Avatar complete with all measurements, Bounding Volumes and Arrangement Points. This will be a great starting point for all your future projects.

MD has the ability to save arrangement files, too. In addition to the project, you may wish to save out the measurement file. The BV and AP have different files and the Save button is at the top of each pane.

You will also want to save your Avatar as an Avatar.

File > Save as > Avatar

The Bounding Volumes and Arrangement Points will save with the Avatar. This allows you to swap out avatars on a project without reopening all the other files.

Using Arrangement Points

To use Arrangement Points, make sure they are visible in the 3D Window. Select a pattern and hover your mouse over a point where you want the pattern to go. You'll see a gray ghost pattern showing you how the pattern will look when you place it. If you like what you see, click and the pattern should jump into place. The pattern will curve slightly, following the Bounding Volume that was used for that Arrangement Point.

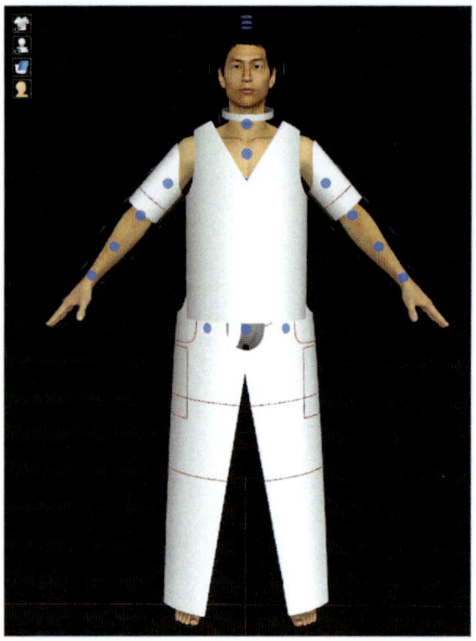

Figure 11-4. Patterns Arranged with Arrangement Points

If you have a lot of patterns scattered all over the 2D Window, it can be difficult to locate them in the 3D Window to select. In this case, select the pattern in the 2D Window and then click an AP in the 3D Window. It will jump over to your Avatar and make quick work of the arrangement process.

You can also use the Object Browser to select your patterns, if you've named them so they are easy to locate.

Arranging Tips

You will often have to fine tune the placement when using Arrangement Points. Use the Gizmo to make sure the pattern does not intersect the Avatar at all. Sometimes, the pattern may overlap another pattern slightly and that shouldn't cause problems. If you are arranging pants, sleeves or other patterns with very narrow openings that must surround the body, take the time to angle the pattern so the sewing lines go outside

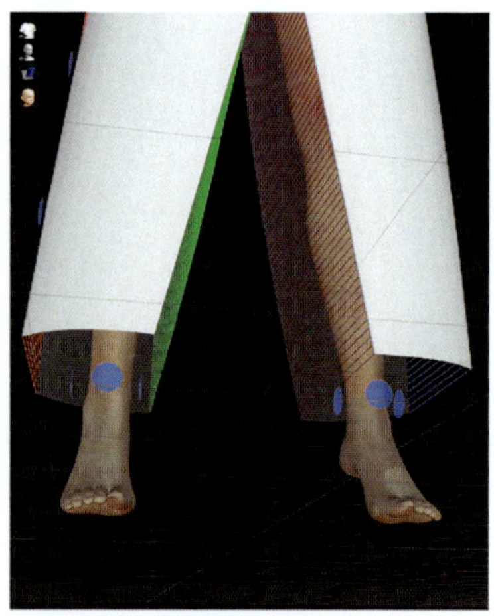

Figure 11-5. Pants Arranged

the body and not through it. This will assist the pattern to wrap and not collide or penetrate the Avatar.

In addition to using the Gizmo, you can make other adjustments after the pattern is arranged. Select the pattern in the 3D window and then look at the Arrangement section in the Property Editor. It will tell you the Point Name that was used for placement and the Shape Style. If you prefer a pattern is arranged flat, just switch the Shape Style from Curved to Flat. You can also use the Offset, Orientation and other sliders to fine tune the arrangement.

If you are arranging patterns on top of other layers or after you have already simulated, freeze the patterns that are already simulated in place. This will preserve their position and not allow additional patterns to distort what you've already done.

Resetting the Arrangement

If you don't like the arrangement of one pattern or all of them, they are easily reset. Select the pattern or patterns that you want to reset then -

Edit > Context Menu > 3D Garment > Reset 3D Arrangement (Selected)

RC the pattern > Reset 3D Arrangement (Selected)

If you want to reset ALL of the patterns, select -

3D Garment > Reset 3D Arrangement (All)

This will reset the patterns back to their position prior to the last simulation.

If you want to reset your pattern layout in the 3D Window to match the patterns in the 2D Window, select -

3D Garment > Reset > 2D Arrangement (All)

You can also choose to reset only selected patterns by choosing -

Edit > Context Menu > 3D Garment > Reset 2D Arrangement (Selected)

RC the pattern > Reset 2D Arrangement (Selected)

Using Superimpose

MD includes another handy tool for arranging your patterns called Superimpose. To use this tool, select the pattern to arrange then -

Edit > Context Menu > 3D Garment > Superimpose Under/Over/Side

RC the pattern > Superimpose Under/Over/Side

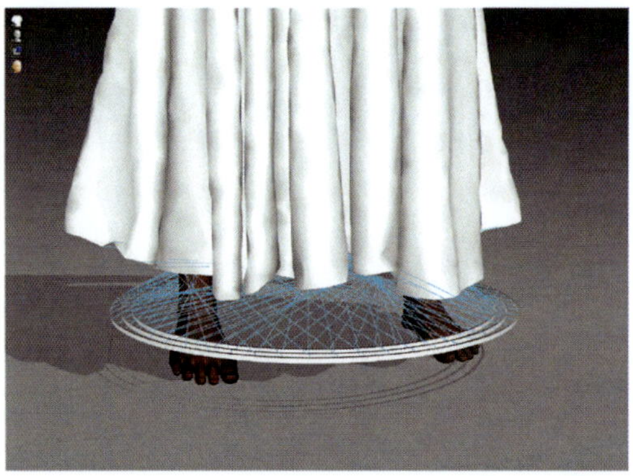

Figure 11-6. Skirt Trim Overlapped Using Arrangement Point

This tool works best adding on detail pieces that are difficult to arrange because they are extremely long or just hard to place. To the left is an image of a very full skirt. There is a narrow piece of trim to be added to the bottom. When the trim is arranged, it is so long that it overlaps itself many times. This would wreak havoc, if you tried to simulate it.

The Superimpose tool evaluates the seam of the pattern piece including the shape of the adjoining piece. Then it places the pattern based on the shape of the adjoining piece. You can decide where it places the pattern by choosing Under, Over or Side.

Figure 11-7. Skirt Trim Arranged with Superimpose Side

The Under option places your pattern under the other pattern, Over places it on top of the other pattern and Side places it edge-to-edge. You see in the image that the pattern was perfectly placed and will simulate easily without distortion.

I will warn you that occasionally MD will flip your pattern over and you'll see the gray backside facing out. You'll want to correct this before simulating, if it happens.

Fold Arrangement

It can be difficult to fold patterns back on themselves or fold down a pattern, such as a collar. MD includes a Fold Arrangement tool for this purpose. To use the tool select -

3D Garment > Fold Arrangement

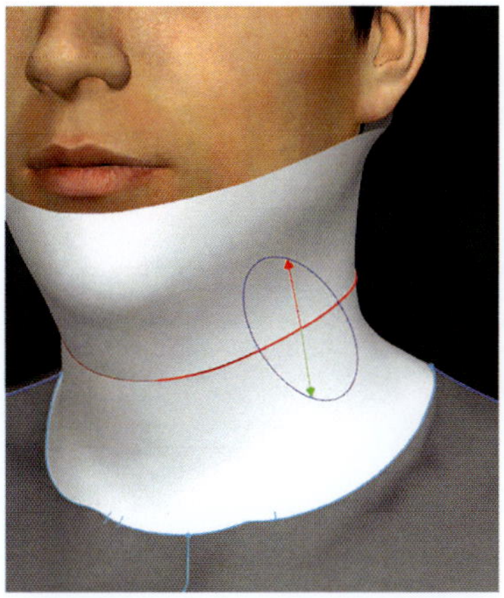

Figure 11-8. Fold Arrangement Tool on Turtleneck

After selecting the tool, select the seam or Internal Line in the 3D Window. MD will display a manipulator that has a circle and two arrows. Each arrow represents the direction of the two patterns on the seam. Click and drag the circle to fold the pattern over.

When you fold a pattern, you can see the wrong side in the dark gray color. On some patterns, the wrong side will be facing out once it is folded. If you would prefer that MD does not show the gray color on the wrong side of your patterns, select -

Display > Materials > Double-Sided Surface

Flipping Patterns

We've discussed the need to flip your patterns so that the correct side is facing out. To do this select the pattern in the 3D Window and then -

Edit > Context Menu > 3D Garment > Flip Horizontally / Flip Vertically

RC > Flip Horizontally / Flip Vertically

The pattern will be flipped and the curve of the pattern will not change.

Another method of flipping is the Reverse Arrange. This option is only available, if the pattern was placed using Arrangement Points. Select -

Edit > Context Menu > 3D Garment > Reverse-Arrange > Horizontally / Vertically

RC > Reverse-Arrange > Horizontally / Vertically

This is similar to a Flip command except the pattern curve will flip, too.

If you have a long pattern that overlaps itself, you can change the direction of the overlap. For example, if it arranges itself with right over left select the pattern and then -

Edit > Context Menu > 3D Garment > Flip Wrap Direction

RC > Flip Wrap Direction

Now the pattern will overlap left over right.

You can toggle the shape style of the pattern by selecting -

Edit > Context Menu > 3D Garment > Flat / Curved

You can also flip the patterns in the 2D Window with the following actions -

Edit > Context Menu > 2D Pattern > Flip Horizontally / Vertically

RC > Flip Horizontally / Vertically

Be very careful with this! The pattern in the 3D Window may change in unexpected ways. I typically would not recommend flipping in the 2D Window.

Normals

Normals are imaginary lines that extend perpendicular to the points (vertices) of 3D geometry. Normals are used for orientation of actions in 3D. For example, when you extrude geometry or map materials, the 3D program needs to know which direction to go. Typically, you will want that direction to be pointing away from the center or facing out.

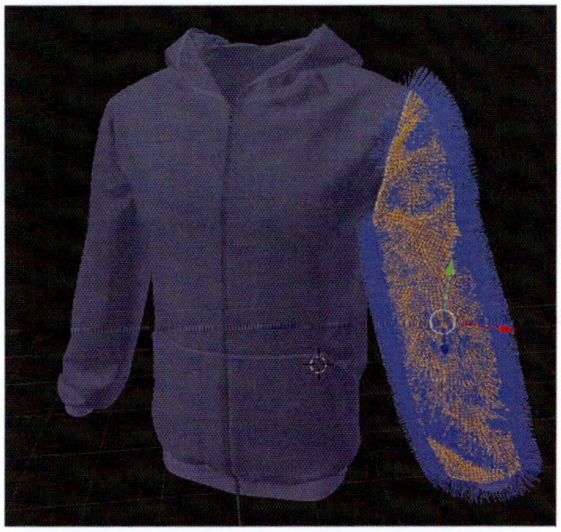

Figure 11-9. Normals Shown on Sleeve in Blender

This is an image from Blender showing the normals of the arm pattern of a hooded sweatshirt. You can't see normals in MD, but they do exist.

The easiest way to tell the direction of normals in MD is by the color of the pattern in the 3D Window (easy to see without a texture). The right side of the fabric is nearly white and the back is dark gray. The normals face out perpendicular from the vertices of the white side.

If you have selected Show Double-Sided Surface, you won't be able to distinguish the difference between the front and the back. The back will no longer be gray and so you can't see the normal direction.

Figure 11-10. Ruffle with Normal Facing Avatar

In the image, the top ruffle has the normals pointing toward the Avatar, not away from it. You will want all your normals facing out, particularly if you are taking the garments outside of MD for further work. Rather than swapping the pattern around and re-sewing it, you can flip the normals. To do this, select the pattern -

Edit > Context Menu > 3D Garment > Flip Normal

RC > Flip Normal

Simulating a pattern after flipping normals can have unintended consequences. Try to place your patterns properly to reduce the necessity for flipping.

Chapter 11 Quiz

1) Always create your Arrangement Points before your Bounding Volumes.

❍ True ❍ False

2) You can choose to reset the arrangement of your patterns in the 3D Window (choose all):

❍ A. Symmetric patterns at once.

❍ B. One pattern at a time.

❍ C. All patterns at once.

❍ D. Chosen patterns at once.

3) To quickly arrange a cuff next to a sleeve use (choose one):

❍ A. Superimpose Under

❍ B. Superimpose Side

❍ C. Superimpose Over

❍ D. Superimpose Next

4) You should name your Bounding Volumes so that it is easier to select them and assign ________________ ______________ to them.(two words)

Chapter 12 - Simulation

Simulation Mode

Marvelous Designer has two modes, Simulation mode and Animation mode. You can switch between the two modes using the drop-down button in the upper right of the program. These two modes are very different.

Simulation mode is the most important mode in MD. Simulation mode is where you will create your patterns, set all of their properties and drape them on your Avatar. In this mode, you'll have the Library, 2D Window, 3D Window, Object Browser, Property Editor and History.

Simulating is the computer process of applying physics to your patterns. The Avatar is a collision object and the patterns will drape around it.

To simulate select -

3D Garment > Simulate

When you click this button, the simulation will begin and the button will turn orange, to indicate that it is running. Click the button again to stop the simulation. You'll want to start and stop the process constantly during your garment creation process.

Sometimes a simulation will go horribly wrong and you'll be left with a complete mess. If this happens, your CTRL/CMD Z (undo) works. It will put everything back where it was before you simulated. You can also step backwards using the History panel.

Interacting with Patterns During Simulation

You have the ability to interact with your patterns in the 3D Window during simulation. Switch to the Select/Move tool by selecting -

3D Garment > Select Move

While the simulation is active, your mouse cursor will turn into a hand holding a blue dot. If you click on a pattern, a blue dot will appear. MD refers to this as a picking point. Click, hold and drag to move the pattern around while it's simulating. You can rearrange and correct pattern problems while the simulation is running.

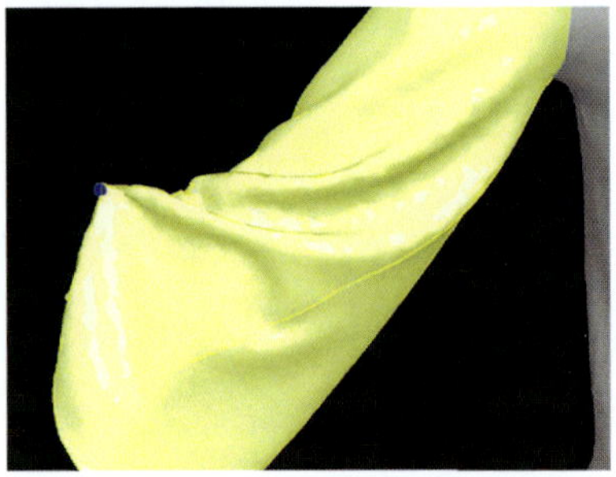

Figure 12-1. Picking Point While Simulating

You'll find this very handy if the Avatar penetrates the pattern or patterns penetrate each other. You can grab the pattern and pull it out. Don't get too aggressive with pulling. It works just like real-world physics. If you grab the pattern and pull really hard, when you release it's going to bounce back and can cause more problems than it solves.

Speeding Up Simulations

If you have a lot of patterns, or just large patterns, simulations may run very slowly. There are several things you can try to speed things up.

Particle Distance

Set your Particle Distance higher. This is the best way to speed up your simulations. If you are roughing out designs, there is no reason to set it low. You can reduce it, when you're ready to simulate your final work.

Hide / Deactivate Patterns

Hide and/or deactivate patterns that aren't being used. You can always un-hide them or activate them again when you are ready.

Freeze Patterns

Finally, you can freeze patterns that you have already simulated. As long as the pattern is where it should be, you can freeze it. Other patterns will still attach with sewing, but that pattern will be left out of the simulation. This is particularly helpful for very large patterns, like a long skirt or coat.

Checking the Fit

After you have simulated your garments on the Avatar, sometimes the fit isn't quite right. It's very difficult to tell where the problem is, just by looking at the final simulation. MD offers a couple of tools that help you see visually where your garment has fit problems.

The first tool is the Strain Map. Select the map with -

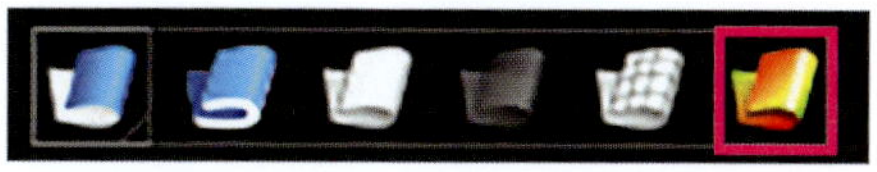

Display > 3D Garment Rendering Style > Strain Map

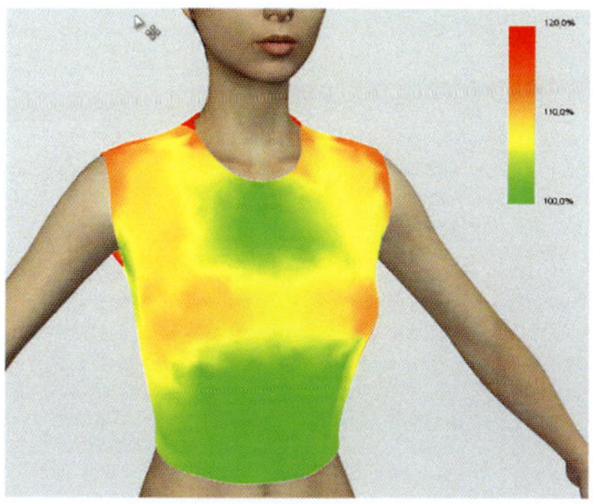

Figure 12-2. Strain Map

It displays a legend showing low strain in green and high strain in red. These colors are applied to your garment. This is an easy way to see where your garment has strain. Generally, you don't want any red areas.

The second tool is Pressure Points. You can find the tool by selecting -

Display > 3D Garment > Show Pressure Points

If you don't see the points in the 3D Window, click the Simulate button and they will appear.

Pressure Points are similar to the Strain Map, but they show points on the garment. The points are either blue or red. Again, red is an indicator of a problem area.

Simulation Properties

To view all the properties of simulation select -

Preferences > Simulation Properties

RC in 3D Window background > Simulation Properties

This opens the simulation properties in the Property Editor.

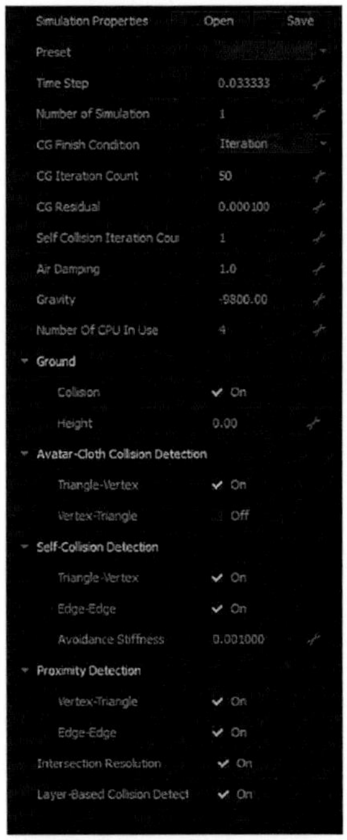

Figure 12-3. Simulation Properties

Complete vs Normal

The first option is a drop-down called Preset, which includes Complete, Normal and Custom. There are two preset simulation settings that MD provides.

The following table outlines the differences between the two.

Setting	*Normal*	*Complete*
Time Step	.033333	.033333
Number of Simulations	1	5
CG Finish Condition	Iteration	Residual
CG Iteration Count	50	50
CG Residual	0.0001	0.00001
Self Collision Iteration Count	1	1

When you go into Animation mode, MD will switch over to the Complete preset automatically. As you can see, the Complete setting refines your simulations. Your garments will look much nicer, but this comes at a high price. Your computer will slow down substantially. Do all of your preliminary work with the Normal preset and switch over to Complete for your final simulation.

If you make changes to any of the settings, the Preset will switch over to Custom. If you create a custom set of simulation properties, you can save them using the Save button as a .smp file to be re-used in other projects. Just use the Open button to import previously saved settings.

I am not going to go into details on these settings, except for Gravity. These settings are beyond the scope of this book and my own experience. Most of you will switch between the two presets and not bother with customization. If you understand what each of these settings does, feel free to change them.

Gravity

The Gravity setting is the one property that you might want to change occasionally. You can determine how much gravity is applied to your 3D simulation. As you know, gravity is an external force. A setting of -9800 simulates like the earth's gravity. If you want to reduce the Gravity, raise the number in the positive direction. As you get closer to zero, your garments will be floating with no downward pressure. This is very useful, particularly if you are making inflatables.

Figure 12-4. Inflatable Airplane in MD

Number of CPU

MD will indicate the number of CPUs it is using. This does not always reflect the actual number of CPUs that are available in your computer. There have been issues with MD not using all available resources on Apple Macintosh computers.

Ground

You determine whether the ground, which by default is the gridded floor plane in the 3D Window, is a collision object. If the checkbox is set to Off, anything

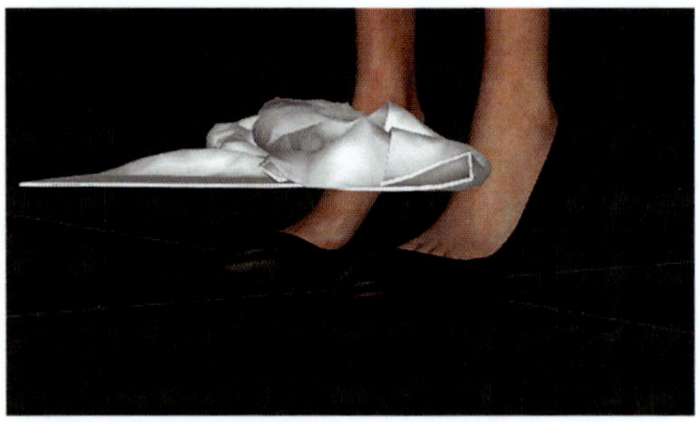

Figure 12-5. Ground Set Higher than Floor Plane

not held on an avatar will fall through the ground during simulation.

You can also set the Height value of the ground above or below the gridded floor plane. This will cause collisions to take place at the level you have specified.

Detection

The rest of the settings have to do with collision detection. These are advanced topics beyond the scope of this book. Try checking the MD manual for details.

Chapter 12 Quiz

1) What are the most common ways to speed up simulations (choose all)?

❍ A. Raise the Particle Distance

❍ B. Deactivate Patterns

❍ C. Hide Patterns

❍ D. Freeze Patterns

2) Strain Maps show where the avatar's body is the heaviest.

❍ True ❍ False

3) You can pull and arrange the patterns while the program is simulating.

❍ True ❍ False

4) The Simulation Property of Complete is the setting that runs the quickest and should be used most often.

❍ True ❍ False

Chapter 13 - Shaping Cloth

Shaping

The basic concept of making clothing is taking a flat, two-dimensional piece of fabric and turning it into a garment that will fit a three-dimensional body. In this chapter, we're going to discuss the techniques used to shape the flat pattern so that it conforms to the human body.

Darts

Darts are very common in garment construction. They remove excess fabric, so the garment conforms to the body. You will find darts used in transition from a larger measurement to a smaller one. For example, on a woman's bodice the bust is generally larger than the waist. A dart is placed at the waist to remove the excess fabric.

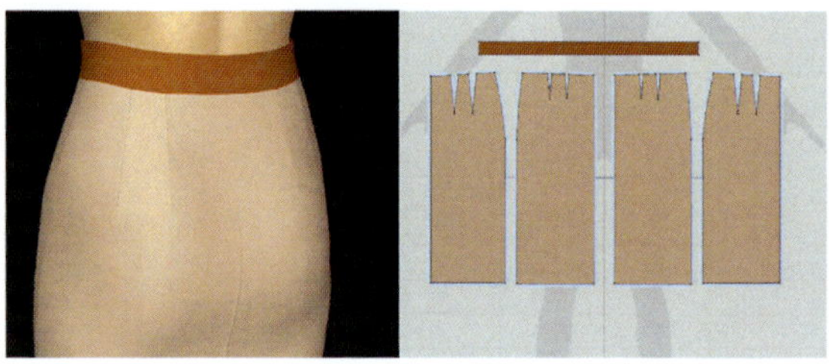

Figure 13-1. Skirt Back Darts

You will find darts in skirts and pants at the waist to transition to the larger hips. You'll also see darts added at the shoulder to fit the shoulder and allow more room in the upper back.

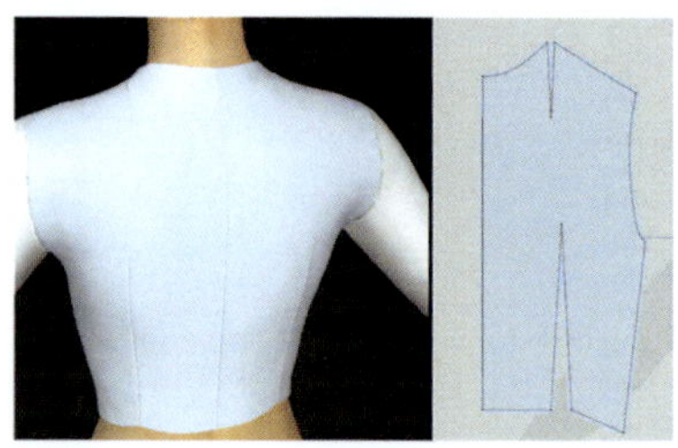

Figure 13-2. Bodice Back Darts

In a fitted sleeve, a dart is placed at the elbow. This causes the sleeve to bend, which matches the angle of a relaxed arm. Our arms are not straight naturally and this subtle detail is the difference between an inexpensive garment and a properly fitted one.

Darts placed on the edge of the pattern are considered single darts. They resemble a triangle and consist of two legs. The legs of a dart must be of equal length, or you will have puckering.

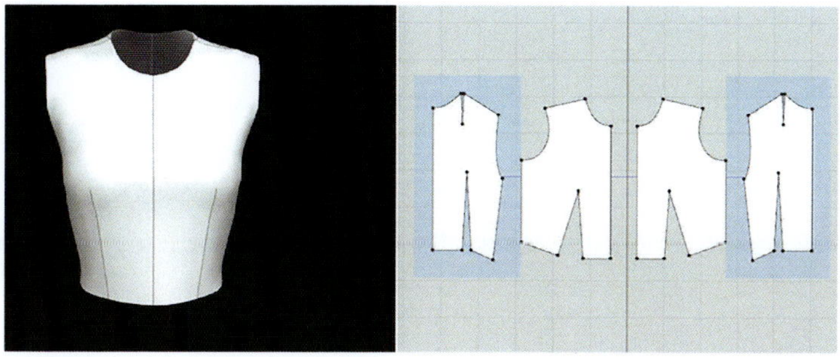

Figure 13-3. Bodice Darts

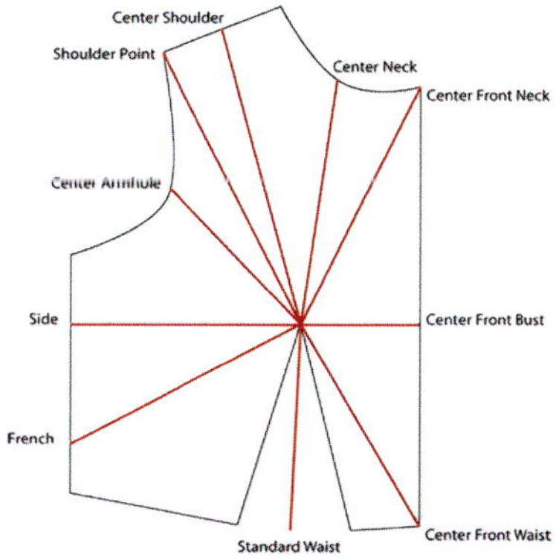

Figure 13-4. Dart Locations for Bodice

Dart placement, particularly on the bodice, can be varied. You don't have to place the dart at the waist. As you can see in the image, the dart can be moved to any position around the bust apex in a full circle. Each change does result in a subtle change in the design of the garment, but they all result in a good fit to the Avatar.

Here is a female bodice showing a bust dart placed at the waist on one side and the dart relocated to the side on the other. This was done only for illustration and looks pretty strange, but you get the idea.

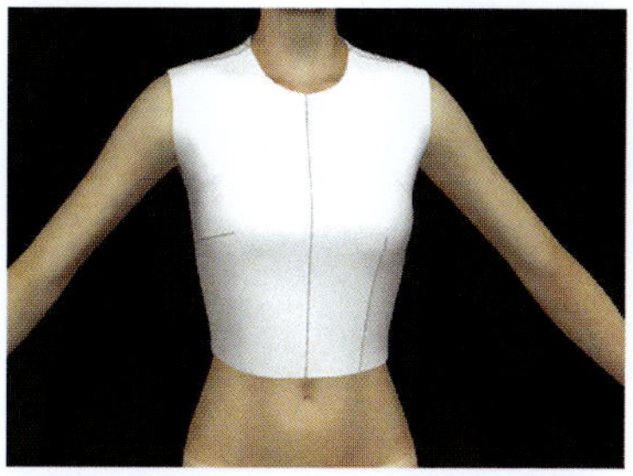

Figure 13-5. Side Dart Left, Waist Dart Right

Standard Darts

A standard dart consists of three points. Two points are placed at the edge of the pattern where you want the dart legs to originate. The third point is placed at the dart apex point. When sewing a female bodice in the real-world, the end of the dart is adjusted to be 3/4″ to 1″ (1.9 cm to 2.54 cm) away from the bust apex for better shaping. You may want to do the same, to reduce the sharp point. Just make sure the dart legs are the same length.

Double Darts

Double darts, also called body darts, look like a very skewed rectangle or two stacked triangles. These darts are not placed on the edge of the pattern, they are put inside the pattern.

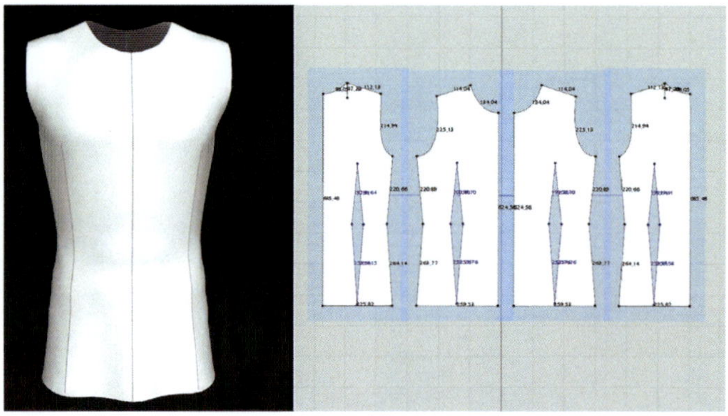

Figure 13-6. Double Darts

These are commonly used in a jacket as a transition from the wide chest/back into the more narrow waist and then back out to the wider hips.

You will also find these on dresses, where you transition from the bust to waist to hips. Double darts are created in MD with the Dart tool. Learn how to use the Dart tool in *Chapter 6 - Drafting Patterns - Internal Geometry.*

Dart Tucks

Dart tucks are another option. The middle of the dart is not cut away. The legs are sewn to each other starting at the pattern edge, just like a regular dart, but the seam stops before it reaches the dart apex point.

This leaves the top open creating a small tuck. You can create these darts using an Internal Line to draw each partial dart leg. Sew the legs together and leave the top open.

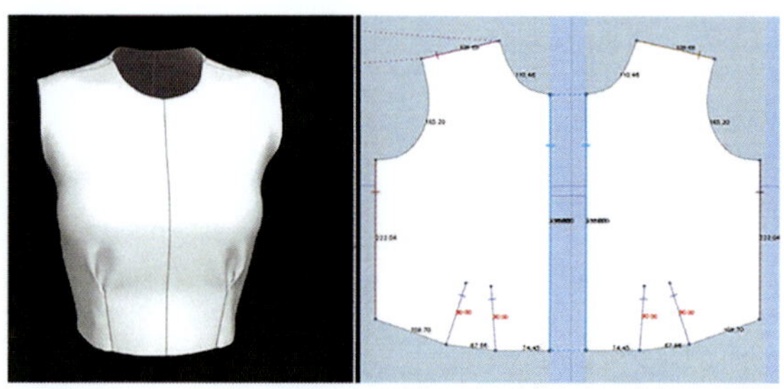

Figure 13-7. Bodice Dart Tucks

Dart Clusters

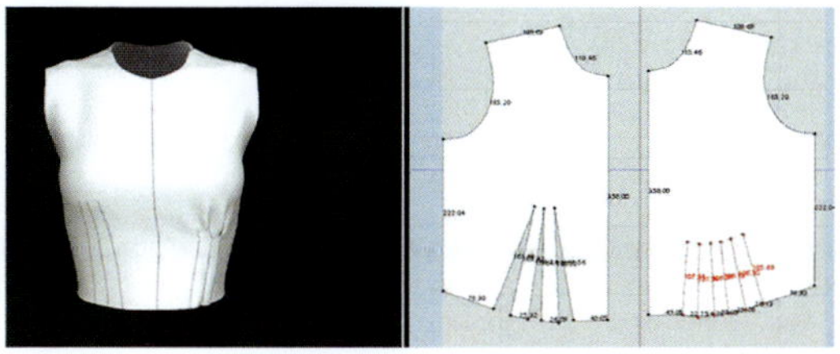

Figure 13-8. Bodice Dart Clusters on Left & Dart Tucks on Right

If you have a dart that is large enough, you can choose to replace one dart with many. These are called dart clusters.

To make a cluster, slash the pattern apart and spread the original dart width over several new darts. You can also use this technique with dart tucks.

Tucks

Tucks serve two purposes, one as a decoration and the other as a means to fit or bring fullness into a garment where it is needed. Tucks can take the place of darts and appears much softer than a dart. A tuck is constructed by sewing two lines together. You've seen examples of tucks replacing darts in prior illustrations.

Pin tucks are purely decorative, but they are a common feature on blouses and shirts. You'll see pin tucks down the front of a man's formal shirt. Additional fabric is added to the bodice draft to allow for the tucks.

Figure 13-9. Shirt Front Pin Tucks

Pleats

Pleating is the systematic folding of fabric. Pleats are held in place by stitching across the top. You can also stitch partially down the pleat fold lines. The most common types are accordion pleats, knife pleats and box pleats.

Pleats are not for beginners and they can take a bit of planning. There are many things to take into consideration before you begin sewing.

MD now has pleat tools for you to use when constructing pleats. This saves a lot of time, because pleats can be extremely confusing to sew.

Understanding Fold Angle

We covered the Fold Angle briefly in *Chapter 8 - Seams*, but you need to really understand this concept before pleating. Fold Angle applies not only to seams, but to Internal Lines as well.

In the Property Editor you'll find the Fold section, which includes Fold Strength and Fold Angle. A Fold Angle of 180° is standard for a seam and it is flat. It means that the fabric to either side of the seam or internal line lays on the same plane.

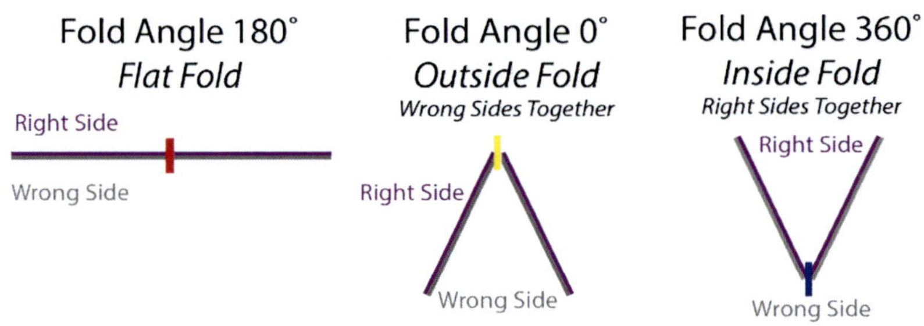

Figure 13-10. Fold Angle Diagram

A Fold Angle of 0° is an outside fold. This will bring the wrong sides of the fabric together on either side of the seam or internal line.

A Fold Angle of 360° is an inside fold. This will bring the right sides of the fabric together on either side of the seam or internal line.

You'll notice that the center mark for each of these folds is a different color in the image above. When you use the pleating tools, MD will assign a color to visually show you how the fabric will be folded. The red color is a standard internal line color. It is flat and at 180° and won't be folded.

The yellow color represents a line with a Fold Angle of 0° and the blue color represents a line with a Fold Angle of 360°. MD will set these for you when you use the Pleats Fold tool. You do need to understand what they represent, because sometimes MD can make errors. You'll want to spot those errors before you simulate and mess up your garments.

Pleat Tools

MD provides you with two tools that are used in combination. I will show you where the tools are located and how they are activated below. You'll want to refer to the sections on each specific pleat for more information before attempting to use these tools.

The first tool is the Pleats Fold. You use this tool to tell MD what type of pleat you will be making and the direction of the folds.

2D Pattern > Pleats > Pleats Fold

To use the tool, you click at the top corner of your pleated pattern, drag and double click at the opposite corner.

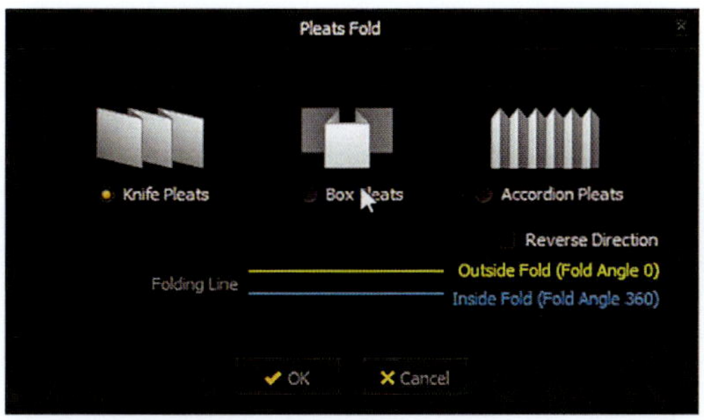

Figure 13-11. Pleats Fold Dialog

This will open a Pleats Fold dialog box and you can choose which type of pleat you want to sew. The dialog also shows you a color code for Fold Angle. Your pattern will show these colors so you understand how it will be sewn. We'll go into more detail on this when talking about each pleat type.

The second tool is the Pleats Sewing tool. This tool creates all the seam line pairs for the pleats. This can be very complex, if done manually. If you use the tool on a well structured pattern, MD does all the work for you.

2D Pattern > Pleats > Pleats Sewing

To use the tool, select the pattern segment that the pleats will be sewn to and then the pleated pattern top just like using the Free Sewing tool.

Accordion Pleats

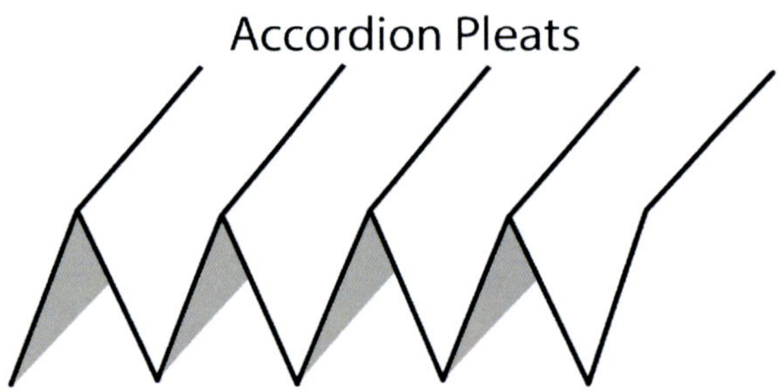

Accordion pleats are the least complicated type of pleat and they are easy to recognize. They look like the bellows of an accordion.

Figure 13-12. Accordian Pleat

These pleats are symmetrical. Both sides of the pleat are the same length. Accordion pleats do not require any extra fabric to make, because they are not sewn closed at the top.

Figure 13-13. Accordion Length

Draw internal lines on your pattern where you want the folds. Accordion pleats do not have any limitations on quantity of lines. You can use an even or odd number. Just make sure the pleat angle starts and stops appropriately for your garment.

Use the Pleats Fold tool across the top of your pattern. Check the Reverse Direction box, if you want to swap the inside (blue) and outside (yellow) folds. Click OK and MD will color code your lines. Notice that they are all blue or yellow. There are no red lines and the pattern will fold in and out all the way across.

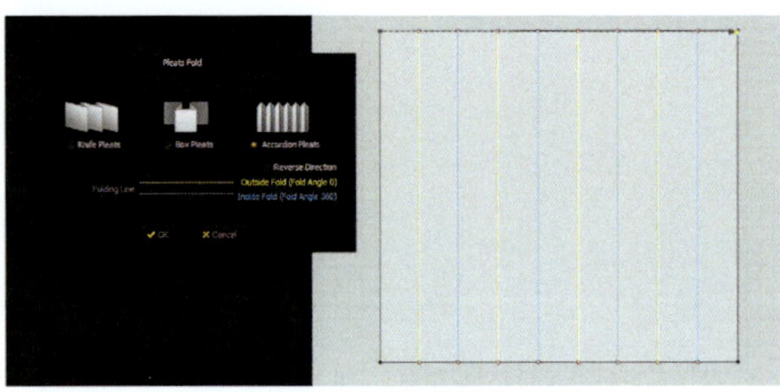

Since accordion pleats are not sewn closed at the top, you won't use the Pleats Sewing tool to finish them. The tool doesn't work at all for this type of pleat.

Figure 13-14. Accordian Pleat Layout in MD

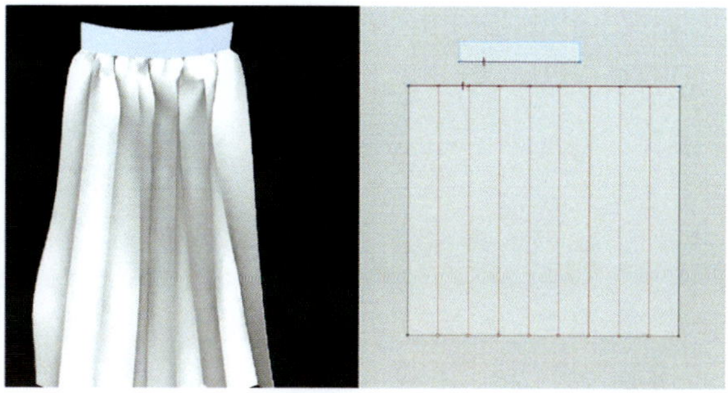

Figure 13-15. Accordian Pleat Sewn

Use the Free Sewing tool to sew your entire base pattern (waistband, in the case of a skirt) to the entire pleated pattern.

Accordion pleats are commonly found on circular skirts. The pleat lines are spaced much closer together at the top than at the bottom.

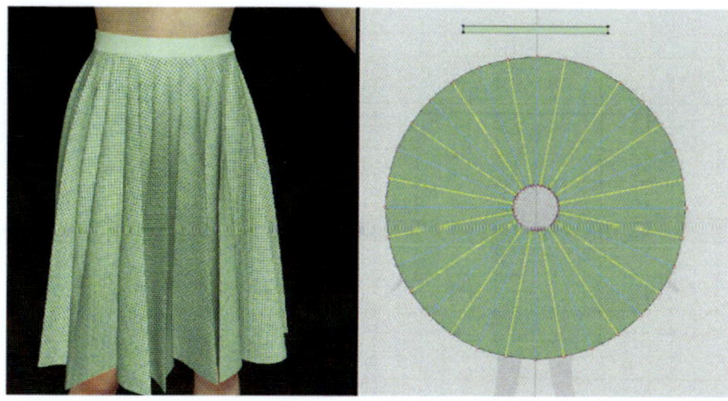

Figure 13-16. Accordian Pleated Skirt

I used the Pleats Fold tool three separate times to make this skirt. Since the tool only works in a straight line, I had to work my way around the waist circle.

If you need to use the tool multiple times, make sure when you are done that the blue and yellow alternate all the way around and you never have the same color next to itself.

Knife Pleats

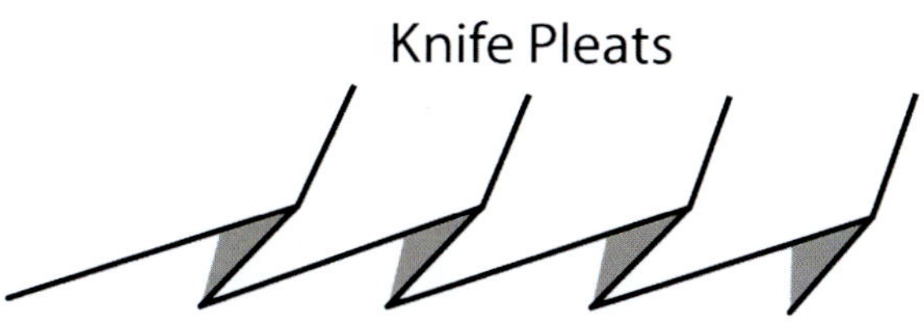

Figure 13-17. Knife Pleat

Knife Pleats, also called Side Pleats, are folds in the fabric that all lay to one side or direction.

Note that one side of the "V" is longer than the other, unlike an accordion pleat that is the same length on each side.

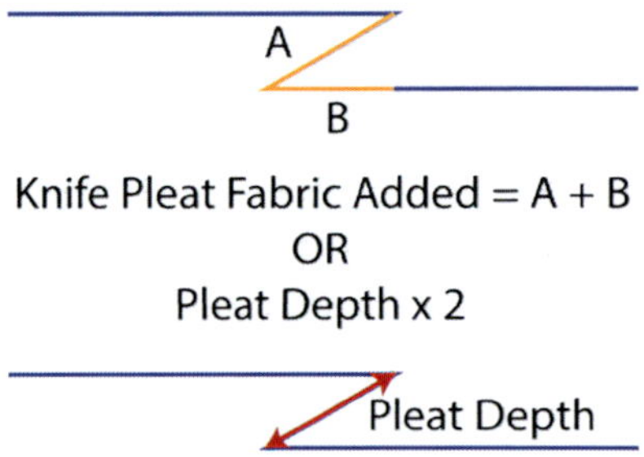

Figure 13-18. Knife Pleat Calculations

You will have to add fabric to your pattern, if you want to add knife pleats. The amount of fabric to add depends on the depth of your pleat. The orange area in the image indicates all the extra fabric needed to make the pleat.

To make a knife pleat in MD, you need to have three internal lines for every pleat. When you draw out your lines, make sure they are divisible by three, or the pleats won't be even and they won't sew properly.

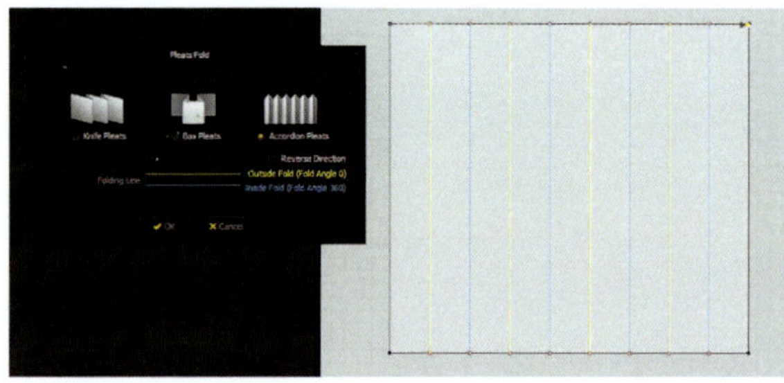

Figure 13-19. Knife Pleat Layout in MD

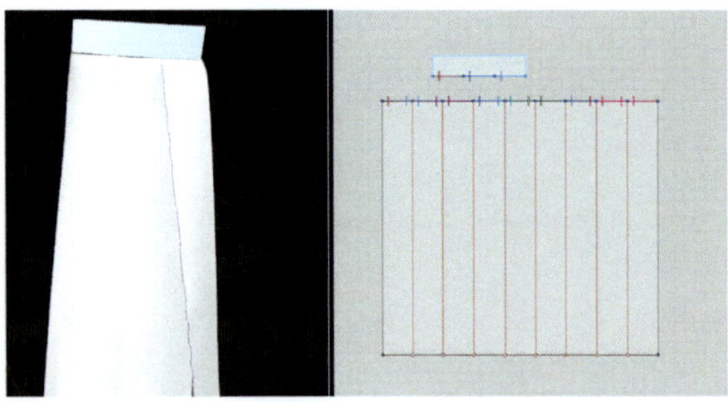

Figure 13-20. Knife Pleat Sewn

Use the Pleats Fold tool to designate your folding lines. Check the Reverse Direction box, if the pleats are folding to the wrong side.

Select the Pleats Sewing tool and click at the start point on the edge of your base pattern (waistband, for skirts) and then click the end point. Now select the start and stop points for the pleated pattern.

The Pleats Sewing tool will fail to work properly, if you have the wrong number of internal pleat lines on the pattern. It will try to select around the edge of the pattern and you'll notice it immediately.

Sometimes this strange behavior will happen even if you have the correct number of internal lines. If this is the case, try adding a standard point to the top of every internal line on the edge of the pattern.

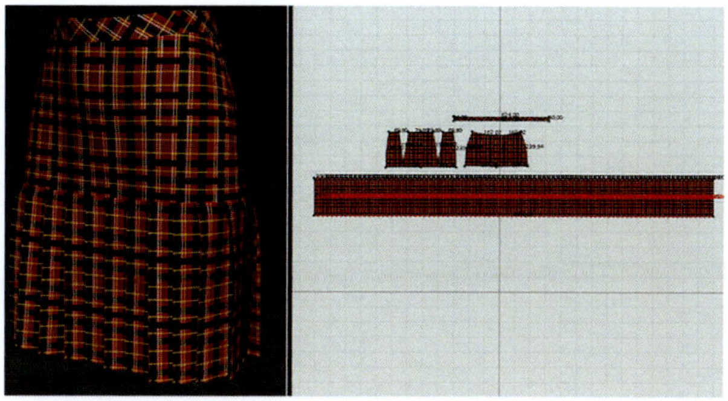

Figure 13-24. Pleated Skirt Using Knife Pleats

Pleated skirts can use a lot of fabric and take some patiencc to create.

Box Pleats

Box pleats are found a lot in upholstery work to allow expansion at corners. A box pleat is two knife pleats that face each other.

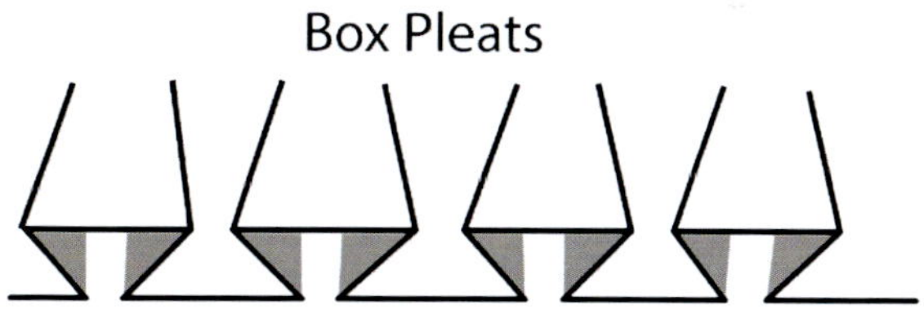

Figure 13-21. Box Pleat

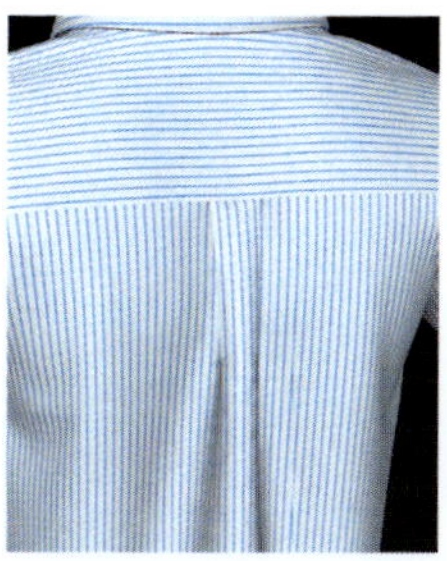

Figure 13-22. Shirt Back Box Pleated

They are also used at the center back of a men's shirt to allow expansion through the back when the person reaches forward.

Box pleats require twice as much extra fabric as one knife pleat. Again, the orange segment indicates the extra fabric needed.

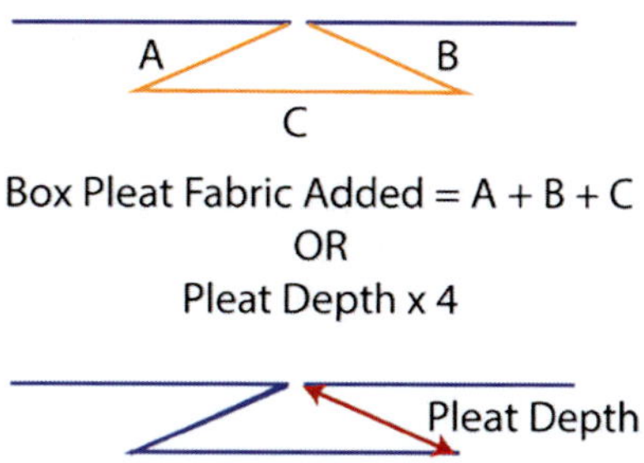

Figure 13-23. Box Pleat Calculations

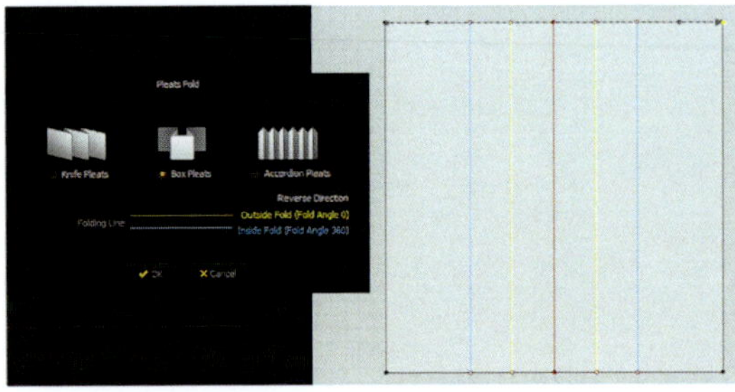

Figure 13-25. Box Pleat Layout in MD

You will need five internal lines per box pleat. The center red line is used for the knife pleat made to each side.

You will use the Pleats Fold tool to designate your folding lines. Drag the tool across the top of your pleated pattern. Check the Reverse Direction box, if the pleats are folding to the wrong side.

Select the Pleats Sewing tool and click at the start point on the edge of your base pattern and then click the end point. Now select the start and stop points for the pleated pattern.

In the image to the right, the back of the fabric is set yellow so it is easier to see and highlights the folding.

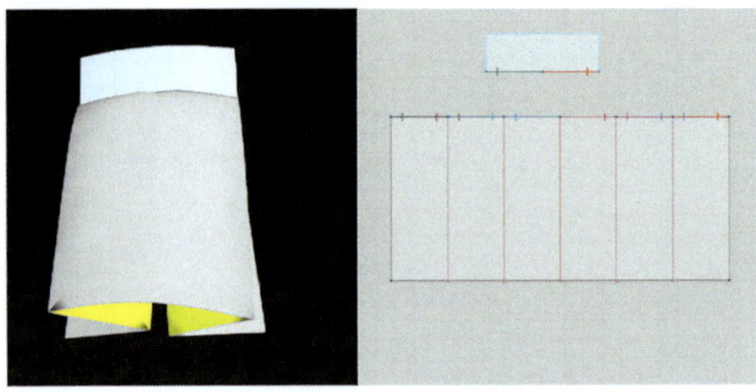

Figure 13-26. Box Pleat Sewn

The Pleats Sewing tool will fail to work properly, if you have the wrong number of internal pleat lines on the pattern and sometimes it just doesn't work correctly on box pleats at all.

If MD is trying to sew beyond the top of the pleated pattern and down the side, you'll know there is a problem. I've found that adding standard points at the top of each internal line on the pleated pattern will fix this behavior.

Another type of box pleat is an inverted box pleat. It is essentially the same pleat, but the "box" portion goes to the inside of the pattern instead of outside. Rather than the edges of each pleat facing out, they will face to the middle when viewed from the front. This is easy to do by swapping the yellow lines for blue lines by using the Reverse Direction checkbox.

Cartridge Pleats

If you are going to create military garments, you'll be interested in the cartridge pleat. This is the type of pleat that is used to create an ammunition belt. The belts are used to feed cartridges into a firearm and most likely this pleat was originally created to make these belts. You will find these pleats used in other home decorating and garment projects.

Figure 13-27. Cartridge Pleat in MD

This type of pleat is called a soft pleat, because there are no sharp folds. Also, you will not use the MD pleat tools to create these.

To create cartridge pleats, determine how many pleats you want. Then create Internal Lines evenly spaced on the base pattern. Create the pattern to be pleated and put the same number of lines on it, evenly spaced and a greater distance apart. Sew each line to the matching line on the base to pleat the fabric.

Kick Pleat

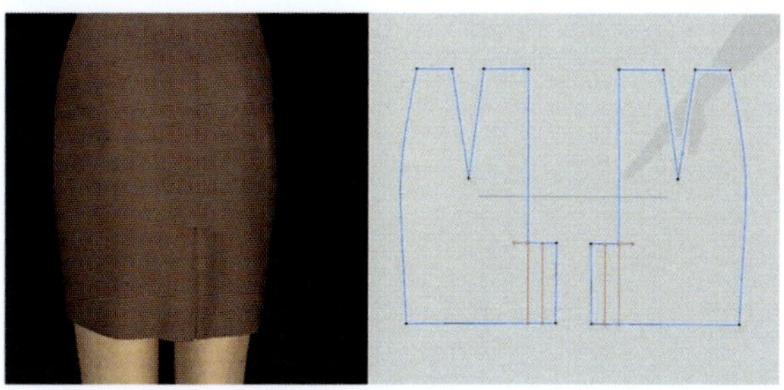

Figure 13-28. Skirt Kick Pleat

Kick pleats are added to the back of a skirt, coat or jacket to add more room. They are necessary when the garment is too narrow to walk in. The pleat will expand open as the person walks and close back up when they stand still.

You are likely to encounter these in more complex garments, so you should familiarize yourself with their construction.

The kick pleat in the skirt shown is actually a box pleat. Extensions were added to either side of the skirt back pattern. The Internal Lines on the center back line have a Fold Angle of 0 (outside fold, wrong sides together). The Internal Lines on the center of the extension have a Fold Angle of 360 (inside fold, right sides together). Then the edges of the extension are just sewn flat to each other.

A small horizontal internal line is added at the top, just inside the center back line. The extension from center back to the middle internal line is sewn to this line to close the box at the top.

Elastic

You can use elastic to make gathers. Elastic is not limited to the edge of a pattern, it can be used anywhere. Elastic in the real world looks like a fabric tape, it comes in all different widths and it has rubber or some other stretchy thread woven in it. No matter how far you pull elastic, it will come back to its original length.

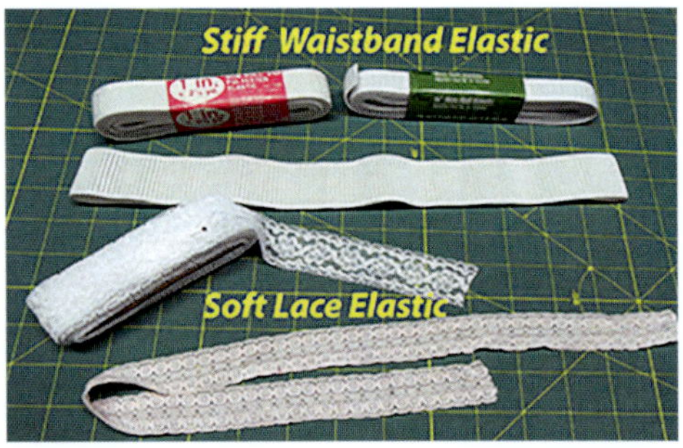

Figure 13-29. Real Elastic

When you use elastic, you can choose how full the gathers are by deciding on the ratio of elastic to fabric.

For example, in the real world, you may have a piece of fabric that is 10 cm wide and you want it to be 5 cm wide after it is gathered. So you cut a piece of elastic that is 5 cm long un-stretched. You stretch the elastic out to 10 cm, pin the fabric to it and sew. When you release it, the fabric is now 5 cm long. MD works the same way.

Select one or multiple lines, external or internal, and look over in the Property Editor. Under the Selected Line section you will find Elastic. Elastic is off by default, to use this property check the box. The segment line will turn green on the pattern in the 2D Window to remind you that elastic has been activated.

Figure 13-30. Elastic Settings in Property Editor

There are several settings for Elastic in the Property Editor. The first is Strength. How hard do you want the elastic to pull? You'll have to make that determination on a case-by-case basis.

The next two settings are actually the same thing, one is the percentage of the other. When you select the edge or lines that you will apply the elastic to, MD gives you the Total Length of your selection. That is shown up above in the Selected Line 2D Line Length property. Elastic by default is set to 80%. The Segment Length number is 80% of the Selected Line length. The Total Length will match the Segment Length, unless the selected line is part of a symmetric pattern. If it is, then Total Length is twice the Segment Length because it includes both patterns.

MD allows you to set your elastic by entering values in any of these boxes or using the ratio slider. It may seem a little strange that MD gives you all these options to set elastic. Most people who don't sew will just move the slider around until it looks good. However, people who do sew have certain percentages they use for different things. For instance, I know that one segment that is 1.5 times as wide as another is a decent gather and that's a 67% ratio. Two times as wide is a pretty full gather and that's 50%.

Anything with gathers is going to require a low Particle Distance to simulate properly, so don't get too crazy with really low percentages.

If you have a garment that needs to be pulled in at the waist, Elastic is a great choice. In the image, the waistband was much larger than the Avatar's waist measurement. Two Internal Lines were used with an Elastic setting to pull the waistband snug to the waist.

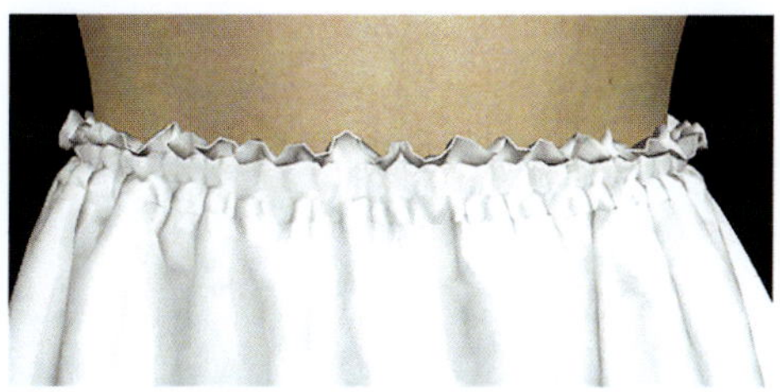

Figure 13-31. Elastic Waistband

Shirring

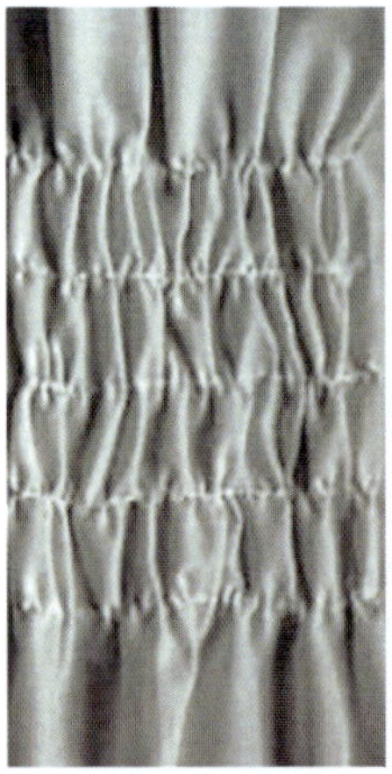

Figure 13-32. Shirring

Shirring is gathering fabric either by pulling threads or using elastic. What makes shirring unique is that it is always done in multiple parallel rows.

To create shirring in MD, you can use multiple Internal Lines. Apply the Elastic setting to the lines to pull the fabric up and create the effect.

Gathers

Gathering is drawing fabric together by pulling on a thread of stitching. In the real world, you gather one edge until it matches another in length and then sew them together. In MD, you can just sew a long edge to a shorter one and MD gathers the fabric for you.

Figure 13-33. Gathered Skirt

Chapter 13 Quiz

1) You can use the ___________ setting in the Property Editor on segments to gather up the pattern.(one word)

2) MD includes tools to create the following types of pleats: (choose all)

❍ A. Accordion Pleats

❍ B. Knife Pleats

❍ C. Cartridge Pleats

❍ D. Box Pleats

3) The bust dart found at the waist can be moved 360 degrees around the bust point.

❍ True ❍ False

4)_________ pleats are used to provide additional room for walking in skirts and coats.(one word)

Chapter 14 - Shirts & Tops

Shirt, blouse, top, and bodice all refer to a garment that covers the upper torso. (I generally refer to these as bodices throughout this book.) They can end at the waist or the hips. They can have collars or plain necklines. They can have sleeves any length or no sleeves at all. The bodice of a garment is the most important, as it brings focus to the most viewed part of the Avatar, the face.

Bodice Fit

It is completely at your discretion, as the designer, to determine the fit of the bodice. They can be closely fitted with darts at the waist and shoulder to conform to the body. You can also choose to eliminate all the fitting and create a very casual, loose style.

Bodice Closure

You need to determine how your bodice will close. Unless you're making a t-shirt out of knit that stretches or a pull-over with a sufficient hole for the head, you will need to slit the bodice to get it on the Avatar.

You can slit your bodice up the back and close it with a zipper, lacing or other fastener. The most common closure is the center front of the bodice using buttons. You'll learn more about buttons in *Chapter 20 - Other Details.*

Men's and women's shirts overlap in different ways. Men's shirts overlap with the left side over the right. Women's shirts overlap with the right side over the left.

Button Extensions

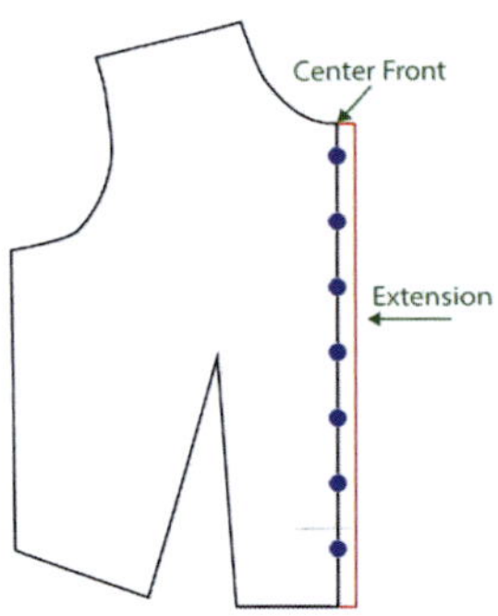

Figure 14-1. Center Front Bodice Extension in Red

For a bodice to fit correctly, the two edges of the center front must meet. When you add buttons, those buttons need to line up on the center front line. You don't have enough fabric to sew a button on one side and create buttonholes on the other. That's why an extension is necessary.

Extensions can be built in to the bodice by extending the width at center front on the front left and right patterns. The extensions will overlap, allowing you to sew the buttons down the center front. Button extensions are typically the width of the button.

The built-in extension is merely an overlap technique for the basic bodice. There is another type of extension that is a separate piece. The separate piece is sewn over the bodice front that is on top when overlapped. This is a decorative element found on many shirts. The separate piece can be referred to as a button extension or a placket, depending on the source.

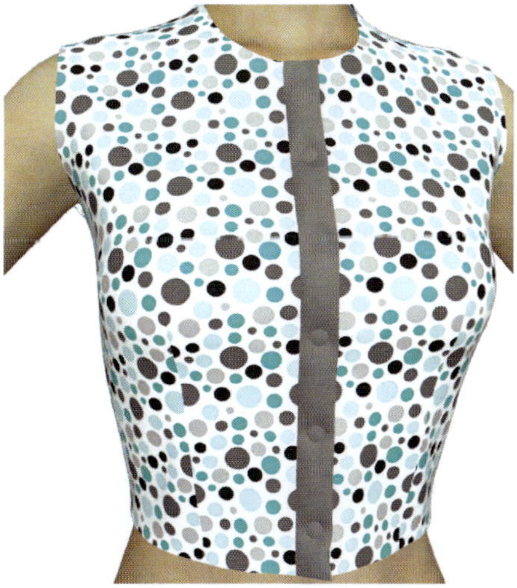

Figure 14-2. Separate Extension Added to Bodice

The separate extension can have buttons on it or not. In some cases, the extension facing has the buttonholes and the extension piece itself does not. This allows a shirt to be closed with buttons, but not have them visible. If you are doing this in MD, completely remove all the buttons. Sew the separate extension on the bodice front that is on top when overlapped.

In the real world, the extension is faced because you have to finish the raw edges of the fabric. This is only necessary in MD, if you intend to view the bodice close up or need photorealism.

Yokes

Yokes are separate pattern pieces that cover the shoulders and extend down the front and the back. To create a yoke, a portion of the front bodice at the shoulder is cut away. Then a portion of the back at the shoulder is cut away. These cut pieces are then combined into one piece.

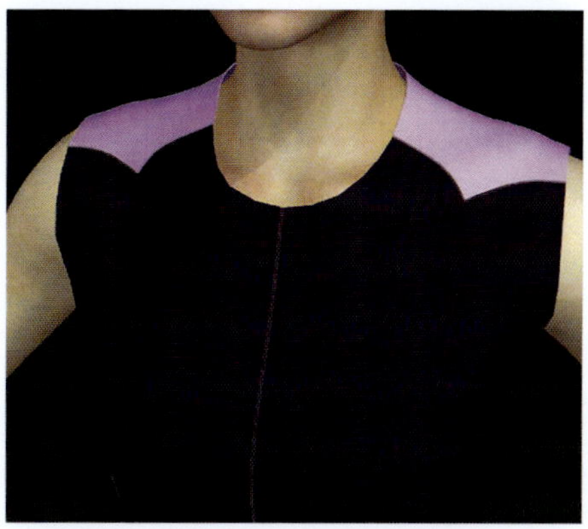

Figure 14-3. Yoke Over Shoulder in Light Purple

Figure 14-4. Yoke Rotated on Men's Plaid Shirt

Yokes help shape the back of the bodice without using darts. They are also a good design element and are often cut on the bias of a textured fabric or rotated 180°. This causes the texture of the fabric to be very different as it goes over the shoulder. This is done because aligning the fabric texture of the yoke to the front and back patterns is nearly impossible.

A basic yoke creates a straight line across the back and front. You can add additional design by adding points and curves to the yoke line. This is often found in western cut shirts.

Chapter 14 Quiz

1) Yokes are made using the (choose one):

❍ A. Front pattern.

❍ B. Back pattern.

❍ C. Both front and back patterns.

2) An extension of extra fabric is needed at the center front of a bodice if you are adding (choose all):

❍ A. Buttons

❍ B. Snaps

❍ C. Zipper

3) ___________ is another term used in the garment industry to refer to a shirt or top.(one word)

4) Men's shirts overlap right over left and women's shirts overlap left over right.

❍ True ❍ False

Chapter 15 - Pants

Pant Terms

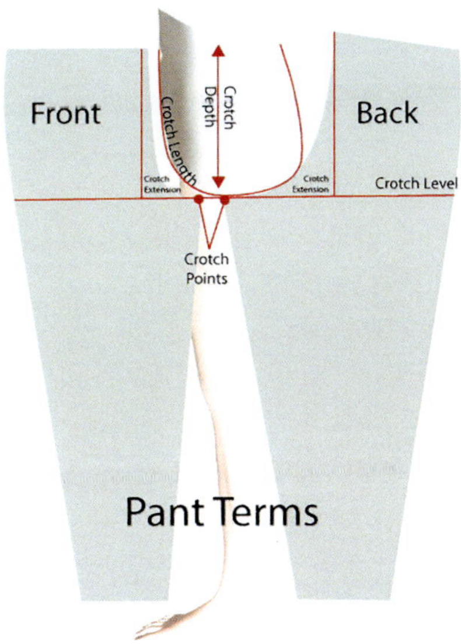

Figure 15-1. Pant Terms

Pants patterns are unique because the most important part of the pants is the part that is missing! Most of the shaping takes place in the waist to crotch area where there is no fabric.

Crotch - Bottom of torso where legs join the body.

Crotch Depth - The distance from the waist to the lowest point of the crotch. Tailor's refer to this as the "rise".

Crotch Length - The distance from the center front at the waist to the center back at the waist passing around the crotch.

Crotch Extension - The distance added to the front and back of a pattern to allow for the depth of the inner leg.

Crotch Point - End of the crotch extension lines.

Crotch Level - The crotch depth distance drawn across the pattern.

Outseam - Side seam joining the front and back.

Inseam - Seam between the legs joining the front and back.

Pant Length

There are specific terms for each length of pants.

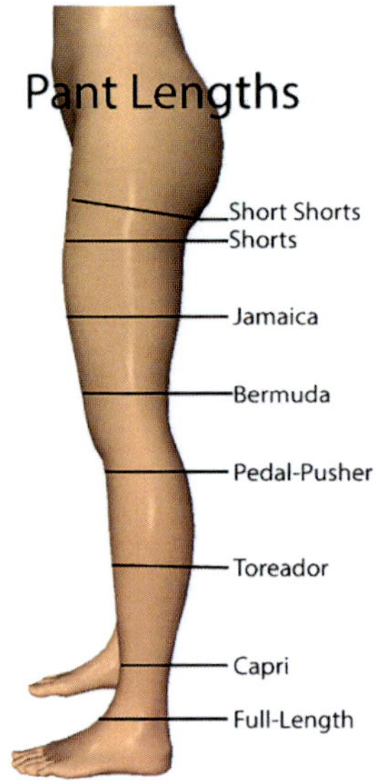

Figure 15-2. Pant Lengths

Full Length - These rest on the top of the shoe and extend nearly to the ground at the heel. The goal is to stay off the ground, so the pants hem doesn't get dirty or wear excessively.

Ankle Length- These stop at the ankle and expose the entire foot/shoe. Most designs hug the ankle using a cuff or elastic on a full width leg or using a close-fitting leg and knit fabric.

Capri Length - These stop 1″ (2.5cm) above the ankle and usual incorporate a close-fitting leg. They are also known as clam diggers, crop pants, three-quarter pants and mid-calf pants.

Toreador Length - These stop halfway between the knee and ankle. This name comes from the pants worn by bullfighters.

Pedal Pusher Length - These stop 2″ (5cm) down from the knee. The name most likely comes from pants designed to be worn when riding bicycles. This same location is used for knickers.

Knee Length - These stop at the knee, but are not a popular design option, as it isn't a very flattering position.

Bermuda Length - These stop halfway between a Jamaica and a knee length.

Jamaica Length - These stop halfway between the crotch and the knee.

Shorts Length - These stop 2″ (5cm) below the crotch level.

Short Shorts Length - These are drawn with a diagonal hem and are located 1.5″ (3.8cm) below the crotch of the inseam and 1″ (2.5cm) to 1.5″ (3.8 cm) above the crotch at the outseam (side seam).

Crotch Depth

Varying the depth of the crotch can change the design drastically. Knit leggings and skinny jeans have a shallow crotch depth and hug the body tightly. Overalls, pantsuits, culottes and hip-hop designs increase the crotch depth. In the case of overalls and pantsuits, this is done to provide additional room when the arms are lifted. In other cases, it is done to make the pants appear baggy for design purposes only.

Fit & Flare

How the pants hug the butt and stomach has a lot to do with design. Loose fit, like culottes, hang away from the butt in the back and the stomach in front. Trousers hang down straight from the most prominent point on the butt and stomach. Slacks cup under the butt slightly and follow the line of the stomach. Jeans follow the contour of the butt and stomach. Leggings are completely form-fitting following every curve.

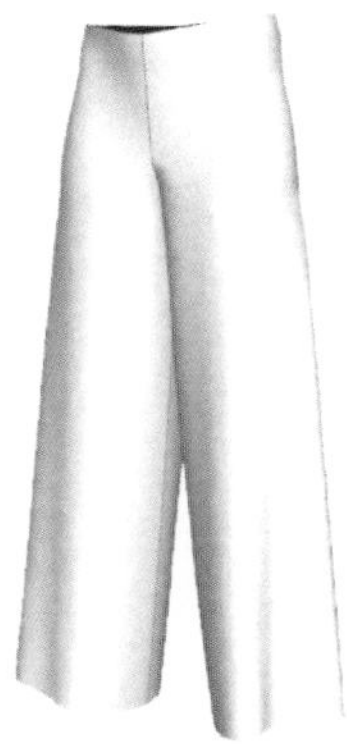

Leg widths are completely subjective. They can vary from form fitting to extremely loose. To flare pant legs in MD, select the lowest point of the leg, down at the hem, and spread it out from center. Spread an equal amount to each side of center on the leg.

Make sure to make the same changes to front and back to guarantee that the seams stay equal in length.

Figure 15-3. Flared Pants

If you want to make the pant legs baggy, but not flared, move the point at the hem outseam away from the body. Leave the inseam hem point in its original position.

Bell-bottoms are a slim fit on the top following by a flare at the bottom. If you want to create pant legs that flare only at the bottom, add a point where the transition will occur using the exact same distance on the inseam and outseam

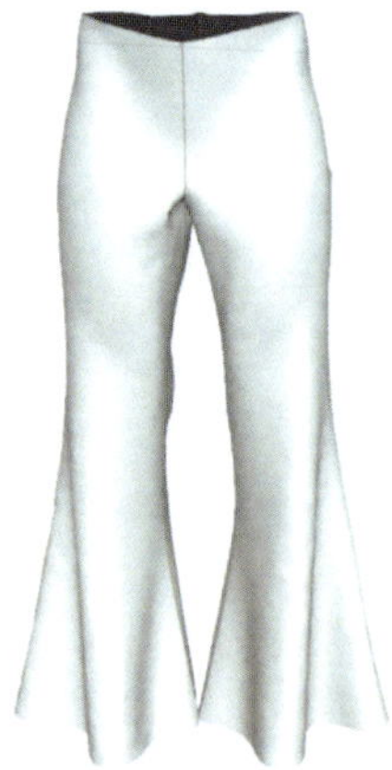

Figure 15-4. Bell Bottom Pants

of the front and back. The transition point can be above, at or below the knee. Now spread the bottom points at the hem further apart. Bell-bottoms in MD look the best when you convert the transition point to a curve point.

Waistline

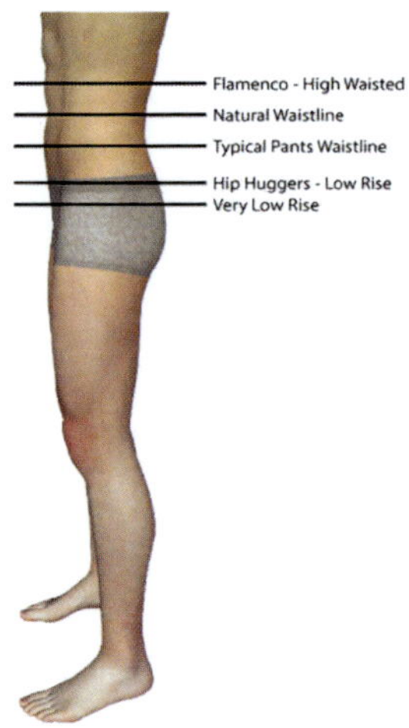

Figure 15-5. Pant Waistline

Locating the natural waistline for your Avatar, particularly males, can be a bit of a challenge. The general rule is that this line should be about where the elbow is when the Avatar's arm is relaxed at the side. You can choose a point anywhere from there to the belly button. This is the location for your waist measurement used to draft the bodice / top patterns.

This location is not ideal for pants. It can place the waistline of the pants much higher than you typically want. Refer to the image to see the different waistline height levels for pants.

As you can see, the natural waistline is where most of us would consider "old man" pants to rest. The Typical Pants Waistline is where most of us would choose, if not lower.

Darts & Yokes

Pants usually have darts at the back waist because there is a big transition from the waist measurement to the hips.

Figure 15-6. Real Pleated Front Pants

Darts in the front of the pants can be used for shaping, but are more often used as a design element. Many times the dart is closed not by sewing it shut, but by pleating the excess. Slacks and trousers often have one or two pleats in the front.

The darts in the back can be replaced with a yoke, like a pair of jeans. The back pants pattern is cut, usually on a slight diagonal, at the top. If there is a waist dart, the dart is rotated closed. Pants yokes are generally left in two pieces, since the center back seam lines up with the center back of the pants.

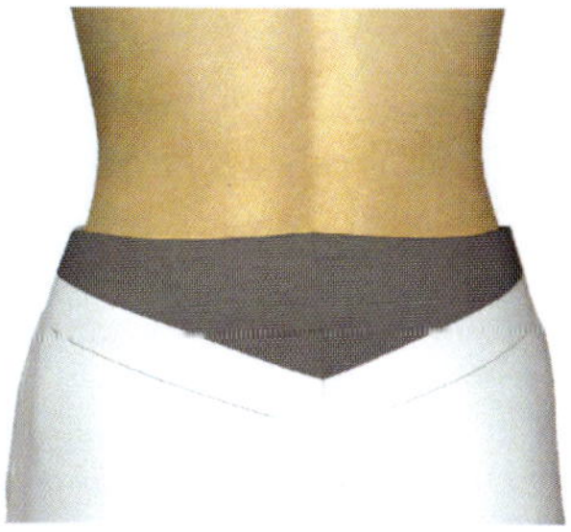

Figure 15-7. Jeans Back Yoke in Dark Gray

Closures

The method you choose to close your pants depends on the design. In order to put on a pair of pants, the waist has to pull over the thighs and hips. You can use a split method, which means the pants separate at the waist or a closed method with no split.

If you are making pants made of knit, you don't have to add a split closure. Also, if your pants are as wide or wider at the waist than your Avatar's hips, you don't need a split. You can use an elastic waist or drawstring for pants patterns wider than your Avatar's waist.

For all other pants designs, you will need to split the waist open. You can put this split at the side seam, center back or center front. How you close the split depends on your design. You can insert a zipper, use buttons or any other type of fastener.

The most common type of split closure for pants is using a zipper at center front with a fly. The construction of a pants fly is rather complicated because you have to create an overlap very similar to a button extension on a shirt.

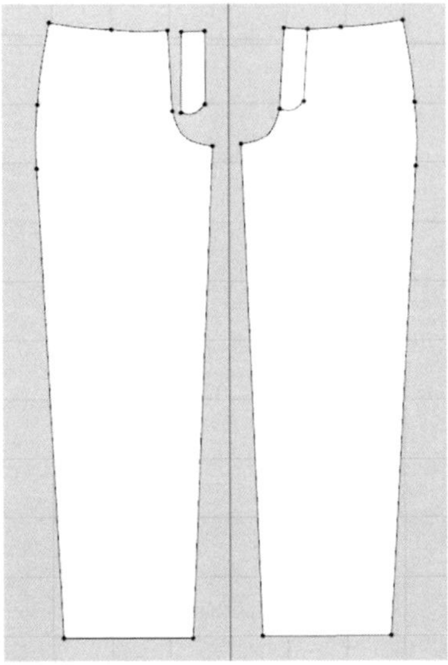

Figure 15-8. Pants Fly

This overlap, called a fly extension, can be part of the pants pattern or a separate piece. In the real world, there are extensions on both sides, right and left. The left front extension is used as a lining and the right front extension is cut on the fold and then folded when sewn in place to finish raw edges. For pants in MD, there is no need to do this. You can apply the right front extension to create the overlap needed. You don't need to worry about raw edges.

The left side of the pants will overlap the right when creating flys and waistbands for men and women.

Waistbands

All pants have a waistband. Sometimes these are sewn on as a separate piece and other times they are just an extension included in the pants pattern. Waistbands that are separate are typically one long piece with one seam.

If you are creating pants with an elastic or drawstring waistband, the ends should meet at center back. Zippered closures usually have a waistband that overlaps with a button or snap. This includes pants with a fly placed at center front.

Even if your zipper or other closure is not visible, there should be a waistband overlap where the slit is. You'll need to secure the overlap to the other side using a button or a small seam to keep it closed.

Belt Loops

Most pants facilitate a belt, which means you'll need some belt loops. The number of belt loops varies with the design. Five belt loops is quite common, with loops placed at the center of the waist on the front left, front right, back left and back right. The final loop is placed at center back, often off-center of the center back seam. The placement of loops also depends on the type of pockets you've chosen and where they lay on the pattern. You may need to adjust your loop placement.

Real world belt loops are pieces of fabric cut twice the needed width. The long edges are folded to meet at the center and pressed. The strip is top-stitched with two rows of stitching. The top and bottom edges are folded over. The loops are placed on the pants and sewn at the top and bottom. The top is on the waistband and the bottom is on the pants themselves.

Figure 15-9. Real Jean Belt Loop

Chapter 15 Quiz

1) The seam located between the legs joining the front and the back of pants is referred to as the _______________.(one word)

2) Pants can have darts and yokes, just like a bodice.

❍ True ❍ False

3) To shorten pants, select the bottom hem segment, hold Shift and drag upwards.

❍ True ❍ False

4) Pants that flare out starting at the knee are called (choose one):

❍ A. Culottes

❍ B. Hip-Hop

❍ C. Bell Bottoms

❍ D. Knickers

Chapter 16 - Skirts

Skirts are very similar to pants and they share many of the same properties. Darts, closures and waistbands are virtually the same. However, because skirts don't have the separation of legs, there are many more options available for fullness and style.

Skirt Lengths / Hemlines

The bottom edge of a skirt is referred to as the hemline. They can range from incredibly short to extremely long. Sweeping hemlines that drag behind while walking are common on wedding dresses, formal gowns and court dresses. These are often referred to as trains, because they trail behind the wearer when walking.

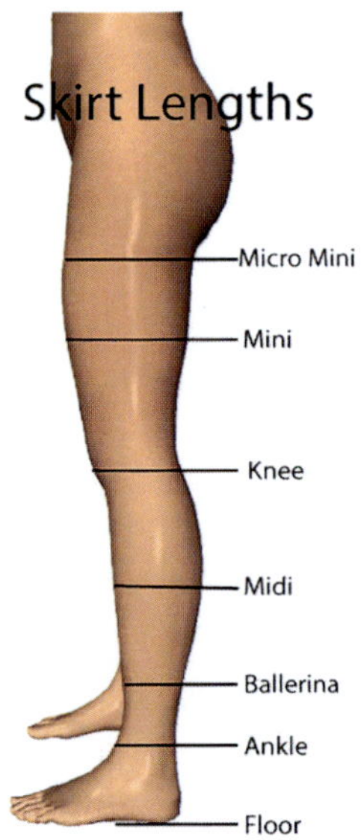

Figure 16-1. Skirt Lengths

Floor Length - Skirts can go all the way to the floor and beyond.

Ankle Length - This is also referred to as the Maxi length. These end at the ankle and rest on the foot or shoe.

Ballerina Length - This is approximately half way between the midi and ankle lengths.

Midi Length - This is mid way between the knee and the ankle.

Knee Length - This will hit just above or below the knee.

Mini Length - This is half way between the crotch and knee.

Micro Mini Length - This is extremely short and usually includes an undergarment that is meant to be exposed.

If you create a skirt that is longer than you want, it is very easy to crop it at any length you need. Generally, you will need to add a slight curve between the side points at the hem and not cut a straight line across or it will hang strangely.

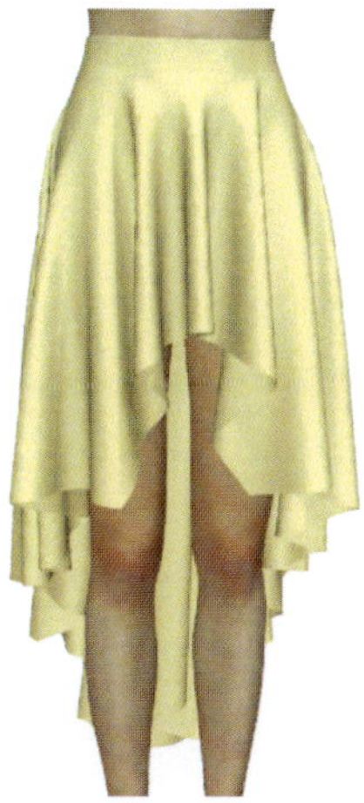

Hemlines don't have to be symmetrical. You can have one side higher than the other or the front and back at different levels. They also don't have to be straight across. Handkerchief hemlines have points all around the hemline and scalloped hemlines are common.

Figure 16-2. Asymmetric Handkerchief Skirt Hem

Yokes

Skirts can have yokes just like pants and bodices. The yoke can be in the front, the back or both. The yoke is typically very fitted to the Avatar and then a full, gathered or pleated skirt is attached. You can create different skirt designs by cutting off the top of one skirt draft and the bottom of another. Then just combine them to make a completely different look.

Gores

When a skirt has four or more separate panels, these are referred to as gores. You can have from four to over twelve gores in a skirt. It is very easy to add width to each gore to make the skirt much fuller. You can also add shape to the hemline of each gore, which will repeat around the edge of the skirt.

Figure 16-3. Fishtail 12-Gore Skirt

Pleated Skirts

Figure 16-4. Schoolgirl Pleated Skirt

Pleats are very common in skirts and the "schoolgirl skirt" is perfect example. Learn more about making Pleats in *Chapter 13 - Shaping Cloth*.

Tiers

Skirt tiers are rows of fabric attached to each other or to a base underskirt. The first tier is typically 1 to 1.5 times as wide as the waist and each subsequent tier is 1.5 to 2 times as wide as the previous tier. Tiers are easy to make in MD, as they are just rectangles. All the tiers can be the same height, or you can vary them. How many tiers a skirt has is completely at your discretion.

Figure 16-5. 3-Tier Skirt

Peplum

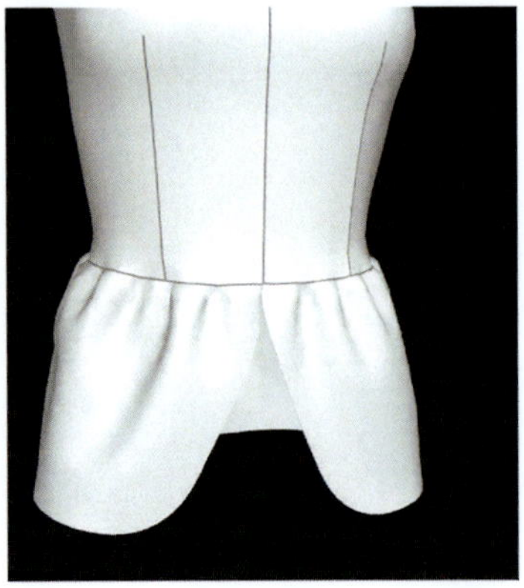

Figure 16-6. Peplum

A peplum is a single tier or very short skirt that is attached at the waist to a bodice. It's actually an extension of the bodice and not technically a skirt at all. You'll find a lot of these in historical clothing.

Godet

Godets are triangular wedges of material inserted in a seam or slit of a skirt or dress to make it flare or just for decoration. The godet does not have to be made of the same fabric as the skirt, so they can be very prominent.

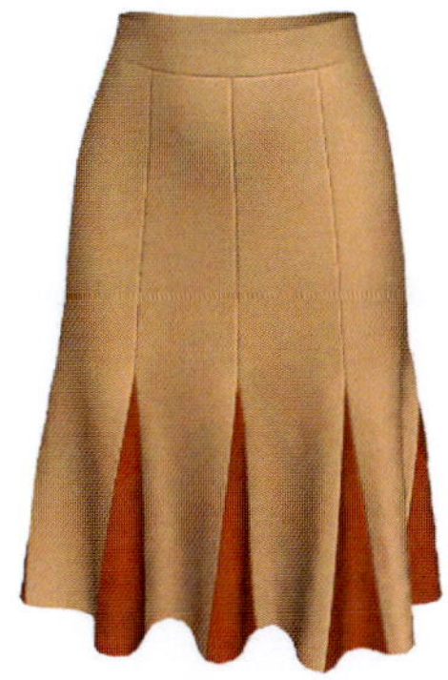

Figure 16-7. Godets Inserted in 8-Gore Skirt

Chapter 16 Quiz

1) Skirt hems should always be the same distance from the floor all the way around.

❍ True ❍ False

2) ______________ are simply the skirt patterns split up into vertical panels. (one word)

3) Tiered or peasant skirts are made of (choose one):

❍ A. Multiple Square Patterns

❍ B. Multiple Rectangle Patterns

❍ C. Multiple Circle Patterns

4) The sweeping hemlines of formal gowns and wedding dresses are called _________________.(one word)

Chapter 17 - Around the Neck

There are essentially two ways to finish off the top of a garment at the neck, you can create a neckline or a collar. You'll have to decide which method is best for the garment you are designing.

Necklines

Necklines are finished edges at the top of the garment neck opening. They are a continuation of the garment itself and don't involve a separate pattern piece.

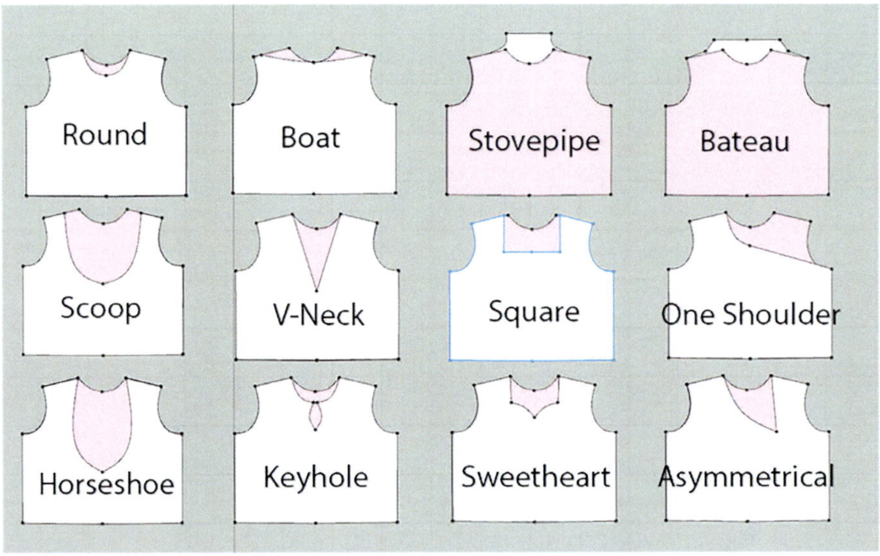

Figure 17-1. Necklines (pink is standard bodice sloper, white is neckline adjustment)

Necklines are easy to make in MD, because all you need to do is modify the neck shape of the pattern. The image above includes 12 common necklines. The pink patterns are an original sloper draft, so you can see the changes made to the white neckline pattern.

Asymmetrical patterns are those that differ from side to side. The One Shoulder neckline is asymmetrical. The Stovepipe and Bateau necklines are built-up necklines, which mean they are taller than the original. In those cases, the sloper was put on the front so you could see the difference.

Collars

Collars are very different from necklines. Collars are typically one or more separate pieces of fabric that are sewn to the neck of a garment.

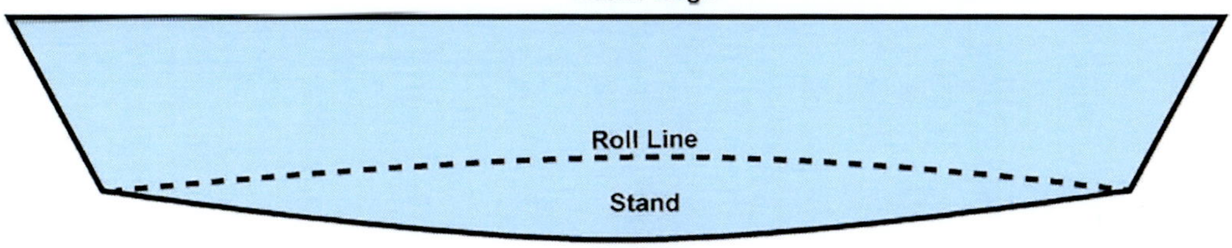

Figure 17-2. Parts of a Collar

A collar may consist of a collar and a stand or just a collar with the stand built in. Either way, the collar consists of the following elements:

Collar Edge (Style Line) - The outer edge of the collar where trim may be added.

Neckline Edge - The inner edge of the collar that is sewn to the garment neckline.

Stand - The portion of the collar that provides the height of the roll. Might be a separate piece.

Roll Line or Folding Line - The point on the collar where it rolls over. Essentially the top edge of a built-in stand.

Collar Shapes

Illustrated on the next page are the basic collar shapes. The collar on your left is a peter pan collar. It is a flat collar that lies on the garment. The collar in the middle is a shirt collar with a built-in stand. You can see that the collar is raised up off the garment shoulders. The last type is a standing collar. Basically this collar is a stand without a collar! The entire thing is vertical to the garment.

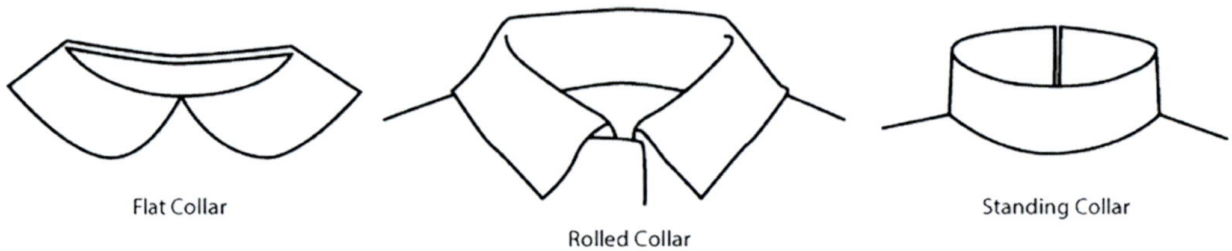

Figure 17-3. Collar Shapes

Convertible Collars

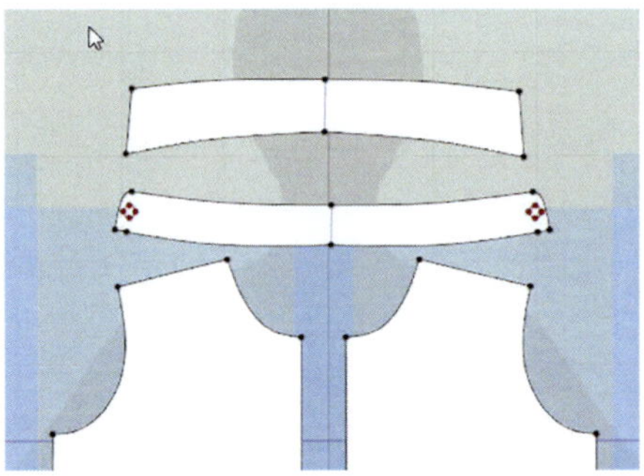

Figure 17-4. Convertible Two-Piece Collar

A convertible collar doesn't follow the curve of the garment neckline. It is nearly straight across, with a slight curve to it.

Convertible collars can be made with a built-in collar stand or two-piece with a separate stand, like the image to the left.

Men's dress shirts most often have two-piece collars, the uppermost part that you see is called the fall (shown in red) and the vertical piece surrounding the neck is called the stand (shown in green).

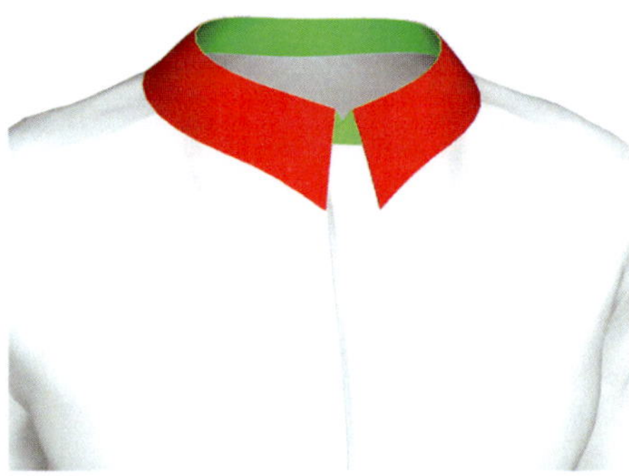

Figure 17-5. Convertible Two-Piece Collar Closed

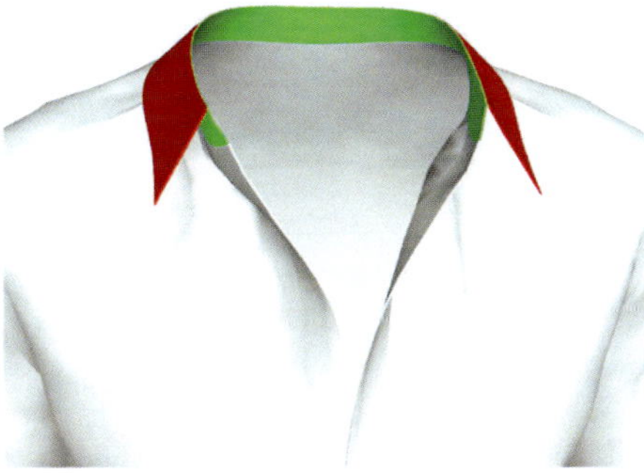

Figure 17-6. Convertible Two-Piece Collar Open

You can close the collar with a button, but when you open it, it acts like a spring and spreads outward. This is because the collar does not follow the curve of the neckline.

Non-Convertible Collars

The other type of collar is a non-convertible collar. The collar follows the curve of the garment neckline. The garment neckline and the neckline edge of the collar are the same length. There is no separate stand. However, the feature of a stand, the ability to raise the collar up off the garment, still exists in a non-convertible collar.

To make a non-convertible collar, you use the front and back necklines of the garment as shown. You line up the necklines by rotating one of the patterns and putting them shoulder to shoulder. Then you trace out the combined necklines and add width in the direction of the shoulder lines.

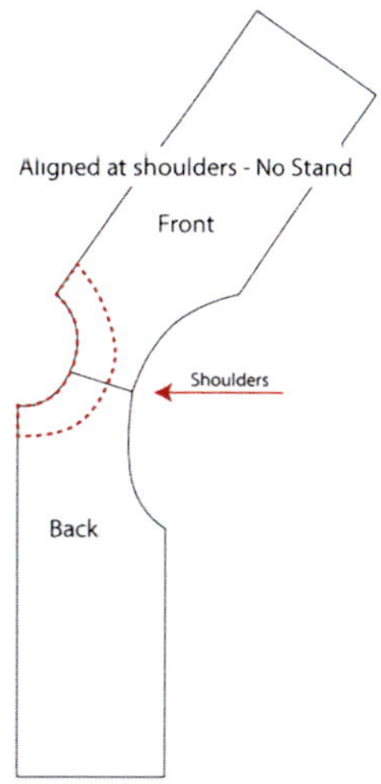

Figure 17-7. Collar (red dashed line) with Shoulders Aligned

A collar created with the shoulder lines lined up will lay down completely (see image to the left). There is no built-in stand.

Figure 17-8. Non-Convertible Collar with Shoulders Aligned

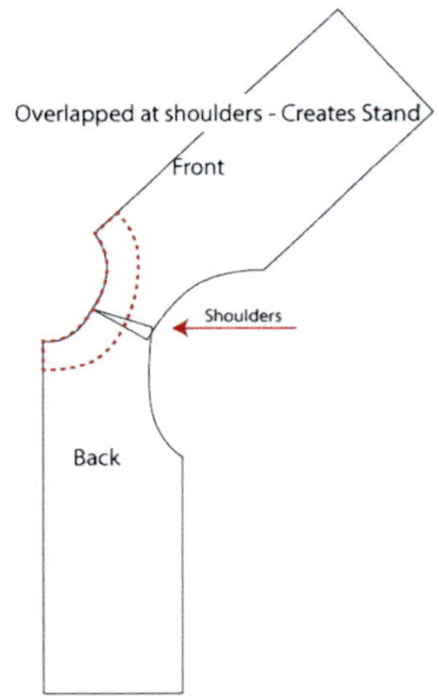

Figure 17-9. Collar (red dashed line) with Shoulders Overlapped

When you overlap the two shoulders, the collar will begin to rise off the garment (see image below).

This is the process of rolling the collar. The more the overlap, the larger the roll and the higher it will crawl up the neck.

The neckline edge of the collar still matches the neckline length, regardless of how much you overlap the shoulder.

What you're doing is straightening the neckline edge curve of the collar. When it meets the more curvy neckline, it pushes the collar up and then it rolls over the little stand that has been created. That's how a built-in stand works.

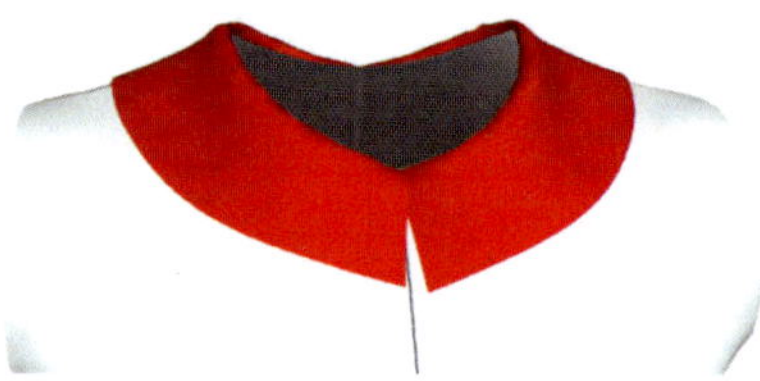

Figure 17-10. Non-Convertible Collar with Shoulders Overlapped

There is a patternmaking technique called 4-to-1 that applies to these types of collars. If you overlap the shoulders by 4″ (10.16cm), the stand of the collar will be 1″ (2.54cm). Since the collar rolls at the top of the stand, this would leave you with a bit less than 3″ (7.62cm) of visible collar. You can see how the collar lifts in the image.

Jabot

You don't see a lot of jabots these days, but they are very important for historical costumes. They are typically an ornamental frill or ruffle on the

Figure 17-11. Jabot in Sheer Fabric

front of a shirt or blouse. These are usually made of lace or other fine trim. They can be added to a neckline, or you can incorporate them with a collar.

Dicky, Vestee & Gilet

You probably aren't very familiar with the terms dicky, vestee and gilet. I thought they were worth a mention, because you may be making garments that could use them. Also, they are a fantastic idea when creating 3D garments. There's no reason to create a bunch of layers, when these types of things were actually worn.

A Dicky is set into a square or rounded neckline and is meant to simulate another shirt. It is essentially a detachable shirt front, collar or bib. Rather than wearing a complete shirt underneath, dickies were added in the neck openings. Rumor has it that the Beatles wore dickies, that resembled t-shirts, under their jackets to keep them from overheating. In the 1940s women used them with suits, so it appeared there was a blouse underneath, but it was all for show.

A Vestee is essentially the same thing as a dicky, but it appears to be a vest rather than a shirt or blouse. Only the front portion was sewn in, so it looked like there was a vest, but it had no back. These were worn under jackets.

A Gilet is a sleeveless blouse that is worn with suits and sweaters. The front and collar may be quite elaborate, but there are no sleeves and it may be short-waisted.

Chapter 17 Quiz

1) Necklines are a separate pattern piece.

❍ True ❍ False

2) Which type of collar has the same shape as the neckline (choose one)?

❍ A. Convertible Collar

❍ B. Non-Convertible Collar

3) Every shirt or top must have either a neckline or a collar.

❍ True ❍ False

4) To make a collar rise up off the shoulders (choose one):

❍ A. Increase the height of the stand.

❍ B. Make the collar wider.

❍ C. Decrease the length of the stand.

❍ D. Make the collar longer.

Chapter 18 - Around the Arm

Sleeves

Sleeves can change the look of a garment more than almost any other part. You can make a sleeve virtually any length from shoulder to wrist and beyond. You can also leave it off completely. The options for sleeves are astounding.

Sleeve Terms

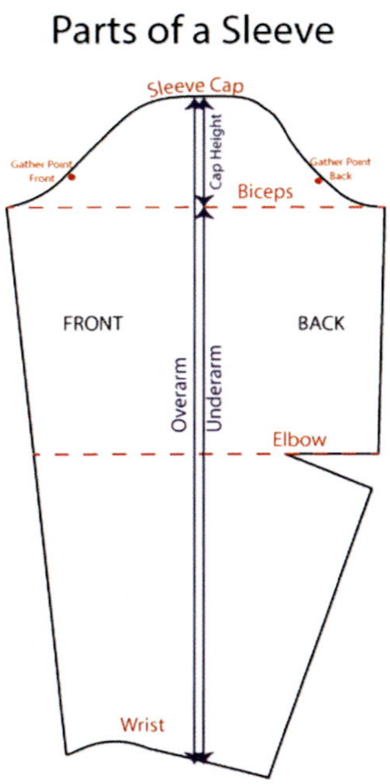

Figure 18-1. Parts of a Sleeve

Sleeve patterns look really strange. The big curve is called the sleeve cap. Sleeves have a distinct top (overarm) and a bottom (underarm). The overarm length is from the shoulder tip point to the wrist. The underarm is from the armpit to the wrist. There's a substantial difference between these two numbers.

You can create a tube of fabric that covers most of the arm and meets the bodice in the armpit, but there's no way to reach up over the arm on the shoulder with a tube. That's where the sleeve cap comes in. It is necessary to make the sleeve fit the body and provides room for arm rotation.

Sleeve patterns are difficult to draft. There are different methods to do so, but none of them is ever a perfect fit to the armhole of the bodice. The sleeve cap edge length on a finished draft may not match the length of the front and back armhole. You never want a sleeve to be smaller than the armhole.

To correct this problem, select the entire sleeve cap edge and note the measurement over in the Property Editor. Now select the entire front and back armhole and note that measurement. If the armholes are larger, you need to modify the sleeve. You can make the sleeve cap taller and/or pull the end points out. If you do move the end points, make sure you move each side out the exact same amount. Remember we have to sew the two sides of sleeve together and they must be the same length.

Cap Ease

In real-world sewing, the difference between the sleeve cap length and the armhole is called sleeve cap ease. Patternmakers often add between 1″ to 2″ (2.5 cm to 5 cm) to the length of the sleeve cap, so it is larger than the armhole. Then this added ease is spread across the top of the cap between the ease points when it is sewn in place. The real pattern image below shows the ease points circled in red and the notches outlined in blue. (Note: This is a multi-size pattern and that is why you can see multiples of things).

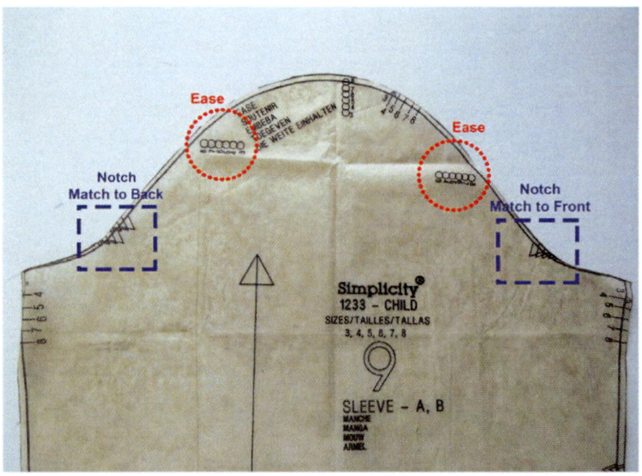

Figure 18-2. Real Sleeve Pattern Cap Ease Marks Circled in Red, Notches Outlined in Blue

This topic is a hot one in the sewing community, because not everyone agrees that it is necessary. It can be a lot of work to ease in a sleeve cap while sewing because you can not have any gathers or puckering. There is no reason to worry about adding sleeve cap ease in MD.

Fullness

Although you don't need to worry about ease, you will probably want to make sleeves that look puffy, which means they are gathered. Your first inclination is to attach these sleeves to the bodice using the M:N Segment Sewing technique. This will not work with puffy sleeves.

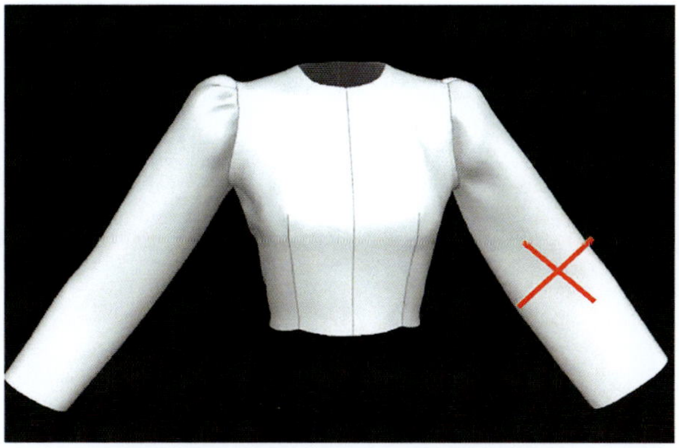

Figure 18-3. Puffy Sleeve Sewn Correctly on Left and Incorrectly on Right

If you distribute all the excess fabric throughout the entire armhole, it will look like the sleeve on the right of this image. It looks awful and poorly fit.

Sleeves must have flat seams without gathering under the arm. All the gathering must take place up high, in the sleeve cap area. You can see the sleeve on the left was sewn correctly. I should mention that these are the exact same sleeve patterns.

If you look at the real sleeve pattern shown previously, you can see notches. There are double notches on the left down low (attaches to back armhole) and single notches on the right (attaches to front armhole). In the real world, excess fabric is gathered above these notches, leaving the area below sewn flat and not gathered.

To do this in MD, you need to place points on the front armhole, back armhole and sleeve.

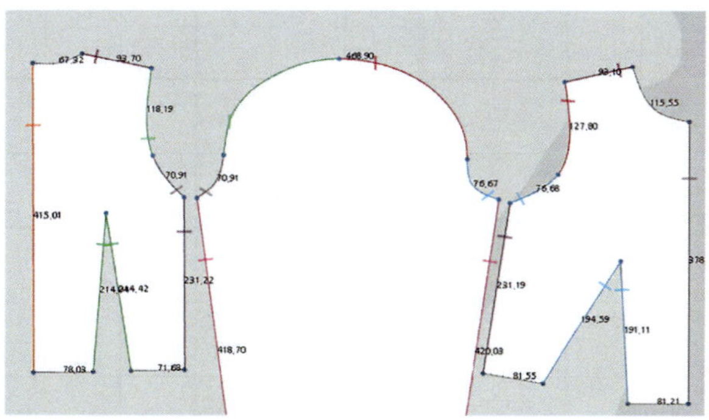

Figure 18-4. Sleeve to Bodice Seams

To determine how far from the armpit to place these points, multiply your front armhole length by 0.375. This will be your point distance. Using the Add Point tool, right click the front armhole curve up slightly from the armpit. Enter the point distance you calculated and click OK. Verify that the point was created that distance from the armpit. Now repeat that same procedure for the back armhole.

Using the same procedure, create matching points on the sleeve. Make sure to put the front distance on the front of the sleeve and the back distance on the back of the sleeve.

This distance is not set in stone. Feel free to vary this amount, depending on the look you want for your sleeve. Just remember to keep the area under the arm smooth and free of gathers.

Sleeve Fit

Figure 18-5. Unfitted Sleeves

Fitted Sleeve

When you make a shirt, you can decide how fitted it is, whether it hangs loosely or hugs the body contour. You have this same option with sleeves.

A fitted sleeve will have a dart at the elbow and a curved wrist line. It will be very close to the arm and mimic the shape of a relaxed arm, which is slightly bent.

Two-Piece Sleeve

The next type is a two-piece sleeve. These are somewhat rare today, but they were very popular at one time. The two-piece sleeve is fitted, but it doesn't have an elbow dart. It is shaped at a slight angle to match the arm and is used primarily for coats and suit jackets.

Straight Sleeve

A slightly fitted straight sleeve will taper down a bit as it reaches the wrist. A full straight sleeve has no tapering and is the same width all the way down to the wrist. You can curve the line at the wrist for better fit or leave it straight across.

Unfitted Sleeve

There are a lot of unfitted sleeves to choose from. They can be very full with pleats or gathers. They can be loose at the wrist or pulled in to a cuff.

Cuffs

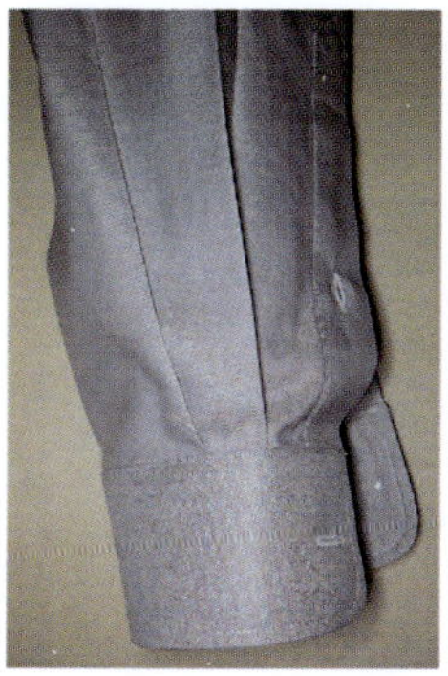

Figure 18-6. Real Shirt Cuff

A cuff finishes off your sleeve design. There are a variety of widths and styles for sleeve cuffs. Cuffs are drafted using the circumference measurement on the arm where the sleeve will end. For a standard long sleeve, this will be the wrist. Regardless of how wide your sleeve is at the bottom, the cuff serves to bring it all together and transition to the wrist measurement.

If your sleeve end is a lot wider than the cuff, you may choose to gather the excess all around the cuff or create pleats. Pleats are very common on men's shirt sleeves.

Simple cuffs are just bands that overlap themselves with a button closure.

Cuffs usually have one or two buttons, but you can add more. Some shirt cuffs are called adjustable because they have two rows of buttons. This allows the cuff to accommodate different sized wrists.

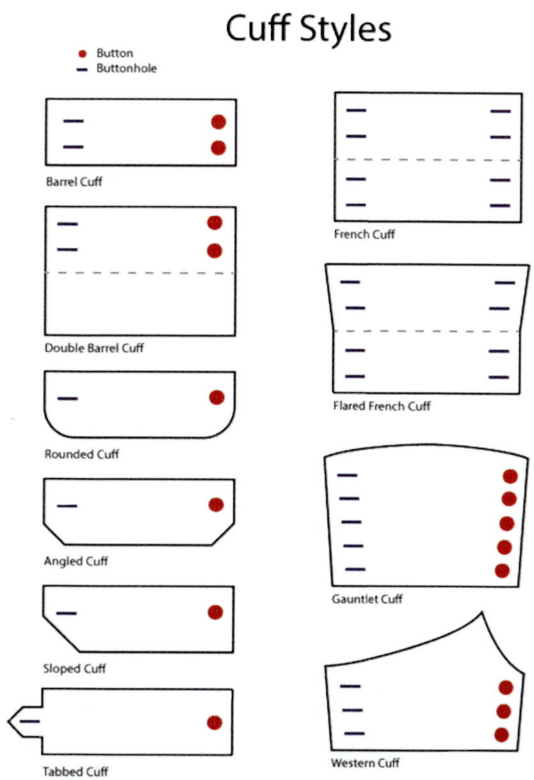

Figure 18-7. Cuff Styles

The style of a simple shirt cuff is changed by how the lower edge of the cuff is shaped.

Double cuffs are cuffs that are created twice as tall and folded back on themselves. A classic French cuff is an example of this style. French cuffs are unique because you don't overlap them. The ends are placed wrong sides together and closed with cuff links.

You can create cuffs that are in excess of 4" (10 cm) tall. These are referred to as the Gauntlet style. To make these cuffs, you must measure the circumference of the arm where the cuff will attach to the sleeve. Then you draft the cuff starting with the wrist measurement and tapering out to the arm measurement. The cuff will contour to the shape of the arm as it rises.

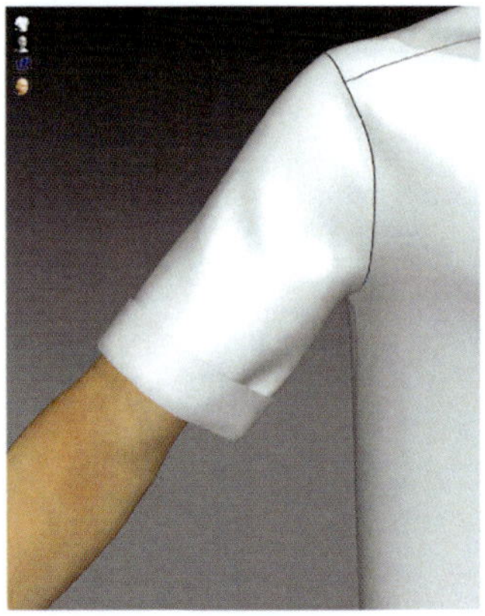

Figure 18-8. Rolled Cuff on Sleeve

The last type of cuff is called a Rolled Cuff. You incorporate the distance of the cuff in the sleeve itself. Then you simply roll the sleeve back on a fold line to make a cuff. These are commonly used to finish a short sleeve as shown.

Other Sleeve Finishes

There are other ways to finish the edge of a sleeve. You can create a casing with a drawstring and gather it up. Many real-world sleeves are just hemmed. In MD, you don't have to put anything on the end of the sleeve, if you want it to appear hemmed. You can also just add a simple band without a button to gather up the edge.

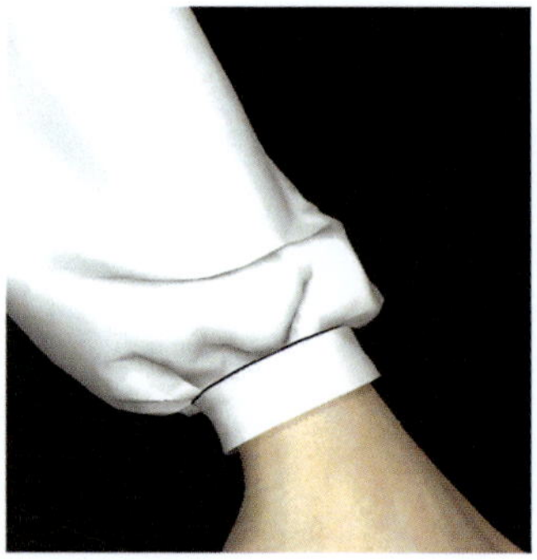

Figure 18-9. Simple Sleeve Band

Sleeveless

The easiest sleeve is no sleeve at all! Create a sleeveless design by simply omitting the sleeves.

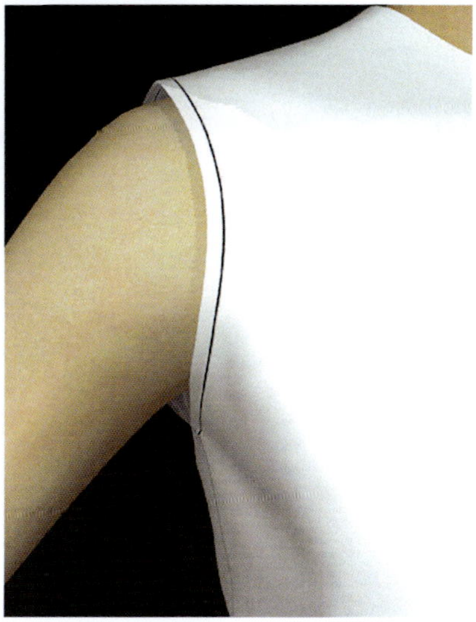

Figure 18-10. Sleeveless

Most sleeveless garments are bound at the armholes. To do this in MD, add together the front and back armhole lengths. Then draft a rectangle that is the length of the armhole and whatever width you like. Make sure that the edges of the trim meet in the armpit (not the top of the arm).

Chapter 18 Quiz

1) The difference between the overarm length and the underarm length is the (choose one):

❍ A. Bicep Width

❍ B. Cap Height

❍ C. Elbow to Wrist Measurement

❍ D. Cap Ease

2) Cuffs that are more than 4″ long are called __________ style.(one word)

3) A sleeve with sleeve cap measurements that are longer than the front and back armhole measurements is (choose one):

- ❍ A. An unfitted short sleeve.
- ❍ B. A sleeve that doesn't fit the bodice pattern.
- ❍ C. A fitted, long sleeve.
- ❍ D. A sleeve that will be gathered into the armhole.

4) A halter top has which type of sleeve (choose one):

- ❍ A. Bell Sleeve
- ❍ B. Puff Sleeve
- ❍ C. Sleeveless
- ❍ D. Short Sleeve

Chapter 19 - Finishing Edges

In the real world, one of the most important techniques in sewing lies in the finishing of edges. Some finishes are purely functional, while others add to the appearance of the garment. If you want your garments to resemble real clothing, you may need to add some edging details.

Fabric in MD technically has no thickness and it doesn't fray. We can leave our pant and skirt edges as they are. That doesn't work in the real world. Raw edges of a garment that are singular, meaning they aren't sewn to another piece, must be hemmed, bound, lined or faced.

Hems

Figure 19-1. Hemmed Edge

Hemming is the process of turning the fabric under and sewing it in place. There are different types of hems and some are very decorative.

Today, most hems are sewn from the top and the stitching is visible. In high-end garments, hems are sewn with a blind stitch, so you can't see it at all. Hems add visual weight to the edge of a garment piece. You may want to use them in MD for that reason alone.

Bindings & Bandings

Rather than turning the fabric back on itself, you may want to use binding or banding. Binding is a separate piece that is twice the finished width needed. The edges of the binding are finished themselves and then the piece is folded in half and put over the edge of the fabric and sewn catching the top and bottom of the binding with the fabric sandwiched between.

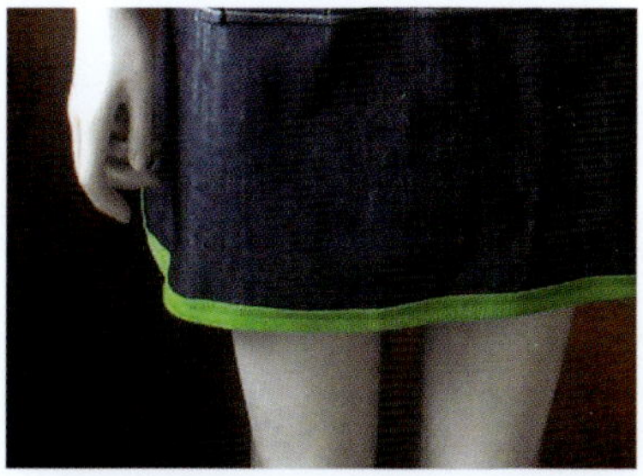

Figure 19-2. Real Apron with Green Binding

Banding is a separate piece of fabric, lace or trim that is sewn to the edge with a regular seam.

Bindings and bandings are used primarily for decoration and can be quite elaborate.

Figure 19-3. Binding Finish Done in Blender

Bindings add substantial thickness to the edge where they are sewn. Binding can be a bit much in MD.

You can fake binding by sewing a separate banding to the edge and then increasing the thickness of just that piece. It will appear to surround the edge. In other 3D graphic programs, try using a thickness modifier.

Facing

Facing is the third method for finishing raw edges. We can make a collar or cuff out of a single pattern and be done with it in MD, not so in the real world.

Facing is a mirror pattern of the piece being faced. If you look at a real shirt collar (see image), you have the top most piece, called the upper collar.

If you lift the collar up, you'll see another collar under there, which is called the under collar. The under collar is a facing.

Figure 19-4. Real Shirt Collar

The collar and under collar are sewn right sides together and then turned right side out to create a nice edge. Sleeve cuffs and button extensions are also faced.

The facing doesn't have to be as big as the original pattern being faced. In a jacket center front edge, the facing may only be a few inches wide. Its only purpose is to finish the raw edge by being sewn and turned to the inside of the jacket.

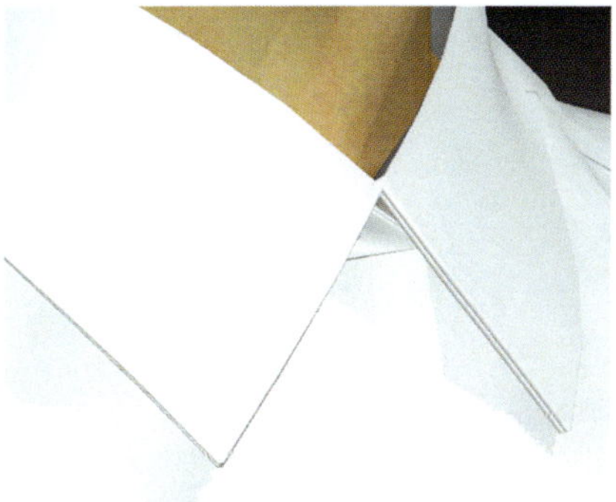

Figure 19-5. Under Collar Done Using Curved Side Geometry

You can fake facings in MD using the Curved Side Geometry option with Double Sided turned on as shown. This allows you to create the illusion of another layer of fabric without using extra geometry or layering.

If you are creating low resolution garments, or those that will only be seen from a distance, there is no need to worry about facings. If you have close-ups or photorealism, you should add the facing pieces.

Interfacing

Interfacing is placed between a pattern piece and the facing. Interfacing should never show on a garment from the outside or inside. It should be sandwiched between two other pieces of fabric. It's only purpose is to stiffen the garment piece.

Collars are comprised of the outer collar piece that will be seen, a piece of interfacing and the under collar (facing) hidden underneath. That's why they are so stiff and hold their shape so well. MD has no use for interfacing and it is an unnecessary piece of geometry that can be ignored.

Lining

Lining is an inner layer of fabric, or other material, to provide a nice inside finish and another option for concealing raw edges. Linings are almost always of a different fabric than the outer layer. They may be fur on a coat to provide additional warmth or perhaps a fine, elaborately printed silk on a vest or formal jacket.

Lining gives you the opportunity to add a lot of character to your plain garments. They do come at a high cost. They are a complete duplicate of geometry and can cause a lot of problems in MD. If possible, fake lining by giving the wrong side of your fabric a different texture than the right side.

Ruffles & Flounces

Ruffles are a separate pattern piece that is gathered. If the ruffle is made from standard fabric in the real world, it is cut double width, folded in half and sewn to the edge. If the ruffle is made out of lace or other fabric that is already finished on the one edge, it is just sewn to the edge without folding.

Ruffles are similar to banding, but the ruffle piece is longer than the edge it is sewn to so it gathers. You don't have to sew the edge to the garment, you can add an Internal Line to use for sewing as shown below. You can make the free edge, that isn't sewn, decorative by adding shapes or scallops to it.

Figure 19-6. Flounce

The image is a flounce. A flounce is essentially a wide ruffle that is sewn on the edge of a skirt or sleeve.

This term is used extensively in my sewing books from the early 1900s. You may encounter it when working with historical patterns.

Piping

Real world piping is made with fabric and cording. A piece of fabric is folded in half (casing) with a cord encased inside. Then the casing is sewn from the outside very close to where the cord is laid.

Piping is usually sandwiched between two other patterns in a seam, rather than on an edge.

If you look at most upholstered cushions, you'll see piping inserted at the seams. You can use piping on a free edge to simulate welting or just for decoration.

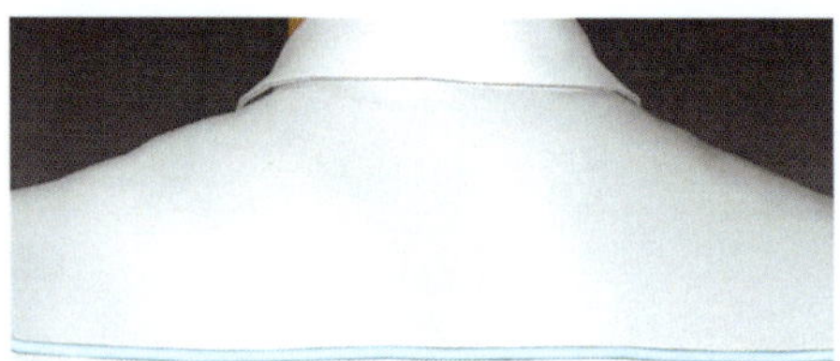

Figure 19-7. Piping Between Yoke and Back Patterns

To see your piping in the 3D Window select -

Display > Materials > Show Piping

RC 3D background > Show All Piping

To hide piping select it in the 3D Window -

RC > Hide

To display hidden piping select -

Display > Materials > Show All Piping

To make piping in MD, select -

Materials > Piping > Piping

MD will put dashes at every point on your pattern in the 3D Window where you can add piping. Click to start the piping and double-click to stop.

Once you've created the piping you can edit it by selecting -

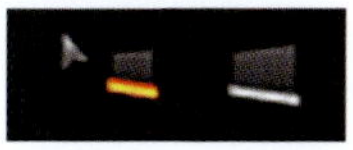

Materials > Piping > Edit Piping

With the piping selected, you can see a number of properties for it in the Property Editor. You can Name the piping and it will show in the Scene tab of the Object Browser.

The Line Length tells you how long your piping is. You can change the size of the piping with the Width value. The Particle Distance on piping is very small and you can adjust this value. You can also choose the fabric for the piping with the Fabric drop-down.

Although MD doesn't draw out a rectangle of piping in the 2D Window, it does exist. When you open the UVGuide, you'll see the piping at the very bottom of the guide. When you are creating textures in another 3D program, place the piping texture in this position.

Other Edging

There are many other ways to finish an edge. Unfortunately, many of them are outside the current capabilities of MD. I'll discuss them briefly so you know what they are when you encounter them in your work. Many of these can be added outside of MD in other 3D graphics programs, like Blender or Maya.

Tassels & Fringe

Tassels and fringe are very similar. Fringe is an edge made of thick threads, ribbons or fabric. Many times the threads are twisted.

Figure 19-8. Fringe in Blender

A tassel is fringe that is gathered into sections and tied. I was successful in making fringe using Blender.

You may be able to cut a band into narrow strips in MD to make heavier fringe, like that found on a motorcycle jacket.

Pom Poms

Pom-poms are little balls attached to an edging piece. The balls are often made of short yarns tied in the middle and then fluffed out. This is not currently possible in MD, but I was able to achieve the look using Blender.

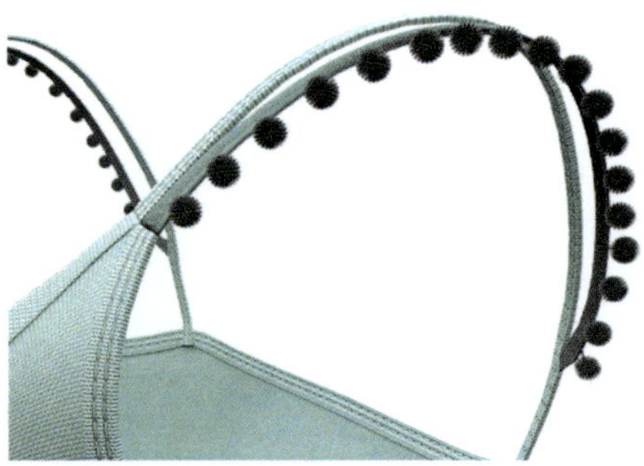

Figure 19-9. Pom Poms in Blender

Chapter 19 Quiz

1) A ____________ is a separate pattern piece that is longer than the segment it is sewn to, so it gathers.(one word)

2) To fake facings in MD, turn on the __________ __________ option on the Curved Side Geometry property.(two words)

3) Piping options include (choose all):

❍ A. Fabric that is unique.

❍ B. Width between 2 and 10 mm.

❍ C. Particle Distance that is unique.

❍ D. UV Guide diagram.

4) Interfacing is hidden and should be left out of MD garments.

❍ True ❍ False

Chapter 20 - Other Details

There are many things added to a garment beyond the basic patterns. These include trims, buttons, pockets and other details. We'll take a look at a few of those options in this chapter.

Buttons & Snaps

Buttons and snaps are a brand new feature in MD version 6. Although we take them for granted on our garments, they can become quite complex. There are lots of different variables that you'll need to consider before adding them to your projects.

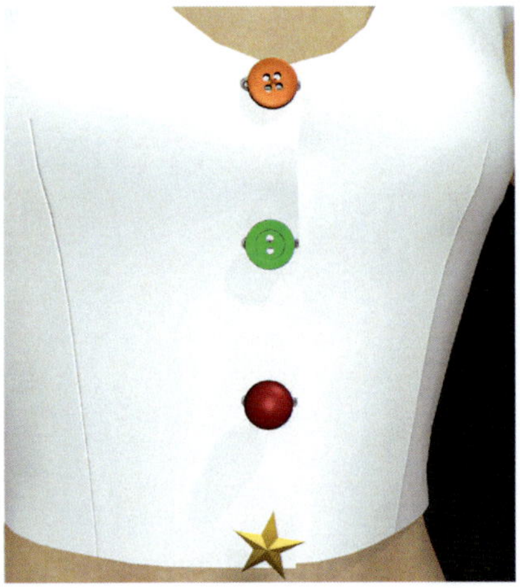

Figure 20-1. Button Samples

Buttons are exported along with your garments and avatars. They are fairly high resolution, so they may not be practical for game artists.

One thing you'll want to keep in mind when applying any type of fastener, is that typically women's garments button right over left and men's button left over right.

Button Basics

Buttons come in many shapes and sizes. The most common buttons are made of plastic or metal, but others are made of porcelain, wood, bone, glass, leather, shell and jewels. There are also buttons that are fabric covered. These are common on outerwear. To make this type of button in MD, simply apply the same fabric to a shanked button as you use on your garment.

You can use buttons with buttonholes, loops, frogs or chains.

Button sizing must relate to the garment design and fabric chosen. Functional buttons generally range in size from 3/8″ (9.5 mm) to 1.5″ (38 mm) in diameter. Purely decorative buttons can be as large as 2.5″ (63.5 mm).

Generally, you'll want to place your buttons an equal distance apart. When working with items that typically gape, like a woman's shirt, you'll want to make sure to place a button at the gaping area. This would be at the bust line.

If you want to be unique, you can group the buttons in clusters, space them irregularly, or use a row of small ones instead of a few larger ones.

There are two types of buttons. A sew-through button has two or four holes for attaching the button to the garment. A shank button has a metal, plastic or fabric shank behind the button with a hole in it sewing the button to the garment. The shank allows room for the overlapping fabric, so that the button rests on top of the buttonhole.

Buttons are sewn on the center front/back lines of tops, skirts and pants. You can use two buttons, placed back-to-back to mimic linked buttons. Linked buttons can be used to close a cuff, vest or cape.

Button Styles & Properties

Before you add buttons to your patterns, you'll want to create the styles you need. Click on the Button tab in the Object Browser. There is one button there called Default Button.

If you want to change the style of button, make sure it is selected in the Object Browser and use the dropdown menu called Shape in the Property Editor. Any changes to a button that is assigned to patterns will change all instances of that button.

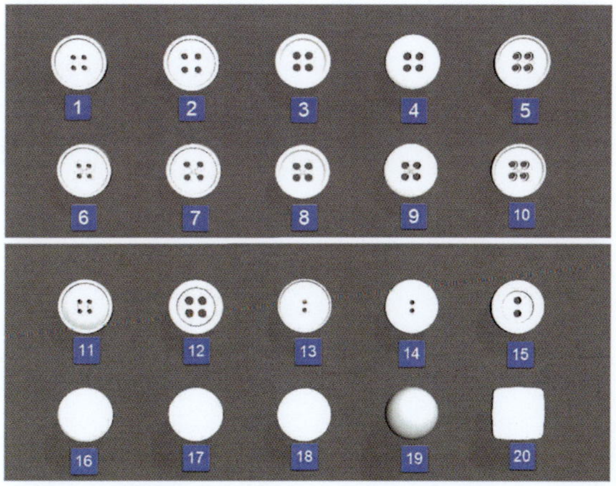

Figure 20-2. MD Buttons 1 - 20

Buttons 1 through 5, 11 and 12 are standard four-hole buttons.

Buttons 6 through 10 are the same as 1-5, but these have threads in the holes showing that they've been sewn.

Buttons 13 through 15 are standard two-hole buttons.

Buttons 16 through 20 are shank buttons.

In the Property Editor, you can change all the properties of the selected button. You can rename your button in the Object Browser, Property Editor or -

RC > Rename

Change the Size value to make your button larger or smaller. The Weight value is how much the button weighs during simulation. If you have very large buttons, or buttons made of a heavier material, you can assign a greater weight to them so they will pull down during simulation just as they would in the real world.

The Material section of button properties is nearly identical to the options for fabric. Read *Chapter 9 - Fabric - Fabric Material Properties* to familiarize yourself with all of the options.

If you want to revert back to the default values on a button, select it in the Object Browser list and -

RC > Reset

Rather than starting over for every new button, you can make a copy of an existing button and change a few properties. Select the button and click Copy at the top of the Button tab to create a copy for you to work with.

If a button is not assigned to any patterns, you can delete it. Select the trashcan next to the button and it will be removed. You can also select -

RC > Delete

Add Button

To add a button select -

Materials > Button > Button

To place the button, click on the 3D garment or place using the crosshairs in 2D window.

If you can't see your buttons in the 3D window select -

Display > Materials > Show Button

There are a number of options for copying and pasting your buttons. Using the Select/Move Button tool select the button you want to copy and -

RC > Copy then RC > Paste

and then click to place the button where you want it.

If you want to create a line of buttons that are evenly spaced, create a button at the beginning of the line. Using the Select/Move Button tool select -

RC > Copy then RC > Mirror Paste

Drag your mouse in the direction of the button line. Hold down your Shift key, if you want to keep straight. You'll see a dashed line attached to your mouse. Right click again and this will open a Paste dialog box.

Figure 20-3. Button Paste Dialog

The value in the Interval field is the length of the line you created before clicking.

As you become accustomed to using this tool, you'll want that line to be the distance between your buttons.

If the Interval is not correct, you can type in a value. Next, the box asks for the number of buttons you want to paste. MD will show you a preview of the buttons in place, so you can determine it is correct before accepting the paste.

Figure 20-4. Button Warning

If the resulting line of buttons, Interval multiplied by the Number of Buttons, is greater than the distance available on the pattern, you'll get a warning that the buttons can't be pasted.

Button to Pattern Depth

You can specify the distance in depth between your button and the pattern it is sewn to. Using the Select/Move Button tool, select the button and adjust the Thread Length in the Property Editor to push it away from the pattern.

Move Button

If you need to move a button select -

Materials > Button > Select/Move Button

Select the button and move it in the 3D or 2D window. You can right click while dragging to open the moving distance dialog and enter a precise distance.

Rotate Button

Use the Select/Move Button tool. You'll see a green circle with a blue line showing the current direction. Click and drag on the circle to rotate the button around its center axis.

You can also change the angle using the Property Editor. Select the button and then use the Angle slider to rotate it.

Button Reset

To reset the button to its original position before simulation, with the Select/ Move Button tool selected -

RC > Reset 3D Position

Button Sewing

By default, the button will be sewn to the top layer of the pattern it was placed on. If you have more than one layer of patterns overlapped, you can tell the button to sew through them. With the Select/Move Button tool selected -

Edit > Context Menu > Materials > Set Number of Sewing Layers

RC > Set Number of Sewing Layers

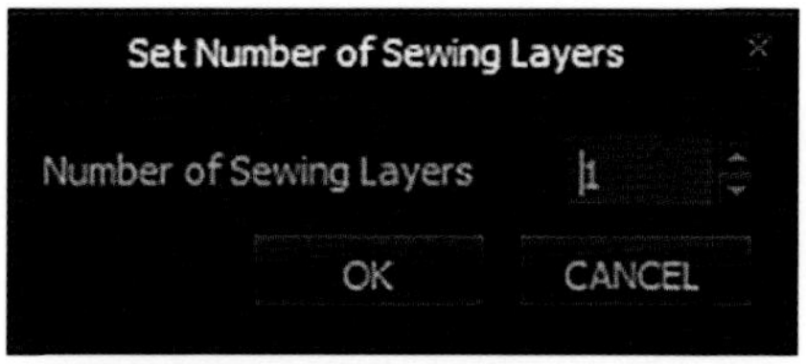

Figure 20-5. Button Sewing Layers

This will open a dialog box that allows you to select how many layers the button should sew through. MD creates a red dashed line between the layers in the 2D and 3D window for a visual reminder. MD also creates a crosshair on the other layers in the 2D window.

By default, the second layer will be sewn through directly under where the button is. If you want to move that position, use the Select/Move Button tool, click the crosshair on the pattern in the 2D window and move it somewhere else.

If the button has been sewn to the wrong side of the pattern, with the Select/Move Button tool selected -

RC > Flip

Now the button will be sewn to the other side of the pattern.

Deactivate / Freeze Buttons

You can deactivate the buttons so that other garments no longer interact with them or recognize their sewing. With the Select/Move Button tool selected-

RC > Deactivate

You can freeze the button, which allows you to adjust the pattern that it is attached to. With the Select/Move Button tool selected -

RC > Freeze

This does not deactivate the sewing, the button will still be attached to the pattern.

Buttonholes

The buttonholes work almost identically to the buttons. You use the same process and Select/Move Button editing tool.

To create buttonholes select -

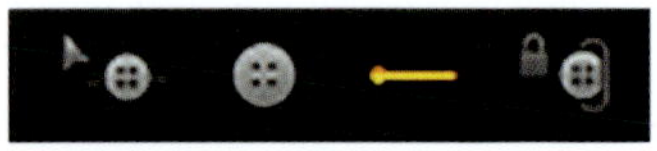

Materials > Button > Buttonhole

MD currently has six different buttonholes.

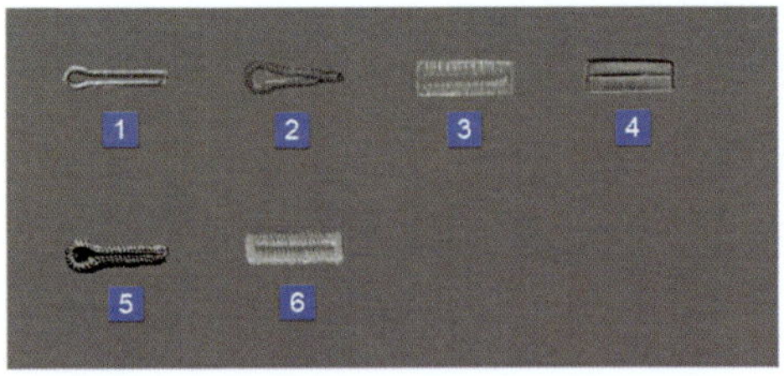

Figure 20-6. MD Buttonholes

Buttonholes 1, 2 and 5 are keyhole buttonholes.

Buttonholes 3 and 6 are standard rectangular buttonholes.

Buttonhole 4 is a welted buttonhole.

Keyhole buttonholes are used on heavy fabric garments like jackets and coats. The rounded end provides more room for the shank of a shank style button.

A welted buttonhole is a specialty item that is not used very often. You would find it on a high-end garment.

Vertical buttonholes are placed running down the center line, with the button in the center. Shirts, blouses and bodices uses vertical buttonholes.

Horizontal buttonholes are placed perpendicular and centered on the center line. Use these on waistbands, coats and jackets.

Fasten Buttons to Buttonholes

MD provides a way for you to bind or fasten your buttons to your buttonholes.

When a button is passed through a buttonhole the button and buttonhole are bound together. The button is considered fastened and the layers of the garment will hold at that point. MD gives you the option of fastening your buttons to your buttonholes so your simulations are very realistic.

To begin select -

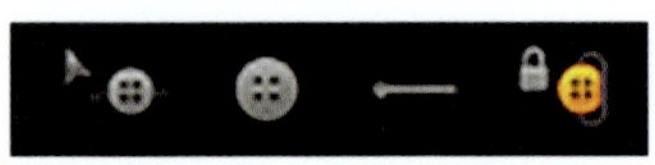

Material > Button > Fasten Button

Use the tool to select the button and then the matching buttonhole. The button will be moved to the buttonhole, if they are in different positions.

Figure 20-7. Button Fastened

MD will lock these two items together and you'll see a padlock in the 3D window. They can no longer be edited or moved. To unfasten the set, click them again with the Fasten Button tool.

Button Bind Position in Buttonhole

If you are fastening buttonholes with your buttons, you have the ability to set the position of the button in the hole. There is a small green dot on the buttonhole in the 2D Window that shows where the button will be fastened. With the buttonhole selected, change the Bind Position in the Property Editor. This will move the green dot to the new location.

Snaps

When you fasten with a button, you simply have the button and the buttonhole. When you fasten with a snap, things can get more complicated.

Snaps are fastened by inserting a stud into a socket. The socket is sewn to the wrong side of the uppermost layer. The stud is sewn to the right side of the lowermost layer.

Snaps can be attached by hand sewing or by using a tool. If the snap is sewn by hand, there are only two parts. There is a socket and a stud.

Figure 20-8. Hand Sewing Snaps (stud left, socket right)

Notice the wide variety of sizing on these snaps. Hand sewn snaps are invisible on the outside. You can't tell that they are there. The only time you need to show a hand sewn snap in MD, is if the snap is not fastened.

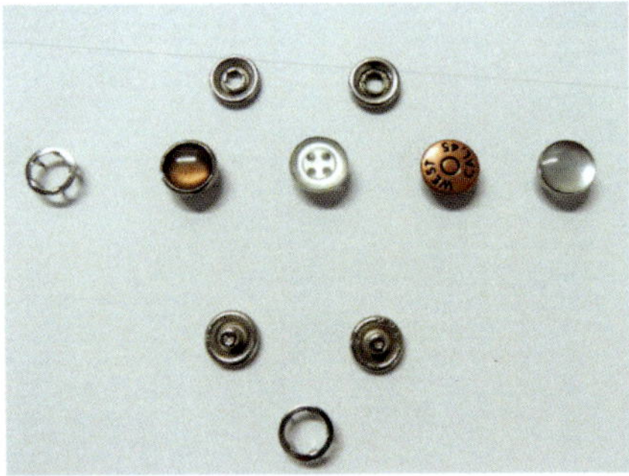

Figure 20-10. Snap Tool Snaps

Snaps that are attached using a snap tool have four different parts. You have the socket and the stud, but you also have attaching units on the side of the fabric opposite from the socket and stud.

The attaching unit for a socket can be a capped ring or an open ring. The attaching unit for a stud can be a post, open ring or capped post.

In the image above, the top row are the sockets, the second row are the attaching rings for the sockets, the third row are the studs and the final row is an open ring for attaching the stud. As you can see, one capped ring looks like a button!

The stud is usually applied with the post of the stud facing away from the body, which means it will be on the inner most layer of the overlap. This is so that the body doesn't get poked with it.

Buttons 21, 23 and 25 appear to be capped rings.

Buttons 22 and 24 are studs.

Buttons 26 and 27 are open rings.

Buttons 29 through 33 are specialty caps.

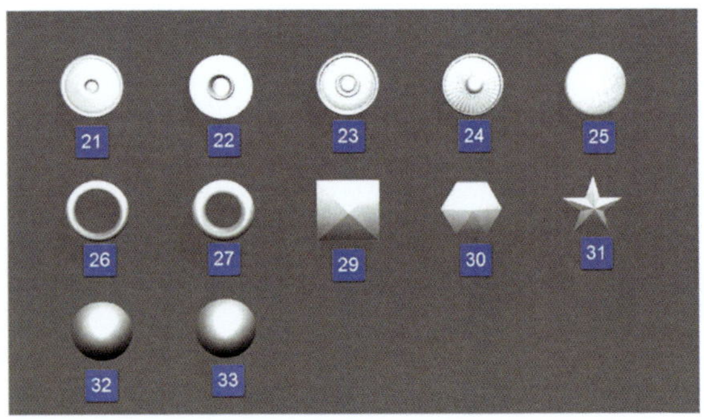

Figure 20-9. MD Buttons 21-33

Note there is no Button #28 and all of these buttons have a Diffuse map on them that makes them appear to be made of metal.

Figure 20-11. Snap Side View

To the left is a side view, so you can see the details of the snap parts better.

MD has supplied you with capped rings, open rings and studs. You will need to determine which ones you will use depending on the level of detail that you want.

If all you see is the outside of a snap fastened garment, all you need to add is the capped or open ring. This is all that would show from the outside.

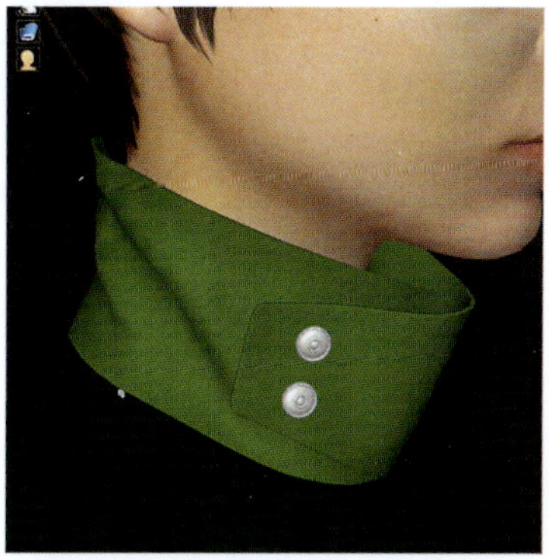
Figure 20-12. Collar Snapped Closed

Figure 20-13. Collar Unsnapped (open)

If your garment has snaps that are not fastened, you'll want the capped or open ring on the right side of the outermost layer. You'll want the snap stud on the right side of the innermost layer.

You can also use the MD snap studs as rivets on jeans.

Pockets

Most pockets are optional, but some are incorporated into the pattern. A side seam pocket on jeans or pants is actually part of the pattern and would leave a hole, if they were not incorporated.

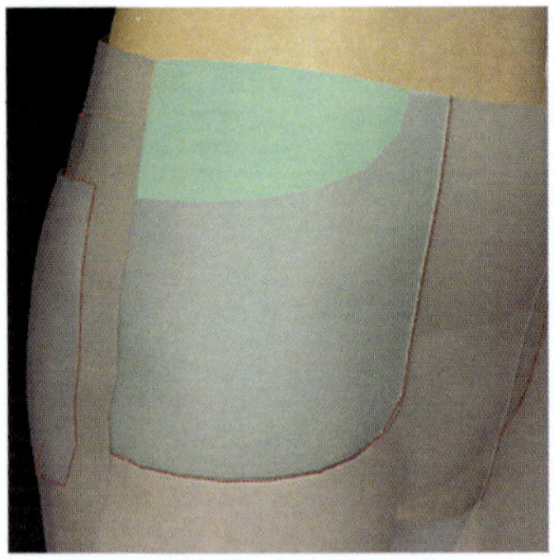

Figure 20-14. Side Pocket (shown in green, pants have opacity turned down)

Pockets can be nearly invisible, showing only the opening. These would be like welted pockets on the back of men's slacks. All you can see is the narrow welting around the pocket hole.

The side seam pocket shown here is partially visible. Most of the pocket is behind the pants leg.

Pockets applied to the outside of a garment are called patch pockets. They are almost always applied with top-stitching. They are as decorative as they are functional.

Different types of pockets define the style of the garment. The patch pockets on the back of jeans include stitching that defines not only the pants, but often the manufacturer as well. Pockets are always an option that you can add to shirts, pants, skirts and outerwear.

Top-Stitching

In a standard seam, you can't see the thread at all from the outside of the garment (refer to the real-world seam image in *Chapter 8 - Seams & Basting*). Whenever you can see the stitching, it is most likely top-stitched. Top-stitching is simply running a line of stitches over the top of the garment on the right side. Sometimes it is part of the seam construction and other times it is purely decorative.

Jeans are a great example of seaming that has a drastic effect on appearance. These seams are called flat-felled seams and are top-stitched with a double needle in order to create the perfectly parallel rows of stitching.

Figure 20-15. Denim Jeans Back

When several layers are top-stitched, the stitches sink into the fabric. They can also pucker the fabric. This is most evident in a well-worn pair of denim jeans.

You can see that the seams don't wear evenly. High spots will wear more quickly and lose their color. The low spots are protected and hold color. In between, the denim fades to a medium shade.

I have seen very few CG jeans that were accurate due to the intricacies of wear on denim and the details of their top-stitching.

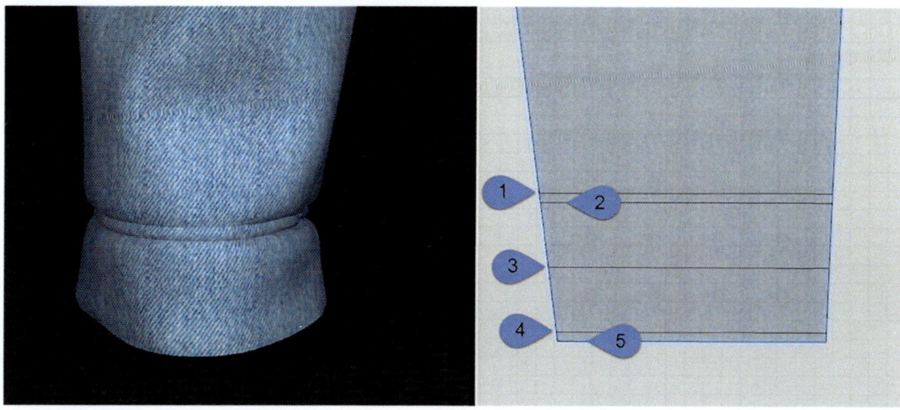

Figure 20-16. Top-Stitching in MD

You can create top-stitching in MD using internal lines and thick textured surface. The hem shown above has a particle distance of 5 and a texture applied. It was created as follows:

#1 Internal Line - has a Fold Angle of 360 and is sewn to #5

#2 Internal Line - has a Fold Angle of 360 and is sewn to #4

#3 Internal Line - has a Fold Angle of 100, is just used for turning and not sewn. It was used with the Fold Arrangement tool to fold the hem to the inside of the pant leg.

#4 Internal Line - has the default Fold Angle.

#5 Pattern - the edge of the pants leg pattern.

If you wanted photorealism, you would create a texture in another program and create stitches that fall on the internal lines. Those stitches would be pulled inside of the folds and look very realistic.

Welting

Figure 20-17. Real Welted Pocket

Some seam techniques will result in deformation of the fabric. A welted or piped seam is such an example. The image to the left is a welted back pocket on a pair of men's pants.

To match the appearance of real garments, we have to improvise and add special effects to simulate the results of these types of seams. Here is a fake welt in MD using piping. You can learn more about piping in *Chapter 19 - Finishing Edges.*

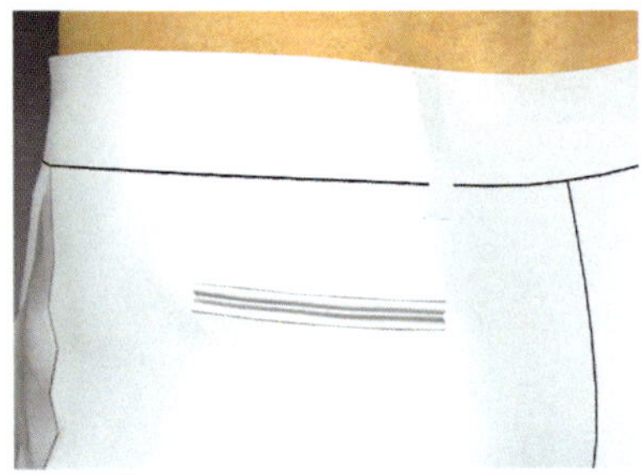

Figure 20-18. MD Welted Pocket

Trims

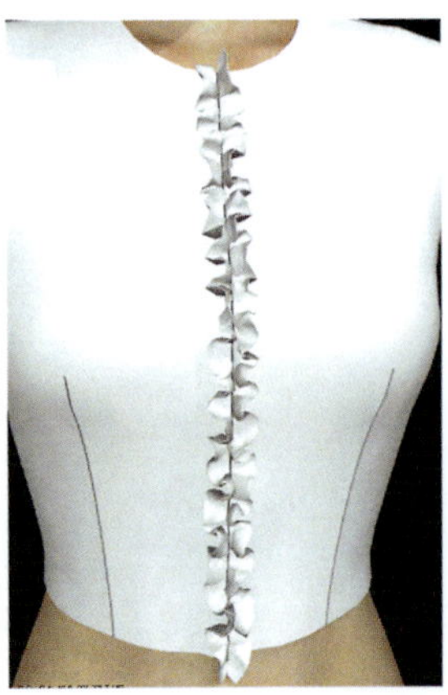

Figure 20-19. Ruche Down Center Front of Bodice

We talked about some trims in *Chapter 19 - Finishing Edges*. These included bandings and bindings that are attached between seams or at the edge.

You can attach other types of trim anywhere you want on a garment. One common trim is called ruche. It is like a double ruffle, with the gathering down the center.

To create ruche in MD, make a rectangle of fabric that is 1.5 to 2 times longer than the edge it attaches to. Create an Internal Line running down the center and sew it to the pattern. You will need to lower the Particle Distance to get a nice simulation.

Bows

The process that MD uses to prevent penetration of objects stops you from making objects overlap themselves or other objects.

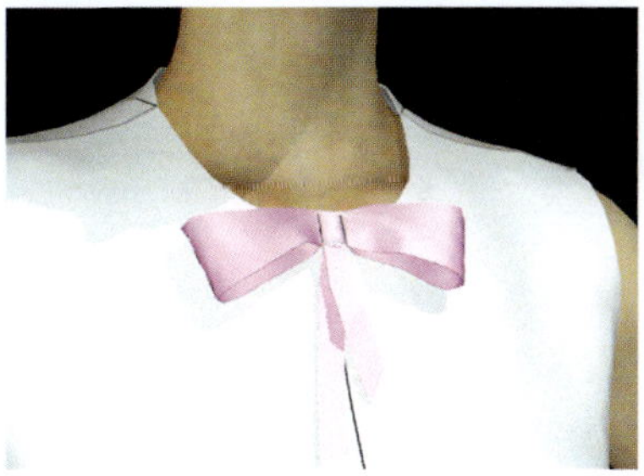

Figure 20-20. MD Bow

This makes lacing, bows and ties very difficult, if not impossible, to do. Rather than using single strips of fabric, you'll need to create many pieces that connect to each other.

The bow above is constructed of four patterns. Take note of the small square pattern at the top. This piece is frozen and I refer to it as the control. The bow tails are sewn to the bottom of the control.

Each side edge of the bow pattern is sewn to the sides of the control. The internal lines on the bow are then sewn to the sides of the control.

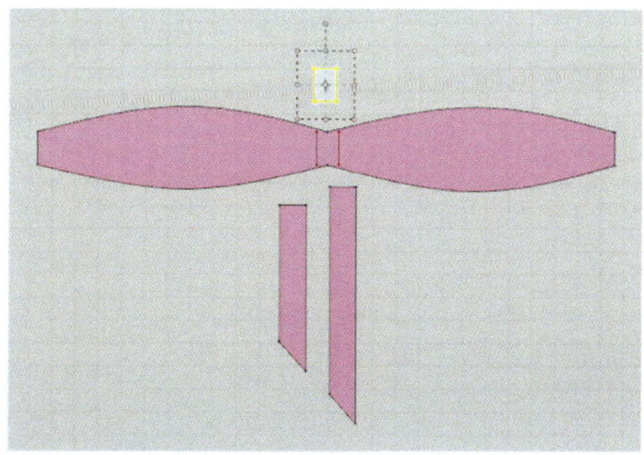

Figure 20-21. Bow Patterns

I like to place the control piece out in space for the initial simulation. This allows me to work with it to get the shape right without interferring with other patterns. Then I select all the pieces and move them into place on the garment.

This can be a significant amount of work and you'll need to determine if MD is the right choice for making these objects. You might find it easier to model these in another 3D program and add them to your finished work there.

Appliqué & Patchwork

Appliqué consists of pieces of fabric that are sewn onto a larger piece. In this way, they are similar to a patch pocket. They are a decoration piece and serve no function in the garment.

Patchwork is smaller pieces of fabric in different colors or shapes that are sewn together to create a larger pattern. MD is very conducive to this type of technique. You can create the pattern as a whole and then use the Cut and/or Trace tools to cut it into many sections. These sections are then sewn back together to create the finished look.

The wetsuit in the image was a standard garment that was cut apart strategically to create the seams found in a neoprene wetsuit.

Figure 20-22. Wetsuit

Plackets

The separate button extension on the front of a shirt is sometimes referred to as a placket. The opening at the cuff is also called a placket. A placket is a finished slit or opening. The polo shirt to the right has a three-button placket on the front.

Figure 20-23. Polo Shirt

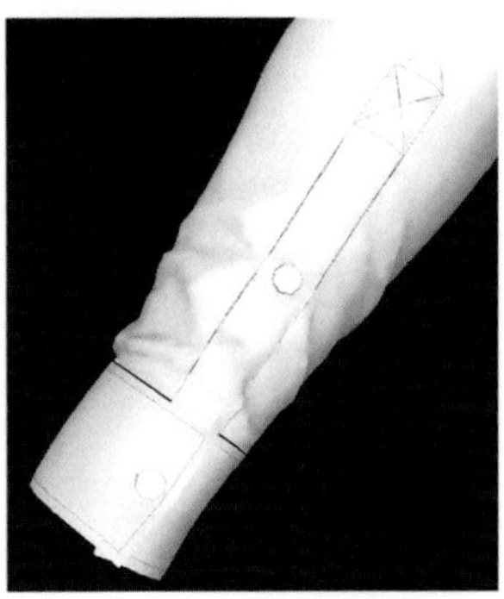

Sleeve plackets in the real world are quite complex and tricky to sew. Sewing them in MD is much easier. However, this level of detail is usually not necessary, unless you are working on photorealism.

Figure 20-24. Sleeve Placket in MD

Steam

MD gives you the ability to steam iron your patterns. You can use this to reduce wrinkles and even out smaller areas of your garments, just like a real-world garment steamer. To open the Steam tool select -

Materials > Steam > Steam

This will open the Steam Brush Dialog box.

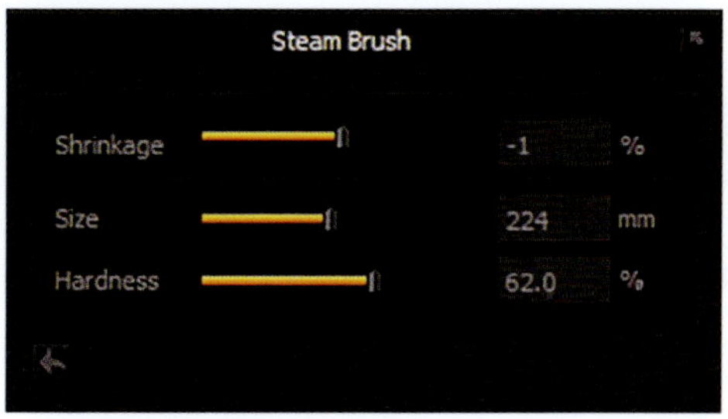

Figure 20-25. Steam Brush Dialog

Applying steam to a pattern will make it shrink. You can select the percentage of shrinkage with the Shrinkage setting.

The next option is Size and this refers to the size of the brush that you will use to paint the steam on the pattern. The size is entered in millimeters.

The last option is Hardness and this is also a percentage. Hardness will adjust the steam brush's fall-off or feathering. Set this to 0% for a soft edge brush and 100% for a crisp edge.

After adjusting the settings, simply click and drag the little iron icon over your patterns. You can adjust the settings at any time during the process.

To remove steam on one pattern, select the pattern and -

Edit > Context Menu > Materials > Remove Steam on Selected Pattern

Materials > Steam > Remove Steam

To remove steam on all patterns, select -

Materials > Steam > Remove All Steam

Pressing

If you have two pattern layers that are sewn on top of each other, they may puff out at the side seams. You can use the Press tool to flatten the turned seams.

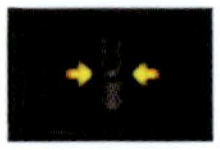

3D Garment > Press

MD will ask you to click on one side and then the other. Simulate and the two layers will come very close together at the seams.

Padding & Cloning

There are many garments that are padded. Any outerwear that is insulated is generally made up of an outside pattern, insulating material and the inner lining. Wherever the pattern and lining are sewn together creates a visible puffing effect.

To create padding you need to have two layers of fabric. MD can create the second layer for you and sew it to the first. You need to specify whether you want the new piece over or under the original. Select the pattern and then

Edit > Context Menu > 2D Pattern > Layer Clone Over / Under

RC > Layer Clone > Over / Under

MD will automatically sew the two pieces together all the way around the outer edge.

Once you have the sewing done, use the Pressure setting in the Property Editor on the top and/or bottom layer to make the layers push against each other and create the puff effect.

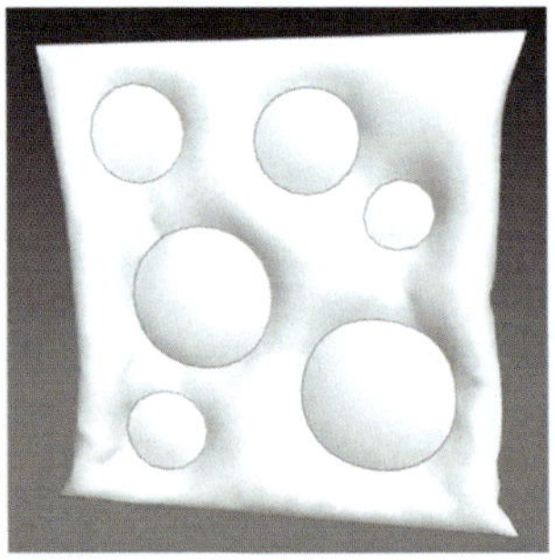

Figure 20-26. Padding

If you want to create top stitching between the top and bottom layers, create your Internal Lines before doing the layer clone. MD will sew the Internal Lines together for you when you clone.

Chapter 20 Quiz

1) Patch pockets are located within the side seam of pants.

❍ True ❍ False

2) You should always include the stud of the snap set on your garments.

❍ True ❍ False

3) Use the ___________ button tool to lock a button to a buttonhole.(one word)

4) You can tie bows and knots in MD.

❍ True ❍ False

Chapter 21 - Mesh / Geometry

With all this talk of sewing and garments, it easy to forget that MD is really just a 3D graphics program. At its core, its only purpose is to create geometry that resembles realistic clothing. Most of you will be exporting the garments out of MD to use in other programs. In this chapter we'll talk about the actual mesh geometry and the ways you can change it and view it.

Particle Distance

The patterns in the 2D Window are very low resolution with only a few points, which are actually called vertices in any other 3D program. These are primitive shapes.

In order to simulate and drape, you must subdivide these primitives. MD automatically puts a subdivision surface modifier on your patterns. If you select a pattern and look in the Property Editor you can see a setting for Particle Distance. By default, this is set to 20. You can change this with -

Settings > User Settings > Others > Pattern > Default Particle Distance

Particle Distance is designated in mm, which I believe is the distance between vertices.

MD creates the garment meshes with triangles by default. To see the mesh in the 3D Window, select -

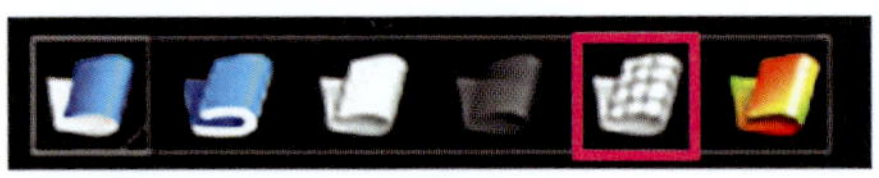

Display > 3D Garment Rendering Style > Mesh

To see the mesh of the 2D Window patterns, select -

Display > 2D Pattern > Show Mesh

Put a sewn garment in the 3D view, select a single pattern and change the Particle Distance to 8. MD makes the mesh more dense and increases the quantity of vertices.

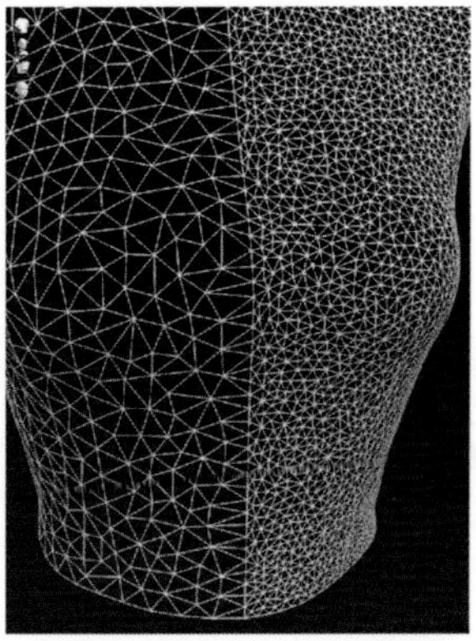

Figure 21-1. Higher Particle Distance on Right Side

If you zoom up real close you can see that not only did MD change the geometry on that pattern, it also changed the geometry on every piece that is sewn to that pattern. For every vertex on the edge of the pattern, there must be a corresponding vertex on the other pieces that connect to it.

Lower Particle Distance is more work for your computer and makes simulations very slow. For that reason, you may want to leave the setting higher wherever you can. You can also keep the setting high and then lower it for your final simulations, which is what I generally do.

Geometry Density

The density of your geometry is particularly important to those of you who will be using MD objects as game assets. If you need to know the vertex count of a pattern, select it and view the Miscellaneous section of the Property Editor.

Figure 21-2. Geometry Properties

Quad Conversion

Many 3D artists prefer to work with quads instead of tris. You can convert all or some of your patterns to quads. You can also convert quad patterns to triangles.

Select your patterns and then -

Edit > Context Menu > 3D Garment > Quadrangulate / Triangulate

RC > Quadrangulate /Triangulate

MD will convert the tris to quads for you. You can also use the Mesh Type dropdown in the Property Editor to make the change. If you have a lot of dense geometry, this conversion can take a while.

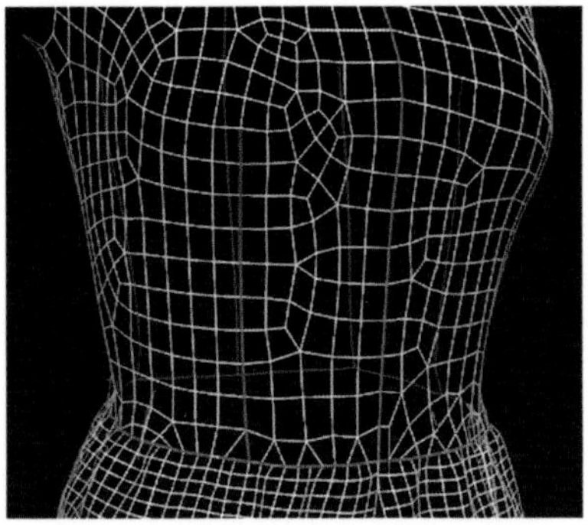

Figure 21-3. Triangles Converted to Quads

Everyone, including me, grouches about what a mess MD makes when it converts. The topology isn't exactly clean. You can see how the mesh isn't well formed in the image.

There doesn't appear to be any reason for these strange edges, when the quads could be much straighter. However, I suspect the problem lies in the huge task MD has in making sure that there is a matching vertex on every side of a seam. You can set the Particle Distance on every pattern to something different and still MD has to match those vertices. When I realized what was going on, I had a new appreciation for what this software has to accomplish. It's not going to stop me from whining about it, but it certainly makes more sense now.

MD is Superior for UVs

I've heard many people speak of the advantages and disadvantages of using MD for garment geometry as opposed to modeling it in other 3D programs. The one thing no one talks about is UVs and this completely baffles me, because this is a huge advantage in MD.

When you sculpt or model clothing in other programs, you need to apply textures when you're done. This means that you have to unwrap your UVs. In the real world, the garment is cut from a piece of fabric using patterns. The UVs for garments must match those pattern shapes exactly to have any hope of resembling real fabric properties.

MD does this perfectly. You have exact lines of all seams in perfect proportion. You can lay your MD UV map on a rectangle of fabric and create realistic textures instantly. Stripes and patterns will line up on the garment exactly as they would in the real world. Applying seam details and normal/bump maps is also very simple when you have the original pattern shapes.

UV Layout

If you are going to take the patterns outside of MD to work with in another 3D program, the UV layout will become important. To view the UV Guide select -

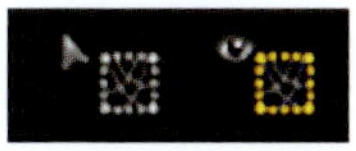

Display > 2D Pattern > Show UV Guide

Display > Materials > Show UV Guide

MD automatically unwraps the UV's for you and creates a layout that surrounds all the patterns.

If you want to take only selected patterns out of MD, you may choose to edit this UV layout. Select -

Materials > Edit UV

At the upper right of the UV box you'll see a double arrow icon.

Click the icon to open a UV grid. The boxes in the corners can be adjusted.

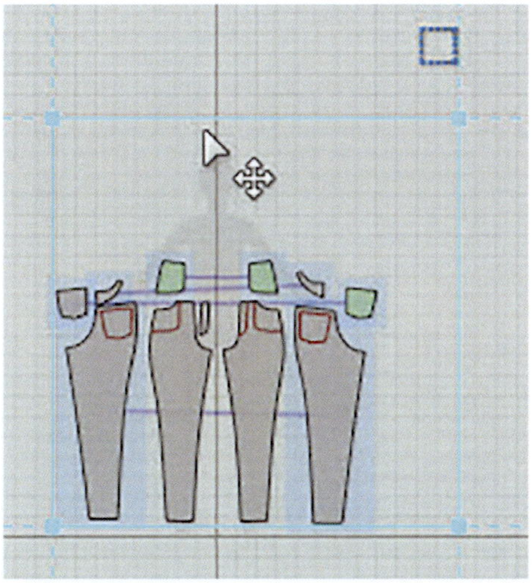

Figure 21-4. UV Guide

Click and drag to re-size your UV layout.

Chapter 21 Quiz

1) MD geometry is quads by default.

❍ True ❍ False

2) You control the density of your garment geometry with the

_____________ _____________ setting.(two words)

3) MD provides the Face and Vertex count of every pattern piece.

❍ True ❍ False

4) You can set the Particle Distance of every pattern to a different value.

❍ True ❍ False

Chapter 22 - Avatars

Avatar Editor

The characters in the 3D Window are referred to as Avatars by MD. The discussion below refers to the MD default Avatars. If you import your own Avatars, many of these features and settings will not exist. You'll have to create them yourself.

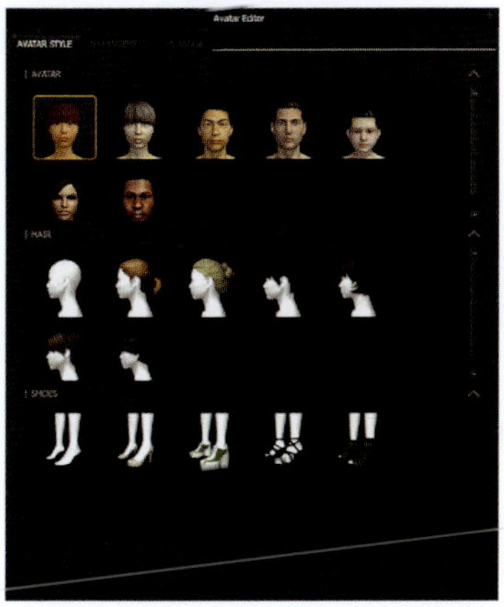

Figure 22-1. Avatar Editor, Editor Style Tab

MD includes seven Avatars in the program. To select an Avatar select -

Avatar > Avatar Editor

This opens a window with three tabs. The Avatar Style tab allows you to choose an Avatar, with hair and shoe choices for some of them. The second tab is Arrangement, which we covered in *Chapter 11 - Arranging Patterns in the 3D Window*. The third tab is Measure and details for this can be found in *Chapter 5 - Avatar Measurements & Fit*.

Showing & Hiding Avatars

If you want to hide an Avatar, select -

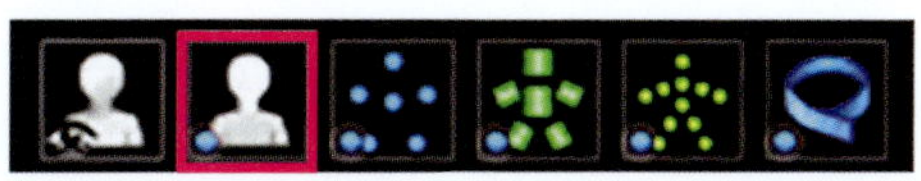

Display > Avatar > Hide Avatar

RC on Avatar > Hide Avatar

This will just make the Avatar transparent, it will still collide and interact with patterns.

To show one or all Avatars select -

Display > Avatar > Show Avatar

Display > Avatar > Show All Avatars

RC on Avatar > Show All Avatars

You can remove one or all Avatars from the scene by selecting -

Avatar > Delete All Avatars

Avatar > Delete Avatar

RC on Avatar> Delete All Avatars

RC on Avatar> Delete Avatar

This will delete all objects that were included in the scene as an Avatar. If you want to delete scenes or props you've placed in the scene, select -

Avatar > Delete Scene/Prop

RC > Delete All Scenes/Props

If you want to deactivate all Avatars select -

Edit > Context Menu > Avatar > Deactivate Avatar

RC on Avatar > Deactivate Avatar

When you deactivate an Avatar it is no longer a collision object and the patterns will no longer interact with it.

Avatar Texture

There are three different textures available for displaying your Avatars.

Display > Avatar Rendering Style > Textured Surface

Textured Surface will apply a material to the Avatar for realistic coloring.

Display > Avatar Rendering Style > Mesh

Mesh will display the geometry that makes up the Avatar.

Display > Avatar Rendering Style > Monochrome Surface

Monochrome will place a grayish white material on the Avatar.

Avatar Properties

Select the Avatar in the 3D Window to view its properties in the Property Editor. You'll see the Mesh Type of the Avatar and its Element Count (which I believe is the vertex count).

Figure 22-2. Avatar Properties

The Skin Offset determines the distance that the patterns are pushed away from the Avatar. If the patterns are too close, they may penetrate. If they are too far away, it won't look natural and you'll see gaping between the pattern and Avatar.

The Friction Coefficient numbers determine the friction of the Avatar during simulation. If the Avatar has higher friction, the patterns will not slide off as easily.

The Material section includes all the information for the material applied to the Avatar. The Diffuse Color is the color of the Avatar when you choose to display it in monochrome. The rest of the settings apply to a custom image map that was created for the Avatar.

Joints

Avatars have skeletons with joints. To view the Avatar joints select -

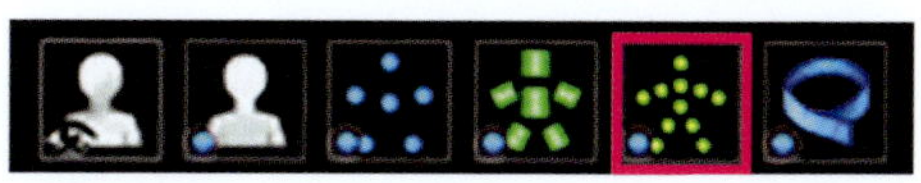

Display > Avatar > Show X-Ray Joints

The Avatar will go into X-Ray Joints mode and the skin will become transparent.

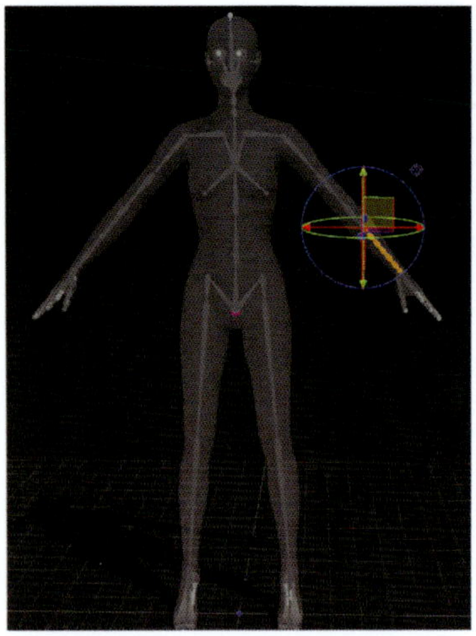

Figure 22-3. Avatar X-Ray Joints

You can select a joint with the Gizmo and rotate and/or move it to change the Avatar's pose. If you want to return a joint to the default position, select a joint and select -

Avatar > Reset Joints

You must have a joint selected for this to work from the main menu. You can also select -

RC on the joint > Reset Joints

Be careful, this will reset ALL joints!

It is possible to import your own character with a skeleton/joints and have them recognized by MD. The import must be COLLADA for this to work.

MD calculates using inverse kinematics, which means that movement of one joint will affect all others further down the hierarchy. For example, if you select the shoulder, you'll see that upper arm, lower arm, hand and finger joints are all selected as well. When you move the shoulder, the other joints will follow.

The highest joint in the hierarchy is the pelvis. You'll see there is a bright pink indicator on the Avatar's pelvis. Select this point to move the entire Avatar within the 3D scene. You can use the Gizmo or just click and drag with the mouse.

When moving joints with the Gizmo, select -

Preferences > Gizmo > Local Coordinates

Now the Gizmo will be placed along the correct axis for joint movement.

Changing the Pose

The position of the Avatar's joints at any point in time is considered a pose. By default, the Avatars are posed in what I refer to as an "A" pose. This differs somewhat from the standard "T" pose in other programs. It is very difficult to drape garments on a character that is in a true "T" pose. If you have a character you want to import to use in MD, I strongly suggest that you put it in an "A" pose before importing or use the x-ray joints functionality to get it that way in MD.

There are many reasons why having your finished garments draped on a character in the "A" pose may not be ideal. Perhaps your character is in the "T" pose for game development or you want a realistic pose for photorealism. Either way, it's necessary to get your garments draped on a character who isn't standing there with their arms raised out to the side.

Figure 22-4. Avatar Posed

There are two ways to change the pose of the Avatar and subsequently, the drape of your garments. Both of these are considered morphing, which is the transition from one state to another.

Use one of these methods to transition "T" pose characters into the "A" pose for draping and then back again before exporting for use elsewhere.

Joint Morphing

MD comes with some pose files for the default avatars. You can open those files for morphing or you can create your own.

To open an MD pose file select -

File > Open > Pose

Navigate to the directories located in the MD installation Avatar > Pose directory. You'll see a folder for each of the default avatars. You must pick a pose file for the avatar you are using. They are not interchangeable. Open the correct directory and select a pose.

You can create your own pose file, if your Avatar has joints that can be manipulated in MD. Either you are using an MD default Avatar or you have imported a fully rigged COLLADA Avatar.

Using x-ray joints, pose your Avatar in the position you want as the final pose.

Do this without any clothing on the Avatar. Save the pose by selecting -

File > Save As > Pose

Using your original Avatar in the "A" pose, put the desired garments on your Avatar. Simulate and finalize their design and placement. When you are done with the garments, you can change the pose.

File > Open > Pose > Select your saved pose

MD will open the saved pose file and the Avatar will animate in the 3D Window slowly morphing into the position defined by the file. You can simulate after the morphing is complete and the Avatar will not move, so you can rearrange the garments and correct any issues.

Vertex Morphing

This method works well if you don't have a COLLADA character or you would rather pose your character in another program. In your favorite 3D graphics program, put your character in the "A" pose and export as an OBJ. Then put the character in your final pose and export that as an OBJ.

Import your "A" pose OBJ character into MD and add the desired garments. Simulate and finalize their design and placement.

To change the pose select -

File > Open > Joint Motion

Then select the second OBJ file with your final pose. MD will morph to the second pose and animation will run in the 3D Window. When the morphing is complete, the avatar will no longer move when you simulate to adjust your garments.

If your final pose is complex, you may want to create tween poses and slowly work your way to the final.

Chapter 22 Quiz

1) The only avatars you can use for making garments in MD are provided with the program.

❍ True ❍ False

2) You can change the body shape and measurements of MD default avatars.

❍ True ❍ False

3) You use _________ _____________ to change the pose of avatars in the 3D Window. (two words)

4) You can change the hair and shoes on some, but not all, of the MD default avatars.

❍ True ❍ False

Chapter 23 - Working with Files

File Extensions

MD provides you the ability to import files for things like avatars and props. You can also export your finished garments to be used in other programs. We'll take a look at those options in this chapter.

MD creates propriety file extensions for most of the files that are saved out of the program. The Color Palette files are .aco, which is the same extension used by Adobe. Many of these files are saved automatically to directories designated by MD.

File Type	***Extension***
Arrangement Point	.arr
Avatar	.avt
Bounding Volume	.pan
Color Palette	.aco
Fabric	.zfab
Fabric Preset	.psp
Garment	.zpac
Motion	.mtn
Pose	.pos
Project	.zprj
Simulation	.smp

Saving & Opening

There are many, many ways to save objects in MD. For example, you can save your character as an Avatar, save it in a project file, save it as a pose and save it's measurements, arrangement points and bounding volumes. The file extension will be set depending on how you save the object or objects.

Avatar

To save your character as an Avatar select -

File > Save As > Avatar

When you want to load an Avatar in the scene you can do so by selecting -

File > Open > Avatar

You can have more than one Avatar in the scene at one time. To add another Avatar select -

File > Add > Avatar

Project

An MD project is everything in the 3D Window scene including the Avatar, all the patterns and all the fabric applied to those patterns. To save the entire project select -

File > Save As > Project

Saving projects is so common that it also has its own choice on the file menu as -

File > Save Project

To open a project select -

File > Open > Project

If you already have a project open, MD will ask if you want to save it before loading the one you've selected.

You can also add another project to the one that you have open.

File > Add > Project

MD will open an Add Project dialog box that shows Project Objects and Translation. Select whether you want to open just the Garment, just the Avatar, or both. You can also designate a Translation to move the added project to a different place in the scene and specify a Unit for scaling.

Figure 23-1. Add Project Dialog

Surface Textures

If you want a reference file that contains all the texture images you've used in your project, MD will create one for you.

File > Save As > Surface Textures

Figure 23-2. Save Suface Textures Dialog

MD will open a dialog asking if you want them saved at their Original Size or Crop to 200 x 200 pixels. The images will be saved in their original file type (jpg, png, etc).

Joint Motion

MD provides motion files for some default avatars. These files have the .mtn extension. Animation data or motion capture data from other 3D graphics programs can be imported as COLLADA files and then extracted as MD motion files using -

File > Save As > Joint Motion

Garment

Saving a garment is quite different from saving the project. A garment is only the patterns and their fabric and properties. The Avatar will not be saved at all. To save the garment select -

File > Save As > Garment

You can open a garment by selecting -

File > Open > Garment

After you select a garment file, MD will ask you if you want the Pose and Avatar Size file to open with the garment. The garment will be added to the scene in the same location it was saved in.

You can also add a garment to the scene by selecting -

File > Add > Garment

MD opens an Add Garment dialog asking for Translation and Unit information. This allows you to re-size the garment and change its position in the scene when it is added.

Importing & Exporting

In addition to the proprietary file formats, MD also plays well with other formats used in the CG industry. The most popular format is OBJ, so those options are shown in detail. Follow these general directions when importing and exporting in other formats.

File Type	Extension	Import	Export
Open COLLADA	.dae	Yes	No
FBX 2014/2015	.fbx	Yes	Yes
LXO	.lxo	No	Yes
OBJ	.obj	Yes	Yes
Alembic	HDF5	Yes	Yes
Alembic	OGAWA	Yes	Yes

Import OBJ

OBJ files are a common file format interchanged between programs. They contain geometry and material information. They are often imported as Avatars or Props into the program.

There is a distinct difference between an Avatar and a Scene / Prop. An Avatar is a collision object and the garments will interact with it. A Scene / Prop is just an object in the scene, most often placed in the foreground or background. OBJ objects imported as scenes and props will not interact with the garments and they will not be draped in the simulation.

An Avatar in this definition does not have to be a body or character. If you want something in your scene that interacts with the patterns, then import it as an Avatar.

To import an OBJ select -

File Import > OBJ

File Import (Add) > OBJ

This will open a dialog box with options. You can select what type of object this will be; an Avatar, a scene / prop or a morph target.

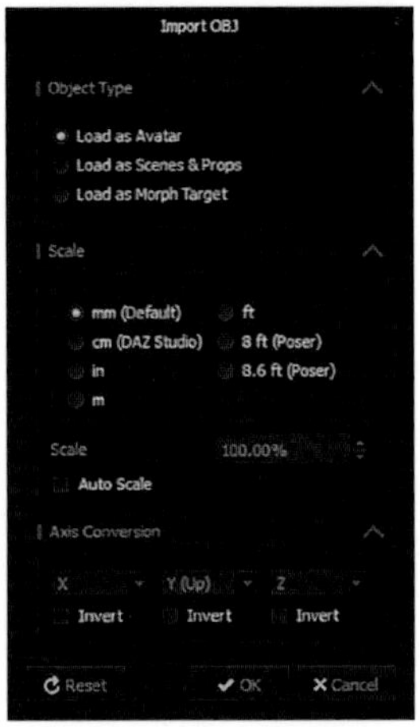

Figure 23-3. Import OBJ Dialog

You need to set the Scale of the OBJ that is coming into MD. Every type of 3D program has a default unit of measure that it uses. Select the unit of measure that was used when the OBJ was created.

MD will convert it so that it fits well in the 3D Window scene. You can also let MD figure out the correct scale by selecting the Auto Scale option.

The last item is the Axis Conversion. The coordinate systems of 3D programs can differ. If the OBJ was created in a program that has a different coordinate system then MD, you should specify what is needed for the conversion on import.

You can import clothing that you've made in other 3D graphics programs to simulate in MD. To import an OBJ to a garment select File Import (Add) > OBJ to Garment. This will open a dialog box that only includes the Scale and Axis Conversion options.

Figure 23-4. Import OBJ to Garment Dialog

Export OBJ

You can export nearly everything in your 3D scene as an OBJ.

File Export > OBJ

This will open an extensive dialog box with many options.

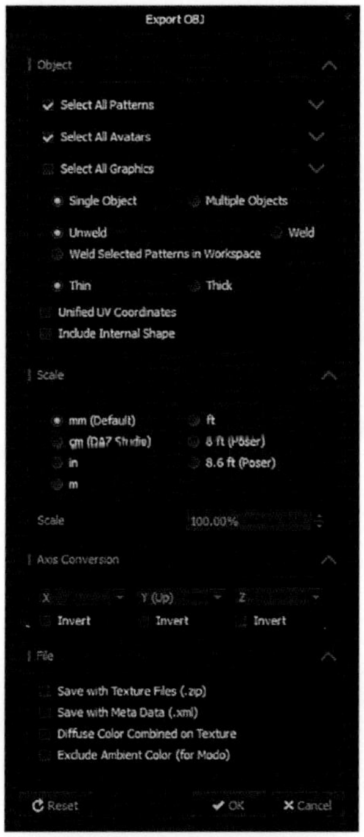

Figure 23-5. Export OBJ Dialog

In the Object section, you can Select all Patterns, Avatars and/or Graphics. You can get very specific about what exports by clicking the down-facing arrow next to each object type. It will open up all the patterns, avatars and/or graphics in your project. You can select items individually to export this way by selecting / deselecting each one.

You can also select a specific item in the 3D Window and choose -

File Export > OBJ (Selected)

This will minimize your export.

The Object section also includes a choice between Single Object and Multiple Objects. This can be a very important distinction. If you are exporting a garment and you select Single Object, the garment will be one single object when opened in another 3D program. If you select Multiple Objects, every pattern of the garment will be exported as its own object. When you select Single Object, you can further refine it by choosing to Weld or Unweld the vertices.

Figure 23-6. Select Individual Patterns to Export

You can choose to export the garment as Thin or Thick. If the garment is Thin, it will be a single plane. If you select Thick, it will have depth (two planes connected with an edge). The depth distance will be what you have specified in the Fabric Thickness.

The Scale and Axis Conversion methods work as described in Import OBJ above. However, now you are converting from MD to the 3D program you will use to open the OBJ on export.

The File section lists some other options you have available. You can zip the texture files and save them with the OBJ. You can save the Meta Data as an xml file with the OBJ. MD will combine the fabric textures with any colors that were assigned or leave them separate. The last item is specific to Modo and allows you to exclude the Ambient Color.

Open COLLADA

COLLADA files are used with other 3D programs, such as 3ds Max, Maya, Poser, DAZ and Blender. They are large files containing not only geometry and materials, but rigging and animation. You can import collada files with -

File Import > Open COLLADA

File Import (add) > Open COLLADA

FBX

FBX files contain geometry, material, joints and animation. They can be imported with -

File Import > FBX 2014/2015

You can also export in this format with -

File Export > FBX 2014/2015

LXO

LXO files are used by the program Modo and contain geometry and material. You can't import these files, but you can export them with -

File Export > LXO

Alembic

The last file type is Alembic, which is a data transfer format for 3D graphics. You can import these files with -

File > Import > Alembic

and export them with -

File > Export > Alembic (HDF5 or OGAWA)

Chapter 23 Quiz

1) You can save in the following formats (choose all):

❍ Avatar avt

❍ Project zprj

❍ Garment zpac

❍ Prop pro

❍ Pose pos

2) MD can save all of the textures you've used in a file for reference.

❍ True ❍ False

3) When you Save As Garment, the avatar is saved with the garment.

❍ True ❍ False

4) In addition to the garments, you can choose to export just the avatar.

❍ True ❍ False

Chapter 24 - Customizing MD

User Settings

You have a lot of things you can customize in MD. The program gives you the opportunity to set it up in a way that makes your work more efficient and more accurate. If you work in other 3D or CAD programs, it's nice to have a similar mapping of shortcuts, so that you don't become confused.

Listed below are the items you can change in the User Settings dialog, which can be opened with -

Settings > User Settings

Shortcuts

The Shortcuts section gives you a complete list of Actions arranged in a tree hierarchy. Click the plus sign next to each Action type to open the individual settings. If MD has set a default shortcut, the keyboard combination will be listed under Shortcut Key.

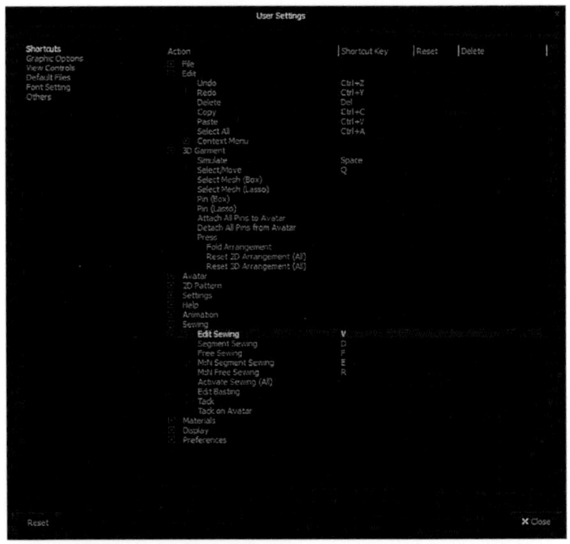

Figure 24-1. User Settings Shortcuts

If you select an Action that has a shortcut key set, you'll see a Reset and Delete button. If you've changed the key to something other than the default, clicking Reset will put it back to the MD default. If you want to remove a shortcut setting, click the Delete button.

To add a shortcut key, click in the box and type your key combination. If the combination has already been set on another Action, MD will show you a dialog box asking of you want to make the change. If you click Yes, the key combination will be set on that Action and removed automatically from the previous Action.

When you hover over buttons in the user interface, MD will show you the shortcut. If you've changed the shortcut keys, MD will update the value on hover. This is very helpful, if you forget your custom shortcuts.

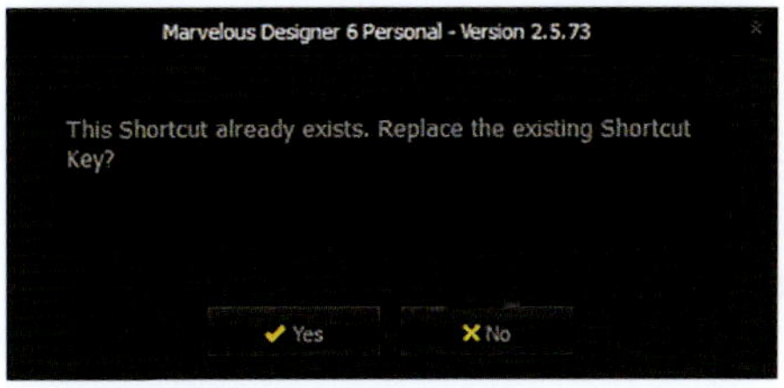

Figure 24-2. Shortcut Change Warning

Graphic Options

The Graphic Options specify the quality of graphics in the program. The Use Shader selection designates whether the shader is used. The shader makes the objects appear smoother.

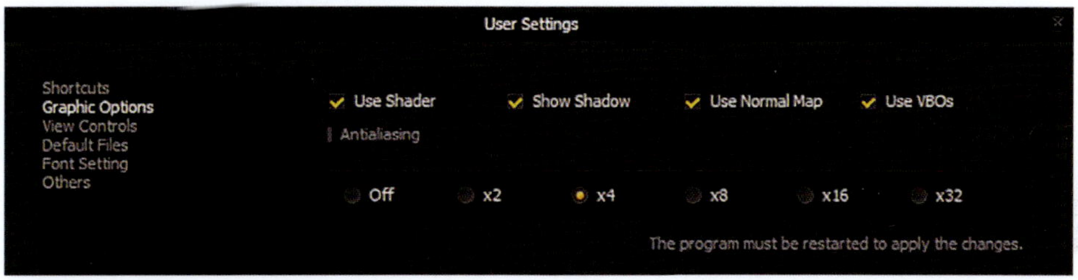

Figure 24-3. User Settings Graphics

The Show Shadow option, when selected, will cause the Avatar's shadow to show in the 3D Window by default. This is an option that can be changed within the program at any time. You might want to set this to your most used preference and change it on a per case basis within the program on each project.

Anti-aliasing is the process of smoothing the outline of objects. The edges of objects can appear pixelated, if they aren't smoothed. Smoothing does come at a price, as your rendering speed will become slower with this option selected.

The Use Normal Map and Use VBOs settings are currently undefined by MD.

View Controls

Figure 24-4. User Settings View Controls

The View Controls section includes your default settings for panning, zooming and rotating. These settings were covered in detail in *Chapter 3 - Getting Started in MD.*

The last item is Pop-Up. MD has an extensive menu system that is available by right-clicking in the application. If you prefer something other than a right click to activate these menus, you can change it to something else.

Default Files

There are a number of file paths that MD stores and you have the option to change. The Avatar & Garment is the project file path that opens when you first open the program. The Materials are paths to saved custom fabrics and stitching. The Simulation Property is where .smp files are saved. Auto Save is where MD will periodically save your project as you're working. This path is used to recover files, if you encounter a crash. The custom Color Pallet is where MD will save the custom color pallets that you create in the program.

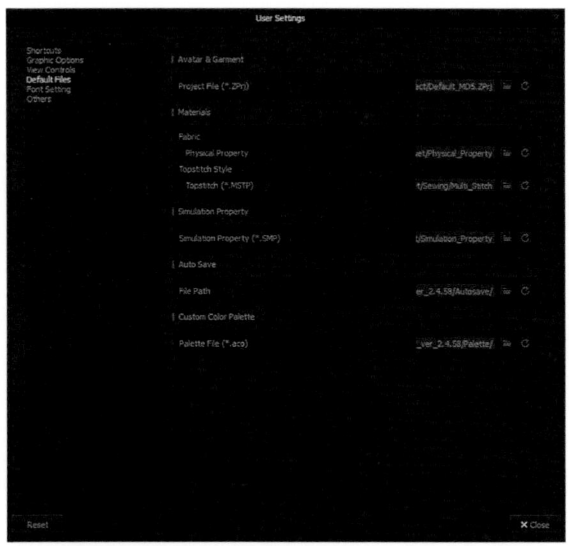

Figure 24-5. User Settings Default Files

Font Setting

Figure 24-6. User Settings Font Setting

You can change the font family and size using the Font Setting options. This changes it throughout the entire program.

Others

Others is a catch-all category for various other settings. The first is Arrangement, where you can set the Default Arrangement Shape Type and the Default Arrangement Point Size. The point size is the size of the blue dots that surround the Avatar when using arrangement points in the 3D Window.

The Pattern section has the Default Particle Distance size. Remember to keep the default low, to reduce computer resource usage while designing.

The Mesh section designates whether your patterns are created by default with quads or tris. If you want good simulations, leave this set to Triangle.

Figure 24-7. User Settings Others

You can change the Unit size in MD from millimeter to centimeter or inch.

The Auto Save Time Interval is the number of minutes between automatic saves by MD. This is very important, if you have a system failure.

The View Point sets the Default Axis Y Position and Default Axis X Angle. Unless you are an experienced user, these are better left alone.

The last section is the Gizmo, which we discussed in *Chapter 4 - 3D Garment Window*.

Button Bars

At the top of the 2D Pattern and 3D Garment windows are button bars. You can control what is displayed on these by selecting -

Display > 3D Toolbars or 2D Toolbars

RC on the bar > Check/Uncheck

My Preferences

The MD preference defaults are pretty good. For the most part, you really don't need to change anything to work in the program. However, I like to be as efficient as possible, so there are some things I change.

Arrow Key Movement

I like to use my arrow keys on the keyboard to nudge points over, rather than dragging them. Dragging is very imprecise and when you want to move the left side of something the exact same as the right, the arrow keys are a better option.

Preferences > 2D pattern Window Properties

The Property Editor will now display all the options. There is a setting here for Arrow Key Movement. It defaults to 10 and I change this to 1. Be aware that this setting does not hold consistently. When you close and open a file, you may have to set it again.

Particle Distance

The default Particle Distance is 20. This can result in rough fabric simulations, so I set my default to 15. Keep in mind that I have a fairly robust computer. The Particle Distance can be set to different amounts for every single pattern. If you are working with a very large pattern, it's a good idea to set this quite high, even higher than the default 20, while you are roughing out your design. You can always lower it for your final work.

Shortcut Keys

Shortcuts are not a priority when you are just learning a program. However, there are some things you will do constantly, even when you are just getting started. The buttons at the top of the 2D Window are easy to use, but eventually you're going to want to speed things up a bit. I like to keep my right hand on the mouse and my left on the keyboard. I put the most used tools easily accessible to my left hand. Here are the changes to shortcuts that I make:

2D Pattern > Edit > Edit Curve Point > C (this deletes the Edit Curvature shortcut, which I never use anyway)

2D Pattern > Edit > Edit Pattern Z

2D Pattern > Edit > Transform Pattern A

2D Pattern > Edit > Add Point/Split Line X

Sewing > Edit Sewing > V

Sewing > Segment Sewing > D

Sewing > Free Sewing > F

Sewing > M:N Segment Sewing > E

Sewing > M:N Free Sewing > R

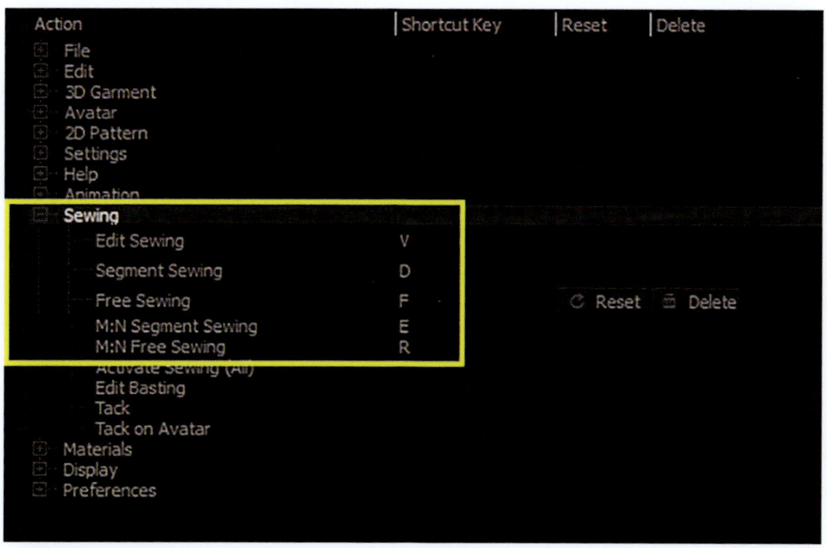

Figure 24-8. My Shortcut Changes

Now the most used tools are easily accessible to your left hand. If you are left-handed, you may want to swap these out so your right hand has access to these tools quickly.

Chapter 24 Quiz

1) You can choose to display or hide buttons at the top of the 3D and 2D Windows.

❍ True ❍ False

2) If you change a shortcut, what happens to the mouse hover tooltip (choose one)?

❍ A. The tooltip shows the default shortcut.

❍ B. The tooltip is no longer shown.

❍ C. The tooltip updates with the new shortcut.

3) You can overwrite, reset or delete almost every keyboard shortcut.

❍ True ❍ False

4) You can change the size of the arrangement points displayed in the 3D Window.

❍ True ❍ False

Chapter 25 - Animation

Marvelous Designer has two modes, Simulation mode and Animation mode. You can switch between the two modes using the drop-down button in the upper right of the program. The layout of these two modes is very different.

As you know, you can drape your cloth using the Simulate button in the Simulation mode. Your avatar and all props will stay fixed. In Animation mode your cloth and the avatar will animate and interact during the animation.

Figure 25-1. Animation Mode

Animation Mode

Some tips that MD offers to make your animations succeed include using elastic to snug garments to the Avatar, increasing the friction on the Avatar, using pins and adjusting the fabric properties of the pattern.

It's a lot of fun watching your avatars walk around in your garments. I can sit here looping the animations over and over and it never gets old. However, you can't model out a scene like you could in other 3D modeling programs. You're also limited to the few MD walking animations and avatars, unless you import your own.

Making an Animation

To animate, you need to clothe one of the MD default avatars in Simulation mode. Currently there are joint motion files for Female_A, Female_B, Male_A and Male_B. To create an animation, switch to Animation mode. Each MD Avatar has walk cycles available to choose from.

File > Open > Joint Motion

You'll see directories for each of the MD avatars. Open the directory for the Avatar you've used and select one of the walk cycles. You must select a cycle labeled for the avatar you are using or you will get an error. Each cycle is titled with a brief description of what happens. These cycles can be from about 400 frames to almost 2000 frames. They are all quite different. For some reason, there are more cycles available for the male avatars than the females.

MD will automatically change your Simulation Quality to Complete for doing animation.

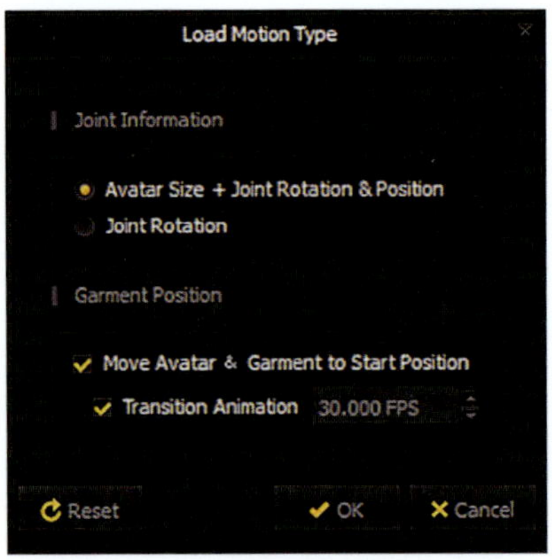

Figure 25-2. Load Motion Type Dialog

Once you've chosen a file, a Load Motion Type dialog will open. If the Avatar in the motion file has been scaled in size, select Avatar Size + Joint Rotation & Position. The Avatar's size will be changed during the animation. If the Avatar size isn't different, select Joint Rotation.

MD can move the Avatar & Garment to the Start Position. If you check this, the avatar will be moved and you can't get it back to the center of the floor plane. Just make sure that you save your project before doing animation, just in case you need to work on it later. The motion defaults to a 30 FPS Transition Animation and that works well.

After you click OK, you'll see that two cycles have been added to the timeline. The first one is Transition and this will move your Avatar to the back of the scene to position it properly before the walk cycle begins. The second cycle is the walk cycle.

The Avatar animation cycles have been pre-baked for you. Now you have to create the garment animation. To do this, select the Record button.

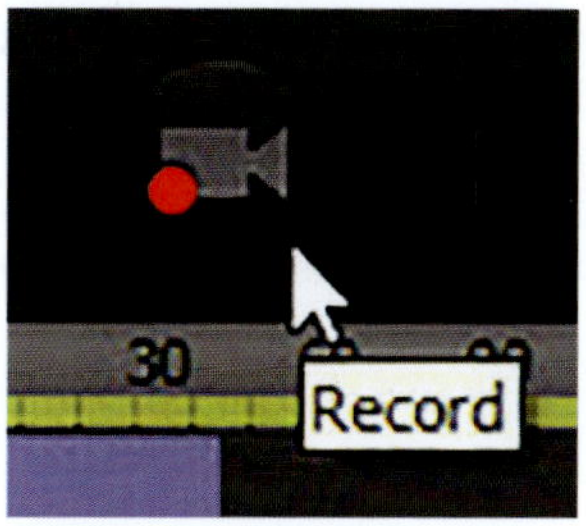

Figure 25-3. Record Button

A third cycle will be added to the timeline and the animation recording will begin. The speed of this process is dependent on your computer and it can take a bit of time. If bad things happen, like pants falling down, you can stop the recording. Go back into Simulation mode and make any necessary adjustments to correct the problem. Then come back to Animation mode and try it again.

Once the recording has completed, you can play with the animation a bit. The Animation Editor is located at the bottom of the program. It includes some button controls and the timeline. You can scrub your animation by dragging the pointer, the vertical red line, on the timeline.

There are the typical video playback controls there for you to Play, Rewind, Fast Forward and Loop. You can adjust the Frame Stepping and Scene Time Warp settings to change the playback.

Make sure to reset your animation to the beginning before returning to Simulation mode or your Avatar will not be in the "A" pose.

Chapter 25 Quiz

1) You can make the avatar walk in Simulation and Animation mode.

❍ True ❍ False

2) You have to load an avatar motion file before you can animate garments.

❍ True ❍ False

3) MD includes several motion files for all the default avatars.

❍ True ❍ False

4) You can model static objects in MD to add to your scene for animation.

❍ True ❍ False

Chapter 26 - Projects

Now it's time to put your new learned skills to the test! I've taught you everything you need to know to make amazing things in MD.

None of these projects are simple. They can't be completed quickly and all of them require you to really think throughout the process. The goal is for you to finish the projects having learned how MD really works when creating actual CG garments. You will find future work much less intimidating, once you've practiced with these projects.

The projects are in order of basic to more advanced. At the beginning of project #1 and #2, you'll find a list of the techniques and tools used in the project. References to the location of the technique or tool in the book are provided.

In projects #3 through #5, the techniques and tools table is simply a list without book references. The list will include only those items that were not covered in prior projects.

The projects do build on each other, so I suggest you start with project #1 and progress from there. The instructions will be quite detailed with lots of images in the simple projects. As we advance, you'll find the instructions become somewhat vague, requiring you to tap into your new skills.

In many cases, I won't give you the measurements you need. I will tell you how to get those measurements yourself. This is the best way for you to learn and be able to recreate these techniques with any avatar, not just the one used in the project.

Some projects require assets to complete. Those assets are available for free on my FearlessMakers.com website. You'll also find all the images in a large format on the site.

You can download my actual MD Project file for every project, too. You can refer to that, if you have difficulty with the instructions.

Project #1 - Starflower Quilt Block

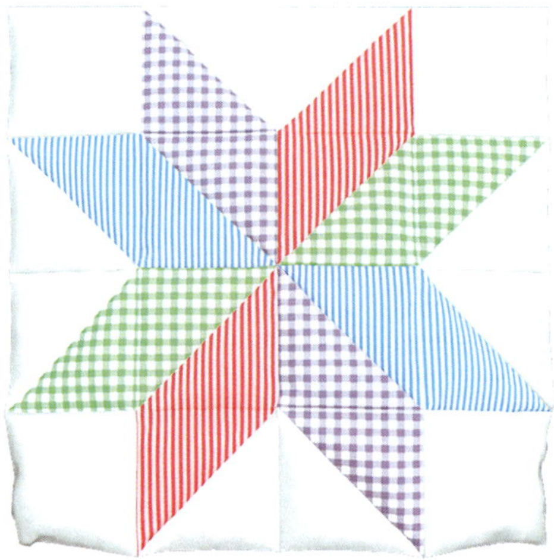

Figure 1. Starflower Quilt Block Complete

This project is a real quilt block design. If you were making a full quilt, you would combine many of these completed blocks to make it the correct size for your bed.

Techniques & Tools

Create Rectangle	Page 46	Internal Line	Page 59
Cut & Sew	Page 67	Segment Sewing	Page 80
Pattern Rotation	Page 51	Mirror Paste	Page 71
M:N Segment Sewing	Page 83	Reset Pattern Arrangement	Page 127
Hide Pattern	Page 27	Pressure	Page 119
Assign Fabric	Page 76	Edit Texture	Page 108
Freeze Pattern	Page 27	Fabric Color	Page 100

Assets from Fearless Makers

- ❑ Starflower Final Project File
- ❑ Texture Image - Gingham in green
- ❑ Texture Image - Gingham in purple
- ❑ Texture Image - Stripe in blue
- ❑ Texture Image - Stripe in red

Instructions

You can ignore the 3D Window until step 15. We will be working in the 2D Window until then.

1. Create a Rectangle that is 100 x 100 mm in the 2D Window.

2. Copy and paste the rectangle to the right of the original in the 2D Window. Hold shift while dragging to keep it aligned.

3. Create an Internal Line diagonally across the square.

4. Cut & Sew the diagonal line (Figure 2 burgundy seam line pair).

5. Sew the two blocks to each other in the middle with Segment Sewing. (Figure 2 blue seam line pair)

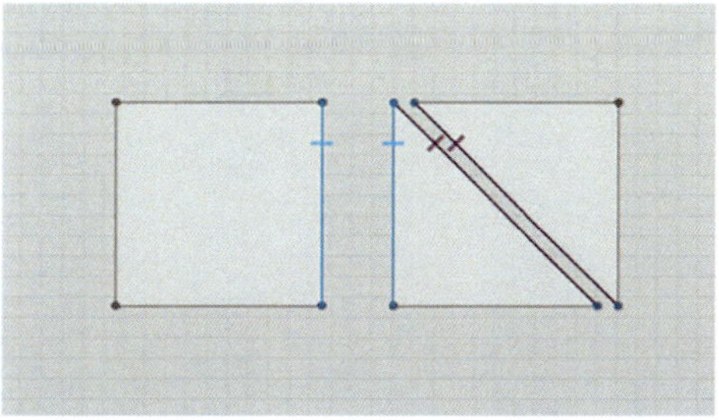

Figure 2. Steps 1-5

6. Select the split block with the Transform tool and copy/paste it twice under the others in the 2D Window (Figure 3)

7. Sew the blocks to each other with Segment Sewing. (Figure 3)

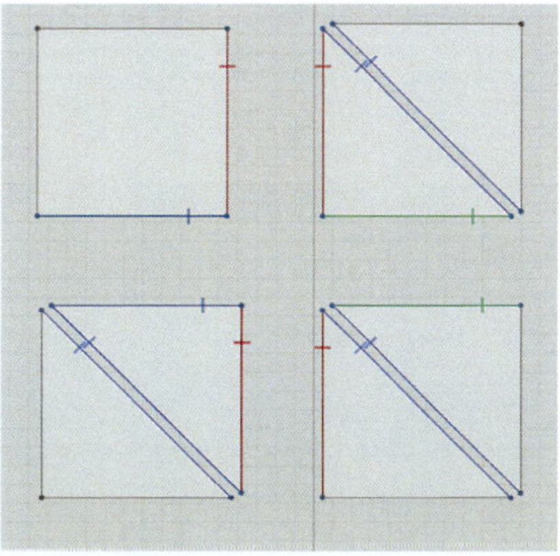

Figure 3. Steps 6-7

8. Select all four blocks in the 2D Window, using the Transform tool, copy and paste under the originals. (Figure 4)

9. Rotate the new set so that the uncut block is in the lower left corner using the Transform tool in the 2D Window. (Figure 4)

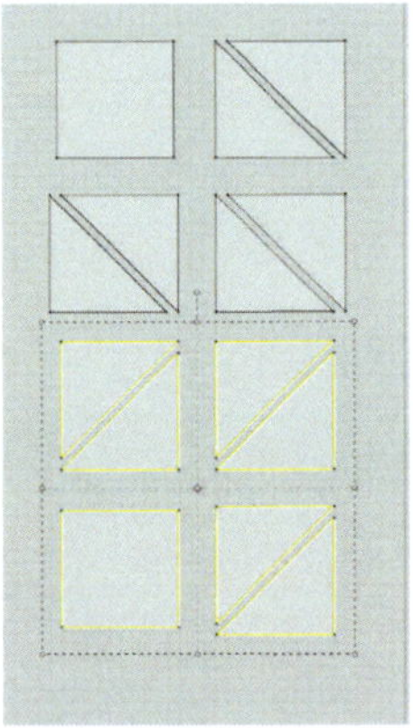

Figure 4. Steps 8-9

10. Sew the two sets together in the middle with Segment Sewing. (Figure 5)

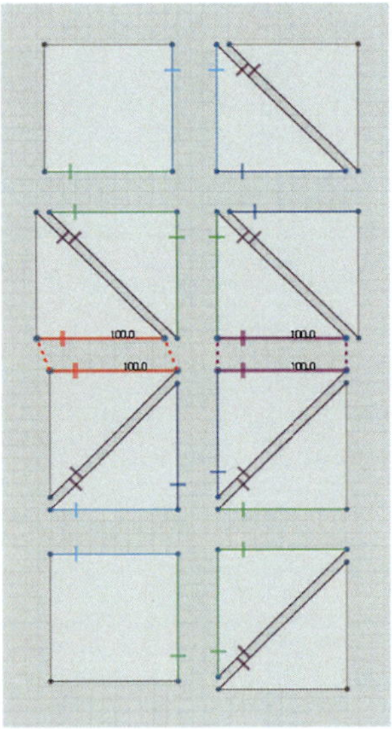

Figure 5. Step 10

11. Select all the patterns in the 2D Window with the Transform tool and copy, Mirror Paste them to the right of the originals. (Figure 6)

Figure 6. Step 11

12. Sew the blocks down the middle with Segment Sewing. (Figure 7)

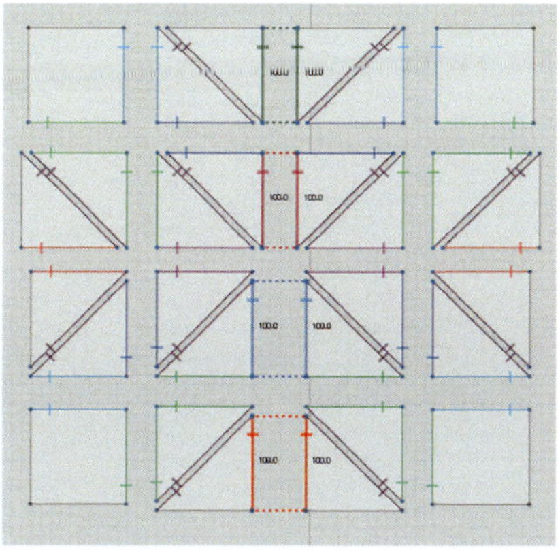

Figure 7. Step 12

13. Create four new fabrics, so now you have five fabrics on the Fabrics tab in the Object Browser. In the Property Editor, change the Color on every fabric so they are all different.

14. Assign the fabrics to the patterns as shown in the image. You can drag and drop the fabric on the pattern in the 2D Window or use one of the other assign fabric techniques. (Figure 8)

Figure 8. Steps 13-14

15. Figure 9 shows the layout of the patterns in the 3D Window. Because of the rotation and mirroring, the patterns are not lined up properly here and they don't match the 2D Window. We can correct this in one step.

Use the Reset 2D Arrangement(all) (located in the 3D Window toolbar) to arrange them to match the 2D Window.

Figure 9. Step 15

16. Now we need to create a holder for simulating. Create a rectangle that is 400 mm wide and 20 mm tall. Place it above all the other patterns in the 2D and 3D Windows.

17. Freeze the holder in the 3D Window and sew the top row of blocks to the bottom of the holder in the 2D Window using the M:N Segment Sewing tool. (Figure 10 - 3D Window left, 2D Window right)

Figure 10. Steps 16-17

18. Make sure you have Show 3D Threads toggled on in the 3D Window. Check all of your sewing in the 3D Window to make sure it looks correct.

19. Simulate. (Figure 11)

20. In the 2D Window, select all of the blocks (not the holder) and Layer Clone Under. These new patterns will be the back of the quilt. Place them to the right of the originals in the 2D Window and assign one fabric to all of them, so it is one solid color.

21. With the cloned layer selected, move them with the Gizmo in the 3D Window so they are lined up a little behind the top layer and then Simulate.

Figure 11. Steps 18-19

22. Select the top layer of blocks (front of quilt) and set the Pressure to 10 in the Property Editor. Select the bottom layer of blocks (back of quilt) and set the Pressure to -10 (negative). (Figure 12)

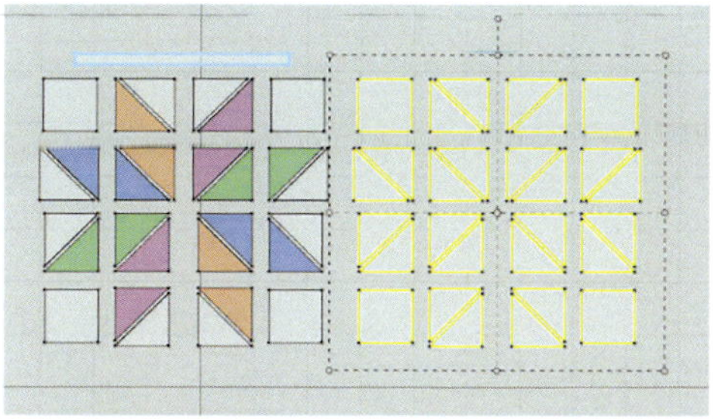

Figure 12. Steps 20-22

23. Make sure your 3D display is set to Thick Textured Surface and simulate. (Figure 13)

Figure 13. Step 23

24. Hide the holder in the 3D Window.

25. Apply image textures to your fabrics to replace the colors. Scale and transform them using the Edit Texture tool to fit the design.

26. Shift select all of the fabric in the Object Browser and change the Physical Property Preset to Cotton in the Property Editor.

27. Simulate

28. You're done with your first project. Great work! (Figure 1)

Project #2 - 1960's Tent Dress

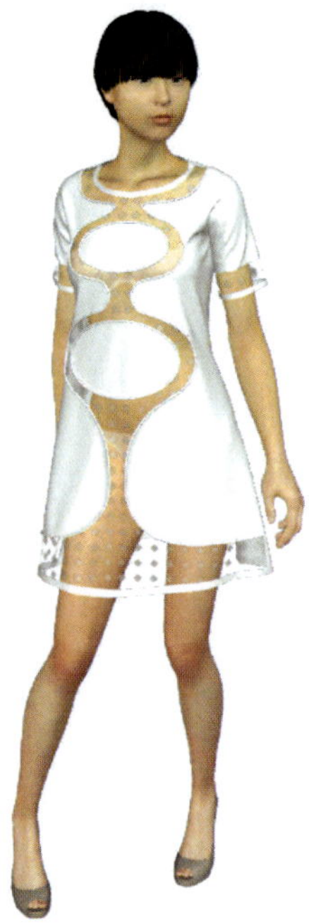

Figure 1. Tent Dress from 1960's

Our next project is a modified tent dress. The inspiration for this comes from a dress designed by André Courréges in September 1967.

As you can see, it was quite revealing and the model's body could be clearly seen through the transparent material.

Feel free to substitute an opaque fabric, if you would prefer something more modest.

Techniques & Tools

Create Polygon	Page 45	Tracing Patterns	Page 113
Clone as Symmetric	Page 72	Free Sewing	Page 80
M:N Free Sewing	Page 84	Arrangement Points	Page 122
Necklines	Page 170	Constrain Editing	Page 48
Internal Lines	Page 59	Internal Circles	Page 61
Transform Pattern Tool	Page 51	Merge	Page 73
Cut & Sew	Page 67	Fabrics	Page 96
Create Rectangle	Page 46	Segment Sewing	Page 80
M:N Segment Sewing	Page 83	Superimpose Side	Page 128
History Panel	Page 20	Piping	Page 188
Pose Avatar	Page 219	Snapshot	Page 30

Assets from Fearless Makers

- ❑ 1960's Tent Dress Final Project File
- ❑ PatternMaker PRO Tent Dress Front Draft
- ❑ PatternMaker PRO Tent Dress Back Draft
- ❑ PatternMaker PRO Sleeve Draft
- ❑ Texture Image - Clover with Transparency

Instructions

This project uses the MD default Female Avatar A. The patterns were drafted using her measurements. Create a new project, open the Avatar Editor and click her picture to add her to the scene.

Dress

1. Trace the front pattern draft. Move it out of the way.

2. Switch the image rectangle to the back pattern draft and trace it. Move the back out of the way.

3. Switch the image to the sleeve pattern. Trace the sleeve pattern draft.

Note that on the sleeve draft, the front of the sleeve is on the left and the back is on the right. This sleeve will not connect to the front and back patterns you have just traced, it goes to the other side. (Figure 2)

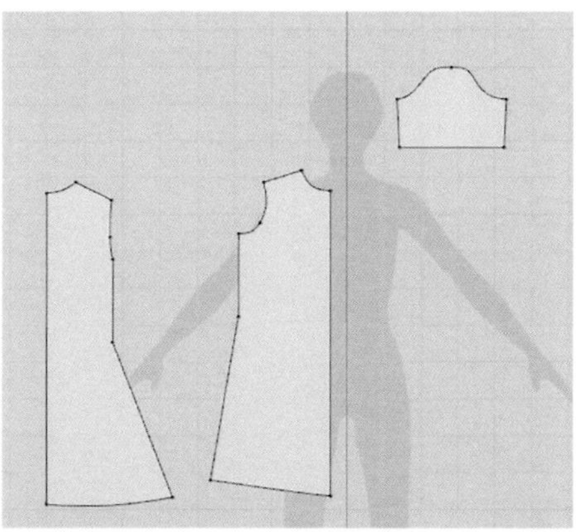

Figure 2. Steps 1-3

4. Select all patterns and Clone as Symmetric Pattern. Now you have all the patterns. Arrange your sleeves so the front side of the sleeve is above the front pattern and the back side is above the back pattern. (Figure 3)

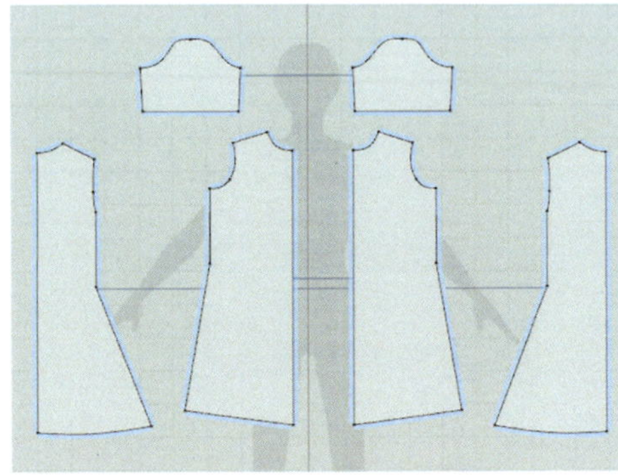

Figure 3. Step 4

5. Sew the front and back dress sides together (everything under the armhole), using the Free Sewing tool. (Figure 4)

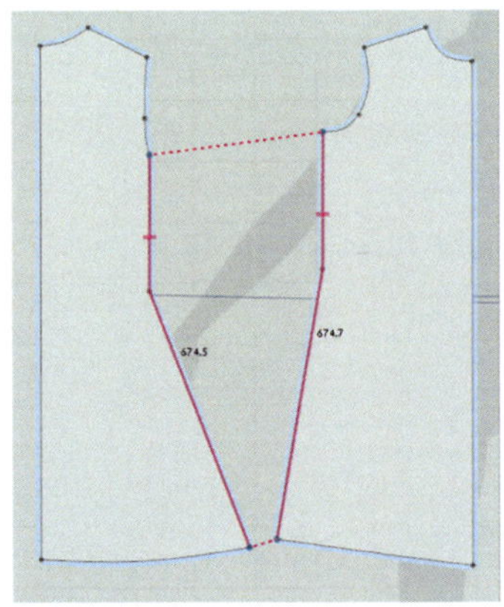

Figure 4. Step 5

6. Sew the shoulders together using the Segment Sewing tool. Remember the notches will be opposite for these. Toggle on the Show 3D Threads and check the 3D Window to verify. (Figure 5)

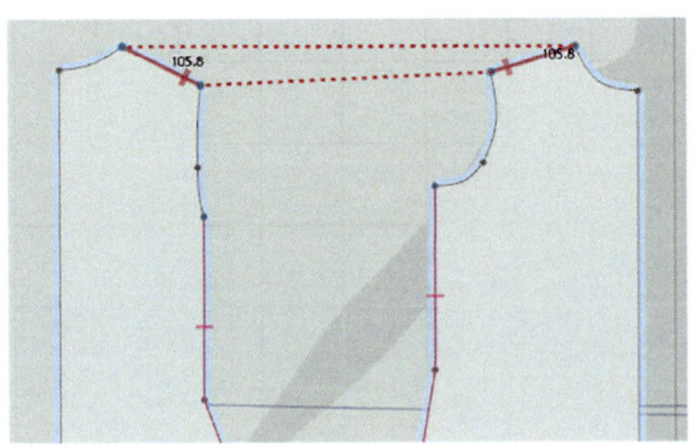

Figure 5. Step 6

7. Sew the center front and center back seams. (Figure 6)

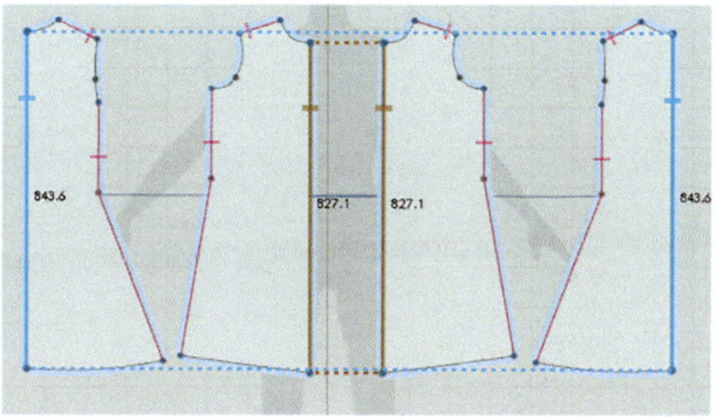

Figure 6. Step 7

8. Sew the underarm seam on the sleeves (the sides of the sleeve pattern). (Figure 7)

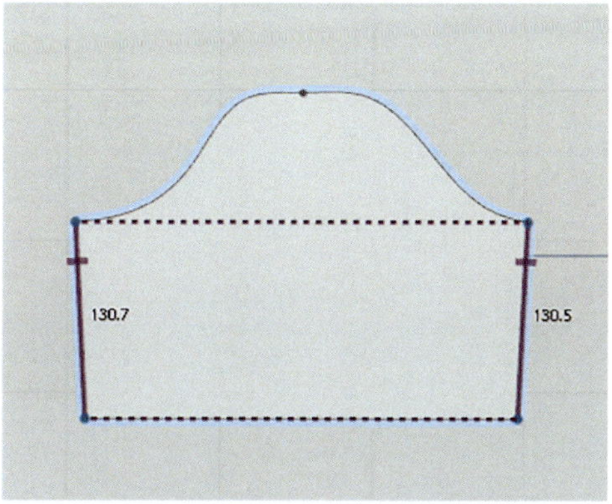

Figure 7. Step 8

9. Use the M:N Free Sewing tool to sew the sleeve cap to the front and back armhole. (Figure 8)

You need to pay attention to where you start the seam on the sleeve. Start at the front side of the sleeve. Select the entire sleeve cap as the M seam, hit Enter. Start the N seam at the armpit of the front, follow the armhole all the way to the shoulder and stop it. Now start at the shoulder of the back and go down to the armpit, stop and hit Enter.

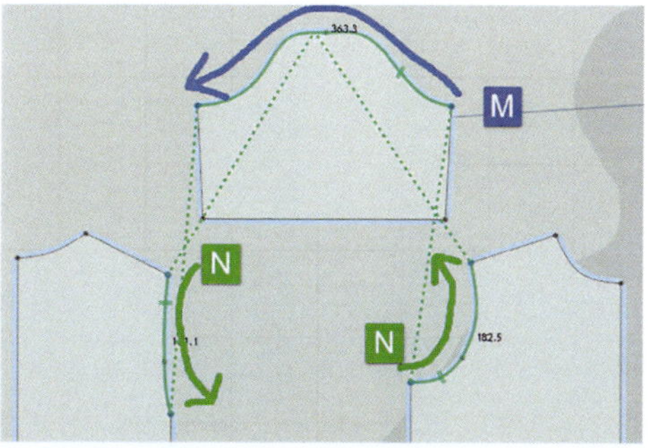

Figure 8. Step 9

10. Arrange your patterns in the 3D Window using Arrangement Points.

11. Verify your seams are correct and Simulate. (Figure 9)

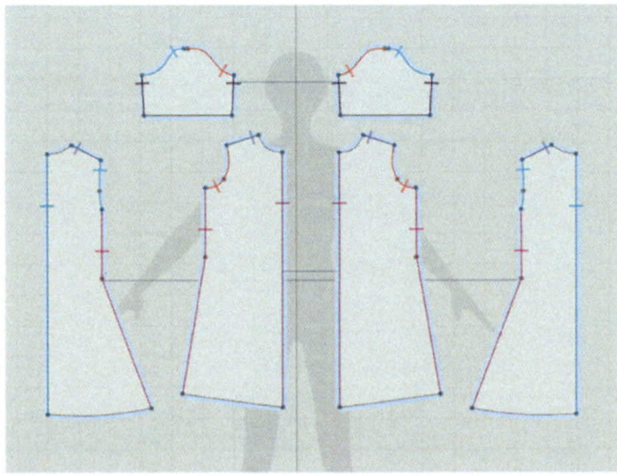

Figure 9. Step 11

Modify the Neckline

12. Refer to *Chapter 17 - Around the Neck* to view the necklines illustration. You want a neckline on the dress that is somewhere between a Round and a Boat shape. Use Chalk to draw on the pattern to visualize your new neckline. (Figure 10)

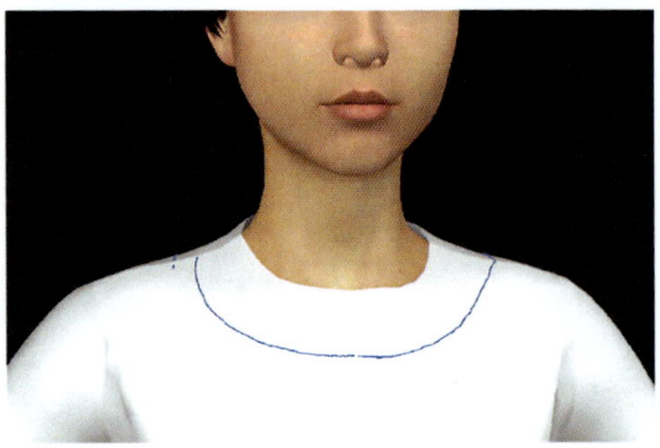

Figure 10. Step 12

13. You can adjust the neckline by moving the shoulder points. As you move the points, hold Control so you don't lose the angle of the shoulder line. Remember that the shoulder seams of the front and back of the dress must remain the same length. When you adjust the center front and center back lines, hold Shift to keep the line straight vertically as you drag downwards.

Dress Cutouts

14. Now it's time to create all the pattern shaping using Internal Lines and Internal Circles. Draw out Internal Circles and then use the Transform Pattern tool to turn them into ellipses. It is okay to have the circles hang outside the pattern. (Figure 11)

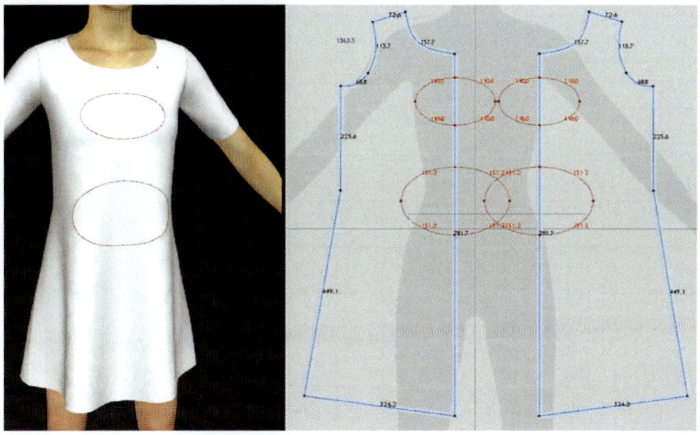

Figure 11. Step 14

15. I copied the ellipses and pasted them over the originals. Using the Transform Pattern tool, I scaled them up proportionally. These will be used as guides for drawing.(Figure 12)

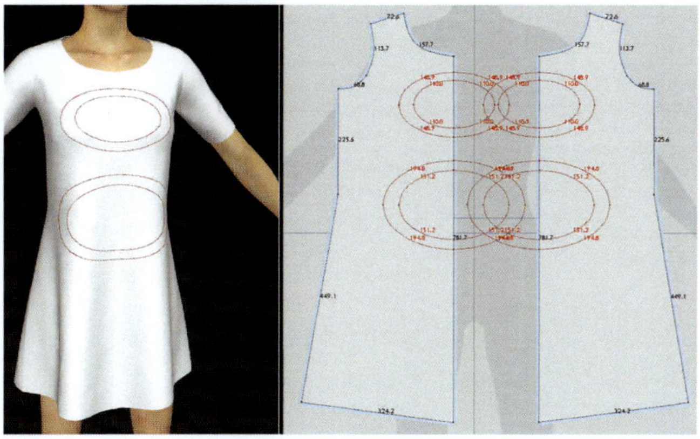

Figure 12. Step 15

16. Use the Internal Polygon/Line tool to draw the vertical cut shape down the front. I used the enlarged ellipses from Step 15 as guides to create nice curves. (Figure 13)

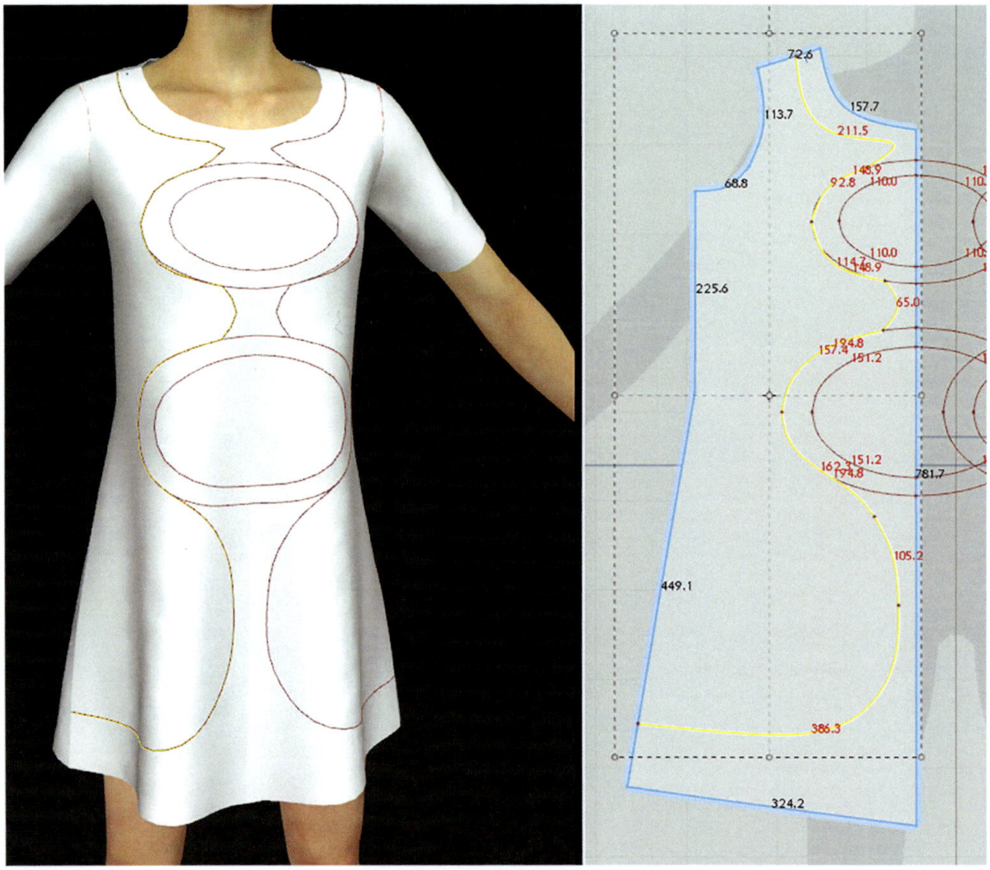

Figure 13. Step 16

17. When you are done, delete all of your guide shapes from Step 15. Then Cut & Sew all internal lines.

18. You can right click, Merge the right and left ellipse shapes at center front so they are one pattern (#1 and #2 in Figure 14), but MD won't let you Merge the other piece (#3 in Figure 14). You'll have to leave that in two pieces, one for each side.

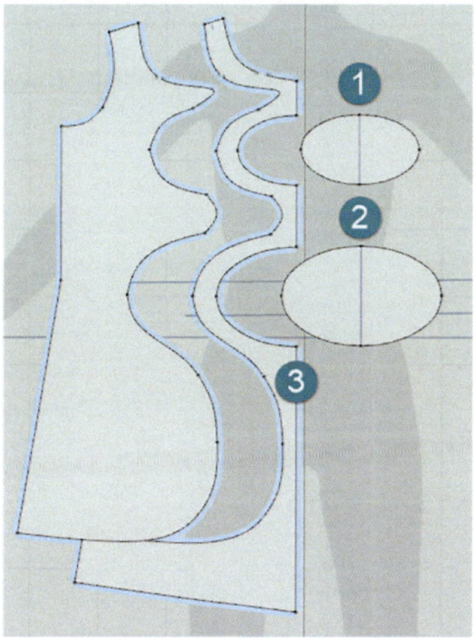

Figure 14. Step 17-18

19. Draw two internal lines across the sleeve and Cut & Sew. (Figure 15)

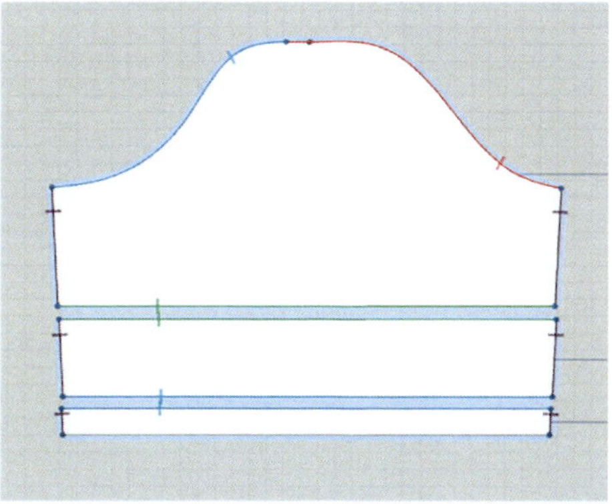

Figure 15. Step 19

20. Create two fabrics for your dress. In the original, one was a transparent plastic with a design on it and the other was solid.

Apply the clover image as a texture or you can substitute a color fabric with the Opacity turned down instead. I added specular color in white to make my fabrics appear to be more plastic-ish.

Apply your fabrics to the dress patterns. (Figure 16)

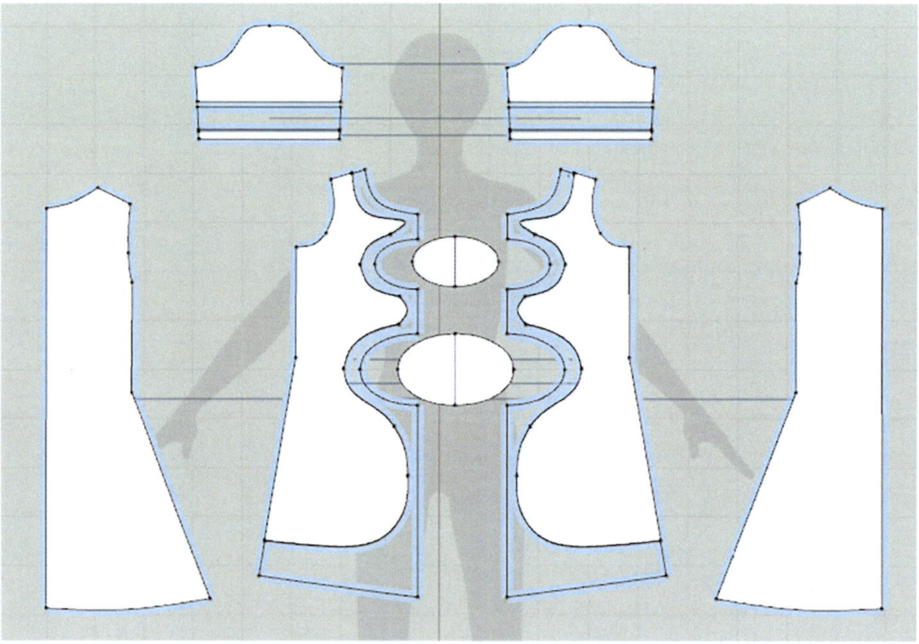

Figure 16. Step 20

Banding

21. Measure the distance of the front and back patterns at the hemline. Create a rectangle that is that distance wide and 15 mm tall. This is a hem band.

22. Sew the hem band ends (short sides of rectangle) together with Segment Sewing.

23. Sew the hem band to the hemline of the dress with the seam at center back. You will use the M:N Segment Sewing tool for this. The M seam is the entire edge of the hem band. The N seam is back pattern, front pattern, front pattern,

and back pattern in that order. This places the seam of the hem band at center back.

24. Arrange it in the 3D Window using Superimpose side. Make sure the hem band is not gray, indicating that it flipped over. If it is flipped, right click it in the 3D Window, Flip Normal.

Select the hem band and pull it down with the Gizmo to make sure your seams are correct. Use the History Panel to put it back, then Simulate. (Figure 17)

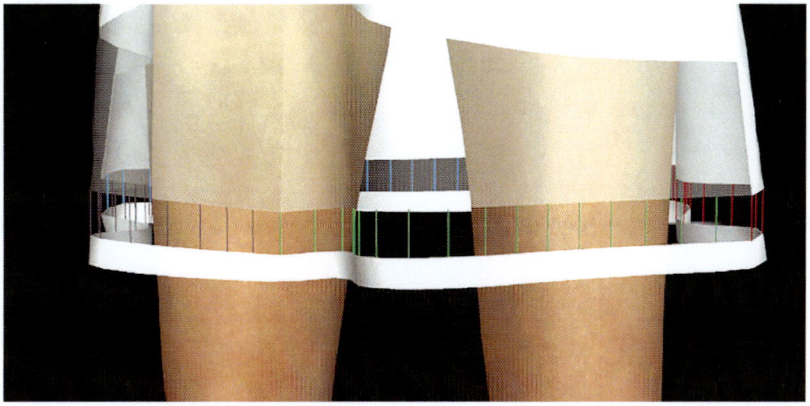

Figure 17. Step 21-24

25. Make a narrow band for the neckline following the same procedure as the hem band. Make it 10mm tall. If the neckband doesn't lay down flat, you can; shorten the length, apply a knit fabric, or lower the particle distance. Any or all of these will help. This is a common problem you will encounter often. (Figure 18)

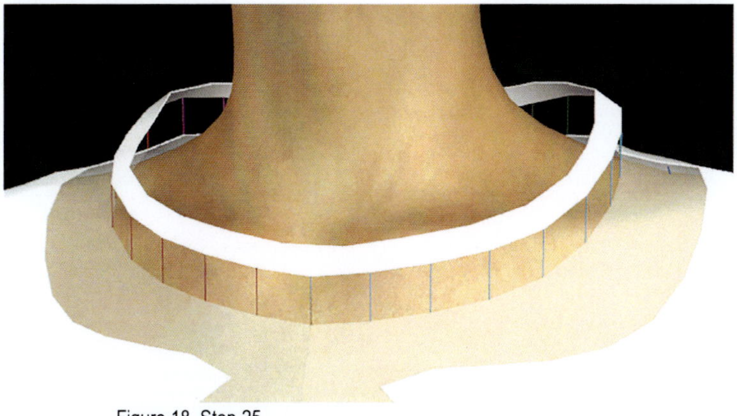

Figure 18. Step 25

Add the Details

26. The dress was originally made of a stiff plastic. Use the Leather or another stiff preset on the dress fabric to make it stand away from the body.

27. Add piping around the ellipses and the shaped line in front. I set my piping to 4 mm wide. (Figure 19)

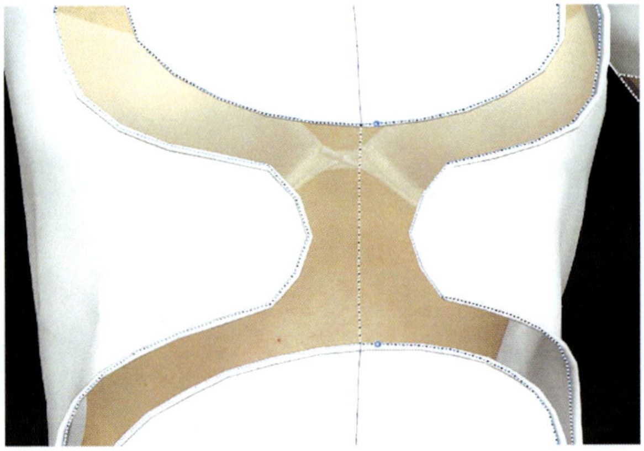

Figure 19. Step 27

28. Lower the Particle Distance as necessary for your final dress simulation.

Pose the Avatar

29. Save your project. open a Pose file for this avatar. You want to look in the Female_A folder. I selected the F_A_pose_04.pos file. Your avatar will morph into her pose.

30. Do a final simulation and re-arrange anything that needs it.

31. Position the avatar in the 3D Window as though you are looking through a camera. Take a 3D Window Snapshot of your final work.

Congratulations, you've finished your first garment project using an avatar. (Figure 1)

Challenge Yourself

Try other cutout designs on this dress. Cut the dress off at the waist and add some shorts for a great summer look. Remove the sleeves and change the neckline to make a fun dress for the beach.

Project #3 - Hero

Figure 1. Hero

Our third project is a hero character and his garments are originals based on patterns from PatternMaker PRO.

I needed an avatar that had a hero physique so I built a custom one. He was created using the Manuel Bastioni add-on for Blender. Visit his website to learn more about this great tool:

www.manuelbastioni.com

New Techniques & Tools

Open Avatar	Bounding Volumes	Arrangement Points
Offset as Pattern	Dragging with Distance	Add Point to Pattern at End
Save Garment	Add Garment	Edit Round Corner
Layer	Unfold Pattern	Additional Thickness
Snap or Button & Buttonhole	Merge	Graphic (2D Texture)
X-Ray Joints	Save Pose	Open Pose - Morph Avatar

Assets from Fearless Makers

- ❑ Hero Final Project File
- ❑ Hero MD Avatar File
- ❑ PatternMaker PRO Bodysuit Draft
- ❑ PatternMaker PRO Cape Draft

- ❑ PatternMaker PRO Sleeve Draft
- ❑ Texture Image - Hero Star for Trunks
- ❑ Specular Map Image - Hero Star for Trunks
- ❑ Texture Image - Leather
- ❑ Graphic Image - Hero Graphic

Instructions

Add the Avatar

1. Create a new project and add the avatar to the scene. I already imported the character into MD and saved it as an avatar for you. No changes are needed, so make sure all the values in the Add Avatar dialog are set to 0.00.

2. The hero avatar comes with a set of measurements that I created so that I could draft the bodysuit, sleeves and cape in PatternMaker PRO. I also created a basic set of Bounding Volumes and Arrangement Points that you can use to place the patterns.

There is one Bounding Volume that you need to make yourself. Create a BV around the avatar's neck and add two Arrangement Points to it. Put one AP at center front and the other at center back. (Figure 2)

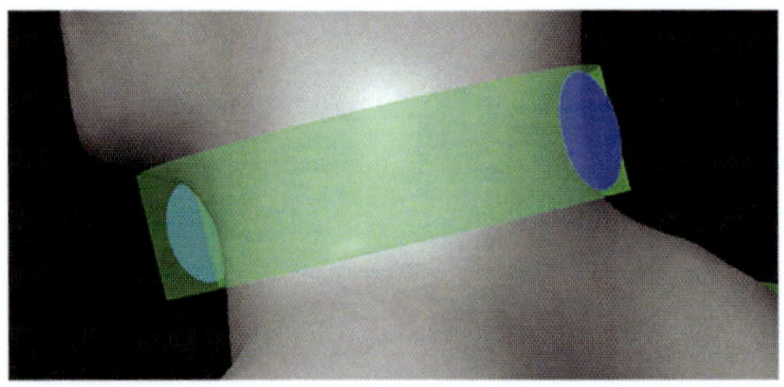

Figure 2. Step 2

Create the Patterns

3. You have three pattern drafts to trace. Ignore the cape pattern for now. Bring in the bodysuit pattern draft and trace it.

You'll notice that there is only one pattern for the front and back. The only difference between them is the neckline. Trace the pattern using the back neckline. Then copy/paste it to the side. This leaves one copy still on the pattern. Adjust the neckline for the front pattern to complete it.

4. Because you traced the bodysuit patterns facing the same way, this front does not attached to this back. Select both and Clone as Symmetric. Now arrange the patterns correctly in the 3D and 2D windows and sew them

together. Arranging the bodysuit is in the 3D Window is challenging because of the narrow legs. Keep the patterns close to the avatar with the 3D Threads to either side of the legs. Simulate the bodysuit.

5. Bring in the sleeve pattern and trace it. I chose not to add the cuff on the pattern. You can include it, if you want.

Make note of the front and back of the sleeve and arrange it to the correct side. Use the M:N Free Sewing tool to sew the full sleeve cap to the front and back armholes on the bodysuit. Sew the sleeve underarm seam. (Figure 3)

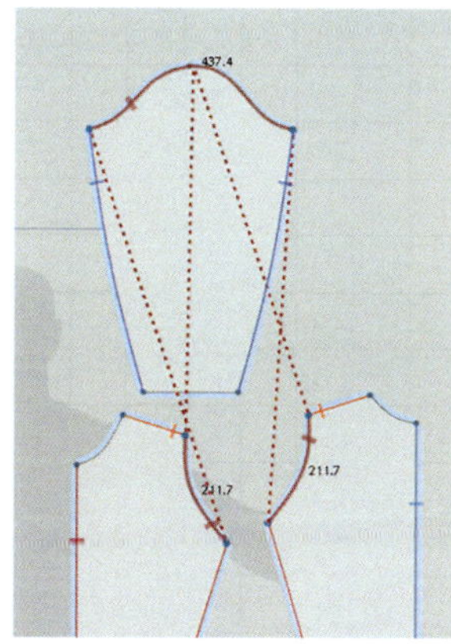

Figure 3. Step 5

6. Use an Arrangement Point to put it into position in the 3D window and Simulate.

7. Right-click it and Clone as Symmetric to create, arrange and sew the other sleeve automatically. Simulate again.

8. The bodysuit and sleeve are very tight fitting and meant for a knit fabric. Create a new fabric and set it to a knit, such as Jersey. Apply to the bodysuit and sleeve.

9. Next you need to create the trunks out of the bodysuit. Use the Chalk tool to draw out where you want the trunks to be. (Figure 4)

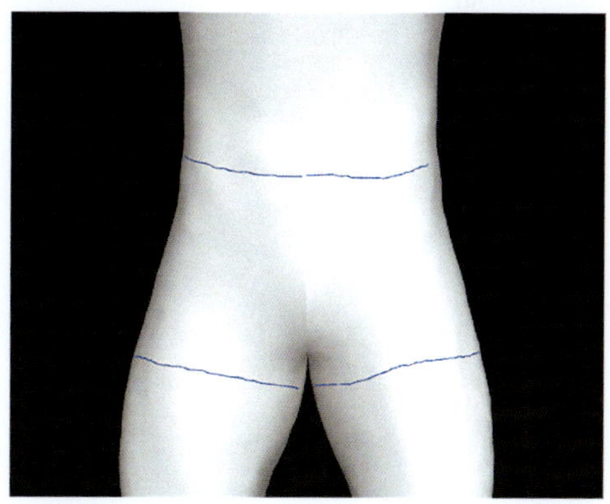

Figure 4. Step 9

10. Using your chalk lines as a guide, add points to the front pattern where the lines hit the pattern edge. You will need four new points; two at center front (waist, leg) and two at the side seam (waist, leg).

Now create the matching points on the back side seam by selecting the Add Point tool and right-clicking. Enter in the same distance that was used on the front for the two side seam points.

This creates the trunk side seam exactly the same length on the front and back. (Figure 5)

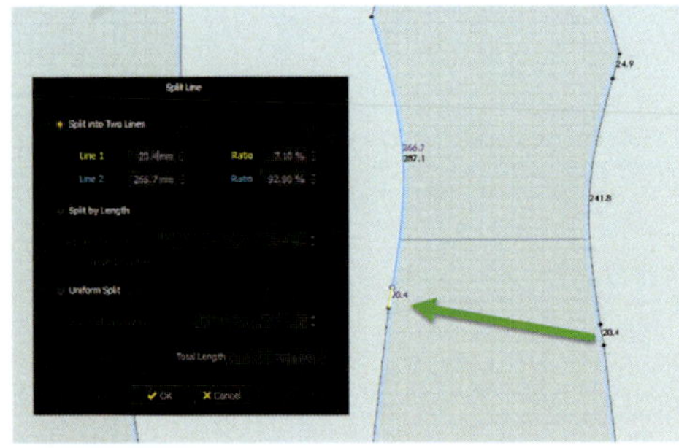

Figure 5. Step 10

Then create the two remaining points on the center back (waist, leg).

11. Create Internal Lines using your new points. Cut & Sew the Internal Lines. Simulate. (Figure 6)

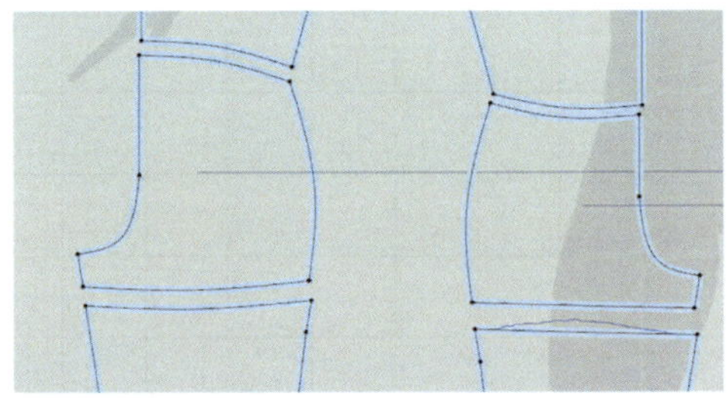

Figure 6. Step 11

Utility Belt

12. Measure the avatar's circumference at the position that you want the utility belt to be. Draft the pattern with that length and a height of 35 mm. Sew the ends together, arrange and Simulate.

13. Create a new fabric using a very stiff preset. Apply that to your belt.

14. Save the project. Delete the avatar and create a new project with nothing in the scene.

Belt Pockets

15. Create a holding piece 100 mm x 20 mm and freeze it in the 3D Window.

16. Create a fabric and set the Back to a different color. I set mine to pink. This will help you visualize the patterns later. Apply this fabric to every pattern you make (except the holder).

17. Create another rectangle 100 mm x 100 mm. Flip the pattern horizontally in the 3D Window. This is the back of the pocket, so we need it flipped with the back facing forward. This will make more sense in a moment. (Figure 7)

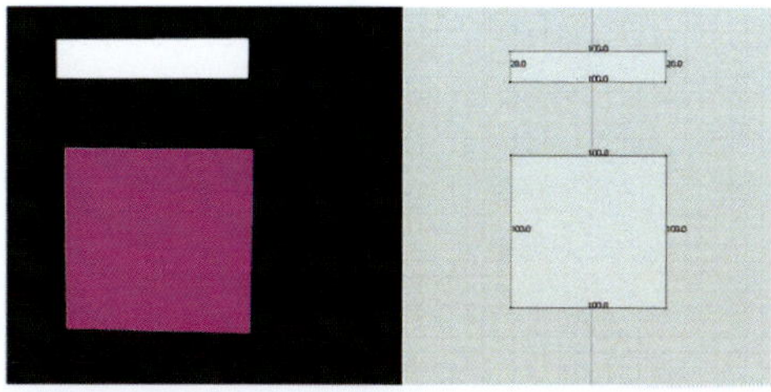

Figure 7. Step 17

18. With the Transform tool, right-click the pattern and Offset as Pattern with a Distance of 25 mm, Unfilled Corners and Internal Lines. (Figure 8)

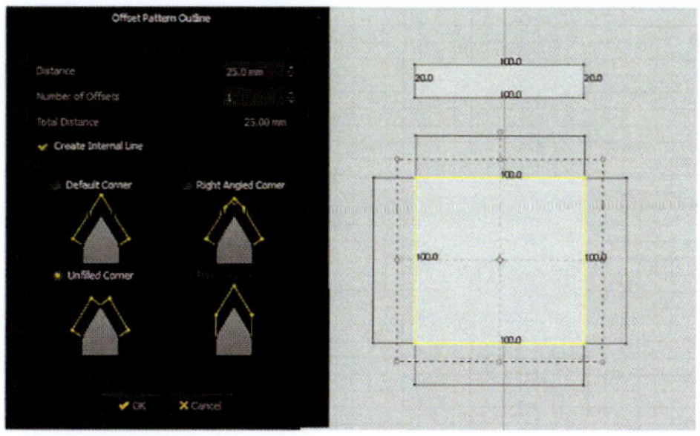

Figure 8. Step 18

19. Select all the new Internal Lines and set the Fold Angle to 0.

20. Select the top segment and start dragging up and right-click. Set the Distance to 50. (Figure 9)

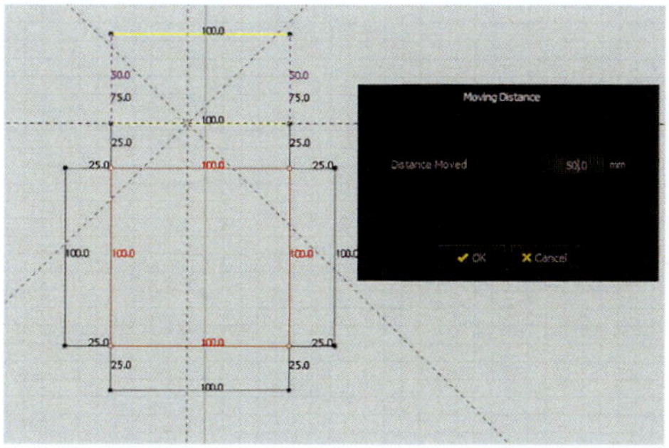

Figure 9. Step 20

21. Sew the corners of the pattern closed. You will need to use the Free Sewing tool for the top corners and stop on the blue dot so the seam lines are equal.

22. Using the Edit Sewing tool, right click the top two corners and select Add Point to Pattern at End. (Figure 10)

23. Create an internal line using those two new points and set the Fold Angle to 0.

24. Draw another rectangle that is 100 mm x 100 mm. This is the front of the pocket.

25. Sew the sides and bottom of the new front rectangle to the outside edges of the back rectangle. Note that because the box is flipped, the notches will sew to the opposite edge.

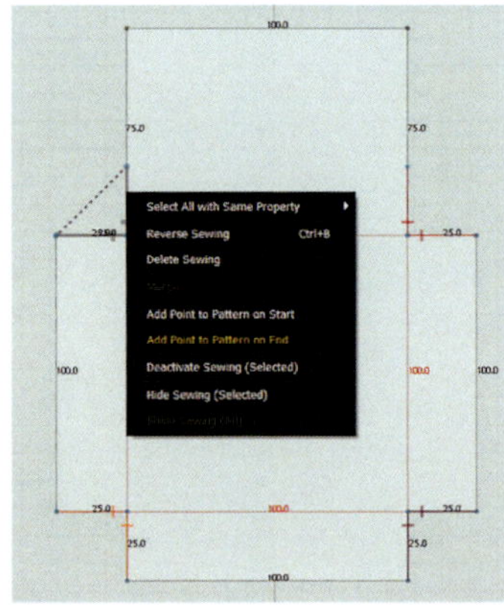

Figure 10. Step 22

26. Sew the back pattern's original top, which is now an internal line, to the bottom of the frozen holder. (Figure 11)

27. Verify your seams in the 3D Window and Simulate. (Figure 12)

28. You should now have a perfect box pocket. (Figure 13)

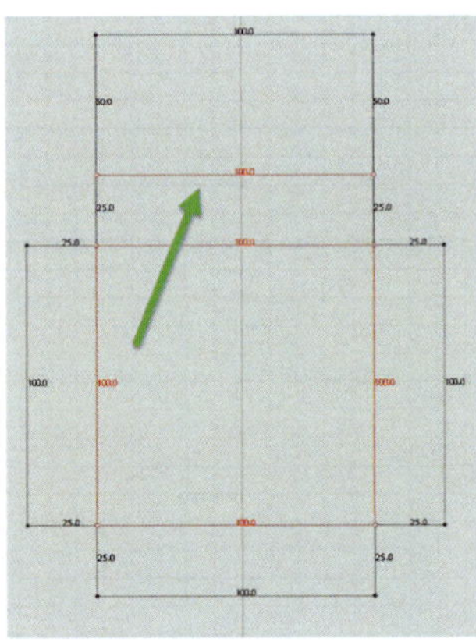

Figure 11. Step 26

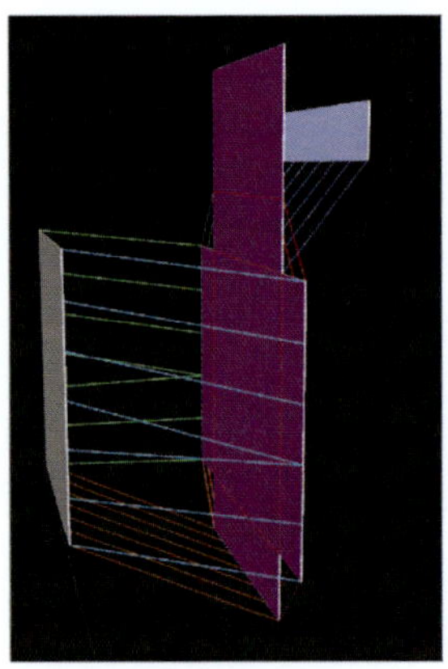

Figure 12. Step 27

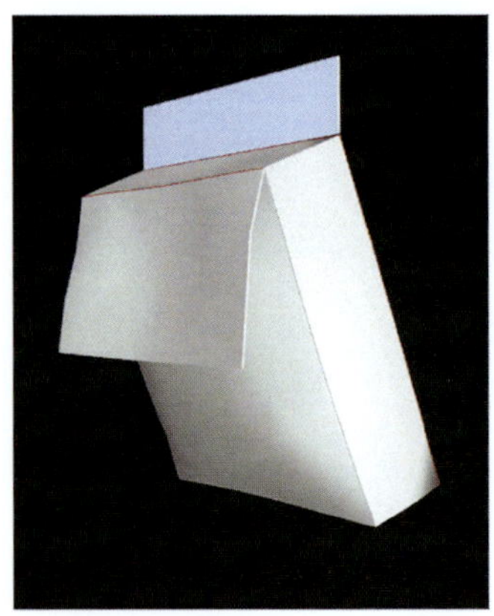

Figure 13. Step 28

29. You will want several different pockets to put on your utility belt. You can make them all individually to practice the technique, or you can copy this one and resize it with the Transform Pattern tool.

30. Save the pocket project. Delete the holder and then save the pocket as a Garment. Close the project and open the hero project again.

Add Garment

31. Select Add Garment and bring your pocket in. Position it next to your utility belt and then sew the pocket to the top of the belt using the free sewing tool.

32. Use the Edit Round Corner tool to soften the corners of the pocket flaps.

33. The pocket may collapse a bit, so you'll want to assign a stiffer fabric. You'll notice that the fabric came in when you added the pocket garment. You can edit that one or delete it and create a new one.

34. If your pockets start flying up off the belt, you may need to add another internal line across the back. Sew that line to the bottom of the belt to hold your pockets down. The pockets will fly up, if you apply a very stiff fabric to them.

35. Sew on as many pockets as you want, but leave some space for the cartridge portion of the belt.

Draft the Cartridge Belt

36. Select a portion of your belt for the cartridge holder. Ideally, the distance will be a multiple of 25. Place points at the top and bottom of the belt at the start and end of the section you have selected. Measure the segment length between the points. Mine was 400 mm.

37. Draw an Internal Line at the start of the cartridge section. Use the Offset as Internal line. Set the distance to 25 mm and keep clicking the Number of Offsets until your entire section is full. (Figure 14)

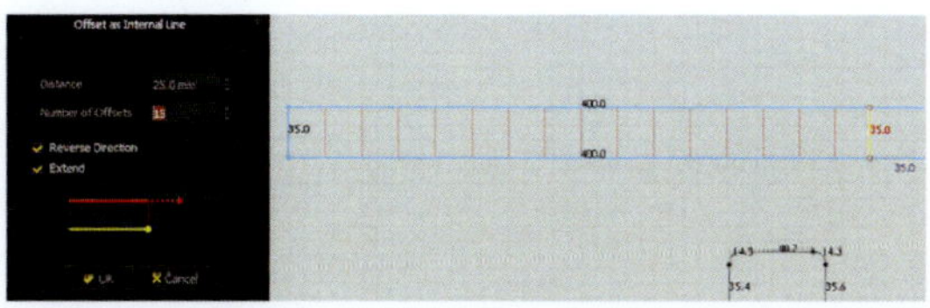

Figure 14. Steps 36-37

38. Create a rectangle that is twice the width as your cartridge section and as tall as the belt.

39. Select one short edge of the rectangle and use the Offset as Internal line again setting the distance to 50 mm. Increase the Number of Offsets to populate the rectangle.

40. Sew all the vertical segments on the belt to the cartridge belt.

41. Create a cotton fabric and assign it to the cartridge belt. Lower the particle distance to about 10. Set the Layer property to 1.

42. Arrange and simulate. When it looks good, switch the Layer property back over to 0. (Figure 15)

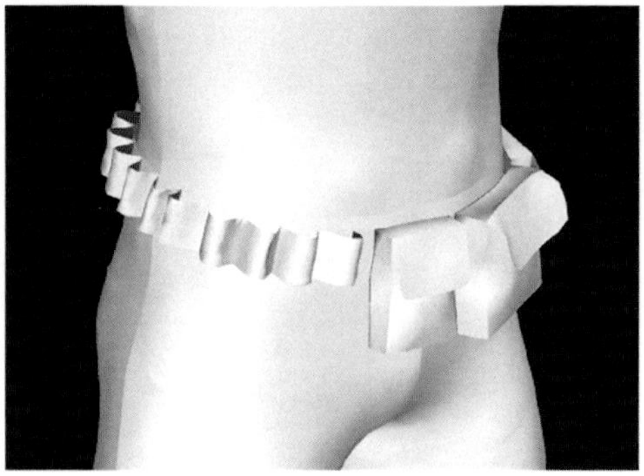

Figure 15. Step 42

The cartridge belt should be the correct size for the ammunition that you will be using. If you are adding guns to the scene, make sure the belt has the correct cartridge size for that gun.

The belt will probably slide around the avatar as you are doing all of this work. Just grab it while simulating and pull it back into place.

When you have knit fabric applied to a garment, it can start to sag with multiple simulations. Turn down the Opacity on your bodysuit and trunks fabric and see if the crotch is falling down. If so, simulate and pull it back up.

43. When everything looks good, freeze all the patterns.

Cape

44. Load the cape pattern and trace it. This is a VERY large pattern. Make note of where the front and back are so you can arrange it properly and then delete the rectangle with the draft image.

45. Raise the Particle Distance on the cape to 40.

46. Unfold the pattern on the center BACK line of the cape.

47. If any of your curves look strange after unfolding, adjust them now.

Neckband

48. Measure the neckline on the cape.

49. Create a rectangle that is the cape neckline width and 20 mm tall.

50. Sew the ends of the neckband. Apply a fabric with the preset Full-Grain Leather to it.

51. Arrange it with the ends in the front, using that new back neck Arrangement Point that you created. Simulate. Freeze the neckband.

52. Sew the cape to the bottom edge of the neckband. Arrange and simulate. The cape weighs a lot, so it will pull your neckband out of shape. When simulating make sure that either the cape or the neckband is frozen from this point forward. (Figure 16)

Figure 16. Step 52

53. With the Edit Pattern tool, select both side seams of the neckband and right-click Offset Pattern Outline with a Distance of 10, Create Internal Line and the Default Corner.

54. The seam is still on the outside edge, so delete it. Sew the new internal lines together. Simulate and the band now has a nice overlap. (Figure 17)

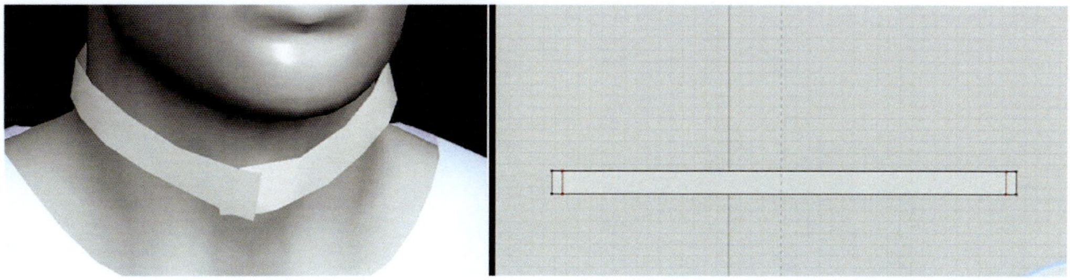

Figure 17. Steps 53-54

55. With the Edit Pattern tool, select the entire edge of the cape. This is everything except the neckline. Offset as Internal Line with a Distance of 10.

56. Make sure you have Thick Textured Surface toggled on in the 3D window. Set the Fold Angle on the Internal Line up closer to 300. This will appear to be a nice hem all the way around the cape.

57. Select the cape and add an Additional Thickness - Rendering value of 2. This adds some weight to the cape.

58. Arrange the cape while simulating to create a nice display. Create a new fabric and apply it. Make it any color you like. I used a Cotton preset.

After it is in place, lower the Particle Distance. Remember this is a huge pattern, so go only as low as your computer can handle.

59. When you like the cape, freeze it to reduce the strain on your computer. Unfreeze everything else so we can add the final details.

Add the Details

60. Add a snap or button at the center front of the neck band. This is where your internal lines are. You can release the seam there after adding the snap, if you desire. (Figure 18)

61. Add snaps or buttons to your pocket flaps on the utility belt pockets. (Figure 19)

Figure 18. Step 60

Figure 19. Step 61

62. Add fake hems using Offset Internal Lines to the wrists, ankles and neckline of the bodysuit. You can also add these to the leg openings and waist of the trunks.

63. You may want to add Additional Thickness Rendering to the trunks so they appear to be over the bodysuit.

Add the Graphic

64. Merge the center front and center back segments of the upper bodysuit to create a one-piece front and back. You will apply a graphic to the front.

65. Use the Graphic (2D Texture) tool to place the outlined star graphic on the front of the bodysuit. Size the graphic and zoom up close to make sure it is centered properly. (Figure 20)

Figure 20. Steps 64-65

66. Finish up details adding additional thickness to anything you like. You may want to add Curved Side Geometry to edges that are visible.

Create fabrics and apply them. I've supplied you with a texture and specular map for the trunks. Set the Specular Color to white, to make the stars extra shiny. There is also a leather texture for you to use on the belt.

Lower the particle distance wherever you think it needs it and Simulate.

Pose the Avatar

67. Save the project. Create a new project, leaving the avatar in the scene. Use the X-Ray Joints to pose the avatar however you want. When finished, save the avatar as a Pose.

68. Open your hero project and Open the Pose file you just created. Your avatar will morph to the final position. Run a simulation and make adjustments until you are satisfied with everything.

69. Take a Snapshot and admire your work. This was not an easy project. Congratulations on completing it. (Figure 1)

Challenge Yourself

If you look closely at the bodysuit pattern, you'll see that it would be nearly impossible to create by just drawing in the 2D Window. Now you understand the shape necessary to create this pattern, you can re-use the design in other projects.

A bodysuit is the basis for lots of different garments. It can be edited into athletic wear, such as jog tops, leggings and bike shorts. It also becomes a leotard or swimsuit with just a few simple changes.

Project #4 - Subway Dress

Figure 1. Subway Dress

This dress is inspired by the one worn by Marilyn Monroe in the movie "The Seven Year Itch" released in 1955. The actual dress sold for $4.6 million in 2011.

In the movie, Ms. Monroe is standing over a subway grate that is blowing air. It caused the pleated dress to flair out and created the iconic image.

New Techniques & Tools

Measuring Avatar	Pattern Drafting	Elastic
Wind	Accordion Pleats	Fold Angle
Select All with Same Property	Adding Garment	

Assets from Fearless Makers

- ❑ Subway Dress Top Garment File
- ❑ Subway Dress Final Project File
- ❑ Avatar Pose File (optional)

Instructions

1. Create a new project and add the default Female Avatar C to the scene. This avatar has a very realistic, detailed texture map. If you find this offensive, toggle

to Avatar Monochrome Surface in the 3D Window.

Dress Top

2. I have created the halter top and torso patterns for you and saved them as a Garment file. Select File > Add > Garment and select the Subway_Dress_Top file to bring the top into the scene. (Figure 2)

The patterns are included and the top has been simulated. Put the top in place in the 3D Window and simulate to place it on your avatar. When you are happy with the positioning, freeze the top before proceeding with the skirt.

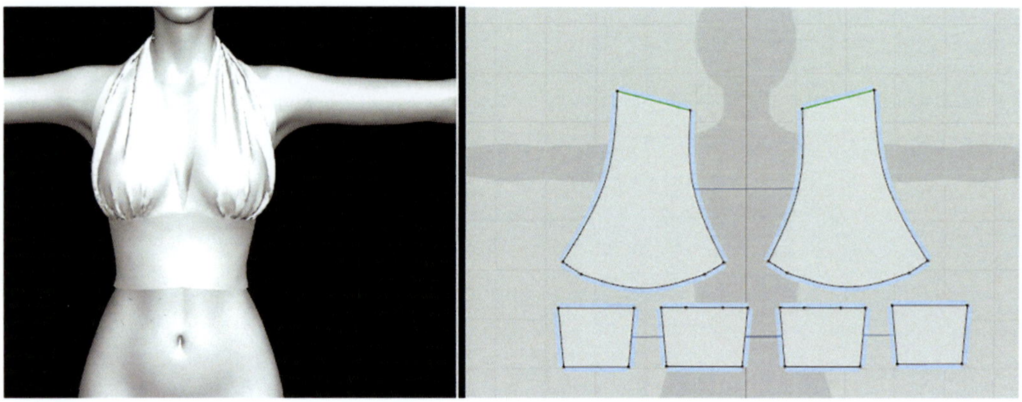

Figure 2. Step 2

Create the Skirt

3. Measure the avatar from her waist to the point on her leg where you want the skirt hem edge to be. I measured just below the knee. This is the skirt length (748.2). (Figure 3)

4. When the wind blows from below, we need the skirt to be nearly horizontal. (Figure 4)

That means that the skirt needs to be very wide. To determine the width, we need to do a little math.

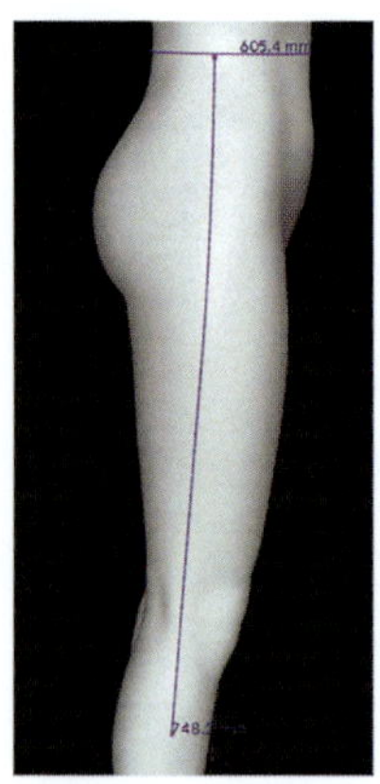

Figure 3. Step 3

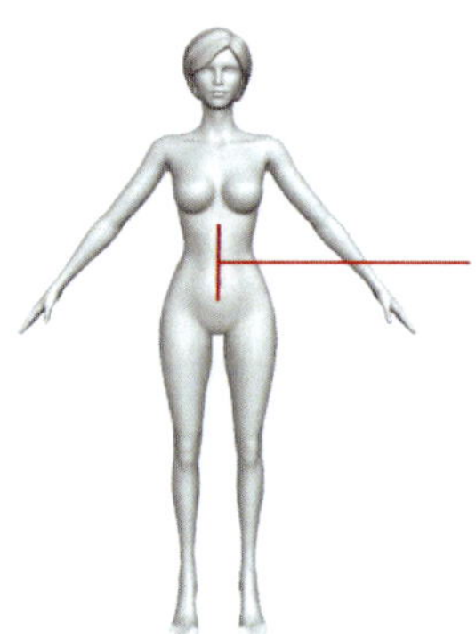

Figure 4. Step 4

5. Refer to Figure 5 showing our skirt from above. You can see that the avatar's waist is in the middle and then the skirt extends from there. You may be thinking that a circle skirt will work, but it won't. We need the same pleating at the waist that we have at the skirt hem, which means we need a rectangle pattern.

Our skirt width will be the length of the Skirt Hem Edge labeled in the drawing, Figure 5. That is the circumference of the circle in the drawing. To calculate that circumference, we need to know the radius of the circle.

We know part of that value because we have the skirt length that you measured. We just need to know the radius of the avatar's waist.

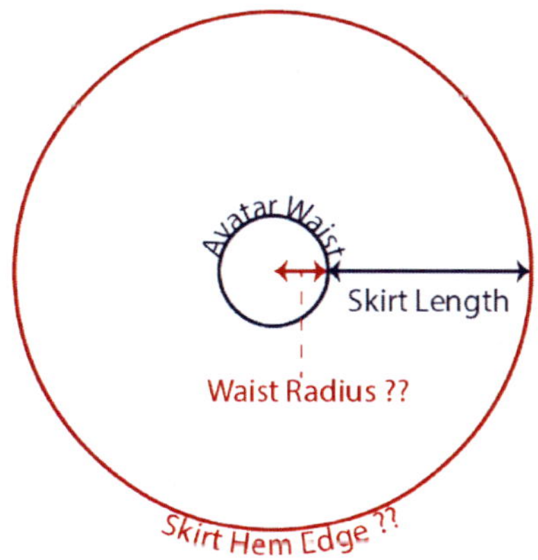

Figure 5. Step 5

The radius of a circle is the diameter divided by 2. The diameter is the circumference divided by 3.14(pi). So our formula is:

Avatar Waist Circumference / 3.14 / 2 = Avatar Waist Radius

For this avatar, I used the following: 605.4 / 3.14 / 2 = 96.4

Now we can add the avatar waist radius and the skirt length to get the circle total radius.

96.4 + 748.2 = 844.6

We can calculate the circumference (skirt width) using the same formula as before, just working it the other direction.

Radius x 2 = Diameter

Diameter x 3.14 = Circumference

844.6 x 2 x 3.14 = 5304

Our rectangle will be 5304 mm wide and 748.2 mm tall. We know that the skirt will be capable of flaring out horizontally when wind is applied.

This may seem a little complicated at first, but it is something you will use a lot. Take the time to really understand this equation and how we've applied it. You'd be surprised how many designs you can make just using this logic for your patterns.

6. Create the rectangle and zoom out so you can see the entire pattern.

7. To create the skirt pleats, we'll use the Offset as Internal Line technique with a distance of 20.

MD will only allow you to offset for a maximum of 100 lines. We have more than that, so we need to use the technique three times. Use the dialog to do the maximum of 100, then select the last line and do it again. The last time you need to watch as you increase the number so you only do as many as necessary to finish the rectangle.

Pleats Fold Tool MD

8. Use the Pleats Fold tool across the pattern selecting the Accordion pleat. When you use the tool, it is not likely that MD will apply the folding across the entire pattern. Every time I did it, it always stopped short.

You'll know that MD did not apply pleats to the entire pattern, because you will still have red internal lines that have no Fold Angle applied. You can see an example of this in Figure 6.

Use the tool until MD does most of the lines, we'll do the rest manually.

If you can't see the color of the lines, switch over to the Pleats Fold tool and they will appear.

(Note that the images provided are just for illustration purposes and are much smaller than your actual skirt pattern will be.)

Finish Pleats Manually

9. The Fold Angle applied for accordion pleats is 0 (yellow) and 360 (blue) on every other internal line. Locate the last line that MD did for you and make note of its Fold Angle. It will either be a 0 or 360 and not red in color (mine was yellow). Select the next line over that has the default 180 Fold Angle (red color). (Figure 6)

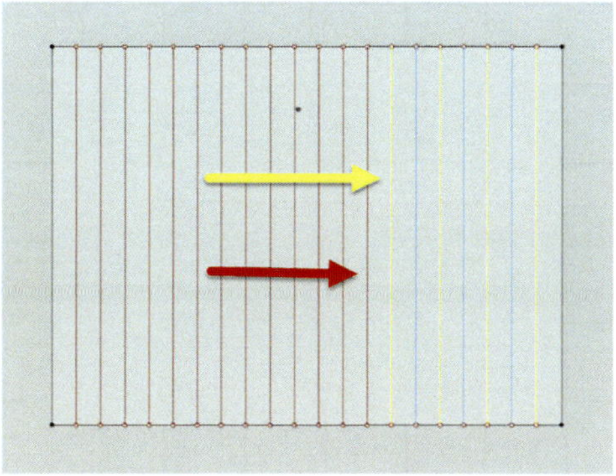

Figure 6. Step 9

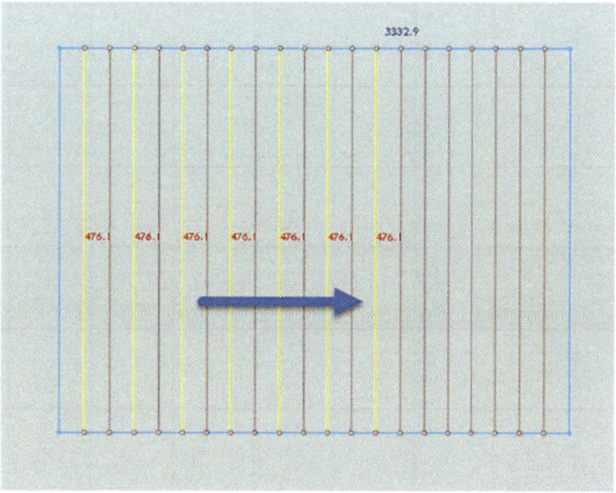

Figure 7. Step 10

10. With the Step 9 line still selected, hold down Shift and select every other line after it. (Figure 7)

11. Set the fold angle in the Property Editor on these lines. If the last MD line is 0, you want to apply 360. If it was 360, you want to apply 0. Make note of the value you apply to these. We'll call it your manual value. (Figure 8)

Switch to the Pleats Fold tool so you can see the line colors. Make note of the red lines that have not been set.

12. Change over to the Transform Pattern tool, if you don't already have it selected. Click on any red internal line that is still set with the fold angle of 180. It doesn't matter which one.

13. Right-click and Select All With Same Property > Fold Angle. (Figure 9)

Figure 8. Step 11

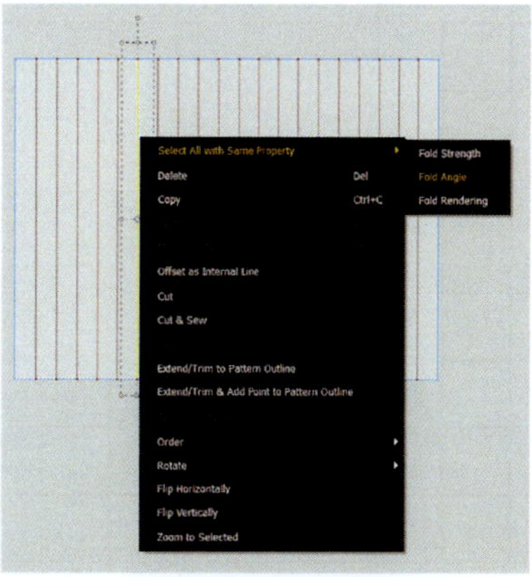

Figure 9. Steps 12-13

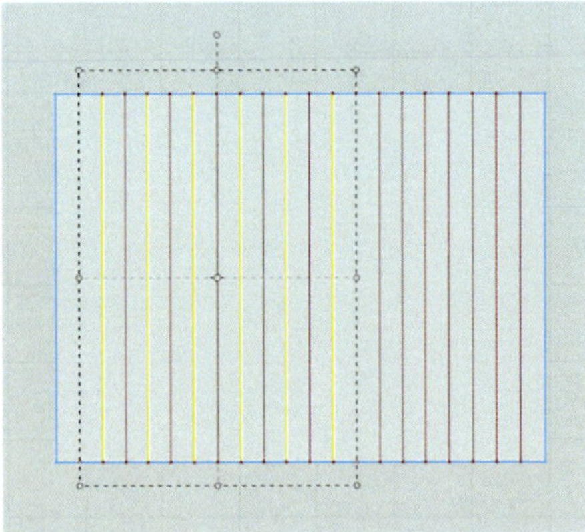

Figure 10. Step 14

Figure 11. Step 15

14. All of the lines left at the default should light up. (Figure 10)

15. In the Property Editor, change their Fold Angle to the OPPOSITE of your manual value (0 if your manual value was 360, etc).

Now your entire pattern should have Internal Lines that alternate blue and yellow in color with no red lines at all. (Select the Pleats Fold tool, if you can't see the colors). (Figure 11)

I wanted to teach you how to apply fold angles manually, because sometimes MD doesn't do the job properly. Now you know how to set them yourself, which means you can make any type of pleat manually, if you ever need to.

16. This avatar doesn't have an Arrangement Point that is large enough to accommodate this pattern. Create a new Bounding Volume using the diameter of the skirt (844.6). See how handy our math measurements can be? Create one Arrangement Point in the center front. Arrange the skirt and sew it to the top torso patterns. The skirt seam should be at center back.

17. We need to make some adjustments before we simulate. This skirt is really big, so turn the Particle Distance way up to 50. The skirt is very heavy, and it will distort the top pattern so make sure it is frozen and then Simulate.

18. Save the project. Open a new project leaving the avatar in the scene.

Pose the Avatar

19. The classic pose for this dress is with the arms in front with the knees slightly bent to the center. You can easily Google this skirt to get lots of inspiration, if you want to see some reference images.

20. You can use the Pose file that I created for you, or you can create a new one.

21. To create a new pose, toggle on X-Ray Joints, pose the avatar and then save the Pose.

22. Open the project with the dress and load the Pose, so the avatar will morph into position. (Figure 12)

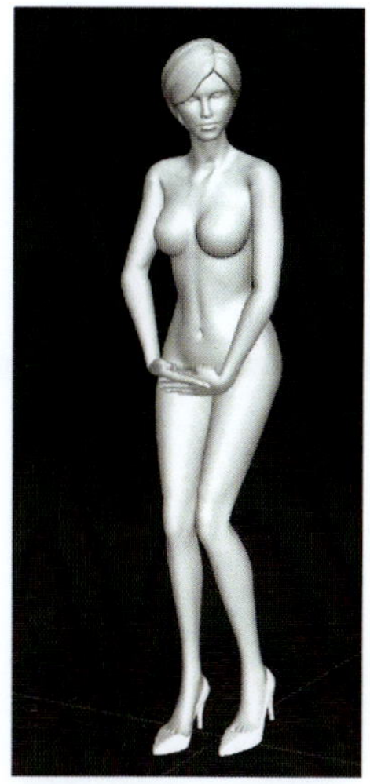

Figure 12. Steps 19-22

Apply the Wind

23. Display the Wind controller in the 3D Window.

24. Place the controller under the dress. You may need to hide the skirt so you can see where you're placing it. (Figure 13)

25. I set the Wind property Type to Spherical and Strength to 8000. You can change these to anything you find pleasing.

26. Run the simulation and be ready to stop it when you see what you like.

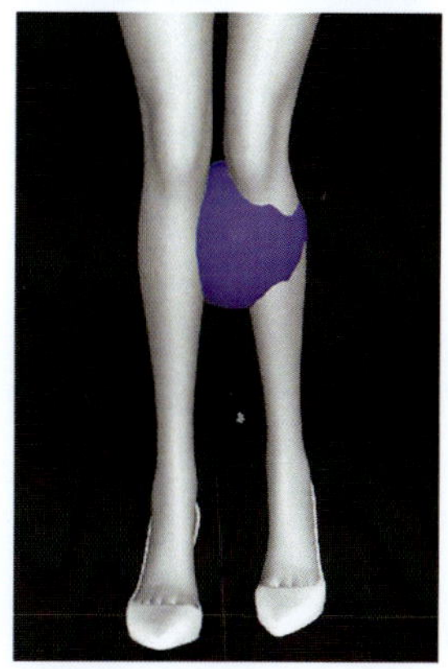

Figure 13. Step 24

Finish the Details

27. Freeze the skirt in position.

I never changed my Particle Distance on the skirt. It was left at 50, which made the simulation run quickly and gave me much more time to work with it. Remember that there is never any need to lower Particle Distance, unless it makes your garment look better.

28. Merge the front torso patterns on the center front. You can also merge the back, if you like.

29. You will want to lower the Particle Distance on the halter part of the top. Work with the gathering as the simulation is running so it looks balanced over the breasts.

30. Finalize your fabrics. I used Full-Grain Leather on the torso patterns and Cotton on everything else. The original dress was a light ivory color, if you want it authentic.

You just created a beautifully detailed dress based on a real-world design and you made the pleated skirt from scratch! That's no small accomplishment.

You also learned the logic behind the patterns, so you can make similar garments for avatars with completely different body shapes.

Challenge Yourself

The real dress included ties and a bow. Feel free to add these details to improve your skills.

Play with the wind and create original compositions.

Project #5 - Drafted Dress

Figure 1. Drafted Dress

We've talked quite a bit about ways to alter patterns throughout the book.

In this project, you are going to use the slash and spread technique to create a new sleeve from a simple sloper sleeve. You'll also create a skirt and collar, drafting from scratch in MD.

Finally, you'll use Animation Mode to bring your creations to life.

New Techniques & Tools

Remove Symmetry	Slash & Spread	Reference Geometry
Sleeve Cap Gathering	Sleeve Cuff	Button
Buttonhole	Select / Move Button	Fasten Button
Button Extensions	Collar	Animation

Assets from Fearless Makers

- ❑ Drafted Dress Final Project File
- ❑ PatternMaker PRO Bodice Front Draft
- ❑ PatternMaker PRO Bodice Back Draft
- ❑ PatternMaker PRO Sleeve Draft
- ❑ Texture Image - Quatrefoil in Teal

Instructions

1. This project uses the MD default Female Avatar B. Create a new project and add her to the scene.

Bodice

2. Trace the bodice front and back patterns.
3. Arrange them in the 3D Window and sew the seams.
4. Select both patterns and Clone as Symmetric.
5. Sew the center front and center back seams and Simulate.

Trace the Sleeves

6. Trace the sleeve pattern and Clone as Symmetric. Read the drafted pattern image to locate the front and back sides of the sleeve. Place each pattern above the correct side of the bodice in the 2D Window.
7. Sew the sleeve underarm. Sew the sleeve cap to the front and back bodice.
8. Arrange the sleeves in the 3D Window.
9. Verify the seams are correct by checking the 3D Threads and Simulate. (Figure 2)

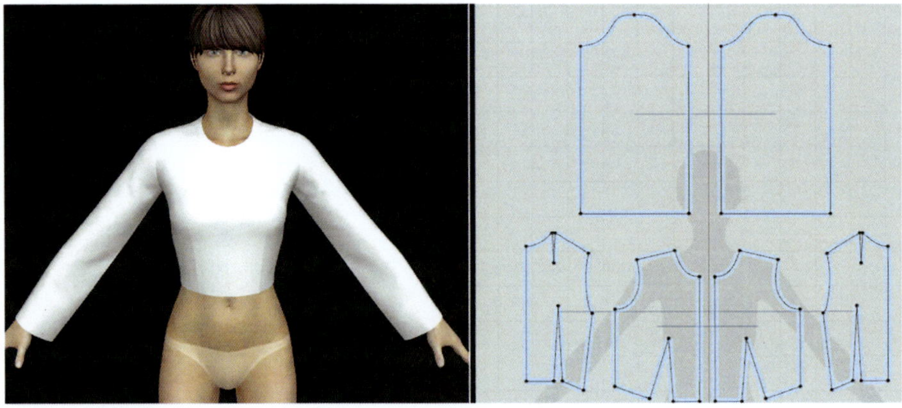

Figure 2. Steps 1-9

Modifying the Sleeve

10. Remove Symmetry on the sleeve patterns. From this point forward, I will be working with the sleeve on the avatar's right. You can keep the original sleeve on her left, just for reference.

11. With the Add Point tool, create a Uniform Split into two segments at the wrist of the sleeve (bottom edge).

12. Draw an Internal Line up the center of the sleeve starting at the new point and holding Shift to keep it perfectly vertical. If the center point at the top of the sleeve cap is not where the new internal line end point is, move it so it is.

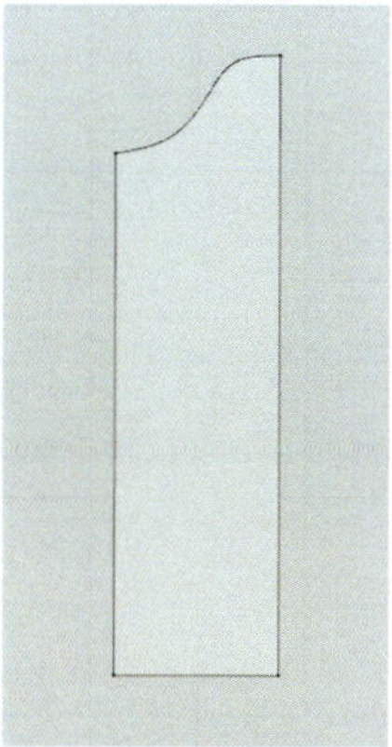

Figure 3. Steps 10-13

13. Cut on the Internal Line and discard the right half of the sleeve. (Figure 3)

14. Create points measuring from the wrist up 160 mm. Use the Split into Two Lines technique to make sure the points are both exactly the same distance on both sides of the sleeve. Select the bottom hem segment and delete it. We just shortened the sleeve by 160 mm.

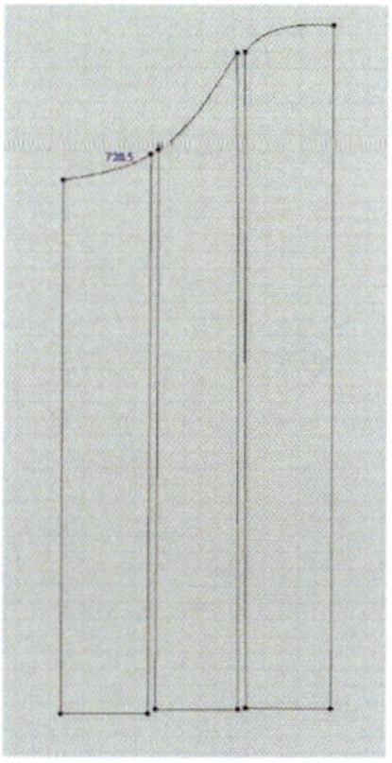

Figure 4. Steps 14-16

15. With the Add Point tool, create a Uniform Split into three segments on the new bottom segment.

16. Holding Shift, draw Internal lines from the two new points up to the sleeve cap. Select both Internal Lines and Cut them. (Figure 4)

17. Zoom in very close. Line up the patterns and place them touching, but not overlapping each other. Note that I have numbered the pattern pieces in the image. I will refer to these numbers, instead of trying to explain which pattern I am referring to in the following instructions. (Figure 5)

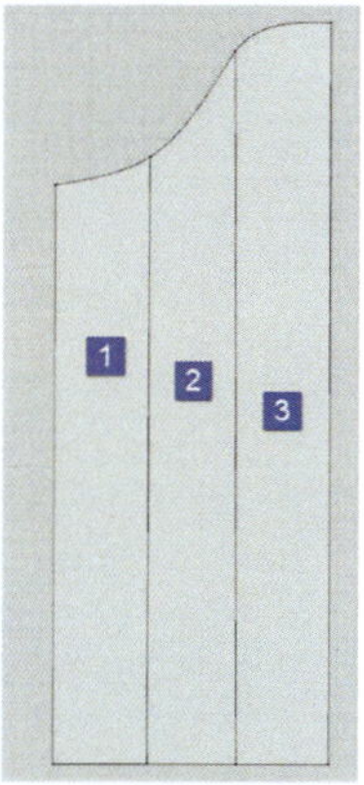

Figure 5. Step 17

18. We need to create a small reference spacer to use when rotating. Create a rectangle that is 65 mm square. I applied a new fabric in orange with 50% Opacity, so it is prominent in the images.

19. Move the spacer so that its top right point aligns to pattern #1 top right point.

20. Using the Transform Pattern tool, select pattern #1. We need to move the rotation point circled in the image. (Figure 6)

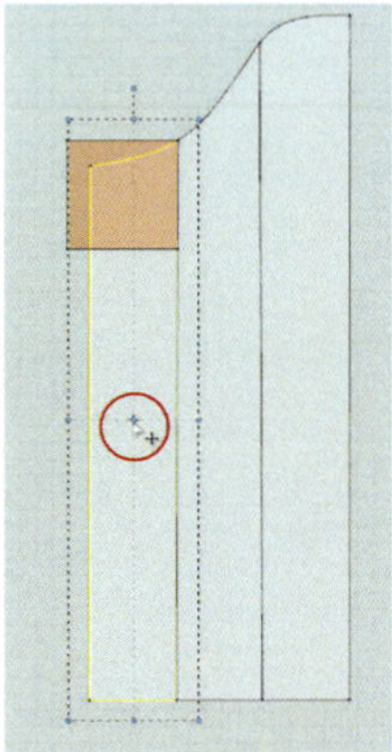

Figure 6. Steps 18-20

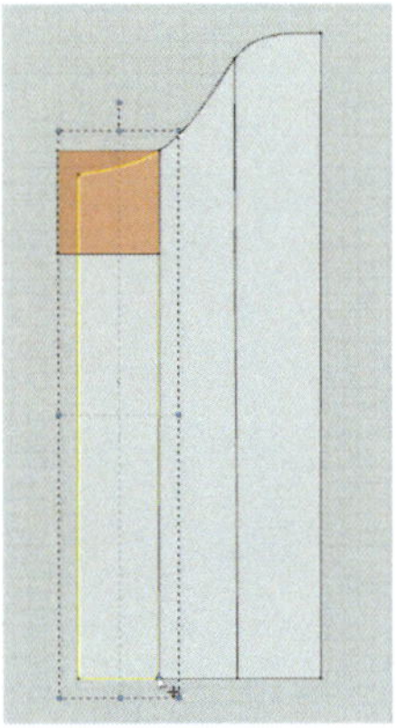

Figure 7. Step 21

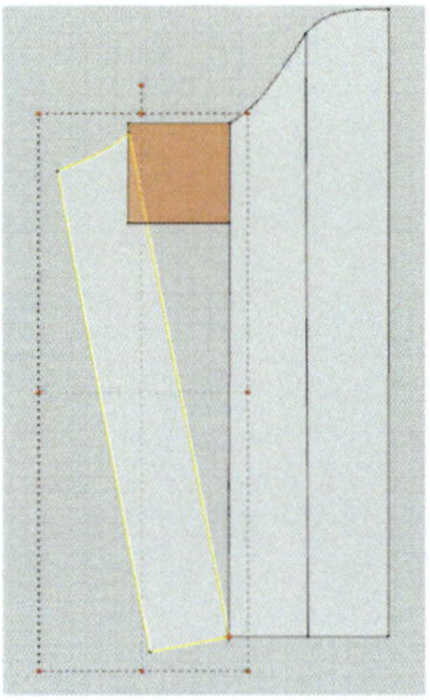

Figure 8. Step 22

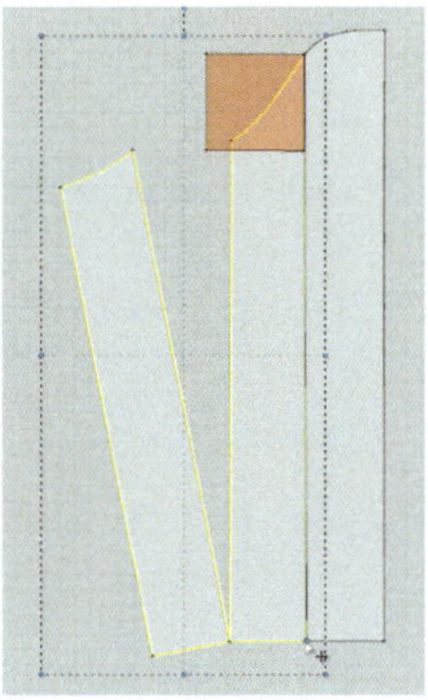

Figure 9. Step 23

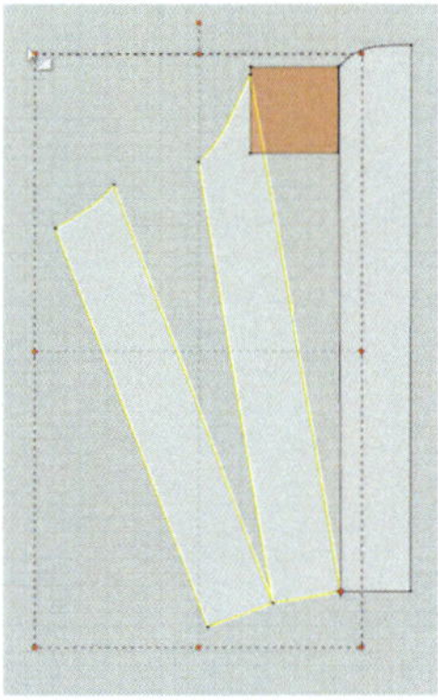

Figure 10. Step 24

21. Select the rotation point and move it to the bottom right point on pattern #1. (Figure 7)

22. Using the Transform Pattern tool, rotate pattern #1 so that its top right point is now on the left side of the spacer. (Figure 8)

23. We are going to repeat that maneuver rotating two patterns pieces at once. Move the spacer to the top right point of pattern #2. Select pattern #1 and pattern #2. Move the rotation point to lowest right point of pattern #2. (Figure 9)

24. Rotate the patterns so that the top right point of pattern #2 is now on the spacers left side. (Figure 10)

25. We are done with the spacer, so you can delete it now.

26. Create a new fabric with Opacity of 0.

27. Using that fabric, use the Polygon tool to trace around the outside of the spread patterns. Refer to the image for the tracing order and points to hit. You will start at point #1, hold Shift and click at point #2. It is very important that the center line is perfectly vertical to the grid. Then proceed around. (Figure 11)

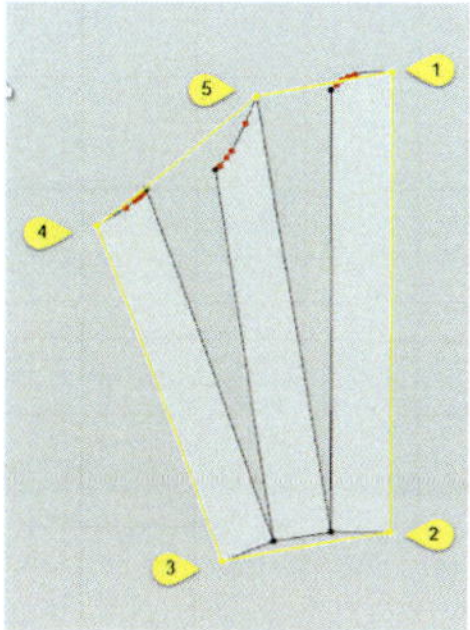

Figure 11. Steps 25-27

28. Switch to the Edit Curve Point tool and create nice curves at the sleeve cap and bottom edge. Refer to the original pattern you left in the 2D Window to get an idea of the shape. (Figure 12)

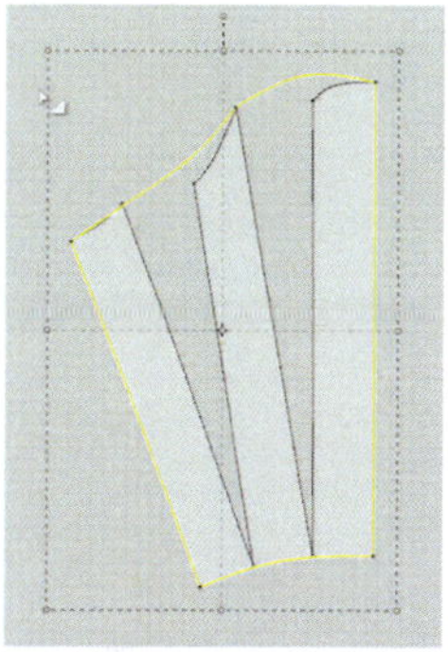
Figure 12. Step 28

29. Move the new pattern off of the slashed pieces. Select the center line and Unfold it. Delete the slashed patterns.

The pattern may look a little strange after unfolding. Make sure it is curved nicely. You may need to convert points to curve points. You may also need to raise the center top point up to fix it. This is a good thing to do, as raising the sleeve cap makes the sleeve fuller, which is what we want. My edited sleeve is shown in orange in the image. The transparent sleeve is my original. (Figure 13)

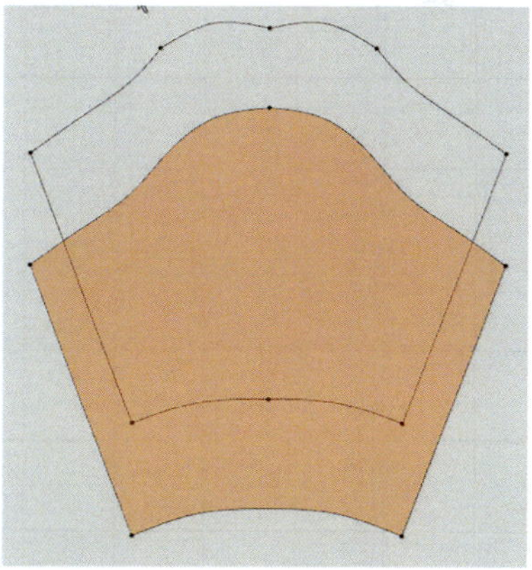
Figure 13. Step 29

30. This new sleeve is very full and has a sleeve cap that is much longer than the bodice armhole openings. We need to mark off the portion of the sleeve and bodice under the arm where we don't want gathering. Refer to *Chapter 18 - Around the Arm - Fullness* for more details.

Multiply the front armhole length by .375. Add a point this distance on the front armhole, measuring from the armpit. Now add a point this distance on the sleeve to match. Repeat this process for the back armhole. Note that the front and back armholes are NOT the same length, so this distance will be different. (Figure 14)

You may have noticed that this point was on the bodice patterns when you traced them. PatternMaker PRO adds these points automatically to the pattern. If you added the point when tracing, just make note of the distance and repeat that on the sleeve.

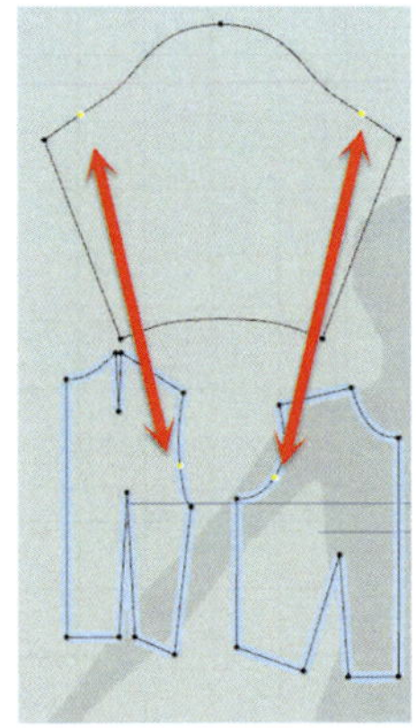

Figure 14. Step 30

31. Now we'll sew the sleeve. You can use the Segment Sewing tool to sew the small segments you just made. Sew the front bodice to front sleeve and back bodice to back sleeve. (Figure 15)

32. To sew the sleeve cap, use the M:N Free Sewing tool. The M seam is the entire unsewn sleeve cap. Make note of which side you select first on the sleeve, front or back. I started on the back of the sleeve, so my N seam started at the back armhole armpit up to the shoulder. The front starts at the shoulder and goes to the armpit. Remember you are following the sleeve shape all the way around the armholes. (Figure 16)

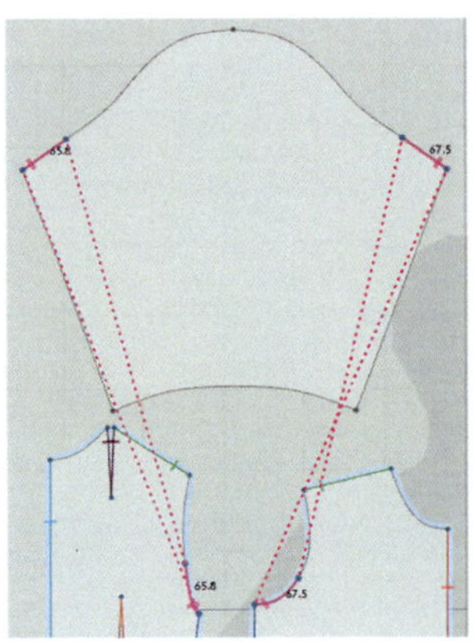

Figure 15. Step 31

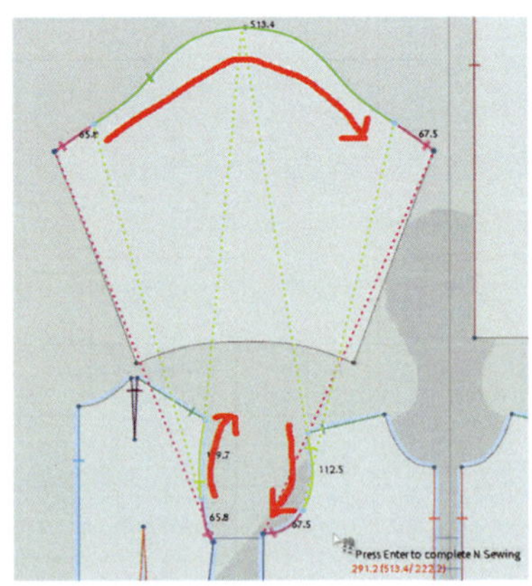

Figure 16. Step 32

33. Arrange your sleeve in the 3D Window and Simulate. Delete the old sleeve on the other side. Select the new sleeve and Clone as Symmetric. Simulate again. You should have two very nice gathered sleeves now. (Figure 17)

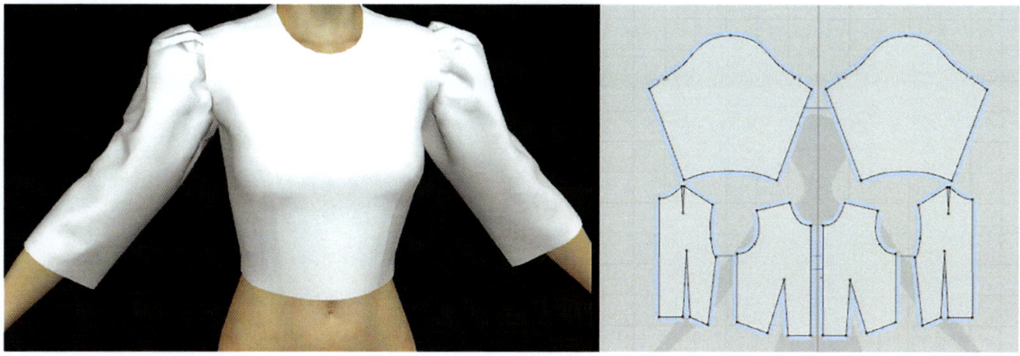

Figure 17. Step 33

Sleeve Cuff

34. Hide the patterns in the 3D Window, so we can take some measurements.

35. Measure the circumference of the avatar's wrist.

36. Use the Surface type to measure up from the wrist circle 160 mm. It may be very hard to reach exactly 160, just get close. Measure the circumference of the avatar's arm at the end point. (Figure 18)

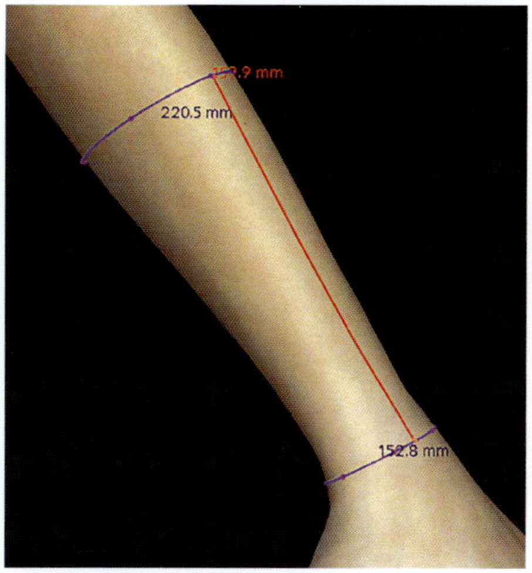

Figure 18. Steps 34-36

37. Draw a rectangle that is the upper arm width and 160 mm tall.

38. Subtract the wrist measurement from the upper arm measurement and divide it by 2. Create new points on the bottom segment this distance to the inside on each side (#1 in image). Delete the old points (#2 in image). (Figure 19)

39. Select the two sides and Offset as Pattern with Distance of 6, Default Corners and Internal Lines. This creates extensions on the cuff for us to add buttons.

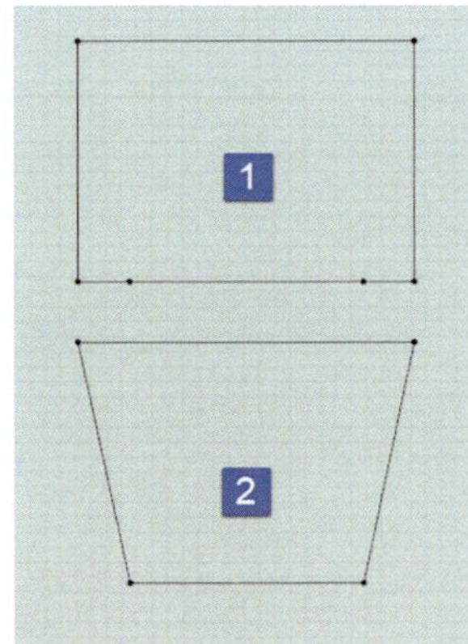

Figure 19. Steps 37-38

40. We want the cuff to button at the back of the arm. This means that the cuff seam will not line up with the sleeve underarm seam. We need to create some reference points before sewing the cuff to the sleeve. Uniform Split the sleeve bottom edge into 4 segments. Now repeat that for the top of the cuff.

41. Arrange the cuff pattern in the 3D Window with the opening to the back of the arm. Use Chalk to mark a line on the sleeve that corresponds to the cuff opening. (Figure 20)

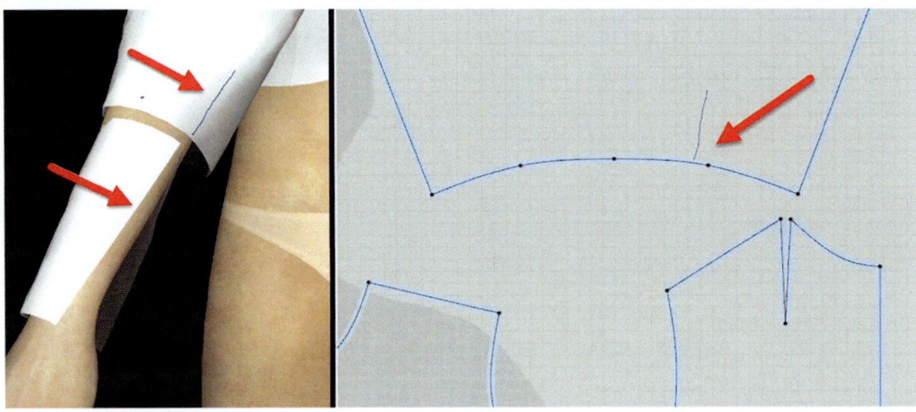

Figure 20. Steps 40-41

42. Using the chalk mark, find the closest point on the sleeve. This is the point where the cuff seam will start and stop on the sleeve. Use the M:N Free Sewing tool to sew the cuff to the sleeve. Do not include the cuff extensions in the seam.

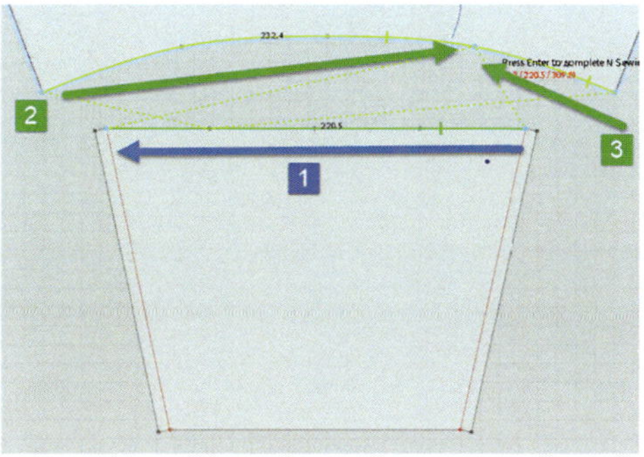

Figure 21. Step 42 In Process

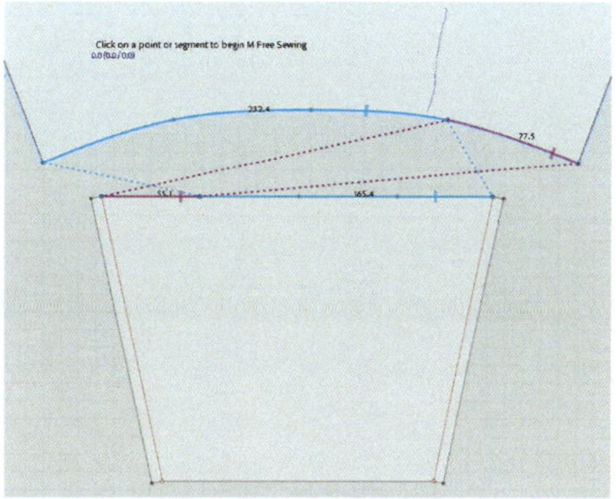

Figure 22. Step 42 Final

Figure 21 shows the seam in process. Notice the change in direction for the second half of the N seam as it wraps around the pattern. Figure 22 shows the completed seam line pairs.

43. Erase your chalk mark and verify your sewing in the 3D Window. Simulate. (Figure 23)

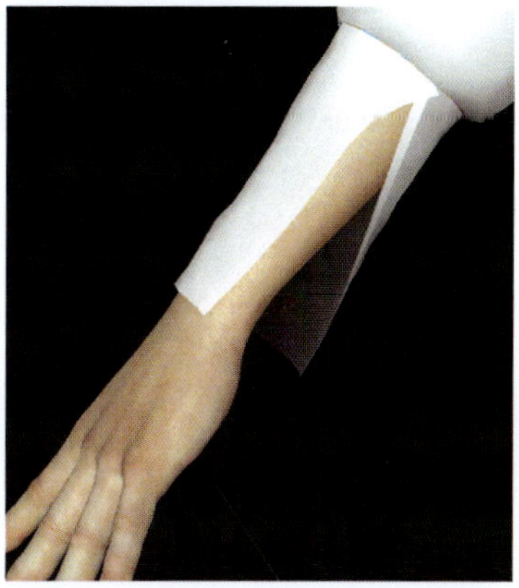

Figure 23. Step 43

Buttons

44. Use the Uniform Split tool on one of the Internal lines at the cuff extension to determine the quantity and spacing you want for your buttons. Repeat the split on the other side. Note the distance between the points you just created. (Figure 24)

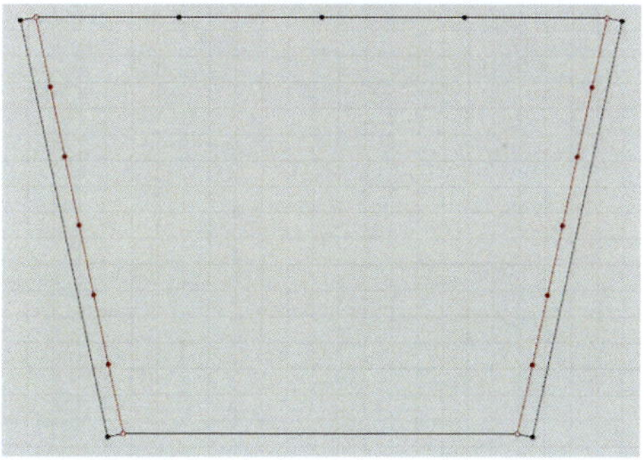

Figure 24. Step 44

As we proceed, you need to keep the cuff wrap direction in mind. Imagine that the cuff is split in half. There is a top half that wraps over the arm and the bottom half that wraps under the arm. The section under the arm is on the bottom of the overlap. The section over the arm is on top of the overlap.

Buttonholes are placed on the top overlap and buttons are placed on the bottom overlap. This may seem strange because fastened buttons look like they are on top. In fact, the button is coming THROUGH the buttonhole on top. Look at a real shirt button, if you get confused.

45. Use the Button tool and place the first button on the point at the top of the Internal Line.

46. Switch to the Select/Move Button tool, select the button you just made in the 2D Window, copy/paste (Control/Command C, Control/Command V) and drag to the second point on the line and right-click. This opens the Paste dialog. Make sure the Interval is correct and use the up arrow next to the Number of Buttons to enter the correct amount. You can see them created in the 3D Window as you increase the number. (Figure 25)

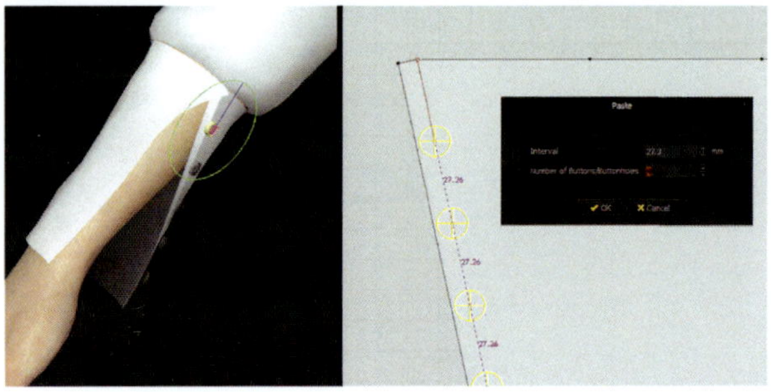

Figure 25. Steps 45-46

47. Use the Property Editor to make any modifications to your button that you want. I changed mine to a small 7 mm shank button.

Buttonholes

48. Repeat this process using buttonholes on the other side of the cuff.

49. You will need to change the Angle of the buttonholes. Buttonholes on cuffs are parallel to the cuff edge. Select all the buttonholes using the Select/Move Button tool and change the Angle property in the Property Editor.

50. Also, a keyhole buttonhole is the default and you want a regular rectangle for this application. Create a new buttonhole in the Object Browser on the

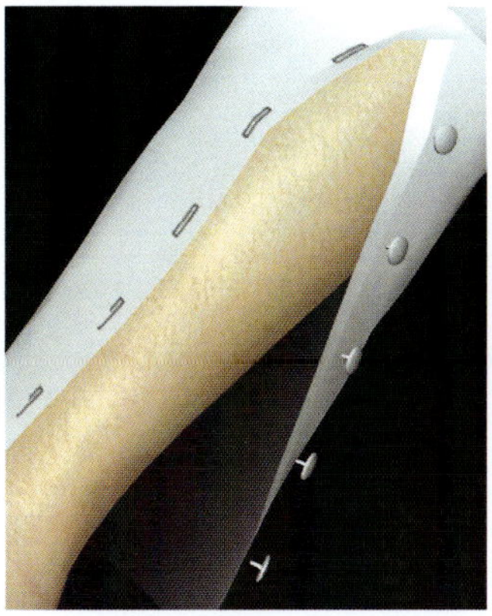

Figure 26. Steps 47-50

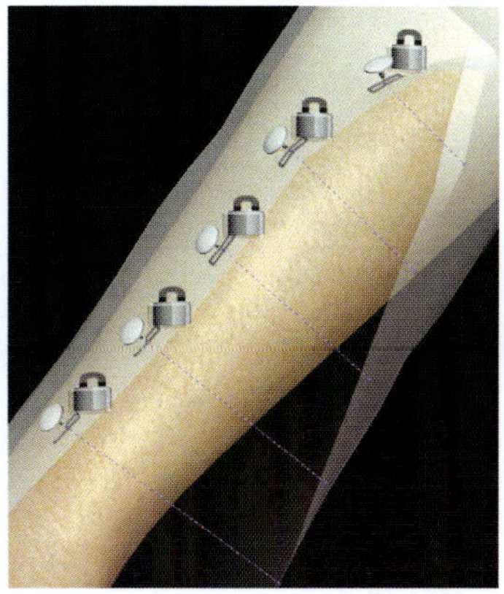

Figure 27. Step 51

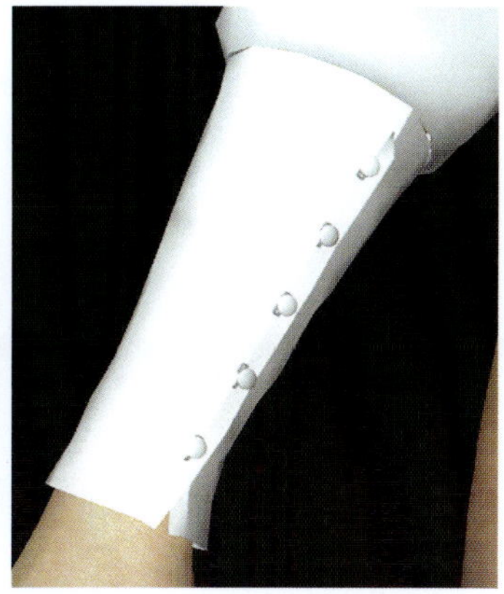

Figure 28. Step 52

Buttonhole tab. Change the Shape to rectangular and also reduce the Size to match your button. (Figure 26)

51. Use the Fasten Button tool to match up your buttonholes to your buttons. (Figure 27)

52. Simulate. If your cuff does not overlap properly, stop the simulation. Freeze the sleeve and then run the simulation again pulling as needed to straighten out the overlap. (Figure 28)

53. Select the cuff and Clone as Symmetric Pattern. Place the cuff to the other sleeve and simulate. Unfortunately, the buttons and buttonholes do not copy.

54. Repeat the button / buttonhole process for the second cuff. Remove the Internal Lines used as reference.

Now that you've had some great experience with button extensions, buttons and buttonholes, you get to do the next section all on your own.

Bodice Button Extension and Buttons

55. Everything you need to know you've already done on the cuffs. However, I'll give you some general outlines based on what I did.

You may want to freeze everything except the two front bodice pieces, just to make sure nothing shifts on you as you are working.

Button extension width should be the diameter of the button used. My front extension is 18 mm wide, as are the buttons. The first button point was placed very close to the top of the center front line and then Uniform Split was used from there. They are spaced 43.4 mm apart. The buttonholes are 18 mm parallel to the center front line.

Remember that women's shirts overlap right over left.

Don't forget to delete the original seam line at center front before you simulate with your new buttons! (Figure 29)

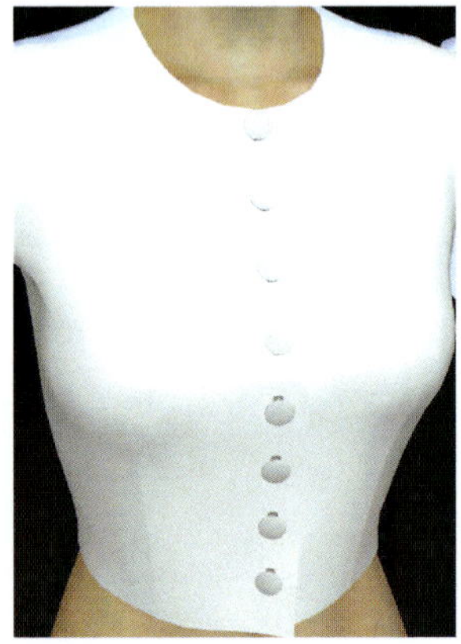

Figure 29. Step 55

Ruffled Collar

56. Select the back and front neckline EXCLUDING the front extension to get the collar width measurement. Look at the Symmetric Line Length in the Property Editor to get the total width.

57. Create a rectangle that is 2 times as wide as the neckline width and 60 mm tall.

58. Before sewing, arrange the collar in the 3D Window with the collar side seam in front, you'll use the back neck Arrangement Point. The collar is long and may overlap itself. Select the collar and use the Offset slider in the Property Editor to expand the collar out so it doesn't overlap itself.

59. Look at the collar in the 3D and 2D Windows. If you sew the bottom of the collar to the bodice the wrong side of the collar will be uppermost. We want the collar normals facing away from the avatar, so we need to sew to the top edge of the collar in the 2D Window.

60. Sew the collar to the neckline with the collar seam at center front. Use the M:N Free Sewing tool and remember to skip the front extensions. (Figure 30)

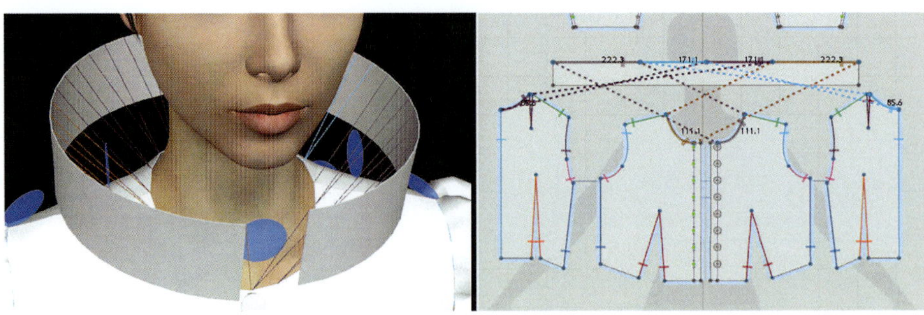

Figure 30. Steps 56-60

When you simulate, you'll see that the collar edges match up perfectly at center front. The collar is very chunky, so lower the particle distance to smooth it out.

61. If the collar isn't laying down, select all the seams on the collar and change the Sewing Line Type to Turned.

62. Use the Round Corner tool to put a nice corner on the front tips of the collar.

Skirt

63. The skirt is going to be very wide, so we need a new Arrangement Point to place it. Create a new Bounding Volume on the floor that is 40 tall and 400 X and Y radius. Create an Arrangement Point at the center front. (Figure 31)

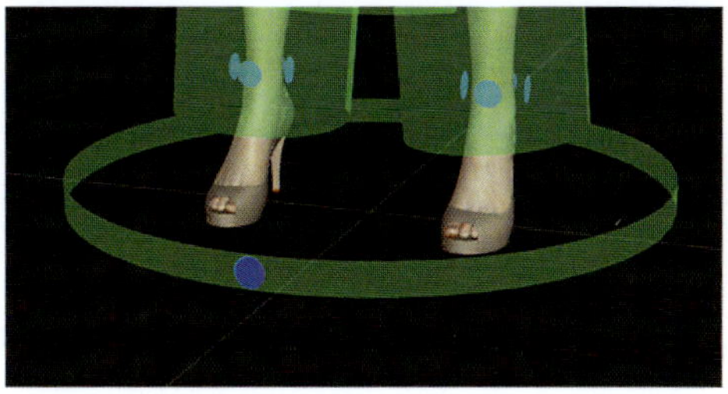

Figure 31. Step 63

64. Use the Basic Tape tool to measure from the bottom of the bodice to where you want the skirt hem to be. This will be your skirt length. (Mine was 1130 mm.)

65. Measure the hip circumference of the avatar or open the Avatar Editor and find it on the Measure tab. Multiply that measurement by 2. This is the skirt width. (880.8 x 2 = 1761.6)

66. Create a rectangle that is the skirt width by the skirt length.

67. Sew the ends of the skirt (side seam) together with Segment Sewing.

68. Sew the skirt to the bodice with the skirt side seam at center back using the M:N Free Sewing tool. Do not include the bodice front extensions in the seam

69. The skirt is very heavy, so you should freeze the bodice pattern before you Simulate.

Add the Details

70. Use the Offset as Internal Line with increased Fold Angle on the cuff edges and skirt bottom to create fake hems.

71. Fabric settings will dictate how this garment animates. You will want to create a bodice fabric that is somewhat stiff, or the skirt will really pull it down.

The skirt, collar and sleeves will be much more puffy with a Cotton preset then they will with a Satin preset. You need to decide which look you prefer.

72. Create all your fabrics and add color and/or texture to all the different components. Lower the Particle Distance on everything that needs it to increase the realism.

Animation

73. Save your project.

74. Load a Joint Motion file. It must be for the Female_B avatar. I used the F_B_Type1_03_no hands pose. Select the Avatar Size + Joint Rotation & Position and the Move Avatar & Garment to Start Position options.

75. Switch to Animation mode. Click the Record button and MD will create the animation. This can take a little while, so take a much deserved break from your computer.

76. After MD has finished processing, you can use the controls above the timeline to play your animation. You can scrub the timeline by dragging the vertical marker. Find a nice pose and take a Snapshot while still in Animation Mode.

That completes this project. It wasn't easy and you used a lot of new skills that will be useful on many different designs. You should be proud of yourself!

Challenge Yourself

In this project, you slashed the sleeve pattern and made it fuller at the sleeve cap by rotating the patterns. Instead, you could have used the spacer at the top and bottom to spread the entire pattern apart. This would have created fullness not only at the sleeve cap, but all the way down to the bottom as well.

I challenge you to re-create the sleeve spreading it apart rather than rotating the top out. You'll create a brand new design and learn more about adding fullness.

If you want another challenge, slash and spread the sleeve by rotating the bottom out and leaving the sleeve cap in place. Now you have a completely different look.

The slash and spread technique works with all types of patterns. Use it on skirts, dresses, tops and bottoms. Keep in mind that every garment you encounter in the real world started out as a simple sloper.

Project #6 - Steam Punk

Figure 1. Steam Punk

This is going to be the most challenging project of the book.

The garments consist of a peasant blouse, corset and skirt. It's all topped off with a hat!

Your job is to recreate the original outfit shown with virtually no help.

This will prepare you for future work when dealing only with images or sketches.

Have fun!

Assets from Fearless Makers

- ❑ Steam Punk Final Project File
- ❑ Open COLLADA Avatar File
- ❑ PatternMaker PRO Corset Draft
- ❑ PatternMaker PRO Peasant Blouse Draft
- ❑ PatternMaker PRO Trumpet Skirt Draft
- ❑ Texture Image - Striped Fabric
- ❑ Texture Image - Satin

❑ Texture Image - Leather

Instructions

Cue the Crickets !

Hints

I'm not going to completely abandon you. I'll give you some hints, instead of instructions. There are also more images of the completed outfit at the end of this project that will help.

Avatar

All you get for an avatar is an Open COLLADA file. You need to add her to the scene. See *Chapter 23 - Working with Files - Importing / Exporting.*

She was created using the open-source Make Human program. You can learn more at www.makehuman.org. (Note that I did use Blender as an intermediary program to create the COLLADA file.)

Make a minimal set of Bounding Volumes and Arrangement Points. You need a BV around the arm and another around the torso. One AP per BV is probably adequate, because of how most of these patterns are placed.

Figure 2 shows the ones that I created.

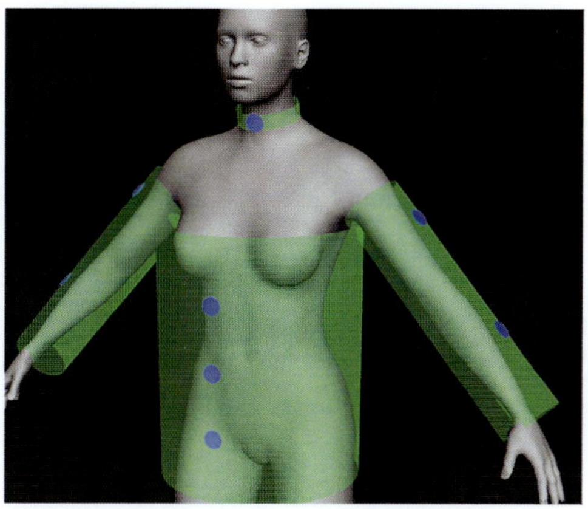

Figure 2. Bounding Volumes / Arrangement Points

Order of Make

I created the garments in this order:

- Corset
- Skirt
- Blouse
- Hat

Corset

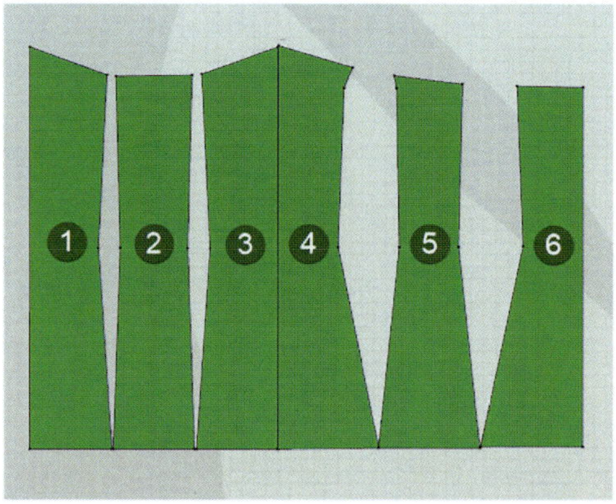

Figure 3. Bounding Volumes / Arrangement Points

The corset is a twelve-panel pattern. You'll have six panels on the pattern draft, three for the front and three for the back.

It can be a bit confusing when you look at the draft to know what is corset and what isn't. Figure 3 shows all the patterns in green. Patterns 1-3 are the front and 4-6 are the back.

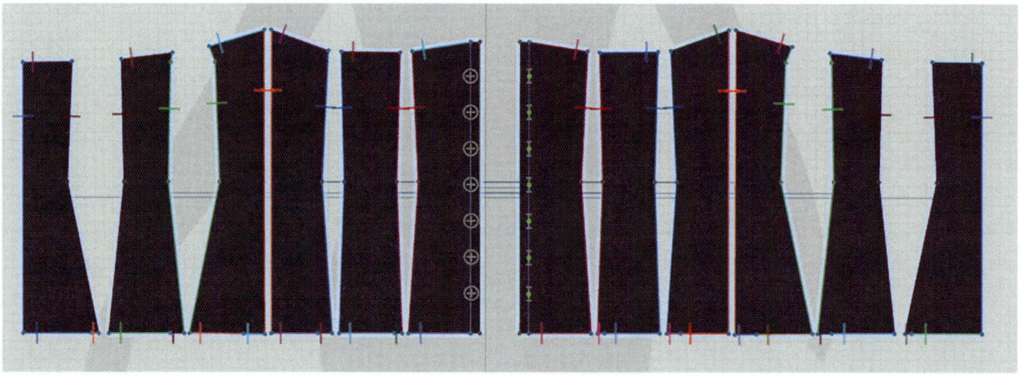

Figure 4. Corset Final in 2D Window

Figure 4 is the corset all laid out in the 2D Window and sewn. I added an extension to the center front panels to accommodate the buttons and buttonholes. The corset stays are done with piping.

You can't use Arrangement Points to arrange all of these in the 3D window. Instead, just create a torso AP in the center front and center back. Snap the front patterns to the front point and then rotate them and arrange around the front using the Gizmo. Do the same with the back. The nice thing about a back Arrangement Point is that MD will flip the back patterns for you.

Skirt

The skirt is a twelve-gore trumpet skirt. It's called a trumpet because of the way the bottom flares out below the knee. The pattern draft is only one gore, so you need to copy it 11 times.

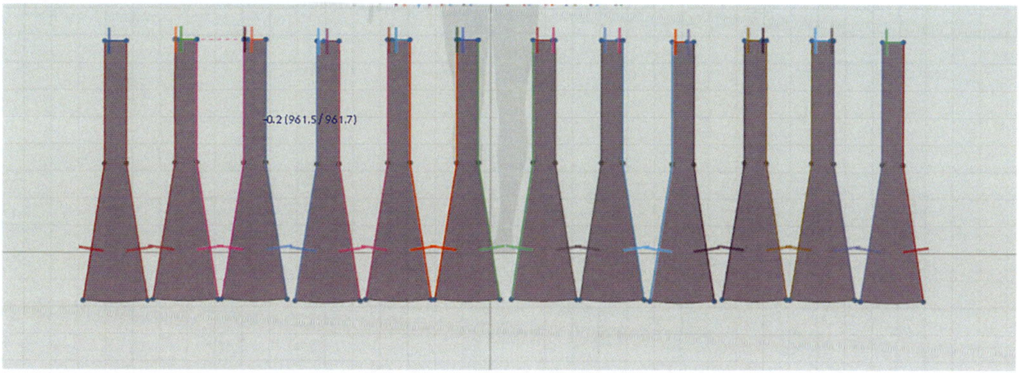

Figure 5. Skirt Final in 2D Window

The skirt pattern is drafted to the avatar's waist. You'll need to cut the top off, because you will sew it to the bottom of the corset. Trying to layer it under the corset would be a nightmare.

Measure from the avatar's waist to the bottom edge of the corset to determine the amount to cut off. (*Hint - Cut off the top before making the 11 copies!*)

Just like the corset, you can't arrange these easily in the 3D Window. Use the same technique as the corset. The bottom of the patterns will cross over each other, but the simulation will fix it.

Blouse

The pattern is a peasant blouse. This is very different from most tops, because the sleeve extends up over the shoulder and is part of the neckline.

I've marked the pattern names in the image.

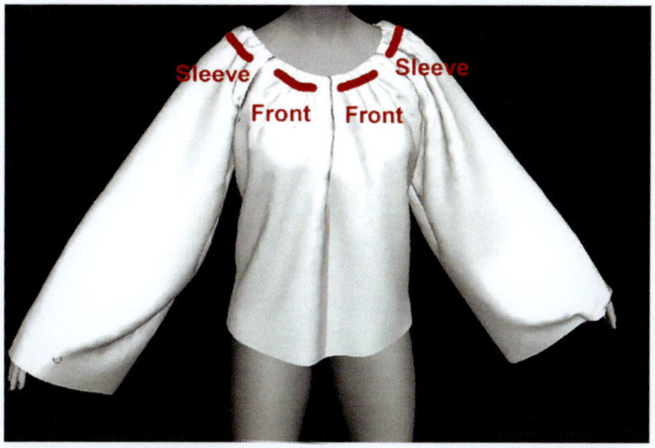

Figure 6. Peasant Blouse

The neckline top of all six patterns is very wide. You need to use elastic to gather it up, so it fits.

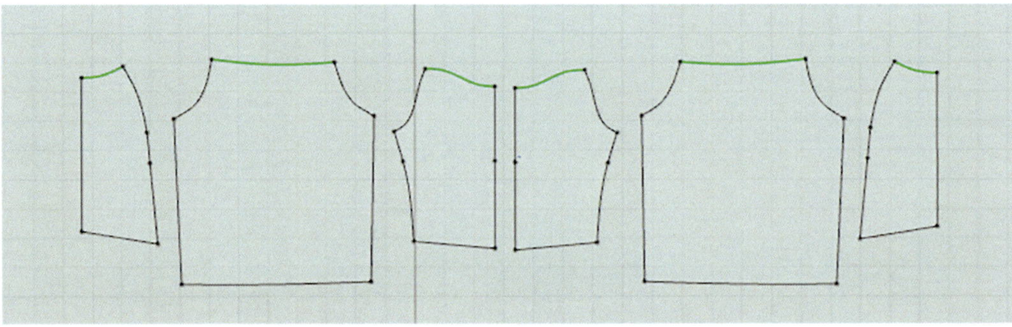

Figure 7. Elastic on Blouse

Figure 7 shows the blouse patterns laid out with the green elastic segments.

Once you sew and simulate, you'll see that the pattern is a full-length blouse. You need to cut off the excess at the bottom and sew the new edge of the blouse to the top of the corset.

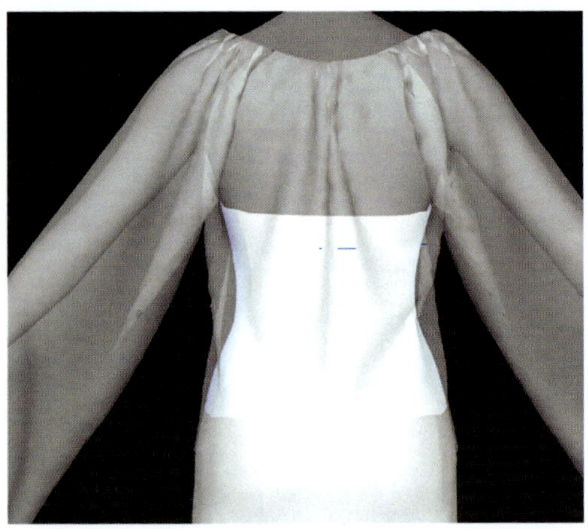

Figure 8. Peasant Blouse with Opacity Turned Down (view of back)

Set the fabric on the blouse with a reduced Opacity, so you can see where you need to cut.

Use the chalk to mark the cut lines. Use Internal Lines and Cut. Discard the bottom portion.

When you cut the front, make sure to leave extra length, because the fabric has to go over the bust and then wrap underneath the bust before attaching. This takes more fabric than you may realize.

You don't want the blouse pulled down tight to the corset. Leave it a bit loose, so you get nice gathers in the final garment.

Figure 9. Peasant Blouse

My blouse also has a separate neckband with ties at the front. The neckband is Full-Grain Leather so it stiffens to hold the blouse.

The ties are Silk / Satin, so they flow nicely. You'll see that I added a loop, so it appears to be tied. All of these are separate patterns sewn together.

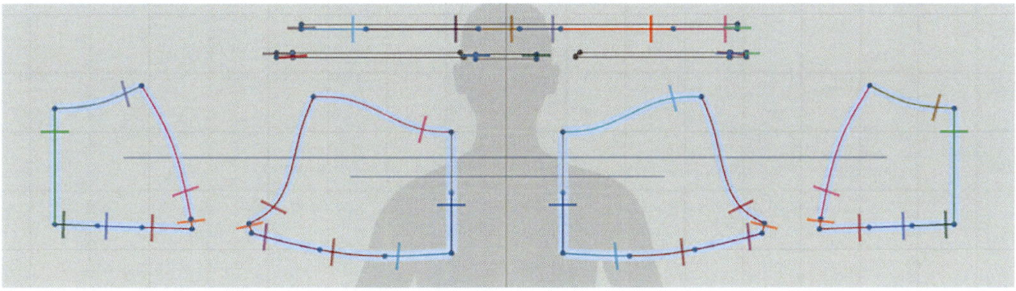

Figure 10. Blouse Front, Back, Neckband, Ties and Loop in 2D Window

To create the leather bands on the sleeves, I cut the pattern using Internal Lines. Then I used the Transform Pattern tool to make them more narrow.

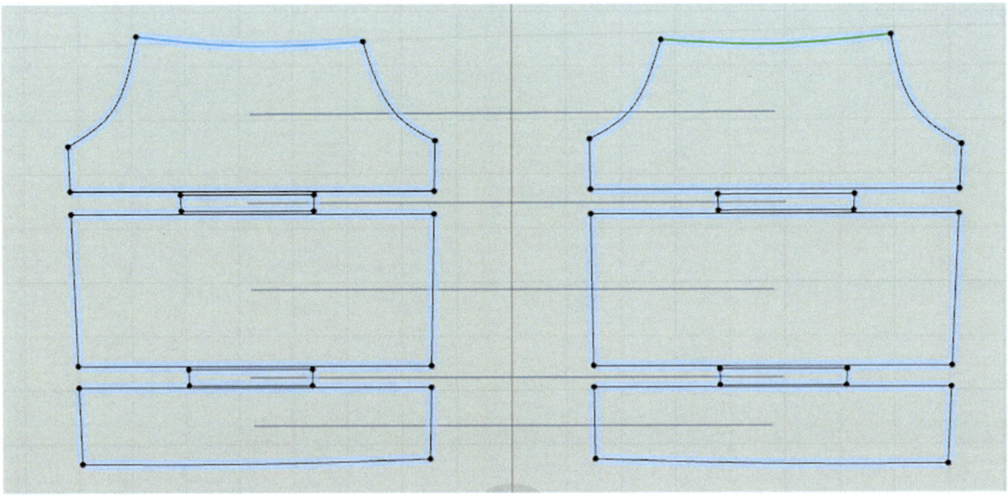

Figure 11. Blouse Sleeve in 2D Window

Hat

The hat was a complete free form design. I didn't use any patterns. The side band of the hat was created first using the avatar's head circumference measurement. The top crown was created next based on the shape at the top of the band. Finally, the brim was added based on the shape of the bottom of the band.

Details

I used Curved Side Geometry on the corset and the hat. They share the same fabric and the Side is set to a different color. This gives a great illusion of depth and creates a darker outline. This is very noticeable on the hat brim and the edge of the corset extension next to the buttons.

I put the leather texture on this fabric, too. The armbands use the same fabric.

The neckband, ties and skirt have a satin texture applied to them. The blouse has a striped texture applied.

Since this was a COLLADA import, there is a full skeleton on this avatar. I created a pose for her and then morphed the avatar. That's the final image you see.

Conclusion

Having the PatternMaker PRO patterns will make this project doable, even for those of you without years of experience. I can't imagine trying it without them.

This is a complex outfit with lots of subtle details. There are so many changes you can incorporate to make a completely different look. Loosen the gathers on the blouse and go off-shoulder. Leave off the corset and the skirt and lengthen the blouse to make a dress. The opportunities for design changes are endless.

In the very beginning of the book, I spoke to you about the difference between my MD techniques and those of most other MD users. If this outfit had been made without real patterns, which I refer to as "sculpting" in MD, the results would be much different.

This outfit may appear to be very tight, which is a characteristic of sculpting, but take a look at my Strain Map in the following images.

Figure 12. Garment Strain Map

These garments are not the least bit tight. Even the corset, that looks very tight in the images, is just snug. They fit the avatar perfectly.

Now you can achieve the same results yourself, because you understand how to "sew" in MD.

Make some well-fitted sloper patterns and then start slashing and spreading. Check out the drafting books I recommended in *Chapter 6 - Drafting Patterns* or give PatternMaker PRO a try.

I hope you found these projects challenging, but achievable. I had a lot of fun designing them and I know that my skills improved in the process. As you've re-created them, I'm sure that yours have as well.

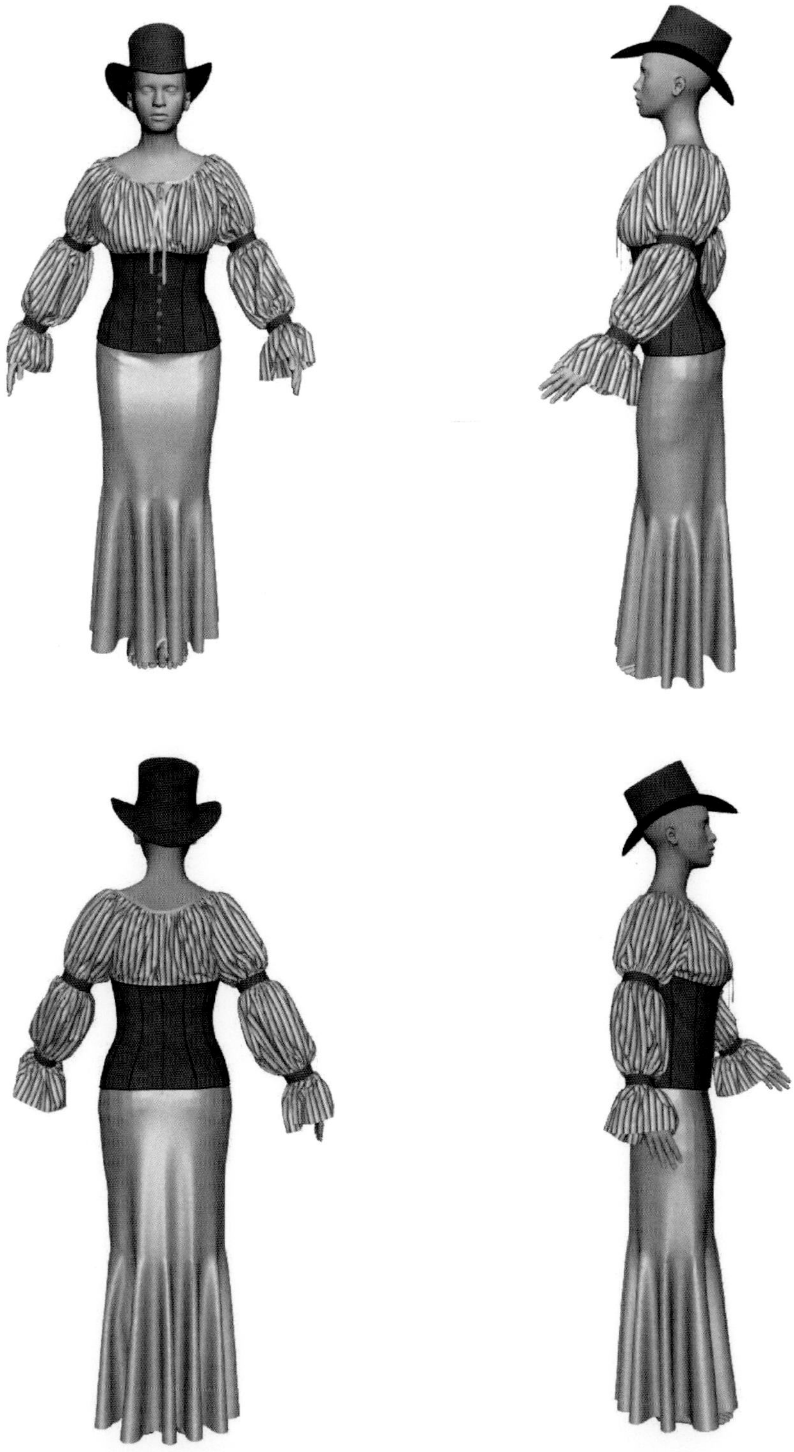

Appendix

MD Fabric Presets

These are the presets for fabric in MD. Use the empty rows at the bottom to write in the custom presets you create.

MD Preset	Stretch Weft	Stretch Warp	Shear	Bending Weft	Bending Warp	Buckling Ratio Weft	Buckling Ratio Warp	Buckling Stiffness Weft	Buckling Stiffness Warp	Internal Damping	Density	Friction Coefficient
0_Default	27	27	9	38	38	80	80	80	80	1	27	3
D_Chiffon	32	32	8	26	80	80	80	25	25	1	35	3
D_Cotton	32	32	23	35	35	50	50	30	30	1	35	3
D_Denim	32	32	29	48	48	10	10	30	30	1	35	3
D_Leather	32	32	32	54	54	30	30	95	95	1	35	3
D_Rib_Knit	32	20	2	50	50	90	90	25	25	1	35	3
D_Silk_Satin	32	32	6	30	30	80	80	80	80	1	35	3
D_Wool	32	32	30	60	60	20	20	80	80	1	35	3
R_20s_Muslin	49	49	42	38	38	10	10	80	80	1	27	3
R_30s_Cotton_Jersey	49	49	6	10	10	96	96	80	80	1	27	3
R_Chiffon	49	49	0	15	15	70	70	80	80	1	27	3
R_Cotton_Gabardine	49	49	33	38	38	80	80	70	70	1	27	3
R_Jersey_20S_Single	49	49	7	5	25	88	88	90	90	1	27	3
R_Lightweight_Nylon	49	49	49	16	16	20	20	80	80	1	27	3
R_Pique_Jersey	49	49	15	10	48	80	80	28	28	1	27	3
R_Polyester_Mesh	49	49	20	50	54	90	90	30	30	1	27	3
R_Ponte_Knit	49	49	15	30	48	90	90	80	80	1	27	3
R_Wool_Gabardine	49	49	15	30	48	90	90	80	80	1	27	3
R_Wool_Twill	49	49	15	23	25	88	88	80	80	1	27	3
S_Full_Grain_Leather	32	32	32	90	90	1	1	99	99	1	27	3
S_Fusible_Rigid	70	70	70	65	65	80	80	80	80	1	27	3
S_Hardware	49	49	49	60	60	1	1	99	99	1	27	3

Stylelines

A styleline is a line or curve in a garment that has a visual effect. A styleline is typically a boundary between two distinct areas of a garment. This line can be created with contrasting fabrics, trims, closures and shaping.

In the real world, stylelines are used to create a flattering garment. Someone with wide hips may add a styleline to their dress that narrows the hips. These same methods can be used to your advantage in CG.

If you are creating a wealthy or well-dressed character, you should choose lines that are flattering, as this is what that individual would choose in the real world. For characters that are better suited to ill-fitted clothing, choose stylelines that exaggerate a poor fit or indicate a poor choice in their clothing selection.

Stylelines that Remove Weight

V Lines	Surplice lines
Asymmetrical lines	Any slanting line, if more vertical than horizontal
Any long line detail - Button/zipper down in line	Plain set-in sleeves
Long sleeves with no fullness	Deep necklines
Long narrow collars	Full length pants with standard width
Shawl collars	Belt-less designs
Straight skirts of easy cut	Straight-hanging draped skirts
Wrap-around skirts	Skirts with knife pleats grouped at center
Slightly flared skirts, if straight at the sides	Skirts with many narrow gores, if straight at sides
Long loose panels in skirts	Thin smooth-surfaced fabrics
Lengthwise stripes, if small	Dark colors
Easy fitting, never anything in the least snug	

Stylelines that Add Weight

Wide collars	High necks with big bows
Soft drapery in bodice, in skirt	Straight-across yokes
Pants that flare at the bottom	Gathers or tucks at shoulders
Full sleeves	Sleeves in one with bodice or yoke
Deep armholes	Gathered skirts
All-around pleated skirts	Fully flared skirts
Horizontal details or trimming	Pockets at bust or hip
Peplums	Bulky fabrics
Checks, plaids, prints	Horizontal stripes
Any shoulder-broadening detail, such as padded shoulders	

Stylelines that Remove Height

Round, high, boat-shape, or square necks	Straight-across yokes in bodice or skirt
Wide flat collars	Cape collars
Full sleeves, long or short	Kimono sleeves
Dolman sleeves	Any deep-armhole sleeve
Two-piece designs, particularly if high contrast	Midriff insets
Pants that are not full length or with bell bottom	Peplums and tiers
Flounces	Any horizontal detail
Big pockets	Bustle and hip effects
Wide belts	Contrasting belts
Skirts deeply pleated all around	Accordion pleats
Skirts with soft impressed pleats	Capes
Horizontal stripes	Bulky fabrics
Gathered skirts	Wide flaring skirts
Stiff fabrics	Heavy fabrics

Stylelines that Add Height

V lines	Deep necklines
Any full-length detail or trimming	Narrow straight skirts
Slightly, flared skirts, if the flare is centered and the sides straight	Knife-pleated skirts, if pleats centered
Long skirts, if not full of soft fabric	Full length pants of standard width
Belt-less waistlines	Long torso lines
Slim sleeves, set-in type	Long loose straight panels
Straight box coats	Slim fitted coats
Lengthwise stripes, if narrow	Fine smooth fabrics
Soft fabrics	

Quiz Answers

Introduction

1) MD is the abbreviation used throughout the book for ______________ ___________________.

Marvelous Designer

2) You must have CG and sewing experience to use this book.

False.

3) The Fearless Makers website includes the following for free:

A. YouTube Videos

B. MD Project Files

D. Written Tutorials

4) There are six projects included in this book located in:

A. Chapter 26

Chapter 1

1) CLO are the creators of Marvelous Designer.

True.

2) Marvelous Designer is a 3D sculpting program like ZBrush.

False. You can't do any sculpting or modeling in MD.

3) You can use Marvelous Designer to make real-world patterns for sewing.

False. MD doesn't facilitate seam allowances or other necessary items that you would need to sew patterns in the real world.

4) Marvelous Designer originates in:

C. South Korea

Chapter 2

1) You can't make a living using MD to create virtual garments.

False. More and more opportunities are available for skilled MD users.

2) MD garments can be used as a selling tool on real-life clothing retailer websites.

True. However, you will most likely need to texture them outside of MD for more realism.

3) You can create photorealistic clothing using MD exclusively.

False. You will need to use another 3D graphics program, like Maya or Blender, to elevate MD clothing to photorealistic.

4) MD can be used by fashion designers to visualize their ideas.

True. Although you can't generate real-world patterns, the software is perfect for conceptualizing.

Chapter 3

1) The layout in MD is fixed and you can't rearrange the panels.

False. All the panels can be resized and rearranged to your liking.

2) Almost all tools can be selected using buttons or through menu choices.

True. There are a lot of ways to accomplish tool selection within the program.

3) You can undo your last action with:

A. Control/Command Z

B. Using the History Panel

C. Edit > Undo

4) The 2D window has:

C. Y, X Axes

Chapter 4

1) When using the Planar type of Wind:

B. Point the cone in the direction you want the wind to blow.

2) 3D Window snapshots are JPG files with an opaque background.

False. The snapshots are PNG files and you can choose a transparent background.

3) The Gizmo can be oriented to:

A. World Coordinates

C. Local Coordinates

D. Screen Coordinates

4) When it comes to lighting:

A. You can change the color and direction of both lights.

Chapter 5

1) The Surface Tape measurement tool:

B. Measures following the curve of the avatar from point to point.

The Height Measurement tool measures from the floor to the end point. The Basic Tape tool measures straight from point to point.

2) A ski jacket would have more ease than a t-shirt.

True. Ease is excess space beyond the body measurements. Outerwear always has more ease to allow for layering of garments underneath.

3) Adding design ease doesn't change the silhouette of the garment.

False. Adding ease makes a garment larger, so it will look different when draped.

4) You can change either end point of a tape measurement with the Edit Measurement tool.

False. All you can do with the Edit Measurement tool is use it to select measurements.

Chapter 6

1) Patterns must always be closed shapes.

True.

2) You can alternate between the Polygon / Line tool and the Curve tool as you are drawing your patterns.

False. You must close the shape when using the Polygon / Line tool before switching to another tool. You can't create curves while drawing, you have to add them to your closed shape.

3) You can make the following conversions with one click:

A. Convert an internal shape to a pattern.

C. Convert a pattern to an internal shape.

D. Convert a curve point to a standard point.

4) You can create holes in your patterns using:

A. The internal circle tool.

B. The dart tool.

C. The internal rectangle tool.

The circle tool is for drawing circle patterns.

Chapter 7

1)You can't edit symmetric patterns.

False. You can edit symmetric patterns. However, any change made to one pattern will be made to the other as well.

2) Use the Edit Pattern tool to resize the entire pattern and move it in the 2D Window.

False. Use the Transform Pattern tool to resize and move your patterns. The Edit Pattern tool is used to select segments and points for editing.

3) You can assign fabric:

A. To multiple patterns at once with the Assign button.

B. To one pattern at a time with drag and drop.

D. To one pattern at a time with the Property Editor Fabric.

E. To one pattern with right click, Assign to New Fabric.

There is no Fabric button.

4) Which statement is not correct:

C. Send Backward - This will bring the pattern two layers to the bottom.

Send Backward takes it one layer to the bottom, not two.

Chapter 8

1) When sewing a seam, MD provides these visual feedback clues:

A. Individual length of each seam line.

B. A blue point showing where the second seam line must stop.

C. The difference between the lengths of the seam lines.

D. The position of the notch for each seam line.

2) Mark which statements are correct regarding seam line pairs:

A. Sew one pattern to another pattern.

B. Sew one pattern to multiple patterns.

C. Sew multiple patterns to one pattern.

D. Sew multiple patterns to multiple patterns.

3) If you wanted to sew only part of one pattern segment to another pattern, which tool would you use?

B. Free Sewing Tool

You can't select only part of a segment to sew with the Segment sewing tool or the M:N Segment Sewing Tool

4) Pattern notches on a real-world pattern are completely different from the pattern notches in MD.

False. Pattern notches in MD work exactly like those found on real-world patterns.

Chapter 9

1) In most cases, the wrong side of the fabric faces out and the right side faces the avatar.

False. The wrong side faces inward to the avatar and the right side faces out.

2) The Fabric Texture Normal Map can be either gray channels or red/blue/green channels.

False. The normal map must use the red/blue/green channels only.

3) How you lay out your patterns in the 2D Window makes a difference in how the patterns will drape in the 3D Window.

True. The 2D Window has a warp and weft grain reference.

4) You can set the following properties on your fabric:

A. Transparency (Opacity property)

B. Pattern/Image (Texture property)

C. Shininess (Specular property)

D. Stretch (Warp & Weft properties)

E. Glow (Emission property)

Chapter 10

1) Use the Layer feature in the Property Editor whenever possible.

False. The Layer feature should be used only when necessary and then turned off. It can cause issues and MD will warn you when you use it.

2) The Pressure property is appropriate for the following:

A. Quilting

B. Inflatables

C. Pillows

E. Mattresses

Aprons are only one layer and will not work well with Pressure applied.

3)The Arrangement property shows "not assigned", if you don't use Arrangement Points to place your patterns.

True. The Arrangement property only relates to the arrangement point that was used to place the pattern.

4)The 2D and 3D Line Length is not accurate if your pattern is one of a symmetric set.

False. The line lengths are still accurate on symmetric patterns. However, you will be provided another set of line lengths called Symmetric Line Length which applies to both patterns.

Chapter 11

1) Always create your Arrangement Points before your Bounding Volumes.

False. You have to create your Bounding Volumes first, because Arrangement Points are assigned to Bounding Volumes.

2) You can choose to reset the arrangement of your patterns in the 3D Window:

B. One pattern at a time. (Shift select, RC > Reset 3D Arrangement (selected))

C. All patterns at once. (3D Window Button - Reset 3D Arrangement (all))

D. Chosen patterns at once. (Shift select, RC > Reset 3D Arrangement (selected))

Symmetric patterns at once is not an option.

3) To quickly arrange a cuff next to a sleeve use:

B. Superimpose Side

4) You should name your Bounding Volumes so that it is easier to select them and assign ________________ _____________ to them.

Arrangement Points

Chapter 12

1) What are the most common ways to speed up simulations (choose all)?

A. Raise the Particle Distance

B. Deactivate Patterns

C. Hide Patterns

D. Freeze Patterns

2) Strain Maps show where the avatar's body is the heaviest.

False. Strain Maps show you where your garments are tight.

3) You can pull and arrange the patterns while the program is simulating.

True. Use the picking point to grab the garment and rearrange it.

4) The Simulation Property of Complete is the setting that runs the quickest and should be used most often.

False. The Simulation Property of Normal is the quickest. Use Complete only when finalizing your work.

Chapter 13

1) You can use the ___________ setting in the Property Editor on segments to gather up the pattern.

Elastic

2) MD pleat tool includes the following types of pleats:

A. Accordion Pleats

B. Knife Pleats

D. Box Pleats

3) The bust dart found at the waist can be moved 360 degrees around the bust point.

True. The dart can be placed from the edge of the bodice pattern to the bust apex point at any place on the bodice.

4)_________ pleats are used to provide additional room for walking in skirts and coats.

Kick

Chapter 14

1) Yoke patterns are made using the:

C. Both front and back patterns.

2) An extension of extra fabric is needed at the center front of a bodice if you are adding:

A. Buttons

B. Snaps

Zippers generally require a reduction of fabric at the center front.

3) ________ is another term used in the garment industry to refer to a shirt or top.

Bodice

4) Men's shirts overlap right over left and women's shirts overlap left over right.

False. Men's shirts overlap left over right. Women's are right over left.

Chapter 15

1) The seam located between the legs joining the front and the back of pants is referred to as the _________.

Inseam

2) Pants can have darts and yokes, just like a bodice.

True.

3) To shorten pants, select the bottom hem segment, hold Shift and drag upwards.

False. To shorten pants, draw an internal line at the new length and use the Cut feature.

4) Pants that flare out starting at the knee are called:

C. Bell Bottoms

Chapter 16

1) Skirt hems should always be the same distance from the floor all the way around.

False. Uneven hems are a design element of some skirts and perfectly acceptable.

2) _____ are simply the panels or patterns of a skirt.

Gores

3) Tiered or peasant skirts are made of:

B. Multiple Rectangle Patterns

4)The sweeping hemlines of formal gowns and wedding dresses are called _________.

Trains

Chapter 17

1) Necklines are a separate pattern piece.

False. Necklines are part of the bodice pattern and not a separate piece.

2) Which type of collar has the same shape as the neckline?

B. Non-Convertible Collar

3) Every shirt or top must have either a neckline or a collar.

True.

4) To make a collar rise up off the shoulders:

A. Increase the height of the stand.

Chapter 18

1) The difference between the overarm length and the underarm length is the:

B. Cap Height

2) Cuffs that are more than 4" long are called __________ style.

Gauntlet

3) A sleeve with sleeve cap measurements that are longer than the front and back armhole measurements is:

D. A sleeve that will be gathered into the armhole.

4) A halter top has which type of sleeve:

C. Sleeveless (Halters have no sleeves)

Chapter 19

1) A ___________ is a separate pattern piece that is longer than the segment it is sewn to, so it gathers.

Ruffle

2) To fake facings in MD, turn on the __________ __________ option on the Curved Side Geometry property.

Double Sided

3) Piping options include:

A. Fabric that is unique.

C. Particle Distance that is unique.

D. UV Guide diagram.

Piping can be from 1 to 15 mm wide.

4) Interfacing is hidden and should be left out of MD garments.

True. Interfacing just creates unnecessary geometry.

Chapter 20

1) Patch pockets are located within the side seam of pants.

False. Patch pockets are on the outside of garments.

2) You should always include the stud of the snap set on your garments.

False. There is no need to include a snap stud unless the snap is not fastened and you can see the lower layer.

3) Use the ____________ Button tool to lock a button to a buttonhole.

Fasten

4) You can tie bows and knots in MD.

False. MD does not allow any type of tying at all. You have to come up with alternative methods to fake results.

Chapter 21

1) MD geometry is quads by default.

False. MD default geometry is triangles.

2) You control the density of your garment geometry with the _________ _____________ setting.

Particle Distance

3) MD provides the Face and Vertex count of every pattern piece.

True. This is located in the Miscellaneous section of the Property Editor.

4) You can set the Particle Distance of every pattern to a different value.

True. This allows you to keep the vertex count down by only increasing the resolution where necessary.

Chapter 22

1) The only avatars you can use for making garments in MD are provided with the program.

False. You can import your own avatars.

2) You can change the body shape and measurements of MD default avatars.

False. The avatars are fixed. You can export them out the program and change them in 3D sculpting software, however.

3) You use ________ _____________ to change the pose of avatars in the 3D Window.

X-Ray Joints

4) You can change the hair and shoes on some of the MD default avatars.

True. Not all avatars have hair and shoe options.

Chapter 23

1) You can save in the following formats:

A. Avatar .avt

B. Project .zprj

C. Garment .zpac

E. Pose .pos

There is no Prop .pro option.

2) MD can save all of the textures you've used in a file for reference.

True. Select Save As Surface Textures.

3) When you Save As Garment, the avatar is saved with the garment.

False. Only the garment and garment properties are saved when you Save As Garment.

4) In addition to the garments, you can choose to export the avatar.

True. You can select whether you want to include the avatar in the export or not.

Chapter 24

1) You can choose to display or hide buttons at the top of the 3D and 2D Windows.

True. Right click on the toolbar background to select and de-select what tool buttons will be displayed.

2) If you change a shortcut, what happens to the mouse hover tooltip?

C. The tooltip updates with the new shortcut.

3) You can overwrite, reset or delete every keyboard shortcut.

True.

4) You can change the size of the arrangement points displayed in the 3D Window.

True. Select Settings > User Settings > Other > Arrangement

Chapter 25

1) You can make the avatar walk in Simulation and Animation mode.

False. You can morph the avatar to another pose in Simulation mode, but you must use Animation mode to make it walk.

2) You have to load an avatar motion file before you can animate garments.

True. You must have a motion file to load or you can't animate.

3) MD includes several motion files for all the default avatars.

False. Not all MD default avatars have motion files.

4) You can model static objects in MD to add to your scene for animation.

False. You can't model in MD at all.

Index

Symbols

A

B

C

D

E

F

G

H

I

J

K

L

M

N

O

P

Q

R

S

T

U

V

W

X

Y

Z

Printed by BoD™in Norderstedt, Germany

9 780998 334288